PRESENTED BY

Dr. Myer Mendelson
and
Margaret Mendelson

1/18/90

KARL LUEGER

This engraving by Schmutzer shows Lueger shortly before his death in 1910. (Author's Collection.)

KARL LUEGER

Mayor of
Fin de Siècle
Vienna

Richard S. Geehr

 Wayne State University Press   Detroit   1990

Copyright © 1990 by Wayne State University Press,
Detroit, Michigan 48202. All rights are reserved.
No part of this book may be reproduced without formal
permission.
93 92 91 90 89   5 4 3 2 1

Library of Congress Cataloging-in-Publication Data
Geehr, Richard S.
  Karl Lueger : mayor of fin de siècle Vienna /
  Richard S. Geehr.
     p.   cm.
  Bibliography: p.
  Includes index.
  ISBN 0-8143-2077-5
  1. Lueger, Karl, 1844-1910.   2. Vienna (Austria) — Politics
and government.   3. Vienna (Austria) — Civilization.   4.
Mayors — Austria — Vienna — Biography.   I. Title.
  DB844.L8G44   1990
  943.6′13044′092 — dc20   89-34449
                                          CIP

Grateful acknowledgment is made to the Lucius N. Littauer
Foundation for financial assistance in the publication of this
volume.

For My Mother

Contents

Preface

*T*his book attempts to describe and analyze Karl Lueger's rise to power and political personality, his influence, and the man himself. It originated in undergraduate researches at Middlebury College in 1958 and 1959. In the initial phase of my study I subscribed, more or less uncritically, to the semi-official view of the man, that of his several Austrian and German hagiographers. My impressions of Lueger started multiplying in 1961, during the first of many visits to Vienna to collect secondary materials. When I was a graduate student at Columbia University in 1963, fin de siècle periodical literature in the New York Public Library showed me another, less positive, Lueger. When I began archival research in Vienna in 1969, further significant impressions began to emerge. The Lueger of this study has thus developed over a period of three decades.

My researches have been facilitated by the generosity of various organizations and enriched by numerous scholars. I wish to thank the Fulbright Foundation for fellowships in 1969–70, 1976–77, and 1985–86; Professor Anton Porhansl and Dr. Günter Frühwirth and their staffs in Vienna; the National Endowment for the Arts and Humanities for a grant in 1974–75; the Marion and Jasper Whiting Foundation for a stipend in 1980; and the Austrian Ministry of Science and Research for an award in 1986. Bentley College granted me sabbatical leave in 1985 and 1986 and provided the resources for retyping my manuscript and for many of the illustrations. Without the efforts of Mr. Charles Thompson and Mr. William Lee Frost and the generous support of the Lucius N. Littauer Foundation in 1988, this book might never have been published.

I owe deep gratitude to Professors Raymond and Susan Tripp who contributed significantly and in various ways to this book. For more than twenty years now, they have encouraged and enriched my researches on "that Viennese mayor." I am most indebted to them in particular for their major role in shaping my thoughts and perceptions, and their many substantive and stylistic additions to the manuscript.

Professor Marsha Rozenblit, Professor Klemens von Klemperer, Professor Jay Baird, and Dr. Karin Brown have read my work, pointed out shortcomings and made suggestions about improvements which I have endeavored to follow. My work is the better for the criticism of Professor Richard S. Levy who painstakingly read and re-read my manuscript. His many insights caused me to reformulate a number of ideas, clarify points, and add needed explanations. I am grateful to him as well for indicating parallels between imperial German and Austrian politics as they affected the Jews of both countries, and for his permission to quote his comments.

I wish to thank James K. Owens and George P. Young of the National Archives, Boston branch, for locating official American reaction to Lueger's mayoralty campaign, and Dr. John Loftus for suggesting that I explore this source. I owe deep gratitude, as well, to Gabriel Alexander, and to Lee Ann Schreiner, Laurel Brandt, Anne Adamus, Thomas Seller, and to the Wayne State University Press staff. A number of unknown readers pointed out errors and made me aware of inconsistencies. I am grateful to them for having done so and have attempted to eliminate the problem areas.

Friends and acquaintances in Vienna have been wholehearted and generous in their support, even though they have not always agreed with my opinions. I wish to thank Hofrat Dr. Franz Patzer and the staff of the Vienna Municipal Library for their unstinting support for the past twenty years, and in particular Ernst Hübsch, Dr. Walter Obermaier, Johann Ziegler, and Dr. Bernhard Denscher. In the early stages of my research the late Dr. Franz Gall of the Archiv der Universität Wien unearthed valuable information about Lueger's student years. Subsequently, Isabella Greiner and Agnes Lössl added to my knowledge of this early period of Lueger's development.

Through her knowledge of Viennese archives Dr. Isabella Ackerl, of the Österreichische Gesellschaft für Historische Quellenstudien, has solved innumerable problems. She and her staff have for many years now diligently searched their own holdings for material about my subject as well. Without her friendship, patience, cheerful support and understanding, my work might have faltered. I am grateful to Dr. Wilfried Posch who answered questions about Lueger's architectural preferences. Dr. Walter Fritz and the staff of the Österreichisches Filmarchiv made available the script, files, and still photographs of the film *Wien 1910*. The actors Erik Frey and O. W. Fischer provided first-hand information, and Ernst Birke arranged a screening of the film and described previous audience reaction.

Dr. Sophie Schick furnished useful materials and a fresh perspective on important aspects of my subject. Herbert Klima shared his wide and deep knowledge and was unfailingly generous. Two Viennese who wish to remain anonymous provided me with primary sources. Clemens Höslinger of Haus-, Hof- und Staatsarchiv, a scholar's scholar and friend, taught me much about his native city and its protean culture. Dr. Maren Seliger of the Wiener Stadt- und Landesarchiv answered numerous questions and suggested fruitful sources of information, as did Dr. Jonny Moser and Professor Wolfgang R. Langenbucher of the Institut für Publizistik- und Kommunikationswissenschaft der Universität Wien. My early enthusiasm for my subject was fed by Professor Adam Wandruszka, the late Professor Friedrich Heer, and the late Dr. Karl Gladt.

Professor Erika Weinzierl has generously assisted my research and provided me with needed information over the years. Professor Roland Sarti solved a problem about one of Lueger's Italian admirers. Professor William E. Wright and Professor Harry Zohn provided encouragement when it was most needed. I wish to express my gratitude to Ina S. Moses, Mary Trimble, and Diane Viverios for retyping the manuscript and correcting my errors in the process. For those that remain I alone am responsible.

My thanks go as well to the staffs of the Austrian Nationalbibliothek, Verwaltungsarchiv, Niederösterreichisches Landesarchiv, Haus-, Hof- und Staatsarchiv, Museum der Stadt Wien, Dr. Andreas Weyringer of the Katholisch-Theologische Fakultät of the University of Vienna, the University Library, the Kriegsarchiv, the Erzbischöfliches Diözesanarchiv, the Evangelisches Pfarramt, A.B. Wien, Archiv der Stadt Wien, and Archiv des Männergesangsvereins.

Finally, I wish to thank my wife, Gerda, for the many hours she has labored on this book. To her is my heaviest debt.

Introduction

*K*arl Lueger was mayor of Vienna for a longer time than any other
mayor of the Habsburg capital during the constitutional era after 1848 —
twelve years, eleven months, and two days. At the time of his death in
March 1910, he was immensely popular, not only as Bürgermeister, but
also as the leader of the Christian Social party in the Austrian parliament,
the Lower Austrian provincial diet, and the Viennese municipal council.
Austrian politicians since have invoked his memory to lend authenticity
and respectability to their own careers. This has led to misunderstandings
of Lueger's political life and the cultural, economic and political conditions of his era. These misunderstandings are rooted in a largely apocryphal tradition. Even today it is taken for granted that Lueger began as a
true "democrat" determined to combat selfish privilege, that his politics
were altruistic and classless and aimed at promoting the lasting welfare
of his native city, that he was never a "true anti-Semite," that he was a
champion of universal franchise, and that his administration marked the
summit of municipal achievement in a sea of inactivity and incompetence.
This apocryphal version of Lueger's career has had an effect. Few in Vienna today remember the name of any of Lueger's Liberal predecessors
as mayor or any real contributions these predecessors may have made to
Vienna's greatness.

Far from being an isolated administrative genius who went his own
way without reference to his Liberal municipal predecessors, Lueger drew
heavily on his Liberal university training and years of practical experience
as a Liberal politician. His politics, cultural views, and political style all

owed more to these early experiences than he or any of his previous biographers have acknowledged. Through him, the past became a significant influence on at least one of his important successors and former opponents—Socialist Mayor Karl Seitz, who held office from 1922 to 1934. Seitz carried an extensive program of communal housing construction to completion on the foundations of Lueger's broader municipal projects. Lueger's career as mayor thus forms a link in the long chain of Viennese development.

Yet, if Lueger were remembered only for his municipal building, he would not continue to stimulate interest and controversy, particularly outside Austria where the meaning of the man as one of the acknowledged mentors of Adolf Hitler is disputed. Hitler admired Lueger's municipal achievements as an attempt to revitalize the heart of the Habsburg Empire. He was also fascinated by—though technically critical of—Lueger's employment of anti-Semitism in mass politics. The Führer referred to Lueger as "the greatest German mayor of all times . . . the last great German to be born in the ranks of the people . . . a statesman greater than all the so-called 'diplomats' of the time," and Hitler was a mourner at Lueger's funeral. But he faulted Lueger's anti-Semitism for its lack of racist focus. Since 1945, Hitler's opinions have embarrassed Austrians who trade on the idea that their country was a victim of National Socialism rather than admitting Austria's complicity in the crimes of the Third Reich. Accordingly, biographers of Lueger writing after 1945 have usually discounted Hitler's praise, or even ignored it altogether. Lueger's good deeds have been used to obscure the compromising events of his career in these books.

To see only Lueger's constructive efforts is to distort historical continuity and lose sight of a purposive movement in a one-sided view of an important political personality. A balanced biographical evaluation argues for a more inclusive picture. Lueger the man shows in his politics as well as in his more tangible achievements. The effect of his personality, thought, and political methods was significant in the formation of the Christian Social party, and in its organization, the attitudes of its leaders, and its course after his death.

Lueger was the undisputed leader of the Christian Socials from 1890 to 1910, the party's most important and influential years. During that time, his power was as considerable as it was varied. He presided over a "royal" court—as would his admirer Hitler. Lueger's party extended its control into primary school education, the cultural life of the city, and even into larger Austrian and imperial politics — as had the Liberals during the 1860s and 1870s. But Lueger's party was tighter, his control more thoroughgoing and pervasive than that of the Liberals. In this he anticipated later totalitarian developments. Lueger's Christian Socials created women's and children's groups as well as a political labor section, each commanded by their own leaders and subleaders within the larger hierarchical party structure. Such intraparty groups had their own newspapers. At least one Christian Social youth organization dressed in uniforms and drilled with rifles. Other groups within the party regularly participated in elaborate paramilitary ceremonies with flags and Christian Social emblems. In these groups, Lueger was extolled as a paternal and all-wise leader, the object of a personality cult. The square in front of the town hall bore Lueger's name even while he ruled. Plaques honoring his municipal achievements decorated buildings and monuments and appeared in front of trees. All of this fed his charisma in a way the world has come to know only too well.

Yet no public image can disguise Lueger's basic nature. He epitomized the successful *arriviste*, the political parvenu. He embodied the ambitions, the resentments, and the disappointments of the lower bourgeois. His people were those who had prospered, acquiring some of the tastes of the upper class without the corresponding education, manners, and sense of belonging. His birthplace on the threshold of the inner city is deeply symbolic. Lueger's considerable operatic talent sometimes failed to conceal his social insecurity. As long as his ambition was satisfied and power preserved, ends outweighed means. During the last decades of the monarchy Lueger exercised more power than any other popularly elected politician. Only the imperial authority stood higher, and for this Lueger's opponents and enemies were thankful.

Lueger was very much a man of his times, and his life casts light upon those times. He was neither merely the product of social forces nor the inheritor of a tradition, but an individual personality who played upon those two things because of who he was and what he wanted. Lueger was more than a picturesque Viennese type, more than the pawn of tradition or socioeconomic forces. Without overselling the importance of a single individual, much can be learned by examining what an individual does with the tradition he inherits and his personal goals. Lueger made a significant impact on Austrian politics during his own day and beyond.

Lueger began his career after Austria's role as the arbiter of Central European affairs had ended. The defeat of Emperor Franz Joseph's forces during the Seven Weeks' War of 1866 reduced Austria to a second-class power and weakened her control over the eastern portion of the Habsburg realm. With the *Ausgleich*, or compromise with Hungary in 1867, Austrians became partners with the Magyars and the Dual Monarchy was created. Lueger deeply resented this turn of events. One of his few consistencies was his hatred of Hungary. But he nonetheless understood the situation, lived with it, and even turned it to his own advantage, capitalizing on anti-Hungarian sentiments in building his own political base.

In his brilliant study *Fin-de-Siècle Vienna*, Carl Schorske has called attention to Lueger's "murky transition from democratic to proto-fascist politics," over which the shadow of anti-Semitism slowly settled. "*I* decide who is a Jew!" Lueger is reported to have said, thereby creating a convenient if honorary category of Aryans. (Hermann Goering would later repeat this.) Lueger was an anti-Semite, not just a hater of individual Jews; his attitude implied long-term action against Jews and denial of equal rights.[1] His influence on Austrian politics lies here, because, unlike most other anti-Semites of his time, he was powerful and facilitated the use of anti-Semitism in Austrian political life. Lueger manipulated anti-Semitism into political success. Under Lueger, anti-Semitism took root in political parties, propaganda societies, and newspapers, becoming an institution in its own right. In this political climate the *source* of ideas, that they were expressed by Lueger in party newspapers, became more important than the ideas themselves. The source became an authority. This was the climate that fostered the growth of the "Jewish world plot" or modern conspiracy explanation of history, the notion that Jews were plotting to take over the world. Later, "the National Socialists knew very well where the roots of Jew-hatred were to be found, and they exploited them to the full."[2] Another saying attributed to Lueger, though suppressed since 1945: "I'll only be happy after the last Jew has disappeared from Vienna," is less ambiguous than the first, and suggests his truer feelings. From the late 1880s, Lueger abetted the growth of anti-Semitism in Vienna and Lower Austria. His political use of it was applauded by foreign anti-Semites as a significant contribution to the larger movement, though there is little evidence to suggest open coordination.[3]

My Introduction to "*I Decide Who Is a Jew!" The Papers of Dr. Karl Lueger* called attention to the likelihood of the mayor of Vienna's debt to Joseph Chamberlain, British foreign minister and also mayor of Birmingham, in municipal socialization.[4] Certainly, Lueger did not invent such municipal reform, though he did introduce it to Vienna. Subsequent researches have not uncovered any direct connection between Chamberlain and Lueger; so Lueger's innovations must now be viewed within a more local Viennese and Lower Austrian context. Lueger's keen awareness of "the political importance of urban environments in achieving community" was perhaps more original.[5] His faith in the physical basis of reform may have been shared with Chamberlain and possibly with another master builder, Louis Napoleon.

This study treats Lueger as a quintessentially Viennese figure who—perhaps fortuitously—always anticipated larger European trends. He was both the epitome and the emblem of his social class, educated in the religious, classical, and Austrian Liberal traditions, a man who came to embody a politicized Lower Austrian Catholicism. Lueger was not a totalitarian; nor is it possible to trace a straight line from him to Hitler. The Austrian path to Nazism was twisted and devious. Lueger was not a true revolutionary. He never aimed to destroy the aristocracy or its traditional institutions. Both he and the Viennese landlord class came to political maturity at the same time. Lueger became this class's leader through luck, opportunism, and skillful politics, rather than premeditation. The haute bourgeois Liberalism that Lueger is sometimes credited with destroying had exhausted itself by the time he became active in organizing Christian Socialism. His political success was a symptom rather than a cause of Liberalism's larger decline. Yet once in power, Lueger tried to perpetuate Christian Socialism, one of the first efforts of modern times to elevate "the masses to a position of influence in the body politic,"[6] not only by enlarging and consolidating party control over electoral bodies, but also by creating special institutions to train party elite. All of this, as well as his restless dynamism, an emphasis on action for action's sake, "militarism, organicist conceptions of community [and] imperialism,"[7] and his political anti-Semitism allowed Lueger to be central in the larger drama of history as an authentic, if unwitting, progenitor of fascism.

1

The Early Years: 1844–1869

Zur Zeit, als ich, Supplent dreier juridischer Lehrkanzeln, täglich das *Theresianum* zu besuchen hatte, gab es dort einen Portier namens Lueger, der mich beim Kommen und Gehen respektvoll grüsste; an seiner Seite sah ich oftmals einen brünetten, sehr beweglichen, auf den Namen Karl hörenden Jungen.
— Cajetan Felder, *Erinnerungen eines Wiener Bürgermeisters*

Der spätere Bürgermeister von Wien war wie alle Männer, die wir Jahrhundertmenschen nennen, schon als Lernender ein Eigenartiger, aber auf ihn passte das Wort Adalbert Stifters vom Knaben im Haidedorf: "Er wird sich wunderbar erziehen und vorbereiten."
— Eugen Mack, *Dr. Karl Lueger und die Jugend*

*K*arl Lueger's beginnings were humble, if not inauspicious. He was born on October 24, 1844, in a service flat of the Vienna Polytechnic Institute. His father Leopold Lueger, the second of three sons of peasant stock, was employed by the institute as a custodian. The times were bad and would soon get worse. A series of crop failures in the eastern provinces were causing serious unrest, and this erupted into an empirewide revolt before the boy reached the age of four. Not until then did Karl speak, and his beginning to talk almost certainly had traumatic origins. He was the fourth of eight children and one of three who lived to maturity. He had already become fond of his five-year-old sister Josefine when first he and then she contracted scarlet fever. When he awoke from his delirium, he noticed that she was not at her accustomed place at his bedside and cried out for her. But Josefine had already died. One of Lueger's contemporary biographers made sanctimonious use of this incident to make the homiletic point that good deeds take time to be achieved.[1] Lueger himself characteristically turned the episode into political capital. As mayor he joked that though he had been silent as an infant, he had since made up for lost time.

The name Lueger — most Viennese pronounce the name "loŏ-ā-guh" — is both common and archaic in Lower Austria. *Lueger* means to "look out at" and stems from the Alemannic dialect. During his years of power Lueger and one of his early biographers recognized the derivation of his name and fully exploited it.[2] His sensitiveness about his name became apparent when he castigated his fellows in parliament who mispronounced it. He asserted — sometimes in racially tinged terms — that such people were not true Germans, so venerably Teutonic was the word.[3] (Unless otherwise indicated, "German" refers to Austrian-German, as distinctly separate from other nationalities in the Habsburg Empire.) Later in Lueger-controlled politics to be non-German and in the opposition was to be at a considerable disadvantage.

Lueger was a consistent Austrian nationalist and conscious of his nation's centuries-old heritage as distinct and separate from that of Germany. He therefore opposed Austrian Pan-Germans who, from the early 1870s, urged the union of the German-speaking areas of the Austro-Hungarian Empire with the Bismarckian Reich. Lueger pursued a sincere pro-Habsburg policy because he believed — like his admirer Hitler — that Austrian Germans were the superior imperial nationality, the one that provided the vital cultural and political impulses for the rest of the empire, the one nationality, in fact, that held the empire together. His beliefs were shared not only by his followers, but also by Austrian Liberals and by at least some of his Socialist foes. This helps explain why some of his opponents respected Lueger as an important bulwark of the empire, as a barrier against the chaos that threatened should the empire collapse. Before World War I, few Austrian-Germans, apart from the Pan-German nationalists, welcomed alternatives to the imperial entity.

Lueger exploited his lineage just as he exploited his personal attributes; he made as good use of his parentage as he did of his stately appearance, bachelor status, and gregarious personality. He seems to have been unclear about his ancestry before his grandparents, which is not surprising for one of his class and background. In the late 1890s, a rival, Dr. Joseph Samuel Bloch, perhaps sensing this uncertainty, challenged Lueger on this sensitive point to embarrass him politically, telling Lueger that he had a Jewish ancestor.[4] If Lueger believed it, this story must have shocked him, for at the time he was considered the most popular anti-Semitic leader in Austria. Dr. Bloch was a parliamentary delegate from Galicia.[5] He had discovered in an ancient chronicle that the wife of a Schebelein had accepted baptism to escape death by fire during one of the periodical persecutions of Jews by the fifteenth-century Duke Albrecht V. At the time of her baptism she received the name Barbara, and she subsequently married Niclas Lueger. The "wife of the Jew Schebelein," Bloch claimed, "was the [sic] ancestress of Dr. Karl Lueger."[6]

Dr. Bloch had not traced the descent over three centuries from Barbara Lueger to Karl's grandfather. The most diligent student of Lueger's heritage[7] has been unable to trace Lueger's ancestry to more than a few years before the eighteenth century.[8] But the allegation of Jewish ancestry was eagerly exploited by Lueger's enemies before he became mayor.[9] In contrast, Lueger's lineage was alleged to be Viennese by one of his supporters, Hans Arnold Schwer, an anti-Semitic Viennese journalist and municipal councillor, who discovered the name Lueger in Viennese documents dating from the fourteenth century.[10] Schwer was silent about any connection between Barbara Lueger and his party leader.

Another story, publicized by Lueger and his sisters,[11] is also unprovable, but bears mentioning because it leads into Karl's paternal history, about which there is some certainty. Karl's patriotic grandfather, Josef Lueger, a farmer and stonemason, was said to have led one of Napoleon's patrols astray and died because of consequent maltreatment by the French.[12] His second son Leopold was nearly six years old when Josef died in October 1812. The following February Josef's widow, Maria Anna, married widower Michael Jandl, who already had his own children. As newcomers, Josef's sons did not fare especially well within Jandl's family, and in 1827 twenty-year-old Leopold was probably happy to escape into military service.[13] While serving in the famous Baron Langenau Regiment, Leopold learned to read and write. He was stationed for a while in Mainz and was mustered out in 1837 as an invalid.[14] Leopold's experience as a soldier impressed itself on his speech. His words to Karl's first schoolmaster, as reported by one of Lueger's early biographers — who probably heard the story from the mayor himself — seem authentic enough: "I've got a little recruit here. . . . I believe he'll do well, for he has a good head."[15]

Despite ill health, Leopold could look back on his military experience with some satisfaction and pride. He had learned to read and write; and he had been exposed to a wider world than that of his native village Neustadtl. This experience would naturally have made him eager to begin a new life, especially because his paternal inheritance had passed to his stepbrothers after the death of his mother in 1832. In any event, he decided to try his luck in Vienna. At first he found menial employment at the exclusive preparatory school Theresianum. This job may have had an unexpected benefit. Years later, after he had ceased to work there, young Karl was permitted to enroll at the Theresianum as a day student[16] when those of humble background were only just beginning to be admitted, thanks to a reorganization of the secondary schools. But in Vienna, that most diplomatic of cities, Leopold's prior affiliation may also have helped open appropriate doors.

Leopold's drudging tasks further undermined his health. Afflicted with "chronic ulcers," and coughing blood,[17] he was admitted to the Wiener Invalidenhaus on April 1, 1838.[18] Yet, this setback proved to be only temporary, for ten months later, as a civil servant with official entitlements, including a small pension and decent living quarters,[19] he became a porter at the Polytechnic. Although Leopold never received more than a modest salary, he was in time promoted to custodian and some supervisory duties. He took full advantage of his official status by furthering his formal education. He registered for technical courses, attended lectures, and "passed exams in three subjects very successfully."[20]

At the height of his fame Lueger is said to have spoken admiringly of his father and his unusual quest for knowledge. But the Christian Social biographies that relate this story[21] may not be fully reliable. Young Karl hints that the relationship with his father was less than loving. In letters to a close friend Karl is silent about his father's protracted terminal illness during the late summer and autumn of 1866,[22] and there are later indications of lasting resentment over beatings meted out by Leopold.[23] Among Karl Lueger's supporters, however, with their paternalistic values and veneration for him as the "uncrowned king of Vienna," the official impression of filial loyalty was preserved.

Leopold had clear ambitions for his son and imagined him becoming a member of the upper class. Karl was consistently dressed in fine clothes. Strangers who saw them walking together occasionally expressed surprise that Leopold and Karl were father and son. Here began the "subtle sense of social superiority despite his lowly origins"[24] for which Karl became well known. On these walks he doubtless also grew familiar with Vienna's landmarks. Architectural aesthetics and history became primers for the future politician.

Karl's mother was the former Juliana Schuhmayer, a Viennese cabinetmaker's daughter who was twenty-seven when Leopold married her on August 18, 1839. Carl Schorske speculates that she was "the real force in the household . . . [a] tough little *petite bourgeois* [who] formed the future 'Lord God of Vienna.'"[25] Lueger's biographer, Rudolf Kuppe, assigned her a traditional role. She was the model . . . German housewife, who applied herself with seriousness and devotion to well-known maternal duties. It was thanks to her prudence and energy, no less than to the father's diligence and thrift, that the family always made out in spite of its increasing size, and the children were carefully brought up though in modest circumstances. The mother shared the education of the children with the father, in whose hearts overflowed the parents' piety and trust in God.[26]

Whatever her contribution, Lueger imbibed ferocious class pride and independence. "Better dry bread at home, than roast at someone else's!" he later recalled his mother's words. "That was the family's feeling, mother's disposition, father's disposition. That was strength that was rooted in the people. . . ."[27]

All agree that Karl revered his mother, though the style of his letters to her as well as to his sisters suggests that familial relations were formal.[28] He displayed mementos of his mother in his office from the time of her death in December 1888 until his death in 1910, even going so far as to insist that her image be included with his in an official portrait in the gallery of mayors in the Vienna town hall.[29] But Lueger's personality was in some respects so completely political that even this gesture may have reflected some unsentimental cunning. He understood only too well the value of instinctive familial emotions and their political uses. When he was a municipal councillor and parliamentary delegate with his eye on the mayoralty, Juliana's funeral was turned into a triumphal procession.[30]

Carl Schorske has observed further that Juliana kept her daughters Hildegard and Rosa "close to her side in managing the tobacco shop through which, after her husband's death, she earned her modest living."[31] He suggests that Lueger and his two sisters bowed to "extreme maternal authority," and that "according to one historian, Frau Lueger exacted on her deathbed a pledge from her forty-four-year-old son that he would remain unmarried to care for his sisters."[32] Yet, one of Lueger's letters to a friend in 1879 suggests that his vow would have been unnecessary in any case. Even at the age of thirty-five, four years after he had entered politics and nine years before his mother's death, he already considered never marrying. As he then put it, "I entered the hostile arena a little too early. Business and politics occupy me completely and won't let go. If someday I tire of politics and could have time for marriage, I'm afraid it would be too late."[33]

The first significant historical event to take place during young Karl's life was the Revolution of 1848, which ushered in a period of turbulence for the polyglot Austrian Empire and for much of the rest of Europe. But the revolutions that abolished once and for all the French monarchy, toppled governments from the municipal to the national level, and forced Prince Metternich into exile did not have much immediate effect on the Lueger family. One fictionalized Lueger biography, *Der Herrgott von Wien*, written in 1940,[34] depicts Leopold as an initial defender of Habsburg hegemony. However, later, after a heated discussion of the implications of the revolution, Leopold becomes disillusioned and rejects as contradictory and divided Franz Grillparzer's celebrated poetic defense of the multinational concept, *In deinem Lager ist Österreich*. In the novel a much agitated Leopold returns home with young Karl riding on his shoulders from a political visit. It would be up to Leopold's little passenger "to try to solve one day the puzzle before which the father stood powerless and questioning in the difficult hour of his people."[35] Little doubt is left to the reader about what the solution would be: the Revolution of 1848 among the German Austrians was a projection of deep longing for a mighty all-German Reich. Until it was achieved there could be no lasting peace and contentment. Germans should therefore shed neither their own blood nor that of their Teutonic brothers for anything but the larger *Volk* community.

Such a conclusion, appearing as it did in 1940, during the high summer of pan-Germanism and the year of unparalleled German victory, tells us much about nationalistic euphoria but considerably less about Leopold's state of mind. Nor is it accurate in hinting that Karl Lueger would solve the riddle of Austria's national ambiguity. Furthermore, it seems doubtful that Leopold would have behaved in any but the most circumspect manner toward civil and military authority, whatever his true thoughts may have been. In fact, there is no evidence that he ever supported anything but conservative authority and the empire as he had always known it. Rather than reject the multinational concept, it is easier to believe that in response to questions about what to do in such difficult times, Leopold "warned against getting carried away by radical fanatics everywhere abroad."[36] And considering the repression after the revolutions of 1848, we can also expect that his friends were afterward grateful for his advice, which they evidently accepted.[37]

Karl Lueger's formal education began in 1850 when he was admitted to the so-called School of the Three Doves,[38] the Taubenschule, in the Margaretenstrasse, in what is now Vienna's fifth district. Many years later in a provincial diet session, in which education, language, and nationalism were central topics of discussion, he remembered his *Volksschule* as "a paradise for poor people." "I owe the *Volksschule* much — everything, and I always recall my teachers with gratitude. . . . The whole world knows that." After describing his studies and his achievements with great pride, he singled out language as a most important subject: "One can . . . only learn a language in the *Volks- und Bürgerschule*; the language must be instilled in the child there. If children don't thoroughly learn their mother tongue in the *Volksschule*, they'll definitely fail to learn it later."[39] Lueger's rhetorical successes attest to the importance of his remarks. Much of his popularity grew out of his superior skill as a speaker.

Leopold tutored his son in fundamental academic disciplines, going so far as to insist that Karl also study during vacations and even on their walks together. One time when he was indolent Leopold chided him: "Now you'll never be first!" whereupon Karl immediately returned to his books.[40] There can be no doubt that he was a gifted student and his achievement was outstanding. Later as mayor, his early academic prowess was praised in *Wiener Kinder,* a Christian Social monthly "for Vienna's German Youth." In the opening story readers were urged to imitate Karl's example, yet not to expect rewards for superior achievement. For as Leopold tells his young son: "It's expected that you do your duty, and that you use your God-given talent well deserves no reward. In school you are a smith and can forge your luck or misfortune according to the way you swing your hammer!"[41]

Reward or not, Karl was admitted as a day student in 1854 to the exclusive Theresianum, where an "elite civil service class" was trained.[42] He continued to achieve distinction in this new environment, as he did throughout his academic career. He steeped himself in classical history, Latin and Greek. Studies of classical history likely taught him that those who were rhetorically skilled earned advancement in the Roman administration — an apt model. As the boss of the empire's most powerful political machine, he remembered how his mother had coached him in his school lessons, made sure he learned his Latin, and insisted that he quote Cicero accurately. Indeed, it may have been Cicero who molded Lueger's early concepts of justice.[43] In any case, Roman studies and Latin came to mark his speeches and influence his attitudes as they did those of many of his political contemporaries.[44] Thus Lueger, the self-styled "tribune of the people," reflected a late-Roman republican attitude in a late-Austrian imperial setting, and repeatedly emphasized his overriding accountability to "the people," rather than to the elective bodies of which he was a member.

It is simplistic to describe the adult Lueger as a complete Philistine, as some have done, and to suggest that his judicial specialization at the University of Vienna prevented him from gaining knowledge of a wider range of up-to-date cultural subjects. As a law student he would have received a well-rounded education in any case. As one scholar of nineteenth-century administrative education put it, "Since the end of the eighteenth century the economic and social sciences in Austrian legal study have always played an importantly greater role than in German legal study."[45]

Lueger's parliamentary speeches show a well-educated man. They are studded with correct Greek and Latin phrases; his letters and impromptu remarks reveal the type of cultural exposure that, at least in part, must have been acquired in his continuing travels. His more formal correspondence and memoranda suggest more than simple awareness of contemporary cultural trends. Rather than dismiss him as a Philistine, it would be more accurate to describe him as a traditionalist in the classical and, one is tempted to say, rigid Austrian pattern, who became increasingly mistrustful of "new" or original artistic and intellectual developments. Lueger preferred pastiches, usually of classical inspiration; he lacked cultural fluency outside his own regional environment, which was nonetheless rich in centuries-old tradition, and deeply rooted in Catholicism.[46]

Young Karl's Theresianum experience affected his spiritual growth. He abandoned his piety. A regular churchgoer during his *Taubenschule* years,[47] whose belief was doubtless also reinforced by his mother's religious convictions, Lueger so disliked his Theresianum religion teacher, Anton Gruscha, later cardinal and archbishop of Vienna, that he remained an indifferent Catholic for the rest of his life.[48] There may have been additional and unknown reasons for Lueger's abandonment of piety, but his personality was subjective and his responses emotional enough, particularly during his earlier years, for him to have been permanently estranged from formal Catholic ritual. Yet, this does not necessarily mean that he was privately or personally irreligious, and the energy that showed as piety during his earlier years seems later to have fueled the pursuit of political goals. Though Lueger may have abandoned his religion early in life, a religiosity remained. As a parliamentary candidate in 1885, he recalled his first high marks in religion, considered exploiting them for their potential political value,[49] and later posed as a devout Catholic. Within Lueger's highly valorized personality, opportunism was one of his more genuine and consistent traits. All in all, however, Lueger's pre-university development appears to have been solid, well-rounded, and stable, but contained little impetus toward genuine experimentation and originality. Yet, it provided a firm base for his subsequent political career, which revealed a good deal of innovation.

Although Lueger's oratory recalls his classical education, his administrative style, his mature preference for elegance and show, his social concerns, and some of his central political preoccupations point toward the influence of his most celebrated University of Vienna teacher, Lorenz von Stein.[50] Lueger enrolled in Stein's *Nationalökonomie* courses during the winter semester of 1864–65, and in *Finanzwissenschaft* during the summer semester of 1865.[51] To touch here on Stein's career and its influence on Austrian education in general, and on Lueger in particular, is neither to deny the several other professional influences on Lueger's development nor to minimize the importance of his other teachers. Indeed, Lueger's notes from Stein's lectures repeat, paraphrase, or summarize much of what Karl had noted in other university courses and are therefore representative.[52] Instead, consideration of Stein is needed to redress the complete neglect of the influence of this theorist on Lueger's mature cultural political attitudes. Stein probably provided some of the theory that lay behind Lueger's exercise of power; and it is necessary to indicate some of the reasons why his contribution has been neglected. At the very least, Lueger's "social concern" had an early theoretical foundation, which preceded his political career. Time would prove that Lueger, the *Primus*, had learned his lessons well. A note in his handwriting from one of Stein's lectures heralds the viewpoint of the mature politician: "An attack on belief is an attack on the social order which defends itself."[53]

Stein synthesized much of the social scientific thought of the nineteenth century and was the last man to treat the social sciences as a unity.[54] "A conservative socialist,"[55] as Lueger himself was to become in some respects, Stein also achieved fame as an economist and journalist. His influence clearly shows through some of Lueger's early essays, suggesting that this great educator helped focus the incipient politician's ideas. Thus Lueger championed the Habsburg Monarchy as the only legitimate repository of political power in the multinational state at the same time Stein was evincing outspokenly pro-Austrian sentiments.[56] Lueger's Austrophile behavior was in marked contrast with that of other Austrian students during the 1860s who were swept up in the pan-German nationalist movement.[57]

When Lueger was attending Stein's lectures, Stein was writing his most important work on the theory and practice of administration, *Das Handbuch der Verwaltungslehre*, completed in 1868. His achievement won him the rank of a hereditary noble that same year. Stein's lectures on administration and jurisprudence were copied down by Lueger in university notebooks. These somewhat arid, theoretical, and occasionally neo-Hegelian jottings do not do justice to the dynamism of Stein's courses, which were among the most popular at the university. His rhetorical style, a vital element in the chemistry between himself and his students, and his ardent social concerns could well have inspired Lueger. Of particular interest in the light of Lueger's political development was Stein's preoccupation with the plight of Vienna's lower classes:

> Students were so thrilled by his utterances that they spoke about what they had heard long after his lecture. His thoughts ran from the philosophical image and experience to abstraction and the other way around. A cotton thread on his suit might serve as the departure for remarks about economic circulation and the division of labor; an image of the miserable quarters of a Viennese seamstress provided the background for exposition of the social question. For Stein himself, the "daily lecture was the source of the eternal youth of the spirit."[58]

It would have been difficult for impressionable young Karl to have ignored Stein even if he had wanted to. Stein's theatrical arrivals and departures at the university were famous. At the height of his career, Stein rode in a stately equipage, as Lueger himself was later to do. Clad in costly furs and reclining in the *fond,* he was attended by his blue-liveried coachman and a servant.[59] Under Lueger, some officials wore a specially designed uniform, too (see illustration), and the mayor was attended by a servant-bodyguard, Anton Pumera. Stein's delight in elegance also extended to fencing, at which he was both expert and ruthless. The effect of Stein's personality and enormous learning was recalled by Friedrich Eckstein, a fencing partner and friend in his student years. Stein, "the very first man to demand the universal franchise for the masses,"[60] praised Fichte's *Bestimmung des Menschen* as having had an especially great influence on him, but added that without

> [an exact knowledge of Kant,] it was also impossible to grasp the . . . ideas of Fichte, Schelling or Hegel and to understand sociological problems; all purely scientific investigations hovered in a vacuum if they were not based on . . . logical philosophical principles. These are the "constants in a continuous flux," . . . the "higher political economy must learn to recognize itself as a servant within the entire development of mankind," for the state was "the idea of freedom in its dialectical process."[61]

Although Stein's concepts were rooted in romanticism, Eckstein added that Stein never denied the close connection between "the idealism of German classical philosophy, the father of modern science, technology, and socialism."[62] Such a connection would become perceptible behind some of Lueger's politics.

Stein's influence extended far beyond the confines of the university, as Lueger's influence was to reach beyond Vienna. Japanese students carried Stein's ideas to their homeland. Shortly before he died in September

1890, he received a commission headed by the future Prince Ito, who had been dispatched by the Japanese government to learn about Western constitutional and administrative practices. Stein provided private lectures.[63] The Serbian party organ *Branik* posthumously acknowledged his pedagogical influence on an entire generation of Serbs.[64] Even Stein's critic Ludwig Gumplowicz conceded that all contemporary administrative literature "was ruled by Steinian ideas."[65] Today, students of jurisprudence at the University of Vienna routinely continue to study Stein's administrative theories.

Early in his career Stein had become apprehensive about the rapidly developing tendency toward specialization of knowledge and the concomitant danger of social disintegration. A similar presentiment appears in some of Lueger's student essays. Both men stressed the importance of community as an antidote to fragmentation, and the will of the state as the means to integrate the community and its functions. "Wholeness" was emphasized over "individualism" to combat fragmentation. Lueger concluded that although "both state and society are expressions of the community . . . the state represents unity [while] society represents fragmentation."[66] There can be little doubt that Lueger favored the unifying idea, that he was a neo-Josephinist, though his later political efforts failed to halt fragmentation, even within his own party.

Of particular interest in the extent of Stein's influence on Lueger's intellectual development is Stein's theoretical position toward women in society.[67] He held that women were of central importance in achieving harmonious community integration, particularly among the lower classes. Although sympathetic to their plight in the increasingly industrial Europe of the late nineteenth century, Stein never advocated any sort of emancipation. Yet, though male workers should bear the burden of social labor, "social feeling," by which Stein implied social awareness, was to be borne by women of the "non-possessing classes."[68] They were thus entrusted with the instinctively "higher task." Armed with this awareness, their role and duty were to harmonize social differences. Lueger used this perception by later appealing to women's "domesticity, to religion, to the education of children,"[69] some of the ostensible ideals of the Christian Social party, in trying to get them to influence their men's votes. He acknowledged their centrality as political agents and posed as the supporter of female suffrage, much to the chagrin and frustration of his Socialist rivals, who realized he had stolen a march on them.[70]

Although Stein was aware of his enormous influence on administrative education, he became dispirited at the end of his life. Perhaps he feared that his influence during his lifetime would be in inverse proportion to his influence after his death. He had educated many students, but he had not developed a school. Possibly he never perceived that an era of theoretical development was coming to an end, that academic speculation was giving way to pragmatic activism. Then, too, the rigidity of his theoretical categories, as well as a fixity about his ideas, may have discouraged imitators. Similarly, Lueger's authoritarian politics, which were often based on the letter rather than the spirit of the law, stifled possible successors, at least in imperial Austria.[71] There can be no effective "interactive" government where such ideas prevail. As he grew older, Stein became authoritarian; Lueger became dictatorial, thus reinforcing an older, deeply rooted outlook.

None of Lueger's biographers mentions, let alone develops, the many avenues of influence that connect the young Lueger with Stein.[72] This silence appears surprising, considering the evidence of Lueger's notebooks, Stein's fame, and his considerable effect on Austrian administrators, of whom Lueger was one of the best known. Yet, this silence is explained if one recalls that Lueger's major biographers, during the early decades of the twentieth century, were Catholic publicists trying to make the best case possible for aggressive political Catholicism during rapid erosion of traditional religious values.[73] Lueger became their standard-bearer; Stein ended as a disquieted liberal and an opportunist, even a reactionary in the eyes of some.[74]

According to the Austrian biographical tradition, which has been somewhat uncritically followed by John Boyer, as well, Lueger received his inspiration as a social reformer from Karl Freiherr von Vogelsang and the circle of publicist priests who formed his coterie.[75] Vogelsang's movement was a reaction against prevailing upper-middle-class Viennese liberalism. Vogelsang vigorously argued that only accredited Catholics could successfully oppose the threat of anarchy that seemed to flow from the liberal revolution of 1848.[76] Not only was Stein in such a context suspect as a Liberal and a Protestant,[77] but he had also participated in the Revolution of 1848, served as a member of the revolutionary Schleswig-Holstein Parliament, and introduced the concept of class into academic discussion before Karl Marx in the 1842 work *Der Sozialismus und Kommunismus des heutigen Frankreichs*.[78] This book probably contributed to his dismissal as a professor of jurisprudence at the University of Kiel during the conservative reaction of 1852. To Lueger publicists, such a man could never have served as the mentor of their standard-bearer.

Following the Revolution of 1848 Stein was obliged to remain in a kind of professional and political limbo, though his articles were still accepted by various journals in an era of imperfect and often ineffectual censorship. He emerged in 1854 and moved to Austria where, the following year, he was appointed professor of *Staatswissenschaften* at the University of Vienna by the minister of education, Count Thun. Although Stein, the former leftist radical, had arrived in the middle of a decade of conservative political reaction, the great economic progress of the 1850s spurred educational reform; and the advancement of a man of such obvious gifts could not long be slowed. Stein's radicalism was soon forgotten, at least by some. Thun carried out a sweeping reorganization of the secondary schools and universities so that "a social élite might emerge which would be sensitive to the requirements of the modern world."[79] Lueger, it will be remembered, began his education at the Theresianum during this decade. Stein, already highly respected for his publications in the German-speaking realm, was a logical choice for this position, and he remained at the University of Vienna, a much honored and productive scholar, until his retirement in 1885.

Upon his arrival in Vienna, Stein found a congenial companion in Karl Ludwig von Bruck, minister of commerce and, from 1855, minister of finance. No doubt inspired by Friedrich List, the men shared the then fashionable views about the need for a central European German federation. As a student, Lueger, too, advocated federalism as a solution to the internecine struggles among the German states. He urged "a large republican federation, that will eventually become one large republic,"[80] a radical beginning for one who later became a strong defender of Habsburg centralism. But Austria should create such a confederation; this was implicit in Lueger's writings and underlies his nationalism.

Through Stein, Lueger may have been introduced to the ideas of Friedrich List, whom he later extolled. As a mature politician, Lueger referred to List as "one of the greatest German national economists." Such a man provided theoretical justification for Lueger's paternalism: "Every state is a family and has to provide for it." Defending his opposition to the gold standard, he added: "[List] the creator of the German customs union . . . founded the strength of Prussia . . . which led to the unity of Germany under Prussia's leadership. I absorbed these teachings, and I am today still of the opinion that the autocracy of the state finds expression through paper money."[81]

"References to past economists can adorn a piece of instant wisdom, but the force of that alleged wisdom will typically lie in its appeal to simple common sense or to a shared prejudice."[82] Both Lueger and Stein before him shared prejudices, if not illusions. They overestimated, for example, the cohesiveness of the imperial idea as well as Austrian strength. Even after Austria had been defeated by Prussia in 1866, Stein continued to view his adopted country as the arbiter of Europe, "a wonderful unity of the most differing elements . . . [where there was] so much new to do and so much to be achieved."[83] Similarly, Lueger adhered to an exclusive Austrian cultural-political concept even after the ruinous potential of nationalism had become apparent.

By 1868 Stein had completed his most important work, the seven-volume *Verwaltungslehre*. Stein believed "administration" would foster a new classless society. Werner Schmidt, Stein's biographer, has condensed and paraphrased his ideas, ideas, it must be underscored, that also permeate Lueger's student essays, as follows:

> Administration is the "idea of state in action," the "actual life of the state," the "working state." . . . Administration . . . becomes "the sum total of all those actual activities of state, whose task and ultimate purpose is the individual growth of all members of the state." . . . Administration constitutes the execution of the will of the state (legislation), as governed by the state idea. . . . The state idea is "the conscience of administration". . . . While within the constitution and legislation some tasks remain possibilities to be realized, within the modern phenomenon of administration, however, they become so imbued with the ethos of human society, that [administration] can be charged with decisive tasks in the solution of social problems, in the harmonizing of interests and the development of the free personality.[84]

Underlying Stein's formulations was the perception that the secular state of the nineteenth century was an outgrowth of medieval church policy.[85] For Stein, sociopolitical attitudes in such a state should be informed with Christian principles, "the equality of man" among them.[86] One of the more positive aspects of Stein's teachings was his effort to retain traditional Judeo-Christian moral substance in his administrative theories, something Lueger's later politics inevitably lacked.

While Stein was his mentor, Lueger studied Austria's municipal legislation since 1848, the theoretical sources of political power, and the major European humanists and philosophers of administrative and governmental theory from the seventeenth century onward.[87] Through Stein, Lueger was likely introduced to the role of class in history and to the critical importance of sociopolitical interrelationships, just as new social groupings were attaining political consciousness. As a student and as a young politician, Lueger advocated a broad franchise, doubtless anticipating that his lasting success would hinge on mass support, or the subtle translation of power that mass support in effect allows.[88] Equally important was his introduction through Stein to the ideas of Saint-Simon, Blanc, Fourier, Owen, and Proudhon.[89] In his quest for power, Lueger condemned the abuses of

industrialism in terms reminiscent of both the early-nineteenth-century utopian socialists and their Christian Social successors.

Stein's neo-Hegelian influence on Lueger also seems apparent. While
he was mayor, Lueger behaved as though he were the will of the party and
the very personification of administrative office. He demanded palpable
achievements, newly created parks and gardens, buildings, and modern
technology, all instruments and repositories as well as emblems of power.
Not only did these achievements bear his personal stamp, but they also
suggested a larger administrative dialectic of Steinian inspiration. Neo-
classical and *Jugendstil* architecture became a memorial, a terminus, a
tomb. Indeed, Lueger and some of the other leading Christian Socials
seemed to be obsessed with elaborate funerary monuments, thus evincing
a characteristic Viennese trait. During Lueger's mayoralty there was a
tomb-boom, which climaxed with the building of the Lueger Memorial
Church in the Central Cemetery.[90] Because of the power Lueger commanded
and the education he had received, such a development may have been
inevitable, for Stein's carefully formulated administrative and social categories, so painstakingly recorded in Lueger's notebooks, and applied in
his essays, left little freedom for any other *style* of expression.

In late-nineteenth-century Europe, where the state's role was yet to
be magnified by technology, Stein's theoretical categories seemed bril-
liantly logical, even prophetic. But they assumed a negative reality in
Lueger's politics and the brittleness of his cultural values. Despite his
youthful political activity, Stein and his world had remained academic,
but for one unsuccessful campaign for the Austrian parliament, the Reichsrat. The realities of practical politics remained a world apart. Increasing
egalitarianism, intensifying nationalism, and other, irrational forces all
grew more important in the world in which Lueger began his political
development than they were in Stein's days. But just the same Stein's administrative theories and dialectical teachings had already been implanted,
and they could be expected to have powerful if subtle effects. In his final
academic exercise at the University of Vienna, Lueger defended forty-six
theses before an examining commission of professors on January 20, 1870.
A handful of these topics look to the future: "All citizens of age who can
read and write should have the active and passive franchise"; "Self-education
is only possible in a state whose citizens have a sense of community"; "The
conditions of the worker demand a much more exact and comprehensive
statistical survey than has hitherto been concluded."[91] Kuppe would have
us believe that Lueger's "defense" revealed "extraordinary courage" during
the zenith "of liberalism in politics and economics."[92] In theory perhaps

so, but as John Boyer has pointed out, "Such statements were not in fact very radical (the literacy qualifications would have denied the franchise to tens of thousands in Vienna alone)."[93] In the light of what Lueger had been studying for years, much of which had been summarized by Lorenz von Stein, it is reasonable to conclude that his defense was in line with his education.

Although one of his theses proclaimed the nationality idea was "an obstacle to the progress of mankind,"[94] it is doubtful that Lueger argued against Austrian nationalism. Instead, he likely condemned the nationalism of the Hungarians, toward whom he was always antagonistic. Lueger's early biographers Tomola, Stauracz, and Kuppe report that young Karl demonstrated outspoken Habsburg patriotism during his university years. According to this biographical tradition, Lueger joined the loyalist "German Academic Reading Society" in 1863, when he was 19. He is reported to have withdrawn from the club when it turned away from Austria and looked toward Prussia for German leadership.[95] "If you cut me, you'll find black and yellow," he supposedly told one student, referring to the traditional Habsburg colors,[96] and to others, after the Prussian defeat of Austria in 1866. "Now we're all Austrians, and no one has to sit on two chairs any longer. That's a great advantage, for we can all attach ourselves more firmly to Austria, to work together with united strength for her greatness."[97]

While Lueger's loyalty seems never to have flagged for long, such anecdotes distort its magnitude by implying an unwavering superpatriotism, and owe more to his biographers' feelings than to young Karl's leanings. Lueger's contemporary letters to a close friend create another impression. In early September 1866, with the Prussians encamped before Vienna, an apparently complacent and self-centered Lueger asserts that he was bored! Karl seems indifferent to his country's defeat, saddened by the absence and misfortunes of his friends in the army, and unenthusiastic about studying for law exams.[98] A month later, he was still complaining about his loneliness, a cholera epidemic in Vienna, and apprehensive lest "the Slavs and Magyars gain complete control" of the Reading Society.[99]

Lueger with this last sentiment reveals that his patriotism had not completely evaporated; but read in their entirety the letters suggest, as one would expect, that he had many practical and immediate things on his mind besides the more remote question of Austrian national destiny. In a subsequent essay he returns to his nationalism and resentment over Hungary's increased power since the *Ausgleich* (1867), as well as regret about the destruction of Josephinian centralism. Lueger's attitudes, therefore, reflect a nationalism coming, not only from student circles, but from a patriotic veteran father. Leopold never lived to see his son receive his diploma because he died, symbolically, in the autumn of 1866, the last year that Austria could have been considered the arbiter of Central European affairs.

For the country this defeat of 1866 may have been a necessary step toward further emergence as a nation of cultural significance: henceforth, energies would be used for something else than maintaining Austria's political and military importance. In any case, the defeated military did not constitute a state within a state, as it did in Prussia, and its relationship with the rest of society was, therefore, more subtly responsive to change. But the effect of this defeat on Lueger is even more difficult to ascertain. His contemporary letters suggest, though, that as a young man of twenty-two in the autumn of 1866, Lueger had had enough of being a student and was ready to embark on the legal career that would prepare him for a life in politics.

2

The Developing Politician: 1869–1889

Certainly Lueger began his career in the Liberal camp; he alone was not Liberal in the sense of the time.
                    —Eugen Mack, *Dr. Karl Lueger und die Jugend*

Nur Derjenige ein echter, guter Mensch ist, der seine eigene armselige Persönlichkeit—und armselig ist auch die Selbstsucht des begabten Mannes—in allen bedeutenden Augenblicken seines Lebens vollständig vergisst.
                    —*Deutsche Wochenschrift*, October 26, 1884

*B*etween 1869 and 1889, Karl Lueger acquired the skills and cultivated the sensibilities that would make him the most popular Austrian politician of the late imperial era. The ways in which he grew largely determined the perimeters of his personality as mayor and party leader. He learned to build coalitions and resolve conflicts among his followers; he developed the most finely attuned political antennae in Austria; and he exploited innovative campaign methods and unexpected opportunities. In addition, Lueger had the common touch, the ability to mingle among his adherents on familiar terms, while yet retaining his authority as leader. Following the death of Vogelsang in 1890, Lueger became the undisputed leader of the Christian Social party, the first modern mass political party in Austria. By then he had thoroughly mastered his craft. A description of his ascent until 1889 is the focus of this chapter; his exploitation of anti-Semitism and socioeconomic discontent to win the mayoralty is the focus of the next.

As a fledgling politician in the late 1860s, Lueger took considerable pride in the achievements of the ruling Liberal party, and he admired at least one Viennese mayor. Though the Liberals maintained their power by means of the restricted franchise, Lueger was at first successful as a Liberal and would have had nothing to gain by attacking his sponsors. Only after Liberalism became too confining for him and unresponsive to change in the early 1880s did he break away. It took several more years for him to emerge as an anti-Liberal. By that time, Lueger's ambitions to create a mass party had become apparent. For above all, Lueger was transparently ambitious. This and his willingness to use any means to achieve his goals became hallmarks of the mature politician.

Lueger was never an ideologist. His well-known rejection of party programs was symptomatic of this. Behind his attacks on Liberalism from the late 1880s may be perceived Lueger's rejection of any and all political philosophies, or of more consistent bodies of political ideas or principles. Neither he nor any of his followers or successors proved capable of creating a coherent ideology, let alone an original one. Viennese Christian Socialism served as a vehicle for Lueger's dynamic leadership but little else. Its emptiness as a political philosophy became apparent as his leadership weakened with the deterioration of his health. Ultimately, Lueger *had* to reject Liberalism or any other systematic body of political ideas, because he could not accommodate his personality to them while he lived. One suspects that he sensed that they would have failed to perpetuate his style once he had gone.

In 1867 Lueger began his legal apprenticeship. According to his own account, he worked as an assistant for three separate attorneys, Hermann Kopp, Anton Edler von Ruthner, and Karl Kienboeck, before setting up his own office in 1874 with Josef Brzobohaty.[1] Lueger's biographer Stauracz emphasizes Karl's selflessness in providing legal assistance to the poor during his early years. According to him, Lueger could have earned a tidy income from a smoothly functioning legal practice, because his professional skills were superior to those of most other attorneys. Instead, he preferred to assist his fellow men without remuneration, even paying for the necessary legal taxes "out of his own pocket."[2]

Although it is probably true that Lueger fought many cases and provided counsel without remuneration — he even defended impoverished Socialists during the late 1870s and early 1880s — he must have accepted fees from some of his clients, or he would not have survived. Possibly his helping the legally indigent also carried a private significance for him by helping others "get even". But it is also possible that he had a sense of social obligation toward the poor. In 1869, again according to his own reckoning, he entered Vienna's political life, though in what capacity he does not make clear.[3] Stauracz states that Lueger joined the newly founded Liberal Landstrasser Bürgerklub in the third district in 1872, at the urging of his friends and because of his own high-flying ambition, and was immediately elected as a second secretary.[4] Yet, this same biographer is silent about Lueger's prior affiliation with another Liberal club, the Deutsch-Demokratische Verein, which was also located in this district.[5] There Lueger met Ignaz Mandl, a radical Jewish physician with ideas of civil reform who was nine years older than Lueger. Neither Mandl nor Lueger could stand the club's tyrannical leader Ignaz Krawani and withdrew some months after joining it. Mandl founded his own rival club Eintracht, while Lueger joined one that suited him, the Bürgerklub.[6] By this time he must have abandoned his ideas of becoming a university professor, if indeed these had ever been seriously entertained.[7] Probably the position of professor would have been too set and continuing for him, as it really was for Stein.

Lueger was realistic about where his talents lay. His ambition took a political form in a pragmatic realization of his goals. The first step for an aspiring young politician such as himself was to attract a following, even though possible supporters may for the moment have lacked the franchise. The turbulent Austrian Socialist movement of the late 1860s gave promise of things to come, a portent that Lueger could not have failed to discern. Though Socialism proved insignificant in Austrian politics until the late 1880s, the party rank and file was a rich pool of potential support for Lueger, who for many years remained uncertain about his political direction, and he doubtless hoped to attract some of them. Providing free legal counsel served both his emotional and political ends as well as those of his clients, for word about the enterprising young attorney who was interested in the underrepresented and underprivileged was spreading.

Karl Lueger was elected a municipal councillor in 1875, representing the second curia from the third district.[8] At that time the Habsburg Empire and much of Europe had been experiencing a worsening depression for nearly two years.[9] In Vienna, the crash of May 9, 1873, "one of the most momentous events in Austrian financial history,"[10] resulted in many business failures and an understandable tendency among the hardworking to mistrust the promises of politicians and financiers.[11]

Many workers who had streamed into the capital during the boom years of the 1860s suddenly found themselves unemployed and without housing.[12] At first, the depression did not seem to weaken the ruling Liberal party, particularly on the local Viennese level. There, all the parties were Liberal, regardless of what they called themselves,[13] and none of them, alone or in combination, could offer opposition to Mayor Cajetan Felder and his powerful backers. A party of the prosperous and well-to-do, the Liberals held on to Vienna, the city that afforded the most opportunity for the affluent, because of their resources, the restricted franchise, and because they met the needs of their major constituents until the early 1890s. Liberal mayors continued to control the city until 1895, though with diminishing support, until they and their party were finally ousted by Lueger and the Christian Socials. However, in the more volatile and variegated, and thus representative, national parliament, Liberal hegemony was decisively broken in 1879.[14] A Conservative-Clerical-Slavic combination was then forged by Count Eduard Taaffe,[15] who held continuous office as prime minister until 1893.

For Lueger, perhaps the most important outcome of the crash was a growing dissatisfaction among the less affluent with the Liberal status quo and a corresponding receptivity to novel political forms and expressions. A new generation of politicians arose, himself among them, whose effect on Austrian politics was great in his own day, and even now is perceptible. On the most basic level, the Socialist movement was further undermined, leaving Austrian workers without effective leadership, and with no representation in the elective bodies at all. Though the depression produced a generally gloomy effect on all parties, few Socialists had any enthusiasm left for politics after the continuing struggle for bare physical existence. The progressive decline had begun after a giant demonstration before parliament in December 1869, when the government arrested and imprisoned 15 of the workers' leaders and dissolved all their political associations.[16] A small Social Democratic party survived, but it remained weak and divided until its reorganization by Dr. Viktor Adler two decades later. Not until the late 1880s did Austria's industrial revolution take off and with it the spectacular growth of the proletariat.[17] No Social Democrats were elected to the Austrian representative bodies until the late 1890s.[18] By that time Lueger and his party had consolidated their control over Vienna and Lower Austria, and in 1907, when he had forged a coalition with the Catholic Conservatives, his became the leading imperial party in parliament. The Socialists would have to wait their turn after his death.

In her study of Karl Lueger as a Liberal, Karin Brown has described the circumstances surrounding Lueger's first election to the Vienna Municipal Council and his early years as a politician. A substantial portion of the following description of Lueger's activities until 1882 is taken from her meticulous account.

Throughout his career, Lueger drew his main support from Vienna's lower middle class, some of whom found an upward mobility in the late 1890s as Vienna and Europe emerged from a lengthy depression. However, in the mid-1870s the Viennese lower middle class was in some ways as hard-hit by the depression as the workers were:

> Income-tax payments had fallen by 40 per cent since 1872, and in 1875 only 50 per cent of the expected business tax was collected; 6,000 (houses) stood empty despite a drastic housing shortage, abandoned by tenants no longer able to pay the high rents; 7,000 businesses, making up 14 per cent of the business tax base, had moved to the outer suburbs to escape the high rents and consumers' taxes in effect inside the city limits.
> The Viennese craftsmen and shopkeepers, who only a few years before had hardly been able to keep up with the demand for new dresses, hats, shoes, furniture . . . did not . . . need statistics to tell them that business was bad; neither were they willing to wait for a general upswing to bring their customers back. What they demanded as a right and necessity for survival was immediate action.[19]

Amid this economic despondency, property-owning citizens of Vienna were particularly sensitive to malfeasance, or even a hint of it, in municipal government. This was the only area of political life in which some few of them, at least, were active.[20] Political clubs sprouted and disappeared like mushrooms. Against this background Lueger and his first, and probably most important political mentor, Ignaz Mandl,[21] a fellow municipal councillor, scored a significant success against Mayor Cajetan Felder, forcing him to resign in 1878. Notwithstanding his Liberal party affiliation, Felder was an authoritarian in outlook. Carl Schorske has trenchantly characterized Vienna's liberal haute bourgeoisie, of which Felder was one of the classic examples, at the time of its zenith: "Morally, it was secure, righteous, and repressive; politically, it was concerned for the rule of law, under which both individual rights and social order were subsumed. It was intellectually committed to the rule of the mind over the body and to a latter-day Voltairism: to social progress through science, education, and hard work."[22] Though Liberalism suffered from many weaknesses all over Europe, the weakness of Vienna's Liberals was its narrow social base, "confined to the middle-class Germans and German Jews of the urban centers. Increasingly identified with capitalism, they maintained parliamentary power by the undemocratic device of the restricted franchise."[23]

For all his shortcomings as a member of Vienna's haute bourgeoisie, Felder was in many ways an extraordinary man and the best mayor the Liberals produced. He was a talented entomologist, linguist, and in general an avid hobbyist, who in his youth traveled on foot throughout Europe and later undertook thirty major ocean cruises. He thus embodied the dynamism of his social class, which had helped move Vienna out of its earlier and more religiously oriented ways. Personally, Felder was an energetic professional and brilliant administrator, whose scorn was feared by those who roused his ire. As a mayor, he started many effective reforms and completed major projects that Lueger subsequently built on, including further reservoir construction, the regulation of the Danube, and the expansion of the Central Cemetery.[24] It is tempting to speculate that Lueger may also have imitated Felder's autocratic style and proprietary attitudes toward city government, indeed toward every aspect of city affairs that he deemed his own province.

Felder mastered all the major European tongues, and was acquainted with some of the Middle Eastern languages. He was admitted to full membership of the Academy of Science, and devoted much of his spare time to the study of insects and butterflies, many of which he collected on his wide-ranging excursions. Never the hard-bitten petty bourgeois who measures everything in self-serving pragmatism, Felder loved esoteric sorts of knowledge for their own sake, not for the political advantages that he might derive from them, according to Richard S. Levy. Felder read Greek and Latin classics, as well as the early church fathers, in their original languages and even undertook the study of Chinese at an advanced age.[25] One cannot escape the impression that he was a compulsive if honestly voracious student. Lueger's studies, by contrast, were fairly well defined even at an early age and mostly served more narrowly focused professional goals. More and more, politics occupied his every waking hour and subsumed his studies, although Lueger had some private life outside politics.

Felder was a private man whose practical politics was balanced by a sensitivity to fundamental cultural interrelationships. Lueger's attraction to power, on the other hand, fostered an increasing indifference to such confraternity. As a student he had acknowledged such social bonds and their importance in shaping the administrative unity within a state. Part of Lueger, the man, thrived on human contact and even more on adulation. Yet, there was a remoteness in him that ran deeper than Felder's apparent imperiousness. A retired Lueger would have been inconceivable because of his fundamental restlessness. But after Felder resigned as mayor, he lived on for sixteen years, dictated his memoirs, which ran to many thousands of pages, became an acute observer of the political scene, and pondered the significance of his impact on Vienna. His memoirs conclude, modestly enough, with the words: "He was a man who did no harm to Vienna."[26]

Lueger's needs went beyond constant activity, which he usually found in full measure in politics; his nature required turbulence and conflict. Only when he was secure in office, did he feel free to travel extensively;

but here again, he traveled for reasons very different from Felder's. For although the Liberal mayor made his journeys primarily to satisfy a wanderlust and intellectual curiosity, Lueger traveled to publicize his politics and himself, and often to negotiate behind the scenes. This style of self-seeking would have been repulsive to Felder, who primarily sought, and found, intellectual enrichment in his own travels. These varied uses and responses to similar experiences show some of the inner differences between the two men. Felder continued to grow in ways that Lueger never did. Felder's dispassionate intellectual curiosity, his personal integrity, and his disinclination to compromise his political principles defined the man. Lueger would rarely take up a political principle that he was not prepared to drop, if expedient.

The conflict that soon arose between the two may have been directly caused by Lueger's ambition to rise swiftly in the political world, but perhaps equally by his frustrated admiration for the mayor.[27] Felder may have held the younger man at arm's length, sensing in him a radicalism antithetical to the established political and social order. Lueger doubtless perceived Felder's positive qualities, and may at this early stage in his career have idealized him and wanted to become his friend, or because he needed other models than those who had merely reflected his own class background. But perhaps it is equally possible that he may have been disappointed that the mayor failed to live up to an ideal.[28] Lueger's teachers doubtless furnished some of his earlier models. Felder's predecessor as mayor, Andreas Zelinka, caused Lueger to confess his ambition to become mayor to his university friends.[29] If for a time Felder served as yet another of Lueger's models, at length, the discrepancy between ideal and reality may have become too great: Lueger's ambition got the upper hand, and he and Mandl challenged the mayor.

Had Lueger been a more conventional politician, less ambitious, and willing to accept an easy path as a Liberal, his career might have been different indeed, even in view of his conflict with Felder. But in rejecting the Liberals' vision of "latter-day Voltairism," or, possibly, not wishing to serve a long apprenticeship in the Liberal party, he gradually discovered his fundamental, if problematic, flexibility. The immediate cause of Lueger's and Mandl's break with Felder was a controversy over a matter that in ordinary economic circumstances might have gone unnoticed. Lueger charged an abuse of power, public waste, and corruption in the purchase of low-grade sand "for which the city had been billed and paid the price of a higher quality."[30] Felder built his house on a foundation of sand. In the ensuing struggle, Vienna's two legally constituted self-governing bodies, the municipal council and the district committees on one side, were ranged against Felder and the Magistrat, or Vienna civil service, on the other. While Mandl criticized Felder for protecting the Magistrat and damaging the city's economic interests, Lueger took another course, demonstrating for the first time in his political career his instinctive grasp of deeper and more subtle principles, and applied this insight to practical politics. He argued on his side that public interests were threatened by Felder's exercise of executive power. Felder believed in and practiced "government by an educated elite."[31] Lueger held that he, as a true representative of the people, should have legal guarantees of that position, for without them there could be no government for the people and by the people. More important, he tried to put these inadequately guarded principles into practice. Brown argues that Lueger's and Mandl's "primary aim was first of all, good government, not a basically different government. The originality of their effort lay in the attempt to shift power not from one party to another, but from one government organ, the Magistrat, to another, the elected representatives in the [Municipal] Council and District Committees."[32]

Felder won the first round of the dispute, which ended in mid-December 1875. He presented the municipal council with a report affirming that the sand in question was of the officially specified quality, stated that further investigation was unwarranted, and declared the case closed.[33] But Lueger and Mandl remained undaunted. They ceased to criticize Felder's conduct of government for the moment, but their retreat was merely a tactic. The two municipal councillors withdrew to the sidelines and waited for further opportunities.

Economic issues continued to preoccupy Viennese voters during the spring of 1876. In district committee elections most of the usual campaign rhetoric, with its pejorative epithets and name-calling, was subordinated to considerations of fiscal questions. Candidates declared as their main goal the prevention of further tax increases. Lueger, running in the second curia from the third district again, but this time for a three-year term, made the same promises as other politicians, and won anyway. Perhaps his individual qualities told in his favor.

In the light of Felder's intense dislike of Lueger and wish to block his reelection, it is not surprising that only fifty-nine percent of the voters cast their ballot for Lueger in March 1876, as against seventy-four percent in the preceding year.[34] Yet, Felder had also lost some of his popularity, if not something of his previously unquestioned authority, in the emergence of Mandl and Lueger. His efforts to get Lueger defeated had not only failed, but must surely also have signaled to him the arrival of a new and potentially dangerous opponent, a maverick rival of subtle mind, singularity of purpose, and relentless ambition.

In describing Lueger's Theresianum education, Karin Brown suggests the importance of school ties in fostering Lueger's professional advancement. At least as important to his advancement as "life-long membership in a fraternity of the empire's ruling elite,"[35] however, were Karl's acute political instincts, intelligence, pragmatism, and also rapport with his constituents. To an older politician like Felder, who had once been highly ambitious himself, the young Lueger may have come to symbolize everything the mayor preferred to forget about himself, or even to reject, at his stage in life. Years of power, but also of travel and reflection, had not left his sensibilities unchanged. Moreover, Lueger was that unusual phenomenon in the German-speaking world of the nineteenth century, a natural leader of humble background. He had won despite all Felder, the older, more worldlywise, or at least experienced, politician could do to defeat him. The mayor had remained proudly aloof, but his self-imposed isolation had proved to be anything but splendid. Lueger had successfully courted the voters and thus isolated the Liberal leader all the more.[36] Had it not been for Lueger and Mandl, Felder at sixty-two might have looked forward to a peaceful and tranquil retirement and to the pursuit of his interests. All of this had now been spoiled, for instead of retirement with honor, the mayor was confronted with the prospect of having to defend his policies and very position against two resourceful and determined foes. It is scarcely surprising that he consigned Lueger and Mandl to the icy regions of his hatred, to a category of men called *"wolfsfrei."*[37] To Felder, this legal term would have characterized Lueger's restless striving and subtle ravening for power, his protestations to the contrary notwithstanding.[38] In his memoirs, Felder gave full vent to his feelings, describing the young politician as "a single-minded villain . . . who wants to destroy anyone who doesn't blindly kowtow, with poison, fire and sword."[39]

For the moment, however, Felder was frustrated. In the months after the spring elections, Lueger and Mandl continued their attacks on the mayor's conduct of administration by reviving the issue of municipal waste. Again Felder brushed aside the two younger municipal councillors' criticism. But the anticorruptionists soon made a discovery the mayor could not ignore. They announced that the third district committee chairman, Mattaeus Mayer, had listed "a part-time city worker . . . under both halves of his conveniently long name, Kirschlehner," and thereby enabled him to receive double pay.[40] Mayer's action, which might have come out of the plot of a Strauss operetta, or perhaps better, anticipated Schnitzler's play *Fink und Fliederbusch*, was intended to aid an elderly local civil servant who had fallen on hard times.[41] But Lueger and Mandl, in their special enthusiasm to tarnish Felder's administration, ignored Mayer's protestations that the district committee had known about his charity to Kirschlehner all along. They threatened to file suit unless he relinquished his post, hoping to replace him with one of their own men. In any event, Mayer resigned, but the pro-Felder minority boycotted the election of the new chairman, and thus deprived the meeting held for this purpose of a quorum.[42]

At this point, the municipal council tried to resolve the impasse by reducing the quorum from twelve to ten, prompting Lueger's sarcastic thanks for the council's "unaccustomed willingness . . . to meet me half way." Felder, himself famous for sarcasm, it will be remembered, refused to tolerate it from others, and especially not from Lueger. Stung by the remark, the mayor demanded that Lueger be called to order.[43]

In the next sessions the confrontation between Felder and Lueger intensified. Early in September 1876, Lueger introduced two motions of urgency charging Felder with conflict of interest in administering the Magistrat and the municipal council, and partiality in conducting the council's business.[44] Felder responded that he would "not go to school to Herr Dr. Lueger,"[45] and, in effect, asked the municipal council for a vote of confidence to move to other matters on the agenda without debating Lueger's motions. The obedient council unanimously complied, indignant that the mayor had been brought to such a pass by the youngest member of the municipal council. Even councillors who had been castigated by Felder revealed a measure of loyalty, or perhaps disorientation,[46] by voting with the majority.

Lueger and his handful of allies were taken to task for their "terrorist" tactics by Felder's journalist allies, and Vienna's papers urged voters to turn the oppositionists out in the district committee elections of mid-October. Lueger and Mandl had been unsuccessful in obtaining the necessary quorum. Lacking practically any journalistic support, except Mandl's paper, the two fought back with the agitational means at their disposal "[sparing] nothing in a desperate bid for votes."[47]

From this time on, Lueger and the Liberal papers became lifelong foes. Lueger fought back in any and every way he could. He sometimes charged them with slander, as against Hermann Fuerst, editor-in-chief, and Franz Singer, publisher, of the *Illustriertes Wiener Extrablatt*,[48] during the autumn 1876 campaign. Interesting in this respect is the retraction he tried to compel the *Extrablatt* to publish, in which the paper was to apologize for impugning his "personal integrity and honorable motives."[49] Lueger was particularly sensitive to suggestions that he was dishonest. From Lorenz von Stein he had learned that "the press [for its part had] an ethical obligation to tell the truth. This sustains and is an integral part of the press."[50] Such ideas also reflect some of the idealism Lueger and Mandl brought to their district committee campaign. The voters responded by a large turnout, but the combined weight of Felder's "influence and prestige"[51] told, and all the Lueger-Mandl candidates were defeated, "overwhelmingly in the Second and . . . First Curia."[52]

In the third curia opposition candidates declined from fifty-three to forty-three percent since the spring, but this was nonetheless a respectable showing, considering the overwhelming superiority of Felder's material resources. Although it remained a local campaign, the district committee election constituted a crucial watershed in Lueger's career:

> Here the effectiveness of a new approach to politics introduced by Mandl and Lueger was clearly demonstrated. . . . If nothing else, Mandl and Lueger had succeeded in reviving a political milieu grown stodgy and out of touch with the feelings and frustrations of the average voter. While the . . . purists had remained content to "speak out of the window" of the *Reichsrat*, and from the pages of a boring newspaper to an imaginary audience of like-minded idealists, Mandl and Lueger filled the galleries with their histrionics, promise of scandal, and concern with problems that could be seen and counted. If they had not yet uncovered a significant case of corruption, at least they had taken the trouble to investigate abuses that affected everyone directly and painfully. Perhaps most important of all, they had . . . gone directly to the voter, wherever he happened to be — his home, coffeehouse, or favorite saloon — and shown an interest in his woes.
>
> With these novel tactics, Mandl and Lueger attracted attention not only to themselves, but to conditions and issues that would keep the political pot boiling. . . . Ignatz [sic] Mandl was the first to understand the art of mobilizing popular support through aggressive agitation, personal contact, and a hitherto unknown degree of self-promotion — the last derided as "popularity seeking" by opponents who persisted in clinging to the notion that municipal politics had everything to do with order and professional competence, nothing with popularity.[53]

Lueger learned much from Mandl, whose own theoretical views doubtless in Lueger's mind aligned themselves with Stein's. Lueger, one might say, took a page from Mandl and wrote a new chapter in self-promotion.

For the time being, however, he had been defeated. He relinquished his mandate on October 20,[54] "explaining that he could not in good conscience continue to represent citizens who had clearly lost confidence in him."[55] Lueger's resignation, which delighted some but disheartened others,[56] was likely prompted not only by political defeat, but probably also by an attendant emotional crisis, the first of his adult political career.[57] Such a deep response points to irrationality in Lueger's personality. In his memoirs Felder mentions a report in the [*Wiener*] *Bürger Zeitung* in which Lueger was said to have become deeply agitated "after his defeat," that he went for weeks with little sleep, food, or drink. But then Felder added: "If it is true . . . the reason [was not] introspection, but rather preparation for that great work of destruction that he felt compelled to complete without delay."[58] The young *wolfsfrei* politician was licking his wounds, studying revenge.

Felder's phrase "great work of destruction," referring to Lueger's attempts to end the mayor's career, was not long in coming. The two had by now become irreconcilable foes; and we can believe that Felder spoke his true feelings when he referred to Lueger as "Goethe's liar, the destroyer, as the old poem paints Mephistopheles."[59] Though out of office, Lueger continued his anti-Felder agitation. He rejected the negative findings of the criminal court in the earlier matter of his slander charges against *Extrablatt* publisher and Municipal Councillor Franz Singer, "an intimate of . . . Dr. Cajetan Felder," and pressed for a "continuation of the investigation."[60] Before the electoral defeat in mid-October, Lueger had been gathering data for a new investigation of malfeasance in the administration of the recently completed Central Cemetery. During his absence, Mandl maintained this pressure on Felder.

Besides Felder and most of the Viennese press, Lueger and Mandl had another less obtrusive enemy, though "the one least comfortable in the role of Felder acolyte . . . the Vienna democrats,"[61] the left faction of the Liberal party. Although Lueger later stated that he had withdrawn from "the old Liberal Party" in 1876,[62] his relationship with the populist democrats was more ambiguous, and he continued his formal affiliation with them until 1887.[63] Some of them, critical of Felder's style of administration if not its substance, had occasionally sided with Mandl and Lueger; but they still disliked their extreme independence. Yet this group was to assume pivotal importance for Lueger:

> Lueger's ambivalent relationship to the Vienna democrats is a major aspect of his political development, and the key to understanding his ultimate break with the liberal tradition and with his colleagues of the (Municipal) Council left. This relationship was from the beginning of Lueger's involvement in district politics, charged with tension. The conflict was basically personal rather than political — between an ambitious self-assertive, exceptionally able young man who knew himself to be superior, and the rather less brilliant, less accomplished men who represented his political values, but by virtue of their seniority and earlier start, blocked his personal advance within the democratic movement.[64]

Had he not been frustrated thus, Lueger's populism might have found expression in an organic form of Liberalism rather than assuming the radical shape it did.

There seems little reason to question that Lueger was exceptionally able, but for all of that, he was ruthless and unscrupulous, and for the moment balked in his ambition. Lueger's career had slowed by the end of 1876, and Mandl's prospects too had also dimmed. However, a core of voters in the poorer area of the third district, the so-called Erdberg,[65] held Mandl's club Eintracht together, and was the nucleus of his reelection campaign in the municipal council elections early the following year. Mandl also hoped to fill two additional seats with his own candidates. With these mandates, he might regroup his forces and mount yet another assault against Felder and his seemingly invincible camp. Lueger campaigned for Mandl's party.

The March election of 1877 was possibly the most turbulent and intense that Vienna had yet witnessed on the district level. Not only was Mandl's municipal council seat at stake, but undoubtedly his entire political career, and indirectly that of Lueger, too, for the latter had divorced himself from any other backing. Mandl's and Lueger's fortunes could not have weathered another defeat like that of the preceding autumn. Besides the practice of seeking out voters in their homes and places of recreation, Mandl's party campaigned among the trade associations, promising to protect them and their enterprises. This was an important and timely innovation, not only because of the continuing depression, but also because in so doing, the Mandl party came to be known for carrying out economic reform at the grass roots level. Also innovative, but far more reprehensible and even ludicrous, was the use of anti-Semitism by the Mandl party, which objected to "a [rival] candidate on the grounds that he was Jewish." The pro-Felder *Konstitutionelle Vorstadtzeitung* dismissed this tactic as absurd, ". . . of warning against a candidate on the grounds he is a Jew, by people whose list is headed by a man belonging likewise to God's Chosen People; one who this time, however, will count with those who are called, but not chosen."[66] Absurd or not, the tactic was significant. A municipal campaign technique in 1877, anti-Semitism was later to escalate into a program to disenfranchise Jews.

Municipal waste and corruption, however, remained at the center of the campaign. And Mandl's fiscal arguments made more sense than ever in the light of continuing economic gloom. Probably his response to real issues, as well as his tireless efforts, swung the election in his favor. In fact, all the Mandl candidates won in a heavy voter turnout.[67] Returned once more to the municipal council with a fresh mandate, Mandl renewed his investigations. But this time he took new steps to stop the mayor from frustrating the disclosure of corruption. Mandl reported "his cases to the State Attorney's Office,"[68] and, assisted by Lueger, deliberately provoked lawsuits, some of which were soon in court, to create a public forum for his investigations. He and Lueger had uncovered evidence of graft at the Central Cemetery immediately before the electoral defeat of October 1876. Among the abuses, Mandl's paper *Fortschritt* had charged "faulty book-keeping, use of substandard materials in paths and walks, unauthorized use of city property by the grave-digging concessionaires . . . and a pay-roll listing more workers than had actually been employed."[69] Felder had dismissed the charges as usual, making the counterclaim that a gravestone dealer, Josef Rohatschek, who had made the disclosures, had been re-warded with a permanent civil servant's job in Mandl's own third district.[70] A complete investigation was nonetheless ordered. A commission an-nounced that irregularities had indeed taken place, but also that none of them entailed punishable offenses. Just the same the case shows that Feld-er's authority was now insufficient to quash the investigation entirely; the efforts of the anticorruptionists were beginning to tell. On Mandl's in-sistence the municipal council kept the investigation open.

The cemetery disclosures were followed by revelations of a different kind. The Magistrat, it appeared, had mismanaged welfare funds for the third district. On this issue Mandl for the first time won considerable sup-port among municipal councillors for administrative reform. "In September 1877 a motion brought by a respected Far Left Councilman, to have the Poor Boards elected by the District Committees [instead of by the Magis-trat], was accepted for consideration by a large majority."[71] Felder's au-thority was being systematically diminished. This same month Lueger and Mandl were further cleared of slander charges in conjunction with their disclosures about welfare mismanagement. The two thus acquired wider and positive publicity, though Felder's journalistic supporters continued to belittle the anticorruptionists' methods, even after one orphanage director, a member of the Magistrat, was convicted and imprisoned for fraud, and another was "placed under disciplinary investigation."[72]

In October 1877 Mandl's reputation as a municipal investigator was dramatically vindicated by the outcome of yet another slander trial in which Lueger defended the editor of *Fortschritt*, Eduard Trexler von Lin-denau. Charges were made against Trexler over the *Fortschritt* article of October 1876 about graveyard mismanagement, but the most shocking . . . revelation . . . was clear evidence . . . of ninety-odd names listed on a payroll sheet for snow shovellers, sixty [of whom] had simply been copied out of the handy burial register. All of Mandl's previous revelations, and his reputation as a defamer and public nuisance, paled before the striking image of this exhumed task force. Lueger had no trouble persuading a fascinated jury that the editor of *Fortschritt* had good reason to believe the story furnished by a former employee of the cemetery concessionaires, which Felder had earlier dismissed [as] "based on lies and heresay." Both Trexler and the informant were acquitted on all seven counts of slander brought against them by two officials in the unsavory business.[73]

In contrast to the brief and noncommittal comments in the Liberal *Neue Freie Presse* about the anticorruptionists' latest triumph, the usually pro-Felder *Morgenpost* reassessed its position on Mandl and thought it likely that "'dead hands' [were] also receiving wages elsewhere" in the municipal service.[74] Felder, 63 at the time, probably wished, because of Mandl's unabated attacks, that he were among the spectral shovelers, but nonetheless decided to run for a fourth term in December 1877. To have resigned at this point would have further abetted his enemies, and the mayor was not a man to give up without a struggle.[75] The lines of battle had been clearly drawn.

Mandl and Lueger carried on their course of agitation against Felder by canvasing Vienna's many district political clubs. In this way they also became more broadly familiar with the political personality and special problems of the rapidly growing imperial capital.[76] Through continuous personal contact, Lueger in particular expanded the foundations of his popularity, and made an impression that few were likely to forget. "He was so conspicuously vital that one had to be blind not to notice him," according to Sigmund Mayer, a municipal councillor.[77] While Mandl and Lueger opposed a fourth term for Felder, Lueger at least was cautious in his rhetoric not to offend the few conservatives who had recently joined the Mandl Party.[78] Both he and Mandl realized that Felder still had too much support to be defeated, and that the only alternative candidate, Second Vice-Mayor Eduard Uhl, had no chance at all unless the incumbent Felder chose not to run. But Lueger's opposing the mayor's reelection even indirectly also served notice that the younger man had returned to active political life, which was perhaps the main reason for this new agitation in the first place. Indeed, several of Lueger's arguing points, including the need to strengthen the voice of the elected representatives, to check irregularities, and to bolster a more democratic exchange of views in the municipal council, would subsequently appear in Lueger's own council reelection campaign the following spring.[79]

Felder won, as expected, receiving seventy-six votes to Uhl's forty. The incumbent cast his own vote for Julius Ritter von Newald, the first vice-mayor.[80] Three municipal councillors were absent. After the election, one municipal councillor offered Felder condolences rather than congratulations. He had won because the opposition had not been strong enough to finish him. He was without friends, his support was completely undermined. Time was growing short for Felder, and he was urged to resign at the first possible opportunity.[81]

The continuing offensive of Mandl's party followed the predictable course. New irregularities and scandals were uncovered. Their popularity was at a new height, and Lueger and Mandl were invited to speak at countless large and often noisy meetings

> that turned out to hear them elaborate a reform program designed to overhaul a representative system grown stale, lazy and unresponsive to the needs of the population. . . . The problem with the city government was less corruption as such, than the underlying source of abuse and mismanagement in a lack of systematic and effective controls; this, stemming in turn from a power imbalance between the representative bodies and the *Magistrat*. By placing inordinate authority in the latter, and giving preference to the judgment of experts, Felder and the conservative liberals [so Lueger and Mandl argued] were inhibiting the fulfillment of municipal self-government; the public was deprived of control over expenditures and a voice in ordering city affairs.[82]

The disadvantage of relying excessively on expert, rather than on informed lay, opinion was brought home on Christmas Day 1877. In three populous districts the water ran out. Before the installation of new pipelines that autumn, Mandl had disagreed with reservoir experts. Both he and Lueger favored maintaining existing house wells in some areas of the city, arguing that the mountain spring reserves were inadequate to meet all Vienna's requirements. But the oppositionists' warnings had gone unheeded. The crisis was precipitated by a severe frost and a resulting drop in the water supply. The emergency prompted Mandl to reiterate his demands for the decentralization of decision making to make government more democratic and therefore more accountable to the voters. As things stood, commissions elected by the council, composed of members loyal to the mayor rather than to the municipal council and its sections controlled the city's technical decisions.

Indeed, decentralization of decision making and administrative reform became the main issues of Lueger's reelection campaign early in 1878, rather than special pleading for the rights of the "little man," as some of his biographers have too simply explained.[83] Lueger was not a democrat at all. He was not really convinced that the common man could rule himself, only that his interests could be better represented by people like Lueger. The "people" would soon become his tool to achieve power. Lueger was much more the demogogue than the democrat who would strive to make self-government and participation a reality.

Mandl was significant in Lueger's reelection, probably inspiring many of his speeches.[84] During his three years in Vienna's political life, Lueger's radicalism was never less in evidence. Far from attacking the Liberal system, he cleverly urged administrative reforms that would make it more responsive to the electorate.

Lueger's speeches during this campaign have a lawyerly quality, and Brown feels that "they suggest a highly practical intellect, given neither to theorizing nor to particularly broad perspectives. They are of interest because, being delivered at a rare time of political security [Lueger's re-election was looked on as certain], they are all but devoid of polemics, and can be taken as a more or less sincere expression of Lueger's premises and political intentions."[85] Lueger delivered his speeches after Mandl, who had provided "a general framework" for Lueger's more detailed expositions. Although it is true that Lueger was not a theorist like his mentor Stein, at least during his political career, and that the range of his thought and tastes was defined at an early age, this "rare time of political security" may not be the best time to fathom the sincerity of Lueger's "premises and political intentions." During periods of crisis and stress the essential Lueger often emerged.

Lueger's nature became increasingly reflexive. As he grew older, his behavior in given situations and his responses to recurring problems became predictable. This suggests that though he was committed to no systematic ideology, there was a pattern to his behavior and one that became set in these early episodes of his career. This pattern was often activated by challenging circumstances, which is why they bear recounting in some detail. Lueger possessed preferences he sometimes compromised, first in his quest for power, and later, after he had won the mayoralty, in retaining this power in given situations. He liked to play the master. To be sure, there were limits to how far his pragmatism could accommodate diverse political situations. The precedents he thus established were sometimes dangerous; and his followers occasionally invoked them to justify some of their own questionable decisions and behavior.

But Lueger was more than the sum total of his actions. He may well have sensed that he would inspire less subtle imitators, and perhaps even desired this to happen. And the subjectivity of his politics, particularly in his later years, inevitably did attract imitators among some of the younger Christian Socials. What would Lueger have done? or, Could this ever have happened under Lueger? became stock queries. Such appeals were indirect but nonetheless significant legacies of the man.[86] In any case, there are several vantage points from which to sketch "Lueger's premises and political intentions," or to infer what they may have been.

Lueger won reelection from the third curia in the third district early in March 1878, receiving 531 out of 956 votes.[87] The following month opposition to Felder now increased by eight newly elected councilmen, united against the aging mayor in a new dispute over mismanagement in the Central Cemetery. Felder had once more sided with city officials after the cemetery investigating committee had released its findings; and this time the committee resigned in protest. In a lengthy ensuing debate, Felder's entire dictatorial mode of operation came under fire. In criticizing his partiality toward the Magistrat and dismissal of corruption charges against city officials, Lueger scored telling points against the mayor. "To 'bravos' from the left and galleries, he . . . drove the Mayor from the chamber."[88] Felder received a vote of confidence from the moderates, but the opposition was now more than ever determined to maintain its pressure.

One of the opposition, Josef Schlechter, spoke of the terrorism of Felder's supporters, who were determined to silence Lueger and Mandl for their revelations.[89] However, in the light of Lueger's tactics, there can be little doubt that the terrorism now emanated from his quarter. Indeed, so effective had the opposition's attacks become that Felder, seriously ill, resigned toward the end of June. Two months later he spoke to his former supporters about a turning point in the city's fortunes and "the administrative battle . . . carried on in such a way as to make it finally impossible for me to persevere in my post."[90] But what Felder had experienced gave only a foretaste of what one of his successors, Johann Prix, would undergo when Lueger's ambitions for the mayoralty ripened some fifteen years later. Some were to say that Prix's untimely death in 1894 was precipitated by the same tactics that Lueger and Mandl had so effectively exhibited during the last years of Felder's regime.[91]

Lueger's and Mandl's journalistic supporters made it clear that Felder's resignation was to be but the first step in a full reorganization of the municipal administration, a revamping in which the municipal council would be principal. Yet Mandl's paper Fortschritt doubted that long-standing and entrenched divisions could be surmounted.[92] Felder's successor, the more conciliatory Julius Newald, who received all but two votes from the council in the mayoral election, was nonetheless warmly applauded from all sides when he promised "to safeguard the esteem of the [Municipal] Council."[93] But Newald failed to pacify the various factions and Vienna's

Liberals continued to fragment. For though individual councillors of the majority Mittelpartei were willing to support a minority candidate for vice-mayor, which post had been vacated by Newald, most of the Mittelpartei refused to go along. The immediate result of the post-Felder maneuverings was the formation of a new group, the United Left, which outnumbered the Mittelpartei by one vote. However, the Mittelpartei could still tip the balance in its favor by aligning with a third faction, the Reform Club. Lueger and Karl Lustig became the secretaries of the United Left, which was chaired by Johann Schrank.

The party program for the United Left reflected some of Mandl's and Lueger's agitation, including economy in spending, abolition of the curial system, and defending the powers of the municipal council against attempts to weaken them in favor of the Magistrat. Two years later, the United Left added to their program the active and passive franchise for all who paid direct taxes, the abolition of food consumption taxes,[94] and the incorporation of some outlying suburbs with Vienna. The most significant new aspect of Mandl's politics at this time, not only for himself but also for Lueger's subsequent career, was an anticapitalist stance. Specifically, this took the form of an "incipient campaign against public exploitation by large unregulated capitalist enterprises such as the private railroads and the Vienna gas monopoly." Lueger may have been flirting with this position when, in 1878, he praised the idealism of Social Democracy, a move long remembered by his subsequent opponents.[95]

But Lueger and Mandl became active critics of the Imperial Continental Gas Association, an English monopoly that supplied Vienna with gas for its illumination and some of its private cooking needs.[96] Despite a drop in the cost of coal, gas prices continued to mount. Mandl concentrated on the city's laxity in ensuring the Gas Association's compliance with contract obligations. Though the rising prices affected relatively few Viennese, the municipality's gas bill was paid by the taxpayers, and the quality of illumination was evidently poor.[97] This entire issue attracted widespread attention in the municipal council and greatly strengthened the United Left. At last Lueger and Mandl could focus their attention on matters more significant than the inefficient use of sand and gravel. Investigating the operations of private companies opened up a whole new range of possibilities. Such diversified projects as an attempt to build an overhead railway[98] and manage a celebration to commemorate the bicentennial of the lifting of the Turkish siege of Vienna in 1883, involving as it did the letting out of contracts to monument manufacturers and publishers, now came under their scrutiny.[99] Particularly ironic in view of Lueger's later endeavors as mayor to create monuments, especially to himself, was his criticism of expenditures on memorials. "Money [thus] being spent . . . would be better applied to 'more useful projects such as the reorganization of the Public Works Department, sanitation, welfare and decentralization reforms.'"[100]

It was not only as a muckraker that Lueger's reputation and status increased over the next few years. By 1881 his knowledge of municipal affairs was widely acknowledged. Mandl had resigned as a municipal concillor in 1879 after his second defeat as a parliamentary candidate. He planned a triumphal return to the council the following year and his hopes were not to be disappointed. However, in his absence Lueger displayed his diverse skills and an expertise of his own. Shortly after Mandl's resignation, Johann Schrank relinquished the chairmanship of the United Left to Josef Schlechter. By May 1880 Lueger had moved up to the vice-chairmanship, and into yet another opportunity to demonstrate his administrative skills. Schrank was elected second-vice mayor in the autumn of 1880.

As the 1880s began, Lueger, for all his activity as an oppositional politician, still hoped that reform in the municipal council would lead to the elimination of the various factions and the rejuvenation of the Liberal party, the leadership of which he perhaps hoped to inherit. However, the final overthrow of the Liberals in parliament in 1879 and the general belief that they could not resolve the serious political and economic difficulties confronting Austrian society cast doubt on any prospects of reform at the lower municipal level. But without a Liberal party, Lueger's politics would have to move in another direction.

Although the United Left became stronger in the spring elections of 1880, this did not increase Lueger's political leverage, and his appeal to the Mittelpartei for cooperation was ignored. The Mittelpartei did agree to some operational compromises,[101] thereby seeming to pave the way for the merger of the two Liberal factions; but further disagreements followed. Moreover, personality conflicts between some of the United Left members and the Mandl-Lueger leadership caused the party to fragment. By January 1881 eight members of the United Left, who had departed under the leadership of Johann Heinrich Steudel, had formed a new club, the Far Left.

During the spring of 1881 Lueger's campaign for reelection marked the culmination of his career as a would-be Liberal reformer.[102] He abandoned the attempt to reform from within the party, though his future path seemed unclear. Yet he had come a long way in the six years since his first election to the municipal council. By 1881 he had learned much about the functioning of municipal politics and had thus tempered his earlier theoretical studies with practical experience. In addition, he had mastered the intricacies of district and committee politics, drafted countless reports for different council sections, served as secretary and vice-chairman of the United Left, and acquired deeper insight into the psychological motivations of his fellow councillors. Very importantly, he had a chance during the municipal council election campaign of March 1877 to see Mandl use anti-Semitism, the political potential of which was yet to be explored in Austria — something Lueger himself was later to refine into a highly effective and destructive agitational tool. In an electoral committee memorandum, Lueger demonstrated a continuing interest in the need for municipal and suffrage reform; but he also struck a nationalistic note by advocating the protection of "German education and culture."[103] In promising party support for individual members, regardless of the district in which they were active, he also evinced an awareness of the need for tighter and more centralized organization.

By 1881 Lueger's popularity, the election results showed, increased from fifty-five to sixty-five percent since the election of 1878. He received 749 votes of 1150. But the United Left could not post any gain, maintaining its strength at forty-five seats. The Mittelpartei possessed forty-seven mandates, the Far Left fourteen and the Independents twelve.[104] It was thus impossible for any one party to command a majority, and the differences between the United Left, Far Left, and Mittelpartei were apparently still irreconcilable. Had Felder still been mayor, he would probably have ignored the differences and ruled through the Mittelpartei regardless of any objections from the minority groups. Newald had proved to be so diplomatic a mayor, however, that little seemed to get done. Not a few of his own Mittelpartei members objected to his reelection during the summer of 1881. This time it was Mandl's and Lueger's turn to defend the mayor, comparing his administration favorably to his predecessor's.

Yet it remains an open question whether any of Mandl's and Lueger's proposed reforms in support of Newald could have been achieved. Unhesitating obedience by most of the councillors to execute authoritarianism may even then have become habitual. Lueger was later to exercise such authority more extensively and in ways that Felder would never have dreamed of. In this respect, Mandl's favorably contrasting "popular representation [in 1881] . . . to the earlier [absolutist system]" is especially ironic. "'Superintend[ing] the executive . . . is negated,'" he added, "'if the . . . council merely acts as a voting machine to cover what has already been done, and approve whatever is put before it.'"[105] As mayor, Lueger, backed by a Christian Social majority in the municipal council, was to employ just such a machine. On July 7 1881, Newald was almost unanimously reelected, receiving 95 of 117 votes.[106] Party divisions continued, but it seemed as though Lueger could continue to circumvent them toward maintaining the coalition needed by Newald. However, in December an event ended Newald's career and nearly put paid to Lueger's. The Ring-theater, one of Vienna's newest and most spacious theaters, caught fire and burned, trapping some four hundred. A controversy arose between Newald and the governor of Lower Austria, Possinger von Choborski, over who should be held responsible.[107] Lueger supported the mayor.[108] In the municipal council, conservative Liberals, backed by the *Neue Freie Presse*, attacked Newald and Lueger. The outcome of the continuing struggle was indicated in January 1882 when, after the death of Vice-Mayor Johann Schrank, Lueger lost an election for that position to Johann Prix. So certain had Lueger been of victory that he drafted a speech of acceptance.[109] Within two weeks, however, Newald, who was ultimately cleared of responsibility for the disaster, had resigned, deserted by most of the municipal councillors. He was succeeded by Eduard Uhl, with whom Lueger was evidently on correct, if not cordial, terms.[110] Prix occupied the first and Steudel the second vice-mayor's position.

For all the apparent ignominy into which Newald and his regime had suddenly been hurled, and Lueger's ill-timed support of the mayor, the younger politician had profited from the experience, if not from the mayor's example. Boyer has summarized the debits and credits of Newald's regime as they affected Lueger:

> Now nearly forty years old, he had established himself as a skillful political leader with experience in managing a city-wide coalition. He came to know the strengths and weaknesses of such an organization. When he had the opportunity to lead a second coalition after 1888, he did not make the same mistake twice. . . . Lueger also gained an appreciation of the utility of a strong party base for a successful mayoral candidate. Newald's fiasco in governing against the majority of the Council showed Lueger that this was an impossibility in the local, faction-ridden world of Viennese politics. He also recognized the need for a strong mayor. As much as he had profited from Newald's patronage, he now saw the merits of Felder's administrative autocracy.[111]

The disintegration of the United Left, which had begun with the secession of Steudel and the Far Left the year before, proceeded apace. Seeing no possibility to repair the damage, Lueger dissolved the party on February 7, 1882. Only two days earlier, he had been explaining to Eintracht (Mandl's Club) members the events that had led to the failure of reform efforts by the United Left, blaming the opposition of powerful financial circles. He mentioned the Ringtheater fire controversy, his support for Newald, and a visit to Count Taaffe, when he had asked for the prime minister's support against the governor during the dispute. He also described the attempted bribery by Bunten and Fogerty and Company to give up his opposition to a belt railway project.[112] However, Lueger chiefly criticized dissension and betrayal within party ranks. He had reached an important turning point in his career. He identified the Liberal party as his adversary for the first time.[113]

On March 6, he elaborated on his remarks. By this time he needed to do so, because he was in a difficult position. Lueger had been fined for failing to prove allegations of bribery against two of those implicated in the Fogerty affair,[114] his party was in disarray, and the majority Liberals were marshaled against him. A draft of a speech, probably written in early March, reveals his state of mind at this time. In it, he mentions his "decision to relinquish [his] mandate," a decision he states to have changed because of the intervention of his "honorable friend . . . [Franz] Hintermayer [who together with] a delegation of my constituents implored me in a polite but firm manner to persevere and not to relinquish my mandate,"[115] As he had done a month before, Lueger charged "treason within our own ranks and blamed external circumstances" for having broken the United Left. He emphasized, as he was to do again on many occasions, his accountability to the electorate, and that their decision to support him or not would determine his future in politics. He was confident of their support, and he believed a decision would be easy because his "life [was] like an open book. . . . If you believe I still deserve your trust, then I will persevere regardless of what may come, for I and my friends will struggle against these enemies, not for ourselves, nor to advance our own interests, but for the people and against their enemies."[116]

His actual speech of March 6, as reported by *Fortschritt*, depicted an approaching confrontation in forceful language: "The power that faces us is a colossus, all but invincible, but we will break it all the same. . . . These financial cliques and gold powers are what have corrupted public life . . . they know no fatherland . . . nothing but the money bag. And against this power of international capital, all must take a stand who have the interests of everyone, and not individual classes, at heart."[117]

At the conclusion of his speech, Lueger was so enthusiastically cheered that the next speaker could scarcely be heard. Lueger's mandate had been thus endorsed and a demagogic future foreshadowed. No one could mistake the implicit anti-Semitism of his remarks, least of all Karl von Zerboni di Sposetti, publisher of the anti-Semitic *Der Österreichische Volksfreund* and father-in-law of Lueger's legal partner. On April 3 Zerboni complimented Lueger as one who had "fought valiantly . . . and emerged gloriously. From such cloth is cut either a minister or a martyr. For both, the reward of posterity is certain."[118] One of the more obscure Viennese demagogues, Zerboni described anti-Semitism as "an ethical, religious, national, political, social, and racial question . . . its cult a boon to humanity . . . its members the governing party of the future."[119] He thereby indicated not only his own convictions, but also those of a growing number of Viennese. A brief comment on the cultural side of anti-Semitism is called for here, not only for its gradually increasing importance to Lueger's career, but also for the light it casts on the changes taking place in Viennese society.

As Erika Weinzierl has pointed out, anti-Semitism in Austrian literature was uncommon, if not rare, before the success of the Christian Social and German Nationalist parties in the late 1890s,[120] but it was not altogether unknown.[121] A relatively early work of this kind was B. Aba's *Moderne Grössen,* published in 1883, which focuses on Liberal corruption of the 1860s and 1870s. B. Aba was the pseudonym of Adolf Freiherr von KriegsAu, a scion of one of the older Upper Austrian aristocratic families. KriegsAu was an influential administrator who held high office, both in the imperial government and in private industry.[122] He was the son-in-law of Prime Minister Alexander Bach and a friend of the novelist Adalbert Stifter. His acquaintance with leading aristocrats in Hungary, his extensive travels, and broad business and political experience found expression in his stories and novels. *Moderne Grössen* describes the lives of four young Sudeten immigrants in Vienna. Of these, Krutý, the most important, abandons his theological studies for a legal career, only to become a tutor in a wealthy Jewish family. His progress happens to parallel that of the corrupt Liberal minister of finance, Dr. Karl Giskra. Krutý turns out to be "an all too accurate mirror image" of Giskra.[123]

When Krutý arrives in the home of the wealthy family Neustätter, the chamber maid introduces him to anti-Semitism of the lower middle-class Viennese variety:

"So, you want to try [your luck] here?" the girl began to speak.

Krutý pulled himself up and withdrew his foot with the ill-fated shoe [which had been damaged] from behind the bench; he shrugged his shoulders.

"They're Jews," said the girl.

"Oh?" replied Krutý.

"Right—Jews, rich Jews, but otherwise nothing—but we, I mean the servants, we're Christians and stick together; naturally, otherwise we wouldn't have enough to eat; the former tutor, Preissgott, acted so strangely; things went badly with him; he left eight days ago; naturally, what should he do without the cook and without us?"[124]

Krutý later marries a wealthy half-Jew and ascends the political ladder. To secure his financial position for good, he engages in stock market speculation, but in the process becomes more and more indebted to the Jews. In exchange for the cancellation of her father's indebtedness, Krutý's daughter is promised in marriage to a financial baron, though she ultimately refuses to abandon her faith and become a Jew. The cynicism of the marriage negotiations is captured in the conversation of Krutý and the father of the prospective bridegroom.

> "There is no absence of sectarianism. No one is non-sectarian, you are not; pardon me, excellency, that I dare to presume upon your philosophy. Edmund can not — therefore, nothing remains but that your daughter — "
> "Becomes a Jew!" cried Krutý.
> "Yes," [said the father]. "Does that seem less possible, than that Edmund becomes a Christian? Why? Because so many Jews convert because of the advantage? We need no advantages; so, service in return for a service. You receive my money — I, your daughter! My compliments!"[125]

In parallel development, *Moderne Grössen* also chronicles the assimilation through conversion and marriage of the financial baron's brother in Hungary. The novel thus plays on the growing apprehension among some Austrians that Hungary, a large and already largely independent part of the empire, might, through Jewish influence, become further alienated from, and antagonistic toward, German Austria. Before the end of the decade Lueger was being enthusiastically cheered whenever he censured "Judeo-Magyars."[126] In this and other ways, *Moderne Grössen* anticipated themes that would soon play a part in Lueger's politics, including class envy, anti-Liberalism, and nationalism.

KriegsAu's work was many-sided. It censured venality and public corruption, as had Lueger and Mandl; it denigrated highly placed political figures, as had they; and it also ridiculed the pretensions and presumptions of the monied classes, particularly the Jews. But most of all, it attacked Liberalism. KriegsAu had said that he was anti-Liberal, but modern. When *Modern Grössen* was published, the splintering of Vienna's Liberals and the rapid but general erosion of Liberalism as a political philosophy had been apparent for a decade. Soon after the appearance of this novel, Lueger made the acquaintance of Albert Wiesinger, a publicist priest who had authored several anti-Semitic novels.[127] Wiesinger's writings resemble *Moderne Grössen* in their attempts to ground anti-Semitism in a nonracist perspective. *Moderne Grössen*, however, provides a more comprehensive picture of the rapid erosion of Liberalism, which Lueger was so effectively to exploit, and without which his career would probably have ended. The complex, if not tangled, cultural roots of Lueger's anti-Semitism, like many other facets of his career, own a general as well as private significance.

After the fall of the United Left in February 1882, Lueger sought a new focus. After briefly aligning himself with a Jew, Adolf Fischhof, to organize the conciliatory Deutsche Volkspartei, he became disenchanted.[128] Although he had already flirted with anti-Semitism by then, Lueger seems to have become disoriented and indecisive. It was perhaps a reflection of his political uncertainty at this time that he became a subscriber to *Die Freiheit*, a revolutionary periodical.[129] Its editor, Johann Most, was imprisoned for sixteen months after publishing an issue proclaiming the paper's sympathy with the assassins of Czar Alexander II.[130] During the early 1880s Lueger also frequently defended Socialists in court and later referred to this as a "repeated honor."[131] He had praised Social Democracy as an ideal as early as 1878, but not until four years later did his sympathy take this concrete form. Perhaps this is why his outspokenly Christian Social biographers have described this period, from the Fogerty trial to the municipal council elections of 1883, as the nadir of his fortunes.

Yet all was not unrelieved gloom. He commanded a loyal following in the third district. Moreover, his earlier citywide campaigning with Mandl had won him important support in the fifth and ninth districts. From the seventh district Albert Gessmann, who became Lueger's most effective organizer, was elected a municipal councillor. He and Lueger worked together politically, but were never real friends, throughout the whole of Lueger's life.[132] Friedrich Funder, a pioneering Christian Social journalist who knew both men, contrasted the two:

> [Gessmann] possessed nothing of the Viennese charm with which Dr. Lueger conquered hearts. Heavy-blooded, almost incapable of more tender emotional feelings, he could be considered the opposite of the jovial, cheerful Lueger, who attracted simply by his handsome masculine appearance. There was actually no inner bond between them, but they stood together for their cause. Dr. Gessmann never had many intimate friends who loved him.[133]

Although he gained an important organizer in Gessmann, he was soon to lose his earliest and most important practical political mentor, Ignaz Mandl.[134] The ostensible cause of their falling out was a lengthy series of disagreements over district intrigues.[135] But the real cause of their split, one suspects, is to be found in the collapse of the United Left, the apparent failure of their several years of oppositional politics, and Mandl's resentment over his own narrow municipal council victory in the spring of 1882. Mandl's personal popularity seemed to be waning while Lueger's held strong and grew. As early as July 1881, Johann Weiss, a district politician and former municipal councillor, tried to repair the quarrel between the two, who once were so inseparable that they had been dubbed "Siamese twins." Although Weiss's letter to Lueger concentrates on Mandl, it implies a good deal about Lueger as well:

> [Mandl] was accustomed to remain in constant contact with you, there were no secrets between you; together you were one heart, of one mind; in all important questions, you consulted with one another; in short, there was a relationship between two true [and] real friends. Then he believed himself being pushed aside by others, saw others come between you and him; that hurt him and he withdrew more and more.—As clever, even brilliant as Dr. Mandl is in many things, in others he is a big child, a child because he doesn't know how to handle circumstances and available human resources, and believes the whole world can be reduced to one particular category. He has also endured and sacrificed much, and, as is natural, is very often inclined to be nervous and wounding.—But the gold in him, his noble core fosters forgiveness [and] reconciliation, more than with an intellectually and morally inferior person. Therefore, I think— and I sincerely beg of you—not to miss the opportunity to come to an understanding should one present itself. You and Dr. Mandl possess two complementary personalities, and if I could look into the heart of one or the other, I would certainly discover the desire and the wish to restore the old trusting relationship.[136]

Weiss's letter hints at a more vital, a more truly symbiotic relationship than Lueger was probably ever to know again. His friendship with Mandl was a natural thing, the kind which, although born of necessity, nonetheless allowed for generosity and emotional give and take on both sides. Lueger, the youthfully optimistic, buoyantly outgoing Viennese, had found an ideal mentor in the Hungarian Mandl, the intense mercurial realpolitiker, who needed an apt pupil to share his hopes and to help carry out his ambitious schemes. Mandl's insights into Viennese politics contributed much to Lueger's political development. Lueger appropriated Mandl's ideas, copied his style, and ultimately surpassed his mentor. Indeed, Lueger eclipsed Mandl and all others in his time as *the* popular agitator in the grand style. Moreover, Lueger carried out the municipalization of Vienna's transportation and lighting systems, and introduced a communal savings bank. These had first been Mandl's projects. Possibly the early rift between the two originated in Mandl's perception that Lueger would abandon anyone or any principle if they became political liabilities. If so, the rift became unbridgeable once the disparity between Lueger as public anti-Semite and private friend of the Jew Mandl antagonized Lueger's power-seeking but powerless anti-Semitic supporters. Here as well as elsewhere Lueger followed the path of political expediency.

In the spring of 1883 the two openly disagreed during an Eintracht meeting. At issue was a proposed amendment to the school law affecting the emphasis to be placed on religion in elementary education. Mandl favored less religion, Lueger more.[137] Lueger argued that to place more emphasis on religion was to oppose the minority Liberals in parliament — and always to oppose the Liberals, Lueger declared, was the purpose of Eintracht. And most agreed with him. Mandl, who doubtless perceived in the proposed measure a threat to the religious freedom of Jewish children,[138] was apparently so deeply offended that a few days after the meeting he refused to stand for reelection as Eintracht chairman and announced his intention of withdrawing from the club and from politics altogether.

Lueger did not see things this way at all. His version of what happened next was revealed in an open letter to Mandl, drafted by Lueger, but signed by another member of Eintracht.[139] Mandl was accused of spreading "false and malicious rumors detrimental to the [club]," of trying to lure its members away to a new club founded by Mandl, and of publicly opposing the real interests of Eintracht. Mandl countered with a series of anti-Lueger articles in *Fortschritt*. Although there were to be several reconciliations over the next few years, there were also to be further disputes, until Lueger's final break with Mandl in 1889. Even by 1883 it was apparent that the deeper rapport between the two during the first few years of their friendship had forever been lost. Lueger's dispute with Mandl suggests his priorities. Personal friendship and loyalty took second place to capturing political objectives. When Mandl died in 1907 Lueger attended his funeral. His presence was noted by a commentator from the *Neue Freie Presse*, who stated that Lueger had "harvested the fruits of Mandl's life-work" and then destroyed his popularity.[140] Lueger was not one to acknowledge his professional indebtedness to others. He kept his thoughts about this, his most important practical political mentor, to himself.

Lueger was, by a narrow margin, reelected to the municipal council in the spring of 1884 after a hard-fought campaign. From the Liberal standpoint probably the best chance ever to defeat Lueger had been missed. Never would he be more vulnerable. Minus Mandl's considerable talents and support, and having failed to win other support in the municipal council, Lueger and Gessmann were ridiculed as the "two-man party." The heat with which this election was fought shows in a letter drafted by Lueger to a Liberal editor three days before the election. Lueger denied that he visited Felder just to garner support for the upcoming election, as his opponents had charged. Lueger did admit, however, to calling on Felder "quite some time ago," but for reasons that were "not a subject for any *public discussion.*" He concluded that he had "never made a secret of . . . [his] *personal* respect for Dr. Felder in spite of my political opposition." Lueger "strongly reject[ed] the attempt to *make political capital out of private relationships*" and denied that the visit had anything "*whatsoever to do with the forthcoming municipal council elections*"[141] [emphases in original].

Felder, who was then the president of the Lower Austrian Diet, has recorded his understanding of the visit. Astonished at Lueger's appearing at all, and having no idea why his "deadly enemy" would be calling on him, Felder nonetheless received him courteously. Because their conversation centered on trivial matters, and Lueger left, "stiffly courteous . . . as he [had] arrived," without betraying a "syllable of anything more circumstantial," Felder could only guess at a more serious ulterior motive. He then told a friend, who in turn told others. Word of Lueger's visit reached the Liberal papers, and his "faithlessness and lack of character" were predictably proclaimed. Felder was upset, because he believed Lueger would blame him for spreading the story. He next told another friend what had transpired and the friend, though an opponent of Lueger, hurried to a Lueger electoral assembly and proclaimed Felder's denial of Lueger's censure. Although Felder also denied that Lueger owed his reelection to him, he added that others thought that he did. "How blind and incalculable are coincidences!" Felder mused.[142]

But "incalculable coincidences" probably had little to do with Lueger's election victory. Felder, here and elsewhere in his memoirs, betrays an injured pride, this time, bemusingly, that he had received so little credit for advancing Lueger's career. There is little reason to doubt Lueger's earlier biographers, Stauracz and Kuppe,[143] that the support of the anti-Semites, led by Ernst Schneider, Robert Pattai, and Josef Porzer, all of whom would remain connected with Lueger in varying degrees for the rest of his life, had tipped the balance in his favor. Although Lueger had been careful not to align himself too openly with the anti-Semites, and avoided such an alliance until 1887, his stance against big business won him their increasing enthusiasm.

In April after the elections, Lueger accommodated the anti-Semites further, in part, perhaps, to repay their support, but probably more to maintain the momentum of his popularity of which they were a considerable part. Lueger had his eye on a seat in parliament, and 1885 was an election year. A new group of voters, who paid five Gulden in direct property taxes, "the so-called Five Gulden Men," would visit the polls for the first time. He needed every vote he could get, and thus sought an issue of national importance to add to the number of his supporters, not just to excite those he already had. Just the right thing was conveniently provided by the controversy over nationalization of the Nordbahn Railroad Company.[144] Lueger's involvement in the Nordbahn issue enhanced his credibility as an anti-big business candidate and a sound critic of inefficiently administered municipal services and privately owned transportation facilities.

In 1836 the Austrian government had granted the Nordbahn Railroad Company a fifty-year franchise, and this now came up for an eighty-year renewal. Although the Nordbahn Railroad Company had already been under fire, the application was at first supported by many Liberals and the Vienna Rothschild Bank. Lueger's opposition to the renewal was only the latest installment in an existing controversy over the Nordbahn and its allegedly exploitative practices. Radical Pan-Germans led by Georg Ritter von Schönerer, a member of parliament, demanded that the franchise be denied. He and his followers stated that the company "charged notoriously high rates and had a stranglehold on the economic development of the empire."[145] Ignoring the storm signals, Prime Minister Taaffe decided to renew the franchise because of practical considerations. Money to purchase the line was lacking, as was skilled personnel to operate it. However, Taaffe's submission of the agreement to parliament for ratification enabled Schönerer to create a national issue. Issues as disparate as German nationalism, anti-Semitism, populism, hatred of the Liberal press, and resistance to private ownership of public transportation all converged in opposition to renewal of the Nordbahn franchise. On April 10, 1884, the government's intention to renew the franchise was made public. Lueger and Schönerer immediately responded by stirring up popular opinion against the Nordbahn. In a large demonstration before the Rathaus, the two condemned the Rothschilds and praised "Bismarck as the greatest social reformer of the century."[146] In the municipal council, Lueger moved to petition the government to request the nationalization of the lines. This motion of urgency, drafted in his own hand, epitomizes his style at this relatively early stage of his career. Lueger denounced the Nordbahn's "ruthless exploitation" [emphasis in original] — in the name of Vienna:

> whose population was practically forced to pay tribute to a private business, whose . . . commerce and trade suffer badly, . . . in fact, whose arteries, necessary for the growth and prosperity of the city, were bled dry. It would go too far to provide documentary proof of the above in all respects. It should suffice to refer to economic reports, to the constant and justified complaints about the transportation of cattle and other vital goods, as well as to state that the transportation and sale of coal have been monopolized through *cartels and abatement abuses*, thereby annually cheating the population of Vienna out of millions that profited only a few.[147]

Lueger's motion, fortified by Schönerer's more than twenty-five hundred petitions to parliament supporting nationalization, was defeated.[148] But Schönerer's continued agitation, intimidation, and obstruction in parliament were so effectively disruptive that Taaffe was ultimately forced to produce a renewal agreement with the Nordbahn much less favorable than the first. Schönerer became the man of the hour, feted by his followers, grudgingly admired by his foes. Even the *Neue Freie Presse* acknowledged that he had won "the first victory for the people in the history of constitutional Austria."[149]

Apart from strengthening Lueger's image with his constituents as a foe of big business and attracting wider attention to his politics, the Nordbahn affair further demonstrated, if further demonstration was needed, the political potential of "intimidation, slander, and emotionalism, combined with an incongruous appeal to legitimate ideals. [Schönerer] and his followers (the Pan-Germans) showed how a tiny but ruthless minority could dominate a majority that in other circumstances detested his ideas and behavior."[150] In parliament a precedent had been established.

Lueger turned his attention to the coming parliamentary elections. The Five Gulden Men—12,243 strong—were to cast their votes in 1885 for the first time.[151] Although these constituted but a small fraction of Vienna's 1,200,000 inhabitants, these soon-to-be-enfranchised voters reflected Lueger's own quarterings, and could thus be expected to support a spokesman who was not only sympathetic to their class interest, but who also symbolized the possibility of realizing their ambitions. The enfranchisement of the Five Gulden Men, those who paid at least five Gulden in direct property taxes a year, signified the arrival of the lower middle class in Viennese politics.

Lueger, running in the fifth district, was opposed by Johann Heinrich Steudel, municipal councillor, Landtag, or Provincial Diet, member, and member of parliament.[152] Steudel was also something of a self-made man. Though he had received no more than a secondary school education, he had prospered as a real estate speculator through selling his family's suburban inn and the lands around it. A Left Liberal oppositionist, he was supported by small-property owners. One significant difference between these two rival politicians was that Steudel, who had matured during the prerevolutionary Vormärz, opposed large expenditures and loans for municipal construction projects; Lueger, a product of the postrevolutionary Vienna, came increasingly to recognize the need for such in the capital's continued growth. During this, his first parliamentary campaign, Lueger further demonstrated this generational difference through his grasp of more comprehensive electioneering techniques, which included the use of women's agitational groups. Furthermore, in his campaign, he demonstrated considerable diplomatic skill as a negotiator by enlisting Mandl's support and that of the anti-Semites and probably some of the lower clergy as well.[153] The outlines of his political techniques had thus become clear at this relatively early stage in his career.

For all his innovations, Lueger fought an exhausting traditional campaign in which he used the good offices of friends, as well as available public political resources.[154] Besides campaigning actively among the voters, Lueger corresponded with individual supporters, composed circulars, handled the details of rallies and related gatherings, both during and after the campaign, and tried to resolve the inevitable conflicts that naturally arose in a coalition of such diverse elements.[155]

By 1885 a distinct polarization had invaded Viennese politics. This had been brought about in part by Lueger's motion that year to eliminate the early spring electoral assemblies where, since 1860, all candidates had had the opportunity to debate their views before the voters. However, polarization had also been fostered by the systematic violation of informal campaigning arrangements by the various clubs.[156] Henceforth, partisans of various persuasions attended rallies only of their respective parties.[157]

Perhaps symptomatic of this development was that Lueger on April 27 should announce a detailed and specific program, such as he thereafter avoided, probably because he believed such statements restricted his flexibility and freedom of action. His 1885 election program outlined his goals as a Democrat, in a way noteworthy for their concreteness,[158] as Boyer has observed. The document is also important because it reveals his development and sums up many of his achievements during his first decade as a municipal politician. It therefore deserves consideration at this point.[159]

After the customary expression of gratitude to his supporters, Lueger said that he hoped to be able to unify the Democratic party on the district level, and regretted that local disunity was a symptom of larger divisions within the empire. If he were elected, he promised not to join any faction, but to adhere to his party and to the larger democratic aim of building on the broad foundation of the entire *Volk*, regardless of class, confession, or nationality. He thereby anticipated the later goal of constructing Christian Socialism on an empirewide foundation. Lueger blamed the failure to achieve a more encompassing democratic vision on the restricted franchise and the overweening influence of special-interest groups. He then elaborated on his political program.

While upholding the present state structure, Lueger stressed the centrality of the Austro-Germans, as he had done and would continue to do till the end of his career. There could therefore be no separation of individual provinces, as the Pan-German Nationalists wanted, he stated, because this would make Hungary insolent and further increase its preponderance. Instead of the youthful free-trade enthusiasm of his university years, Lueger upheld protectionism for Austria's industries, as he and Mandl had done since the late 1870s. Universal suffrage,[160] a stiffer press law to protect the Volksparteien, religious and national equality — all received his endorsement. Lueger knew his constituents, by 1885 a grouping of lower-middle-class shopkeepers, artisans, petty bureaucrats, and some workers. Instead of solving the social question "through police measures,"[161] he urged reform. This was doubtless a gesture, not only toward his laboring constituents, but also toward greater consistency, for, as we have seen, he had recently defended workers as a trial attorney.

He indeed "hit hard at 'large capitalism,'"[162] reveling in his victory in the Fogerty affair; and he reminded his listeners of his struggles against foreign utility owners who gouged the taxpayers. Along more constructive lines, Lueger recalled his efforts to make cheap capital available to aspiring entrepreneurs through supporting a municipal mortgage bank scheme. For related reasons, he had opposed the "peddlers" who threatened to undermine domestic tradesmen. This side of his program received his continued support throughout his mayoralty.

While proclaiming his support for religious equality and remaining silent about the Jews, there was nonetheless an element of latent anti-Semitism in his opposition to "peddlers" as well as in his promise to promote "the creation of laws and institutions"[163] to prevent exploitation of the middle class by the capitalists. Even his less astute listeners could hardly have missed the drift of this last promise. Of central public interest was the continuing struggle over the Rothschild-supported Nordbahn. Lueger took credit for initiating the entire railroad nationalization issue, just as he was later to take credit for achievements decidedly not his own but that he had in fact opposed at one time or another.[164] This portion of his speech especially is thus remarkable for the appearance of a flexibility of technique he was subsequently to refine.

The main issues of the upcoming 1885 election were clearly of broader significance than Lueger's program indicated, but in mentioning local as well as large parliamentary problems he reminded his listeners where his heart really lay. In this local category was the need to amend the Poor-Relief Law and food tariff barrier, to abolish the food consumption tax, and to confront the question of creating a greater Vienna by incorporating the outer suburbs.

While conveying the impression that he represented a distinct and distinctive standpoint, Lueger had in part borrowed larger and more useful themes from rivals. He also appealed to a variety of sentiments, of class, economic, religious, nationalistic, and populist nature. In so doing, he offended very few groups, with the exception, perhaps, of his old enemies the Liberals, and the German Nationalists, with whom he nonetheless remained intermittently allied for years to come.

During his first parliamentary campaign, Lueger demonstrated a political sophistication and dynamism that undoubtedly tipped the balance in his favor on June 1. For all of that, he defeated Steudel by fewer than 100 votes, 1,403 to 1,346, in a heavy turnout.[165] Once in parliament, Lueger pursued other avenues, by magnifying and reinforcing this at first narrow local prestige, and provided himself with additional opportunities for extending his influence. More important, Lueger in parliament was no longer merely a local politician. He was still only forty but he stood on the threshold of wider power. He had been unsuccessful in building his own party, yet his very lack of affiliation drew diverse groups in need of representation to him. Lueger was nearing the end of his political *Wanderjahre.*

Parliament convened on September 22, 1885. Lueger began the new phase of his career by criticizing the scandal-ridden commerce department and the *Statthalterei,* or governorship, for favoring the Vienna Tramway Company at the expense of the municipality. This tactic was reminiscent of his opposition to Felder and the Magistrat, in that it focused public frustration on a specific individual and body of officials who could easily be blamed for apparent public ills and mismanagement, but who had somehow remained unaccountable. In picking such a target, Lueger played spokesman for one area of general public concern, while he signaled to his own constituents that municipal interests remained of paramount importance to him. His new role in the national assembly created the impression that his enthusiasm for municipal reform was clearly undiminished. This shrewd position grew out of his objective perception of the limits on his own power. Only two other Democrats, Anton Kreuzig and Ferdinand Kronawetter, had been elected that spring, and they had their own connections. The latter would join Viktor Adler and Engelbert Pernerstorfer the following spring in continuing efforts to organize the new Social Democratic party.[166] Robert Pattai, though also a member of the far left with the Democrats, was officially an "anti-Semite" and for the time being remained independent.

Though Schönerer's victory in the Nordbahn affair had revealed the potential of political anti-Semitism even to the Liberals,[167] not until 1887 would Lueger become outspokenly anti-Semitic, in his support of Schönerer's Jewish exclusion bill.[168] However, there were earlier hints, in parliament and in the municipal council, about which way he thought the wind was blowing. In parliament he referred to "the pseudo-Magyar press in Hungary, and the just as pseudo-German press in Austria."[169] Although this statement might be interpreted as merely underlining the mistrust he had entertained for the press all along, he had cooperated with the anti-Semite Ernst Schneider and his followers in the spring municipal council elections of 1886. A consistent pattern of cooperation had begun in 1884 and 1885.[170] (The 1886 elections resulted in "a Democratic Left" consisting only of eighteen members, most of whom looked to Lueger for leadership and for a more radical and implicitly anti-Semitic politics.) Whatever tactical advantages he may have enjoyed by embracing one splinter group or another, they were fast being eroded by an increasing radicalization of politics on all levels of society. Lueger could not long put off a decisive choice of one group over another and expect to retain his supporters. His outspoken antipathy toward the Magyars, however, was still another sign of his growing radicalism at this time. This most consistent aspect of his political personality had shown itself at least as early as the years immediately after the Ausgleich.[171] Though he radiated Austro-centrism in parliament, he was careful not to preclude Austro-Slavic cooperation against the Hungarians. The thrust of his ideas was that the two groups were held in common bondage by the Magyars.[172] Many years later, Gessmann recalled this in referring to Lueger's initiation of the united struggle of various Aryan nationalities against the Jews, though Gessmann went further than Lueger did at the time.

Lueger's participation in parliament brought him into contact with some of the leading social reformers of the day at a time when legislation was being enacted that would place Austria in the forefront of European socialization. Although many of these new laws were disregarded, the movement to limit working hours and improve conditions in factories, shops, and mines at least turned the public eye on the abuses and fueled new political movements, of which Christian Socialism and Social Democracy became the most important. Prince Alois Liechtenstein and Lueger won the admiration of their followers, in part because of their open discussion of labor issues.

Liechtenstein, who was to become second only to Gessmann in importance in the party hierarchy, had been a member of parliament since 1878. As early as 1874, however, he had raised social issues in Austrian Catholic conservative circles. As a diplomat in England, Liechtenstein had had the opportunity to study economic and social labor questions in the country where the Industrial Revolution had begun, but whose effects were yet to be felt in full measure in Austria. He continued his study in Germany after abandoning his diplomatic career. Here he was introduced to the reforming ideas of Wilhelm Emanuel Ketteler, bishop of Mainz. In 1873 Liechtenstein made his political debut by criticizing Liberal short-comings in a speech in Graz.[173] The following year he promoted the idea of a Catholic labor movement, urging the creation of a kind of trade union as well.[174] Considering his noble lineage, and at a time when most of the Austrian labor leaders had been jailed and their movement disbanded, Liechtenstein's ideas were radical indeed. In parliament he led the Taaffe coalition and advocated "social security measures, the confessional school, and moderate advancement of the non-Germans of Austria."[175] During the Nordbahn affair he criticized the Rothschild Bank, asserting that any losses it might incur because of the new Schönerer-inspired arrangement would be made good in a subsequent loan "floated for the state."[176] By 1890 Liechtenstein had tired of leading the Taaffe coalition and, with Lueger, formed the nucleus of the Christian Social party in parliament.

As early as April 1886, Lueger had supported the draft of a labor, health, and accident insurance law on which Liechtenstein and leading Catholic conservatives had collaborated. In this way a working partnership was formed, though a deeper alliance was precluded for a time, probably because Lueger was as yet uncertain of where his own political future might lie.[177] He remained a Democrat, or more precisely, a member of the "Democratic Left," as the new club was called in the municipal council, until late November 1887. At that time he accused the Democrats of "open cooperation with the Liberal [municipal councillor, Karl] Wrabetz,"[178] and formally withdrew in an apparent gesture of indignation. Lueger's break with the party had little to do with indignation over Democratic-Liberal "cooperation," but more with his changing tactics. As early as the municipal council spring elections of 1886, Lueger's fellow Democrat Kronawetter, referring to Lueger's collaboration with Schneider, had complained of "'pollution' of the democratic movement through anti-Semitism . . . 'political pestilence,'" having Lueger's collaboration with Schneider's supporters in mind.[179] At the time of his 1887 municipal council reelection, which he won, 2,057 to 1,197, Lueger was still "collaborating," yet he also, to some extent, tried to distance himself from anti-Semitism, allegedly in the interest of "national peace." If actions speak louder than words, however, in May 1887 he backed the proposal of the above-mentioned Jewish exclusion bill. The next month he delivered an anti-Semitic speech in his home district, Margareten,[180] and finally followed this up with another in September, in which he also defended the right of the lower clergy to agitate politically.

Since May, then, he had clearly accommodated the anti-Semites and made plain his availability to the clericals as well. The merging of the two groups into a new alliance became a fact shortly thereafter, as circumstances would have it, though "the grand alliance had been forming for some time."[181] A seventy-one-year-old Liberal member of parliament and provincial diet representative, Johann Ofner from St. Pölten, had died the preceding summer and by-elections were held that autumn.[182] A Pan-German Nationalist named Ursin, who had also received the endorsement of the local Catholic establishment, defeated his Liberal opponent in both races, much to the surprise of the Catholics, who had struggled without success against Liberal hegemony for years.

The significance of these victories was not lost on Lueger. He implied that his was the credit for previously urging the very kind of coalition that had just come into existence. He had done little in fact to initiate it and, in all probability, little to help it to victory. However, the advantage of belonging to, and perhaps leading the variegated coalition represented by the "United Christians," as the new grouping came to be called, must have been immediately obvious to him. In the face of objections from some Democrats to his compromises with the anti-Semites, and the general ineffectuality of that party, he could not long afford to vacillate: he had either to remain with the Democrats or to move decisively toward the anti-Semites. Lueger now revealed "what was probably the most delicately attuned political sense in Austria."[183] In contrast with the less flexible and more doctrinaire Schönerer, he recognized that the new coalition would serve him best, and acted accordingly. In January 1888 he joined the new anti-Liberal Bürgerclub, which had supplanted the Democratic Left in the municipal council. He thus signaled yet a further accommodation with anti-Semitism.

That same month, Lueger received a letter from a disaffected Socialist, Josef Schatzl. The letter, which Lueger valued highly enough to preserve, and some of whose objectives he was to try to translate into concrete politics, underscores the "delicate atunement" of his political sense. Outspokenly anti-Semitic in content, Schatzl's letter urged the creation of "a Christian Social, though also loyal, patriotic labor association" that would provide benefits to the sick, aged, and invalids:

> a daily, rock-bottom inexpensive . . . Christian Social newspaper . . . which represents the interests of workers, artisans and farmers . . . an association for Christian literature and popular education (*Volksbildung*), that includes the editions of inexpensive anti-Semitic social pamphlets, such as poems, novellas, novels, plays, etc.; . . . [and] the creation of a Christian Social public reading room.[184]

Schatzl added that for the realization of these suggestions, of "great physical and moral use to the workers," Lueger's party could expect unconditional support, and "that the power and influence of Jewry will and must disappear."[185] Beyond its gathering specific demands, Schatzl's letter further hinted at that very kind of systematic—that is, inflexible—program for their realization, which, as we have seen, Lueger disliked. Schatzl's suggestions may, in fact, have inspired some of Lueger's remarks before a group of United Christians in February 1888.

The February meeting of the United Christians, organized by the Christian Social Association, was, if nothing else, anti-Semitic.[186] Only Liberals and Pan-Germans were excluded. The relative solidarity and momentum of the new grouping were tacitly recognized.[187] Its very homogeneity obviated any need for an offical program, which was lacking until 1889. When it did appear, the usual demands for restriction of Jewish immigration to the empire and exclusion from various professions were reminiscent of the proposed 1887 German National bill. By 1889 the United Christians included points calling for a customs union with Germany and for denominational schools.

Meanwhile, after a premature newspaper report of the death of William I, emperor of Germany, an event was to have an important effect on politics in Lower Austria and on Lueger's career in particular. Schönerer and a group of his inebriated followers led a foray on the offices of the *Neues Wiener Tagblatt* on the night of March 8, 1888.[188] Arrested, tried, and convicted of assault,[189] Schönerer stated that his action had been motivated by justified outrage over Jewish attempts to exploit German "race love" for the dying emperor, that is, that the premature obituary would affect stock market prices. Schönerer was imprisoned for four months and lost his patent of nobility and his political rights until 1893. In the aftermath of this incident, his party nearly disintegrated.[190] As a member of the Reichsrat, Schönerer enjoyed immunity and received a parliamentary hearing before it voted to surrender him to the legal authorities. Lueger and others defended him in parliament. To the amusement of his listeners, Lueger related how a Bohemian at a party meeting had urged him not to vote for Schönerer's surrender, for "there are enough Jewish journalists in Vienna, but only one Schönerer." Referring to Schönerer, Lueger added, "He's a little rough, perhaps; he's perhaps . . . whatever, but Ritter von Schönerer is no criminal."[191]

Although the reasons for Lueger's defense of his intermittent rival remain uncertain, Schönerer's absence from the political scene during the last four months of 1888, and the consequent loss of control over the activities of his party members, provided Lueger with the opportunity to consolidate his own position. And this began the period of his close tactical cooperation with Karl Freiherr von Vogelsang. Their correspondence between July 1888 and May 1890 affords insights into Lueger's activity as an "anticorruptionist," as well as into the motivations of a highly ambitious politician eager to enlarge his following.[192] To Vogelsang he also confided his anxieties about electioneering, internecine journalistic struggles, rival politicians, and the fragility of the United Christian coalition. A recurring problem was control — control over some of the more volatile coalition members, such as Ernst Schneider,[193] and over reports in *Das Vaterland*.[194] This important Catholic organ, the chief mouthpiece of the United Christians, was published by Vogelsang between 1875 and 1890 when he died from a traffic accident. Lueger admired Vogelsang and a friendship developed, though its tenor remains unclear, in part because of the survival of but three of Vogelsang's letters to Lueger.[195] Lueger was occasionally fawning, probably wishing to cultivate the most harmonious relations possible with the man who was doubtless his last important mentor. At one point, Vogelsang played father, comforting Lueger when his mother died in December 1888, praising his "self-sacrificing work" for their mutual cause,[196] and sending his collected essays "to the courageous and untiring leader of the 'United Christians' as a humble sign of [his] gratitude."[197] Lueger had evidently met Vogelsang as early as 1883,[198] but it was another four years before the possibility of a political alliance was seriously considered and longer still before a partnership was formed.

Vogelsang was a minor Mecklenburg noble who had become disenchanted with Liberalism after the failure of the revolutions of 1848. According to Seliger and Ucakar in their comprehensive political history of Vienna from 1740 to 1934:

[He] developed intensive publicistic activity in Catholic papers, especially in the *Vaterland*. . . . Through his pre-eminent *engagement* in the social question, he soon came into conflict with the state, the conservatives, and above all, with the high clergy.

Vogelsang was preoccupied with the solution of the "social question" through a professional class order based on medieval models. Vogelsang exerted great influence on later Catholic social thought through his criticism of Liberalism, and he played a prominent role in the creation of a uniform Catholic political movement. He criticized Liberal political theory, because it aimed to take power from the state, [and] to regulate social and economic affairs. For this reason, industrialists and capitalists could freely exploit economically weaker groups without fearing state intervention. The Liberal bourgeois state was therefore used by those who created it. Vogelsang attempted to mediate the conflicts between the two Catholic parties, the feudal conservatives and the later Christian Socials. "He was a Catholic conservative, the spokesman of the feudal, the representative of tradition, descendant of Romanticism; and he was a Christian-Social, a teacher and educator of the rising Lueger movement in the 1880s, which wrested the helm of Austria from the Catholic conservatives during a fierce struggle."[199]

In Lueger, Vogelsang found the man who could popularize his social teachings. As a disenchanted Liberal struggling to build his own party, though if as yet unsuccessful, Lueger was gradually acquiring a loyal and energetic constituency. He had, as well, already won the reputation of a municipal reformer. Still in his early forties, Lueger possessed the legal and political knowledge and organizational skills that Vogelsang, nearing seventy, lacked. Lueger must indeed have been attractive to Vogelsang, for Lueger could transform his social teachings into a vital social politics that refuted the evils of Liberalism. Vogelsang, the journalistic theoretician, was the perfect complement to the rising politician and popular leader.[200]

At a private birthday celebration for Vogelsang in September 1888, Lueger allegedly delivered "a brief but impassioned" speech that caused Vogelsang to proclaim him the leader of the United Christians.[201] Vogelsang then added: "The word Christian will remain; we'll replace the word united with social, for we have to work socially for the people in the Christian sense."[202] Lueger then enthusiastically accepted Vogelsang's suggestion. Although this incident may have prompted Lueger to accept the new political grouping as the nucleus of a Christian Social party,[203] the term *Christian Social* had been around for some time, and the political nucleus already existed in the municipal council and parliament.

After defending Schönerer in parliament, Lueger continued to support Catholic school legislation in parliament and thus ensured Vogelsang's approval. From the beginning of his career Lueger had demonstrated an energetic interest in school matters, so his parliamentary activity in this area cannot be dismissed as simple opportunism. Lueger was most certainly aware of the importance of schools as an immediate political issue far beyond their long-range educational usefulness. Now that he had become a member of parliament, the arena of his endeavors naturally expanded, and so in like measure did the effect of his educational politics.

The political thrust of Lueger's attention to schools was trenchantly put by Erich Graf Kielmansegg, governor, or *Statthalter*, of Lower Austria from 1889 until 1911, except for a brief period in 1895 as prime minister, who was watching Lueger's rise along with the Christian Social party.[204] He saw right away the use the Christian Socials were making of educational matters. The lowest common denominator of the primary school was the *Volksschullehrer*:

The influence which the *Volksschullehrer* (primary school teacher) had on the voters in the simple rural communities was and will always remain important, for these teachers are in continuous contact with single families, often act as community secretary, are advisors in this or that capacity and represent, next to the priest and the curate, the intelligentsia of the little community.

"The party that has the priest and teacher on its side will win political elections."[205]

The school issue was to remain a chief bone of contention between Lueger and the Liberals for years, and later after Liberal power was broken, among Lueger and his rivals, the German Nationalists and the Socialists. As mayor, he would fire supporters of rival parties from their jobs and distribute the positions among his supporters. Such practices were to embroil Lueger and the Christian Socials in some of the most acrimonious debates and causes célèbres of his mayoralty.

During the summer of 1888 Lueger called all anti-Liberals and anti-Semites to join together in one party. Whether he believed that just such a party already existed in the United Christians, whether the United Christians could be reshaped, or whether an entirely new party would have to be created remains unclear. His appeal followed his public endorsement of "Pope Leo XIII's pleas for Christian unity,"[206] and suggests that Lueger was, at the least, exasperated by the internal struggles of the United Christians. In any case, this inchoate party at present consisted of "democrats and clericals, German National and Austrian patriots, aristocrats, artisans, peasants and workers."[207] In other words, the party already included most of those who would comprise its mature membership. This distribution probably encouraged Lueger to believe that reorganization would enable him to eliminate the undesirable, consolidate the desirable, and establish his control over the result.

Lueger's endorsement of Leo XIII's plea also underscores his cooperation with the devout Vogelsang and the need to present himself as a pious individual. Such gestures became permanent ingredients of the public Lueger at about this time, aimed at making him acceptable, not only to his more godly lay followers, but also to the lower clergy, who (as Kielmansegg saw) in increasing numbers urged their parishioners to support him. In 1889 Lueger confessed himself a convert to Vogelsang's Christian Social concepts. This set the seal on his politics. Lueger had in this move emerged from the political wilderness. This year also saw the final rupture between him and Mandl. By then Lueger had learned to stand on his own. He was evidently reluctant, however, to lose Mandl as a friend and ally after so many years.[208] But Lueger was never one to allow sentiment or friendship to get in the way of political goals, in this case maintaining some unity within the United Christians. Political causes assumed religious priority.

Kuppe provides a dramatic account of Lueger's acceding to the more radical anti-Semites during a rally in February 1889 when they demanded that Mandl be expelled from the United Christians. Led by Cornelius Vetter, the radicals "proved" Mandl's "betrayal" by showing Lueger a handbill announcing Mandl's appearance as a speaker at a Liberal meeting. According to Kuppe, Lueger, thunderstruck at the revelation, responded as though the shade of Julius Caesar hovered: "So, he too!"—and then and there declared his affiliation with Mandl dissolved. Lueger's words had a cathartic effect on his listeners, who "broke . . . into a storm of applause."[209] As surprised as he may have been, Lueger's indignant response to the ostensible betrayal may have been clever posturing. There is no denying the theatrical in his nature and this gesture in particular. He had responded similarly in 1887, before resigning from the Democratic party. And yet, as with other things about Lueger's behavior, it is difficult in this instance to calculate the ratio of his sincerity. There were many layers in the Lueger personality, and here as elsewhere it is impossible to determine where genuine hurt left off and cunning political calculation began.

Nonetheless, his break with Mandl doubtless worked to consolidate his popularity among the anti-Semites. Though dissension was to continue, Lueger may have won over some of the German Nationals who were more attracted to Lueger's anti-Semitism than they were put off by his clerical affiliation. The publication on the next day of the United Christian program in the recently established paper *Deutsches Volksblatt*[210] revealed that more than a third of the points were anti-Jewish. These focused on segregating Christians from Jews and limiting further Jewish immigration to the Habsburg Empire. The next phase of Lueger's career attests his skill in harnessing the energies released by decaying Liberalism, anti-Semitism, and the discontent of the landlord class, hitherto inadequately represented by the Liberals. The master politician had arrived.

3

The Master Politician: 1889–1897

It can hardly be said that [Lueger's] party was the expression of positive aspirations. Rather, it was a compound of negative attitudes—of the fears and insecurities of the lower middle classes. Lueger appealed to the hostility among these groups to large-scale capitalist enterprises.
— Edward Timms, *Karl Kraus, Apocalyptic Satirist*

*T*he March municipal council elections of 1889 marked a significant increase in anti-Liberal strength. Forty out of a total of 120 seats were contested. The Liberals remained the majority party, but Lueger's Bürgerclub doubled in strength, increasing from twelve to twenty-five members. Among those defeated was Mandl, who never again held public office.

The year 1889 also witnessed the birth of the Social Democratic party, whose founding sessions were concluded in Hainfeld, Lower Austria, on January 1.[1] Though the Socialists were to become the principal rivals of the Christian Socials, the restricted franchise and gerrymandering kept them from commanding a majority in any of the elective bodies until after Lueger's death. The immediate concerns of the Socialists, however, were practical, not ideological, matters: how to win suffrage for the workers and peasants and how to initiate social reforms.[2] Excluded from representation and, therefore, a forum to voice their demands, they and their leader, the moderate and practical-minded Viktor Adler, recognized the importance of having a party newspaper. This need was met by the *Arbeiter Zeitung*, which first appeared in July 1889.

Lueger, who had been embroiled in journalistic controversies since his early days in Viennese political life and whose letters indicate he realized the importance of the press,[3] did not direct his efforts toward the creation of such a party paper. Like his admirer Hitler, he prided himself on his dynamic speaking and may for this reason have scanted personal journalistic endeavors. He was, further, sure of the support of *Das Vaterland*, at least as long as Vogelsang was alive. Then, too, an independent effort by Lueger to create another paper would almost certainly have complicated an already difficult situation. Since December 1888 the radical anti-Semitic mass circulation *Deutsches Volksblatt*, which sometimes favored the United Christians and sometimes the German Nationalists, became a bitter rival of *Das Vaterland*.[4] This situation was exploited by Schönerer. His paper, *Unverfälschte Deutsche Worte*, criticized the *Volksblatt* and the *Vaterland* and added to the already rampant dissension among the anti-Semites. This journalistic struggle did not always follow political lines and demonstrated the lack of cohesiveness of the United Christians, which, if a party at all, required drastic reorganization if it were to survive.

The same month that witnessed the birth of the Social Democratic party also saw the first meetings of a sociopolitical society founded by Vogelsang and Prelate Franz Schindler.[5] Organized in response to "the New Socialist International"[6] and held at the hotel Zur goldenen Ente, the "Ente Evenings" became "the cadre school for the political elite of the Christian Socials."[7] They attracted a mixture of old and young conservatives, anti-Semites, members of parliament, clergymen,[8] and, later, members of university fraternities. Lueger regularly attended the Ente Evenings from April 2, 1889.[9] Later that month he spoke at the Second Katholikentag, an assembly of clergymen and laity with a great interest in political developments. His words were probably calculated to dispel the doubts of some clergymen that he "didn't want to have anything to do with church and religion"[10] as much as they were intended to differentiate "*his* politics from the dangerous rhetoric of the Schönerians."[11] At this point Lueger needed the backing of this Catholic reform group, which in theory at least transcended nationalistic rivalries and symbolized imperial unity. At the outset of his speech, he emphasized that he had "dedicated his life to the service of the Christian people."[12] He then struck a conciliatory note, remarking that the multinational composition of his audience presented "a picture of Austria," with the difference that the members of this group were at peace with one another, rather than in conflict. Just as Christianity had been founded on the masses, so it had been spread among the masses, he added, thereby suggesting that something like a new gospel was at hand, of which he was the (implicit) apostle elect. Both gospel and apostle were needed, because Austria and Vienna were threatened "by a great danger," just as they had been threatened more than two centuries ago by the Turks. But now the enemy was "far more dangerous," because it attacked from within. This enemy was "anti-Christianity," and the struggle would be decided within Vienna. As the First Austrian Katholikentag had been a rallying point for the parliamentary struggle, the Second should continue to be so. Whether city or country dwellers, "whether we are Germans or Slavs or Italians, we all want to be one, brothers in Austria and brothers in Christ."[13]

Lueger's speech, conspicuous for its militant religiosity and demagogic tone, was interrupted at many points by "stormy applause" and cheers. Without naming a specific group, he managed to suggest with his reference to "anti-Christianity" that the Jews were the enemy and that only unified mass support by the Christians could defeat them. He praised the "picture of Austria" presented by the "Germans, Czechs, Poles, Ruthenes, Slovenes and Italians" of his audience, but he significantly omitted the Hungarians. By this time, "Judeo-Magyars" were becoming a frequent target in his parliamentary speeches, with significant effects. A more specific identification of "the enemy" was neither necessary nor prudent.

The Second Katholikentag "marked the zenith of Vogelsang's influence" on his followers.[14] It also afforded Lueger the opportunity to resolve a controversy that had divided Schindler and Vogelsang, and thus to reveal those considerable negotiating skills that were to be of key importance in Lueger's success as Christian Social party leader years later. At issue was the question whether to adopt an antiusury resolution. This point had been raised during the Ente Evenings, with Vogelsang opposed and Schindler in favor. The subject was of relevance to Lueger's career, because of his reputation as an anticapitalist, and the possible objection to his leadership on the part of some Katholikentag participants who were small-property owners and shareholders. Not until the Katholikentag had he taken such a position, but when he did it proved to be decisive and rendered any resolution superfluous: "Gentlemen! We Catholics are generally poor people, but each of us has a few annuity bonds and debentures. In my humble opinion, it would create considerable anxiety among our people if they became worried about a few coupons by such a resolution. I therefore strongly suggest, gentlemen, that we refrain from drawing up such a resolution."[15] Such was his gift for taking a position and at the same time sidestepping the decisive implications of saying so outright.

For the rest of the year Lueger tried to resolve continuing conflicts among the United Christians. At the end of October 1889, Schönerer, who had been behaving ever more erratically since his release from prison the preceding December, disavowed both Lueger and Pattai for having betrayed German nationalism for Catholicism.[16] Lueger lost no time in turning this to his advantage by appealing to Schönerer's followers early the following year in the name of anti-Semitism and unity.[17] Meanwhile, he also continued to speak at Christian Social gatherings throughout the autumn,[18] gaining confidence in his growing "leadership role" and asserting at the end of November that he was the leader of the Christian Social party.[19] In parliament on February 13, 1890, he proudly referred to himself as "one of the few representatives of the Christian Social party."[20] His power continued to grow throughout the year in his reelection to the municipal council and his election to the Landtag, or provincial diet.

By 1890 Lueger's popularity was firmly enough established among his constituents to make his reelection to the municipal council that spring relatively certain. He emerged with a substantial majority over his Liberal opponent, the outspoken anticlerical Friedrich Dittes,[21] and the Bürgerclub increased its strength from twenty-five to thirty. The perceptible decline of the Liberals became even more apparent with the results of the Landtag elections later that fall, when anti-Semites became a significant force. Had it not then been for the assistance of large–landed property owners, the Liberals would have lost their majority.[22] Uhl, who at seventy-six had tired of the strife between the majority Mittelpartei and the Bürgerclub, had resigned as mayor in November 1889.[23] But his resignation was by then little more than a formality. The more vigorous Johann Prix, who as first vice-mayor succeeded Uhl, had for some years been providing much of the impetus for the conduct of business, if not the actual leadership of the city. Prix was forceful and aggressive, his style somewhat reminiscent of Felder's. His clash with Lueger was inevitable.

But the events of the next few years, until Prix's death in 1894, proved to be anything but a replay of the earlier Felder-Lueger rivalry. Lueger had long since left his tutors behind. He commanded a growing, if volatile, coalition; and even if he could not altogether control all his followers, he became at least a powerful activator of the radicalism that would characterize Viennese electoral politics for years to come.[24] Moreover, by 1890 there were more significant issues at stake than petty municipal graft and influence peddling. At the municipal level, there was the incorporation of Vienna's outlying districts — the creation of greater Vienna — to be considered, not to mention accompanying commodity tax reforms that would adversely affect the outlying area's rapidly growing poor and lower middle classes. So far as Lueger was concerned, his dream of becoming mayor seemed to be coming closer to reality in the fact of declining Liberal popularity and a notable lack of outstanding rivals for leadership positions. Yet several years of intense struggle lay between him and the Rathaus.

Lueger's position on the incorporation of the outlying suburbs reveals ambiguity. During the early 1880s he had favored incorporation, but late in 1890 he opposed it.[25] Later, as mayor, he would change positions yet again, support the incorporation of an additional district, and even pose as the creator of greater Vienna.[26] The probable reason for his original change of mind was that the incorporation would entail taxes on food where few had existed among his increasingly important constituents in the as yet outlying districts. To have supported such a measure would have cost him votes in the Landtag.[27] At no point in his career were Lueger's political skills more adroitly deployed than during this consumption tax-incorporation issue. In parliament early in 1890 when the tax issue arose, Lueger remained silent, doubtless because his fifth district constituents would benefit by its passage, and he wished to present the appearance of tacit support. Moreover, to have blamed "Vienna's financial isolation on . . . agrarian privilege," which the Taaffe ministry sustained,[28] would have meant offending the peasants Lueger hoped would support him in the autumn Landtag elections. To remain silent about the consumption tax was in effect to favor it, and with it, the incorporation of the outlying areas. But after the elections, which netted him and the anti-Semites important success, Lueger attacked the incorporation in the Landtag. This had no effect on the outcome of the issue, because the Liberal majority supported it. Lueger and his followers thus appeared to have championed suburban interests all along and won valuable support from this area in subsequent elections.

Since 1889 the significant losers in Austrian politics had been the Pan-German Nationalists, Schönerer's followers. By the end of 1890 they were confronted by three formidable sociopolitical developments led by the Socialists, Christian Socials, and a German *völkisch* national group, which became known as the Deutsche Volkspartei in 1893.[29] Lueger displayed his anti-Semitic rhetoric during the 1890 Landtag election campaign, which was marked by unusual intensity. In fact, the entire year was scarred by anti-Semitism. Before Lueger's spring municipal council victory, police had intervened to separate Jews and anti-Semites on election day.[30]

Lueger's personality as leader of the anti-Semites was becoming an increasingly prominent election issue. During his reelection campaign for his parliamentary seat in March 1891, the *Volksblatt* stated that it had become impossible to speak of an anti-Semitic victory without having reelected Lueger.[31] Although he was once again victorious, Christian Social elation was dampened by Liberal municipal council victories a month later. This had come about through new franchise legislation.

> The franchise provided for a [Municipal] Council of 138 seats, divided, as in the 1850 franchise, into three electoral curias. Each member of the Council would be elected for a six-year term, as opposed to a three-year term previously in force. A major change was made in the way in which the curia members would be reelected. The 1850 franchise had prescribed that one-third of the members of each curia would stand for reelection each year, so that no year went by in Vienna without a municipal election. According to the new regulation, elections would be held on a staggered basis every two years, and at a given election the seats of a whole curia would be subject to reelection. To start the system, a general election for all three curias was called for March/April 1891. The next election would then be held in 1893, at which time the seats of the wealthiest curia, the First, would be vacated and reelected. Elections for the Second and Third Curias would follow in 1895 and 1897. The cycle would begin again in 1899.[32]

The idea behind the recent legislation was to slow the momentum of the anti-Semites. As things had stood, annual municipal council elections had provided the Liberals little respite from adversarial agitation.[33] Under the new system, the curias would vote in numerical order, instead of the third voting first as before. Because the first and second curias contained a majority of affluent pro-Liberal voters, the Liberals hoped to gather momentum, and thereby reduce the impact of third curial elections, which had invariably returned radical, or lately, anti-Semitic candidates. Lueger had predictably opposed the new arrangement.[34] To improve their chances further, the Liberals gerrymandered the municipal council seats. The majority would be occupied by municipal councillors from the first ten districts whose residents had benefited from the 1890 Liberal tax and incorporation revisions. These districts received ninety-three seats; the remaining forty-five were allocated to the nine newly incorporated districts.[35]

Although the anti-Semites won the third curia elections, as had been expected, the Liberals secured a majority in the other two curias. Their strength now stood at ninety-four. The anti-Semites possessed forty-two seats, and two independents were elected. Later in April 1891 Prix was reelected mayor. For the next three years Lueger carried on aggressive and disruptive agitation in the municipal council, leaving no doubt about his impatience to take control of the chief executive's position.[36] When Prix died from a heart attack in February 1894, many Liberals blamed Lueger.

Meanwhile in parliament, Alois Liechtenstein, who had been reelected in March 1891 after a two-year hiatus,[37] outlined the details of a Christian Social program.[38] The salient points included a response to Franz Joseph's call for a solution to the social problem. Echoing Pope Leo XIII's encyclical *Rerum Novarum,* he urged reform measures to alleviate peasant debt burdens,[39] support for small crafts, and improved conditions for workers. Liechtenstein expressed qualified support for collective bargaining, worker representation in parliament, and the universal franchise. He also defined anti-Semitism as part of the social question, being careful to describe Christian Social opposition to Jews as economically, rather than religiously or racially, motivated. Catholic Conservatives, the cream of Austrian society and at that time one of the vital segments in Taaffe's Iron Ring, mistrusted the Christian Socials because of their anti-Semitism, as well as their emphasis on the social, rather than the Christian, aspect of their program, seeing in these the emblems of lower-middle-class inferiority and radicalism. It was in part to refute the designation of "second class Catholics"[40] that Liechtenstein spoke at the Third General Austrian Katholikentag in Linz the following summer.[41] Predictably, when the Christian Socials seized the opportunity to present their views, the Catholic Conservatives were peeved, and the Katholikentag ended in disunity. About the only positive thing to come out of this meeting from the standpoint of the Christian Socials was the decision finally to found a paper, *Die Reichspost.* This major political organ, whose life span corresponded approximately with that of the Christian Social party,[42] proved to be more politically reliable than either Vergani's *Volksblatt* or Vogelsang's *Das Vaterland.*

Not until November 1894, after the collapse of the Taaffe Ministry the preceding year, did the Christian Socials and at least some of the Catholic Conservatives conclude a truce at a conciliatory meeting. But the Archbishop of Vienna, Cardinal Gruscha, Lueger's former religious preceptor at the Theresianum, made his attendance conditional on Lueger's and Gessmann's nonappearance as speakers.[43] Though the names of the two were omitted from the program, Gruscha failed to appear. In the event, Lueger delivered the opening speech. Friedrich Funder, later the editor-in-chief of the *Reichspost,* was at the conciliatory meeting, a provincial Lower Austrian gathering, rather than the successor to the larger Linz Katholikentag, as had originally been planned, and described what took place. Lueger welcomed the assembly, delivering a speech that Funder praised as "one of the noblest flowers of Catholic rhetoric."[44] Read today, it anticipates William Jennings Bryan's "Cross of Gold" oration in its imagery.[45] The conclusion of Lueger's remarks bears quoting for what it reveals about his religiosity and his calculations on contemporary instincts. Greeting his listeners as "the Catholic Volk of Vienna and Lower Austria," he informed them that the state needed Christianity, rather than the other way around. To those bewildered by years of anarchist violence, exposures of corruption in high places, and Socialist propaganda, Lueger's words were just what they wanted to hear:

> The body of mankind bleeds from innumerable wounds. Eyes look up beseechingly to Him, flayed and crowned with thorns, who died for the people. They in turn acknowledged the religion of love, of justice and mercy in contrast to the theory and relentless hegemony of the powerful over the weak. They also acknowledged the religion of the poor and the oppressed. Their hearts were comforted again, and they spoke once more that beautiful greeting that a pious mother . . . had taught them, . . . the greeting that I believe will become the victory cry for all mankind—the greeting with which I too welcome you: Praised be Jesus Christ![46]

Lueger's words produced the desired effect. Funder speaks of "an indescribable scene. Men stood pale with emotion and with tears in their eyes; from the tribunes and galleries waved the handkerchiefs of women bent over the balustrade, cheering the speaker. Applause and cheers thundered without end."[47]

Lueger's parliamentary attacks until the mid-1890s concentrated on the Hungarians, by this time frequently "Judeo-Magyars," against the introduction of the gold standard, and big business corruption. Lueger favored paper currency and silver, much as did Bryan.[48] After one parliamentary anti-Semitic diatribe against the financially troubled Donau-Dampfschiffahrts-Gesellschaft in February 1892,[49] Lueger was challenged to a duel by Heinrich von Etienne, a company official and brother of the cofounder and publisher of the *Neue Freie Presse*. Unlike Schönerer, who fought several duels,[50] Lueger responded by saying that "a person cannot be held responsible in the manner proposed by von Etienne for statements made in the performance of one's official responsibilities," that he did "not consider a duel an appropriate way to handle the matter and therefore refuse[d] to accept the challenge."[51] Lueger's response is telling and would be repeated on several occasions.[52] Though he was a firm opponent of dueling in principle as stupid and wasteful of life, Lueger's response suggests that in his mind, a public forum admitted broad limits on what he was permitted to say. He was prepared to go as far and beyond what was permitted, if he could get away with it. He frequently did.[53]

Lueger's agitational speeches focused on citywide affairs, thus suggesting his tangible goal. The mayoralty was the great prize, but before it could be won Liberal power in the municipal council had to be destroyed. There, Christian Social agitation frequently made the conduct of business impossible. The decisive year was 1895. Lueger's popularity had increased since 1891, and many developments augured well for his continued success, the most important of which was largely economic.[54] The Liberals had been unable to slow the inflation of consumer commodity costs. Some voters undoubtedly believed the anti-Semites' agitation,[55] blamed hard times on Jews, for some had sided prominently with the Liberals, particularly in Vienna, and therefore favored Lueger who promised to bring "Jewish mismanagement" to an end. But his success among the electorate had other causes as well. Lueger was recognized as a sincere populist leader when populism was reaching flood tide. Public approval of him and of his style of politics was attested by a flood of Lueger-inspired memorabilia, most of it kitsch, including pipes, statues, beer mugs, and cups with his picture. Many poems and musical compositions were dedicated to him as well. The Lueger memorabilia industry that grew up in the 1890s in response to his popularity fed on it, and was in turn fed by it.[56] Despite protestations to the contrary, Lueger thrived on this personality cult, which later became a significant part of his public presence. The appearance of these objects should have been a warning to higher imperial officials who opposed Lueger that they were dealing with something more than a skillful politician who commanded a loyal and growing following. Lueger was a highly dynamic leader; more than that, he was a new sort of phenomenon making full use of media potential, which extended to leading European cities outside the Habsburg Monarchy. Lueger's was a forerunner of twentieth-century dynamic leadership. There was nothing comparable to it in Europe at the time, except briefly General Georges Boulanger. And unlike the general, Lueger's popularity was to grow importantly for the next fifteen years until his death in 1910, and beyond.

Lueger's bid for the highest elective position in the Habsburg Monarchy was precipitated by Prix's death. Prix had been a particular target of oppositional attacks in the municipal council. He had resigned in October 1893, only to be reelected in a vote of confidence the following month. His opponent was Lueger and the outcome of the contest, eighty-one to forty-five, showed the Liberals still in command of the municipal council.[57]

What followed Prix's death in February 1894, however, not only revealed Liberal disarray, but pointed to more serious difficulties. Prix's logical successor, First Vice-Mayor Albert Richter, proved unacceptable, in large part because he was married to a Jew, and also because to marry her, he had declared himself nondenominational.[58] A few days before the

March 14, 1894, election, he had converted to Catholicism, something that made his opportunism in Vienna, that most Catholic of all imperial capitals, all too apparent. While there were no legal obstacles to mixed marriages, the more subtle one of public disapproval proved all too formidable. Accordingly, the second vice-mayor, Raimund Grübl, who was also married to a Jew and who became the target of anti-Semitic attacks, became the Liberal candidate. He defeated Lueger eighty-eight to forty-three, suggesting that some of those who had favored Lueger in November 1893 had since become more sympathetic to the Liberals. Yet the second curial elections in April 1895 resulted in an increase of sixteen new seats for the Christian Socials and a major defeat for the Liberals. After the results were tallied, the Liberals retained sixty-six seats, the anti-Semites sixty-four. Eight independents controlled the balance. Of great importance to the anti-Semites' victory had been the dissaffection of municipal officials — formerly staunch Liberal supporters — over broken Liberal promises.[59] In the spring of 1895 they voted against the majority party. Lueger had exploited the Liberals' factionalism in masterly fashion. This had become apparent as early as 1893, when enough disaffected white collar workers, ineptly handled by the Liberals, had deserted their party to elect Lueger to the recently created city council (Stadtrat).[60]

Rather than trying to rule with the weak majority he possessed, Grübl resigned in mid May, after having been reelected, together with his first vice-mayor Richter. This had been Prix's strategy in 1893. Lueger, who had been elected to replace Richter,[61] accepted the results and assumed his office as first vice-mayor. In resigning, the Liberals may have been trying to expose the Christian Socials' administrative incompetence, because they were considered incapable of governing, or perhaps to force imperial intervention in one form or another.[62] Whatever the outcome, the Liberals could have functioned as an effective opposition. Yet another election followed on May 29, 1895. This time, Lueger was elected mayor, receiving seventy votes during the third balloting,[63] but he refused to accept for the same reasons as Grübl two weeks before.

Vienna was now without a chief executive, and its autonomy was suspended. Assisted by a fifteen-member council, District Chairman Hans Friebeis was appointed imperial commissioner by Kielmansegg, the governor of Lower Austria, and ruled in the mayor's stead, for the council had been dissolved by Kielmansegg. The issue that plagued Kielmansegg as much if not more than the mayoralty election crisis was the more than theoretical one of Lueger's possible amassing of power: what would happen if he were to become mayor and retain his positions in the provincial diet and parliament, thus uniting the office of mayor with his position as a powerful parliamentary leader.[64] For the summer, however, this possibility remained academic. In a subsequent interview with Lueger, when Kielmansegg mentioned this issue, Lueger tellingly responded that only if he retained his parliamentary position, could he as mayor adequately represent the municipality.[65] Lueger thereby served notice that he would make no deals or compromises. He had a winning hand and intended to play it out to the end.

Meanwhile, Lueger's supporters furiously agitated for further curial elections that were to be held in September. A Liberal, Robert Weil, described the atmosphere in Vienna at the time:

> An agitation developed such as no metropolis in the world had yet seen. Demagogy, incitement, and slander celebrated veritable orgies. Sanguinary posters grinned from every street corner; every evening agitated meetings filled the halls, taverns and such, lasting until dawn; Dr. Lueger was often on hand, cheered by his followers, to harangue the masses, to shake the hand of the faltering, and to expose the enemy parties to ridicule and contempt. And since nothing seemed low enough to injure his opponent, he revitalized the specifically Viennese custom of disrupting opposing meetings by force, and bloody attacks were the order of the day.[66]

Lueger's popularity had received an additional and dramatic boost that spring from none other than Pope Leo XIII. Rejecting the advice of Cardinal Schönborn, the archbishop of Prague and senior Austrian cardinal, to disavow the Christian Socials because their party contained "unhealthy and rotten elements,"[67] for inciting "insubordination among the lower clergy" and for instigating anti-Semitism,[68] the pope sent Lueger a message: "The leader of the Christian Socials should know that he possesses a warm friend in the pope who blesses him; he values the Christian Social efforts and has complete understanding for certain difficulties, 'but they will be overcome.'"[69] With that, the lower clergy had also received approval to continue their pro-Lueger agitation, for their political engagement had also long been a bone of contention with their superiors.[70] Lueger must have been particularly grateful for the papal sanction. He was no revolutionary and seems to have needed constant reinforcement from respected sources for what he was doing to undermine established practices and attitudes.

Not only did the Vienna mayoralty crisis attract Europeanwide attention that summer, it also became the subject of intermittent comment in American diplomatic correspondence. Bartlett Tripp, a member of the United States legation, described the situation in early June:

The municipal government of Vienna, which in importance is almost a co-ordinate part of the general government, is rent in pieces by the great question of party politics. The antisemites were partially victorious in the recent municipal election, to such an extent at least to deprive the liberals or any consolidated party of a majority, and to enable themselves by the aid of some independent votes to elect Dr. Lueger, their acknowledged representative in Vienna, Mayor. He however was wise enough to know that his election, with no majority behind him, would be injurious rather than beneficial to his party, and would destroy the aim of his personal ambition. The result is that the municipal council has been dissolved and the government of the city placed in charge of a commission of fifteen, until a new election can be held which will probably occur in September. Here is a new and serious complication. The antisemites, which is not, as the name seems to indicate, wholly a party of opposition to the Jews, but rather of the small tradesmen and common people against the capitalists, it is expected will have a working majority in the new city government, the effect of which in part will be to weaken the liberal party of Austria which already is obliged in the present ministry, to combine with the Poles and conservatives to obtain a majority in parliament and to strengthen the clericals and the opposition and thereby to weaken the bond which unites the dual government. The great strength of this nation, up to this time, lay in the united power of Austria to overcome the factions of Hungary struggling for the independence of that half of the monarchy. If Austria develop [sic] at home and in her own capital an opposition to and hatred of the duality of the monarchy itself, the nation will have received a wound which would seem to be fatal to the continuance of the alliance which alone gives it rank as one of the great powers of Europe.

I hand you herewith a double leaded editorial from the London Times of June 4th on the situation which is very accurate and gives a very full description of the condition of affairs here. The very fact that the London Times devotes a column and a half editorially to this question is evidence that the situation is of such moment that it may well be viewed with serious consideration if not with feelings of alarm.[71]

Two weeks after Tripp's dispatch, "the present ministry"—the Windischgraetz Ministry—did collapse, though not because of the mayoralty crisis. Ernst Plener, the Liberal minister of finance, had approved appropriations for parallel secondary school classes to be conducted in Slovene instead of German, in the Styrian town of Cilli. The Liberals repudiated his action and withdrew from the coalition, stating that "the inter-Party agreement had been broken."[72] The collapse of the Windischgraetz Ministry proved fateful for Lueger. Its successor, formed in October by Casimir Badeni, a Polish noble, would effectively postpone the necessary sanction for Lueger's election.[73]

Meanwhile, Lueger's campaign was aided not only by his unorthodox electioneering during the summer months when many Liberals were vacationing, but also by the ineptitude of the interim Kielmansegg Ministry. Kielmansegg took a dim view of the increasing politicization of the bureaucracy and the teachers and tried to halt it through a decree restricting the political participation of these groups.[74] But nonetheless, teachers and bureaucrats continued to participate in political — and usually anti-Liberal — rallies, thereby deepening the already existing rift between the upper and lower strata of society.

The elections returned the anti-Semites with a majority of seats to the municipal council. When the mayoral elections were held on October 29, 1895, Lueger received ninety-three out of 137 votes.[75] He immediately accepted the results, in a speech that was both nationalistic and anti-Semitic.[76] This acceptance made it imperative for the emperor to act: should he or should he not sanction the election? Lueger-watchers were split roughly along class lines, the upper level conservatives and higher clergy favoring nonconfirmation, his lower class supporters enthusiastically endorsing him. There was some exceptional support from the Catholic Conservatives Lueger had won over in 1894 at a regional Catholic gathering in Vienna. The Hungarian Prime Minister, Baron Desiderius Bánffy, was predictably opposed to the confirmation, also the Liberals and bankers such as Rothschild, who, according to Kuppe, threatened to withdraw his capital and move to Budapest if Franz Joseph approved the election.[77] Kielmansegg was qualified in urging the emperor's sanction, repeating an opinion he had voiced the preceding spring, that Lueger's political bark was worse than his bite: once he had assumed office, his radicalism would decline.[78] The key man at this stage of the crisis was the new Austrian Prime Minister Count Badeni, who, after some behind-the-scenes intrigue, voted against confirmation.[79] Lueger received official word of the emperor's negative decision on November 6.

Two days later, he and his supporters responded angrily by introducing a motion of urgency in parliament inquiring about the reasons for the nonconfirmation.[80] Additional supporting interpellations were submitted by German Nationalists and Czechs. In his reply, Badeni, who may have been irritated by this challenge from a lower authority, flatly denied that Lueger possessed the "objectivity" and "rationality" to run the capital.[81] Although this sort of strong unequivocal response was what had won Badeni praise as former governor of rural Galicia from military authorities during an earlier crisis,[82] his similar behavior in these altered circumstances only revealed his ignorance of Vienna. Badeni's reply also determined Lueger and his men on a more radical course of action — to challenge Badeni and Kielmansegg. The Bürgerclub called yet another election in the municipal council. On November 13 Lueger was reelected with ninety-two votes.[83] He once again accepted the results in a speech that emphasized his patriotism, independence of the government — by which he alluded to the autonomy of Vienna — religious devotion, and resistance to the temptations "of the golden calf."[84] As soon as he had finished speaking, Friebeis, the head of the provisional municipal governing committee, declared the council dissolved. Lueger shouted back that Friebeis had broken the law. Pandemonium now broke out in the municipal council chamber and outside the Rathaus. Some of Lueger's supporters wanted to storm the town hall but were restrained by the police. Lueger, probably recognizing the possibility of a bloody confrontation, and with it the collapse of his political ambitions, tried to calm the crowd. When some of his followers started for the royal apartments to confront the emperor, they were restrained by the police.[85]

The government's response to the mayoralty crisis produced a twofold effect. Agitation for Lueger continued, formally and informally, and negotiations were undertaken to ease a Christian Social puppet into the mayor's position, to be quietly retired and replaced by Lueger after a few months. Although Franz Joseph had informed Kielmansegg during the autumn of 1895 that "so long as [he] rule[d], Lueger [would] never be confirmed as mayor of [his] imperial capital,"[86] he had begun to waver by the end of December. In a letter to Empress Elizabeth he confided:

> The day before yesterday I received the enclosed letter from Valérie [their younger daughter] as well as the additionally enclosed letters of old Princess Arenberg, née Auersperg in Salzburg, to Valérie and to Baroness Vécsey, in which Lueger and his party were most warmly recommended to me. Anti-Semitism is an uncommonly wide-spread sickness that has penetrated into the highest circles and the agitation is unbelievable. The core is actually good, but the excesses are terrible. [*Der Fond ist eigentlich gut, aber die Auswüchse sind entsetzlich.*][87]

A week after the municipal council had again been dissolved, Bartlett Tripp again commented on political events. He wrote Secretary of State Richard Olney that he had been surprised on returning to this post that the usual tranquility of Vienna had been disrupted and that "the unrest, which now seems epidemic in Europe, has assumed a violent phase," yet

> the most remarkable thing of this whole matter . . . is, that during all this excitement and in all the noisy demonstrations upon the streets and discussions in public places and otherwise, while the most bitter feeling is exhibited against the Government of the province and the ministry, while the cry "down

with the foreigners," "back to Hannover with the 'German'" (the Governor of the province Count Kielmannsegg [*sic*] is a German) "back to Galicia with the minister" . . . not a word is ever heard against the Emperor himself even in private conversation.

Two reasons may be urged for this, first the great respect amounting almost to veneration in which the person and name of the emperor is held, second the severe penalty for offenses against his Majesty. But it is difficult to conclude that it is the latter rather than the former reason that restrains any expression of feeling against the head of the royal and imperial house, when it is remembered that almost equally severe penalties are openly and constantly incurred in the epithets used and public demonstrations made against the ministry and other official heads of the departments of the Government.

The personality of the Emperor Francis Joseph is felt everywhere among the people and I can best convey to you an idea of the feeling entertained for him by the people by repeating the remark made by a strong partisan of Dr. Lueger . . . in reply to the suggestion that it was the Emperor who refused his sanction not the ministry nor the Government. "O the Emperor is too just, too humane to allow any discrimination between classes or races of his people.!!" commending in the Emperor the same thing he had already so strenuously and earnestly condemned in those who were mere agents of the imperial will.

It is now believed that the crisis has passed and that the tide of public excitement is at its ebb.

The firmness and ability exhibited by the new minister Count Badeni during the continued period of intense excitement and public demonstration has [*sic*] won him warm commendation at home and abroad and has [*sic*] given his administration an impetus to apparent future success.

The City government moves on under the imperial commission with no appreciable difference so far as the intents of the public are concerned and it is hoped by all friends of good government that the questions which have brought about so sudden and abrupt a termination of the recent City government may now find some proper solution before the next election be held.[88]

By the time the next curial elections took place in late February and early March 1896, Lueger and Badeni had made a deal that settled the mayoralty crisis. It is said that fate sometimes selects peculiar agents to further its ends. On this occasion the solution to the mayoralty issue was facilitated by Badeni's son, who had a toothache, the son's dentist, and an insecticide manufacturer.[89] The result was a face-saving measure for those principally concerned. According to his father's wishes, Louis Badeni had attended a Landtag session in which Kielmansegg had been bitterly attacked by Lueger's party. Evidently disturbed by what he had seen and heard, Badeni, Jr., told his dentist about the session. The dentist's brother-in-law, an insecticide manufacturer, was a friend of Lueger, who by then earnestly wished to speak to Badeni about the crisis. A secret meeting was arranged late the following evening in the ministry of the interior. Lueger insisted on becoming mayor, but agreed that his close friend Josef Strohbach should occupy that position for a few months and then retire. In the interim, Lueger would serve as first vice-mayor and subsequently move into the vacated position. In return, only token resistance to Badeni and his Liberal, German, Czech coalition would be offered by the Christian Socials in parliament. Peace would return to the Landtag as well. As a final major condition for his cooperation, Lueger also demanded an audience with the emperor "in order to assure the latter of his loyalty and to be able to prove to the Viennese population, that he stands in his good graces, and that his party has no occasion to demonstrate against his majesty, as had happened."[90] Badeni believed that the realization of this last condition would be difficult, an impression he later confirmed to Kielmansegg. "I feel so weak, as if I had just gotten over a grave illness, but it was just as difficult and painful for me to arrange the requested audience for Lueger with his majesty and to win his supreme highness for the later confirmation of Lueger, after I had asked for and received the non-confirmation not long ago."[91] Although Lueger probably had reason to reassure Franz Joseph, it is impossible to escape the impression that the audience with the emperor was also intended to assuage Lueger's injured vanity and to nourish his ego. He later boasted to his followers that only he and Franz Joseph knew what had transpired between them,[92] a claim that carefully held confidences had been exchanged, perhaps, but a remark also redolent with exclusivity: Lueger had made it to the top. In fact, Lueger had vindicated his shrewdness in refusing to relinquish his mandate the preceding year. By holding to his course, he had brought Badeni and Franz Joseph to the bargaining table, and revealed his increasing control over party activity in the political arenas.

After the curial elections in February and March, events moved according to plan, and Lueger's party worked like the well-oiled machine it had become. The Christian Socials had picked up four new seats for a total of ninety-six in the municipal council. The Liberals with forty-two were now outnumbered by more than two to one.

Although the outcome of the elections was never in doubt, the Christian Socials were opposed for the first time by the Social Democrats, an increasingly effective foe who supplanted Lueger's party as the parliamentary majority in 1911, and as Vienna's leader in 1919. Viktor Adler in 1889 had characterized Austrian liberty as "a façade, German in form and Russian in practice," adding that the "government was deliberately inhibiting the political and economic development of the working class."[93] His own party had become structurally centralized by the mid-1890s and may even have surpassed the Christian Socials in efficiency.[94]

Nationally, however, the Social Democrats suffered from the faults implicit in their virtues. The Czechs resented the interference of the central Austrian leaders on the hitherto autonomous local level. In Vienna, Social Democratic defeat was a foregone conclusion, but although he had anticipated the outcome, Adler insisted that the Social Democrats campaign to gain experience for the parliamentary elections in 1897.[95] It was then that the franchise was to be extended, and Adler's hopes were rewarded, for the Social Democrats for the first time won fourteen seats.

For the time being, however, Lueger was the man of the hour and the Christian Socials continued to score victories. On April 18, 1896, he was again elected mayor, receiving ninety-six votes to Grübl's forty-two.[96] Lueger accepted the results perfunctorily, referring to "the mayoralty question" as "a part of the great struggle for the liberation of the Christian people."[97] Friebeis noted the result and closed the sitting. This time, however, there were no disturbances as there had been in November. Nine days later, Franz Joseph received Lueger in the Hofburg, a personal triumph for him and for his followers. During this interview "Lueger's natural feeling for social distinction . . . in relation to the more unbending bourgeois breed [of] . . . his foes, a subtle sense of social superiority despite his lowly origins," may well have come to the fore.[98] He would have been afforded no better opportunity to demonstrate "the sensibility of the well-trained servant, who knows breeding better than the classes do that lie between his master's and his own."[99] On April 28 Lueger relinquished his victory. This produced consternation among some of his constituents, although most of the party elite had realized for some time that an elaborate charade was now being played: Strohbach would become mayor while Lueger as the real power behind the scenes served as vice-mayor for a few months. Early the following year, Strohbach would resign, Lueger would be elected for the fifth time, and Franz Joseph would duly sanction the election. There was brief uncertainty over who was to become second vice-mayor. The more strident German Nationalists advanced their own candidate, Paul von Pacher, but their efforts were ineffectual, and a majority of anti-Semites supported a more moderate nationalist, Josef Neumayer. He would succeed Lueger as mayor in 1910. On May 6, 1896, Strohbach was elected mayor, ninety-four to forty-two. The imperial sanction followed a few days later and Strohbach took the oath of office on May 20.[100] Vienna thus became the first "major metropolitan area in the modern urban political history of Central Europe [to fall] to non-Liberal rule."[101]

A week before, Lueger had explained his tactics to a mass rally in Vienna's Musikvereinssaal. Pressing municipal business had necessitated a solution to the mayoralty crisis, he stated, and "a personal sacrifice" rather than the "surrender of [his] principles" had been demanded by the emperor.[102] On May 22 he and Neumayer were elected first and second vice-mayors and duly sworn in. Even though Strohbach was soon to be succeeded by Lueger, according to plan, Strohbach never let him forget that he had been the first Christian Social mayor,[103] something that Lueger, who hated to be upstaged, must have resented.

Although it was clear that Lueger remained at the head of the party and was thus the actual power, the election of Strohbach was nonetheless significant. A self-taught, self-made man, Strohbach was a *Hausherr*, or landlord, and his election thus symbolized the arrival of that class in Christian Social politics.[104] This was the very group that the Liberals had slighted to their detriment between 1891 and 1895, and became "the last stage in an ascending hierarchy of Bürger interest groups upon which [Lueger's] party based its electoral strategies."[105] Some of its members, including Strohbach, were friends of Lueger, though it is perhaps significant that Lueger's elitist education may have prompted him to maintain a distance from them. This was once suggested by Lueger's request for second-class train tickets for another landlord, Karl Hallmann, Strohbach's colleague, and his wife, while Lueger rode in his own first-class coupé.[106] As mayor of Vienna, he would have traveled first class; but it is nonetheless hard to escape the impression that Lueger's handwritten request reflected more than mere protocol, an impression that is strengthened by Lueger's later insistence on his prerogatives.

All the same, Lueger's perception of the importance to the party of the landlords helps explain why little municipal housing was constructed during his mayoralty.[107] The Christian Social party was far from monolithic, being a conglomerate of interest groups, which Lueger tried to harmonize with differing degrees of success. In no instance is this better illustrated than in his handling of the landlords. Their support for his municipal socialization projects, beginning with the gasworks in 1896, was crucial.[108]

As mayor of Birmingham, Joseph Chamberlain had revealed the political possibilities of gas and water socialism in the 1870s and thus anticipated Lueger.[109] Mandl had agitated for municipalization of the gas works then as well, predicting, falsely as events turned out, that twenty-five percent of Vienna's income would be supplied by profits from this operation.[110] (Prior to 1914, scarcely ten percent of the city's revenue was provided by the gas, electrical, and tram systems combined.) But it fell to Lueger and Strohbach to carry out this project.[111] The elimination of private foreign ownership and diversion of gasworks revenues to the municipal treasury were aims the landlords and all taxpayers could approve during rising nationalism and hard times. But what delighted property owners was the increased value of their property once it was supplied with municipal gas, a service qualitatively superior to that of the English company.[112] Rather than buying them out, the Christian Socials decided to build a new gasworks to supply the needs of the first eleven districts, though this proved to be more expensive than purchasing the foreign plant.[113] But by 1896 even more important than the cost was the need to show results after years of agitation and electoral promises: "The pressure to succeed, which Lueger felt, was certainly great, since the municipal construction of the gasworks had become a matter of prestige for his party, just as the propaganda against the foreign capitalists had been an effective instrument in the struggle for power in the town hall."[114]

Despite Liberal predictions of failure, the gasworks was completed on time on October 31, 1899, without interruption in service, and ultimately fulfilled the hopes of its creators by increasing municipal revenues without drastically raising taxes.[115] Refused credit for this project by leading Austrian banks, the gasworks was eventually financed by the Deutsche Bank of Berlin, prompting Lueger's comment that "the dependence on Jewish capital had only changed its location."[116] The apparent success of the gasworks established a precedent for further similar municipal undertakings. Transportation and electrical services were municipalized, and the construction of a second mountain spring reservoir was undertaken.

It was imperative for the Christian Socials to prove their mettle as leaders of municipal affairs, but they were also obliged to continue their campaigning for the autumn Landtag elections and for the Reichsrat elections of March 1897. They thus expended their energies in several ways. Lueger was the stellar attraction, whether in the representative bodies in Vienna, the hamlets of Lower Austria or Bohemia, or even in Munich, where he accepted an invitation to speak about "farmers and tradesmen as the twin pillars of the state."[117] Although the tradesmen had been among the Christian Socials' most important constituents for years, the farmers were eventually to eclipse the former group in importance, particularly after World War I. However, even before the conflict, Lueger's party sensed future developments by devoting legislative efforts to supporting its agricultural constituents. Fueling some of these endeavors was the apprehension that economic weakness would strengthen the appeal of the Social Democrats;[118] yet, it is significant that during the late 1890s Lueger sometimes chose a *völkisch* approach to the farmers, calling them "the core of the German people," and "the roots of the German race."[119] He thereby again demonstrated his famous insight into crowd psychology at the most workaday level and foreshadowed a type of rhetoric that was to become increasingly popular during the interwar period.

The spring run of anti-Semitic victories continued throughout the autumn of 1896 and beyond. From early November the Christian Socials and Nationalists outnumbered Liberals in the diet by nearly two to one. Lueger's appeals to the rural electorate yielded tangible results, and the Liberal hold declined still further. The Christian Socials were no longer merely a municipal power, but could base their politics on Landtag support. Because of the extended franchise, some five million voters, instead of two million, went to the polls to elect a new parliament. In the spring parliamentary elections of 1897, the Christian Socials won thirty seats; the Social Democrats received fourteen. The Liberals and the German Nationalists were the heaviest losers. Lueger easily won reelection, defeating his Social Democratic rival Nemec by four thousand votes.[120] Although it had been taken for granted that Lueger would take over as mayor in January, he had agreed with Badeni to wait until after the parliamentary elections.[121] Lueger's great moment had arrived. Following Strohbach's resignation on March 31, 1897, Lueger was elected for the fifth time on April 8, receiving ninety-three out of 132 votes.[122] Strohbach and Neumayer were elected first and second vice-mayors. Grübl, who once again opposed Lueger, received but thirty-seven votes. With this election, the Liberals ceased to be a significant political force.

The day after the election, Kielmansegg drafted an official letter to Badeni.[123] Though the governor recommended confirmation, he again expressed reservations about Lueger's ability to function effectively as mayor and parliamentary representative, reservations which he repeated to Lueger. Lueger replied that only as a Reichsrat delegate and mayor could he effectively represent Vienna's interests, because "negotiations in the representative body very considerably affected the interests of . . . Vienna."[124] He added that were his election confirmed, Viennese matters would assume priority, in the Rathaus and in the Reichsrat; and here he was to prove as good as his word. In replying thus, he not only underscored his considerable ambition, but also suggested his full understanding of a political comprehensiveness that embraced local and national politics. This was something none of his predecessors had shown. He nonetheless acknowledged the centrality of the state by promising to support its administration "in his capacity as head of the Vienna Magistrat."[125] This last remark signaled his obeisance to the higher authorities of governor, prime minister, and emperor, but it remains an open question whether he believed it.

Kielmansegg cautioned him about continuing his agitation while trying to rule as mayor. Lueger said that if his election were sanctioned, he would appear less frequently at public meetings, and only then with due regard to his mayoral duties. To Lueger's way of thinking, such an assurance afforded him wide latitude. For several years after he became mayor, until his health gave out, he continued to appear at public meetings, assemblies, and rallies — contact with the electorate was a mainspring of his existence — to the delight of his followers, though to the doubtless irritation of Kielmansegg, who had a long memory about Lueger and his broken promises. On April 16, 1897, Franz Joseph sanctioned Lueger's fifth election as mayor, and he was sworn in four days later. The police kept close tabs on political activities in the city during this time, anticipating that clashes between the Christian Socials and Social Democrats would continue to be a feature of Viennese politics.

In his speech of acceptance, Lueger took his cue from Kielmansegg's opening remarks.[126] The governor had stressed the importance of improving the city's provisioning services and municipal transportation, of creating a new building code and constructing more churches, themes that Lueger developed. Early in his speech he emphasized the importance of the religious aspect of his oath, that his appeal for divine assistance was "no empty legal phrase," but a public acknowledgment of his faith. Such a declaration would doubtless have reassured his more religious followers; but it also showed his fervent determination to forge ahead with his projects. The "construction of new churches" received priority.

Second only in importance to construction was the obligation to preserve "the historical character of the city" through reasonable zoning. Lueger thereby served notice that he would uphold environmental considerations, to leave "room for light and air." He may also have wished to indicate to his landlord supporters that he would not undertake projects that would undermine their interests. As he had done for years in his speeches, Lueger attacked "the unauthorized . . . middle man who enriches himself at the expense of the producers and consumers, and who represents an apparently invincible power." This was a thinly veiled anti-Semitic remark, for some of Vienna's retailers were Jewish, and a boycott of Jewish stores had been carried out by Lueger's followers the preceding year.[127] One of his earliest and continuing agitational issues, the need to increase the water supply, received but passing notice, possibly because he felt that the theme was so well worn that it hardly bore repeating, but also because recent Liberal decisions had already made the building of a second reservoir a probability.[128]

Of particular importance in this speech were his references to municipal personnel: inadequate wages and inequitable promotion policies would come under scrutiny. He thereby reiterated earlier campaign pledges to improve the lot of the municipal civil servants, one of his most important constituencies. Realizing that any fundamental change in their material situation would depend on increased revenues, which were also needed to support the unemployed who had flocked to Vienna with the acceleration of industrialization,[129] Lueger hoped that "the municipal gasworks, once in operation, [would] provide . . . considerable revenues." But there were to be more sources of city income as well, from "municipalization of insurance and loan businesses." He thus indicated the comprehensiveness of the plan he hoped to introduce.

During his speech, Lueger touched on the inherent inadequacy of the city council.[130] Although he suggested that it be replaced by departments, Lueger was to change his tune once in office, and this body continued throughout his mayoralty, a bastion of Christian Social power. By citing the need to strengthen the Magistrat, as well as the need for increased centralization, Liberal priorities were here emphasized. Trade associations received his predictable endorsement as well. In view of the empirewide nationalism and Lueger's outspokenly pro-Habsburg orientation, no speech of this sort would have been complete without reference to Austro-German nationalism. Lueger equated social reform with the protection of the German working classes. He thus tapped one of the most potent wellsprings of emotion and played on socioeconomic anxieties as well. Lueger's acceptance speech ended with the obligatory acclamation for Franz Joseph.

Lueger's acceptance was a remarkably self-contained unit. It summarized many of his earlier efforts and indicated future priorities. Lueger's words "made a strong impression," according to Kuppe.[131] He describes the appearance of the Rathaus at the time:

> Thousands were drawn to the town hall in order to witness the festive activity. From all sides marched groups and associations with flags in ordered files. These were the delegations of Christian and craftsmen's associations. In long rows of coaches municipal dignitaries rode to the town hall with their wives, the high and highest officials of the state, provincial diet and parliamentary delegates, representations from all parts of the empire, from foreign countries as well, emissaries of the clergy, and of all professions.
>
> In the broad festive hall of the town hall, richly decorated with flowers and greenery and by a forest of flags, standards and pennants, the most festive mood reigned, despite the pressing throng. The sounds of the fanfare announced the arrival of the Governor Count Kielmansegg. He was followed by Dr. Lueger with the vice-mayors.[132]

The only thing missing from this description is an indication of the mood of the city beyond the immediate environs of the Rathaus. A band of some forty of Lueger's followers chanting *Der Dr. Lueger soll regieren und die Juden sollen crepiren*[133] had to be dispersed by the police in one district. In another, a group of Lueger's female supporters, "Lueger Amazons," clashed with a rival Social Democratic women's auxiliary.[134] However, the most striking contrast to the festivity in the town hall was afforded by the darkness of the inner city and the workers' districts. In the former Liberal stronghold and the proletarian quarters, few shared the elation of Lueger's followers. Many feared the implementation of a radical politics.

Lueger was born in a service flat in one of the buildings to
the right of the Karlskirche. (Author's Collection.)

Lueger as a young lawyer. (Courtesy of the Historical
Museum of the City of Vienna.)

Lueger's most famous university teacher Lorenz von Stein, whose administrative theories and flair for the flamboyant may well have influenced Lueger. (Courtesy of the Austrian National Library Photograph Collection.)

The Ringtheater fire of December 8, 1881 in which nearly 400 perished. The aftermath provided a cause célèbre during which Lueger achieved a certain prominence. (Courtesy of the Austrian National Library Photograph Collection.)

Lueger as swell. "The pragmatic politician crystalized into a style as elegant and brittle as the jewelry and gems he came to wear in his later years" (Richard Geehr, "I Decide Who Is a Jew!" The Papers of Dr. Karl Lueger, 7). (Courtesy of the Historical Museum of the City of Vienna.)

As his years in power passed, Lueger was obliged to spend more and more time at recreation, because of declining health. (Courtesy of the Historical Museum of the City of Vienna.)

Salon rustics. Lueger is second from the left. As the Romantic Age waned and cities burgeoned, rural backdrops became popular with professional photographers. Lueger looked back with nostalgia to "simpler" and "happier" ages, as this scene suggests. He claimed that "there never were such sad conditions as there are now in the time of the Enlightenment." Shortly before his death he supported the construction of a Viennese hall of fame in Greco-Roman style with Christian and Germanic adornments. Archbishop Simon Aichner admonished Lueger to cease his support for a "heathen cultural place" as a cornerstone for Christianity, which "hinders the good success of the Catholic missions in Central Africa and elsewhere." In his Germanic and medieval preferences, as well as in his taste for blending paganism with Greco-Roman style, Lueger anticipated major themes of Nazi culture. (Courtesy of the Historical Museum of the City of Vienna.)

Lueger and his vice-mayors, following the death of First
Vice-Mayor Josef Strohbach. Left to right, First Vice-Mayor
Josef Neumayer, Lueger, Third Vice-Mayor Heinrich
Hierhammer, Second Vice-Mayor Josef Porzer. (Author's
Collection.)

An unofficial photograph of Lueger during his mayoralty.
(Courtesy of the Handwritten Documents Collection of the
Vienna Municipal Library.)

The master builder and the seeds of the future. Lueger at the cornerstone laying ceremony of the second mountain spring reservoir. (Courtesy of the Handwritten Documents Collection of the Vienna Municipal Library.)

Lueger and municipal garden director Hybler. Lueger is said to have instructed Hybler to plant vines to conceal Jugendstil ornaments he disliked. (Author's Collection.)

*Lueger took credit for the Marienbrücke. When visiting
German Emperor William II asked "how such an atrocity could
(have been) constructed, Lueger is reported to have responded
with "a very impolite answer." (Author's Collection.)*

The Prissnitz Monument in the Türkenschanzpark, Vienna, eighteenth district. After a municipal councillor repeatedly objected to proposals for this monument, on the grounds that nudity would offend public morals, Lueger replied that he would write to the pope and ask him to close the Vatican art collection, because it contained too many nudes. (Courtesy of the Austrian National Library Photograph Collection.)

Lueger was sworn in as mayor for the last time following
his seventh election in April 1909. During his last years
municipal officials, clad in special Lueger "court uniforms,"
appeared at all ceremonies, anticipating a similar practice at
Hitler's "court." (Courtesy of the Austrian National Library
Photograph Collection.)

Lueger delivers a nationalistic speech before the Schiller
monument on May 7, 1905 praising Schiller as a German
poet. Photographs of Lueger orating are relatively uncommon. (Courtesy of the Austrian National Library Photograph
Collection.)

Lueger as orator. "And in parliament he wielded his speech like a flag, then like a whip and then like a hammer" (Felix Salten). (Author's Collection.)

During his struggle for power, Hitler always carried a Lueger medal in his wallet.

Franz Opelt, leader of the Christian Social Knabenhorte.
This militaristic organization won the admiration of the
young Hitler who said it was "good for youth to be politically trained" in this fashion. (Courtesy of the Austrian
National War Archive.)

A Socialist comment on Lueger as honorary member of the
first Knabenhorte. The praying figure behind him satirizes a
portion of the high altar triptych of the Lainz home for the
aged in the thirteenth district. In the original triptych,
Lueger and his parents pray to Mary and the infant Christ.
(Courtesy of the Austrian National Library.)

*Archduke Rainer reviews a detachment of the Knabenhorte
in his palace park auf der Wieden. (Photos courtesy of the
Austrian National Library Photograph Collection.)*

Lueger and the Christian Social elite at a mass children's demonstration at Schönbrunn Palace honoring Emperor Franz Joseph's sixtieth jubilee on May 21, 1908. Lueger's sight was severely impaired and he wore sunglasses to protect his eyes. Franz Opelt, the leader of the Knabenhorte, is seated on the reviewing stand, second from right. (Author's Collection.)

At this demonstration the children were arranged so as to complement the pattern of Schönbrunn's formal gardens. The ornamental use of masses anticipated the Nuremberg rallies of the 1930s. (Author's Collection.)

The Christian Social childrens' periodical Wiener Kinder —
paid for by public tax revenues, distributed to Vienna's
public schools, and printed by Third Vice-Mayor Heinrich
Hierhammer — reflected the tastes of its sponsors. Wiener
Kinder featured allegories on Christian Socialism and Socialism, "Die Zwillingsschwestern," glorifications of technology
and particularly the achievements of Lueger in this area, ro-
manticized historical tales, and anti-Semitism. See also the
following three illustrations. (Photos courtesy of the Vienna
Municipal Library.)

Die Zwillingsschwestern.

Ein Märchen von Karoline Faller-Schmid.

Mit zwei Originalzeichnungen von Richard Reinmer.

Einer guten, frommen Mutter brachte einst der Storch statt eines gleich zwei kleine herzige Kinderchen, zwei Mädchen. Diese sahen einander so ähnlich, daß niemand sie unterscheiden konnte, selbst die eigene Mutter

Der Jude im Dorn.

Brüder Grimm.
Originalzeichnungen von H. Chytra und K. Jobit.

s war einmal ein reicher Mann, der hatte einen Knecht; der diente ihm fleißig und redlich, und wenn's eine saure Arbeit gab, so stellte er sich immer zuerst daran. Als sein Jahr herum war, gab ihm der Herr keinen Lohn und dachte: „Das ist das Gescheitste, so geht er mir nicht weg." Der Knecht schwieg, tat das zweite Jahr seine Arbeit und als er abermals keinen Lohn bekam, ließ er sich's gefallen und blieb noch länger. Als auch das dritte Jahr herum war, bedachte sich der Herr, griff in die Tasche, holte aber nichts heraus. Da fing der Knecht endlich an und sprach: „Herr, seid so gut und gebt mir, was mir von Rechts wegen zukommt; ich wollte mich gerne weiter in der Welt umsehen." Da antwortete der Geizhals: „Ja, mein lieber Knecht, du sollst mildiglich belohnet werden." Er griff in die Tasche und zählte dem Knecht drei Heller einzeln auf: „Da hast du für jedes Jahr einen Heller, das ist ein großer und reichlicher Lohn." Der gute Knecht, der vom Geld wenig verstand, strich sein Kapital ein und dachte: „Nun hast du vollauf in der Tasche, was willst du sorgen."

Da zog er fort, sang und sprang nach Herzenslust. Nun trug es sich zu, als er an einem Buschwerk vorüber kam, daß ein kleines Männchen hervortrat und ihn anrief: „Wo hinaus, Bruder Lustig? ich sehe, du trägst nicht schwer an deinen Sorgen." — „Was soll ich traurig sein," antwortete der Knecht, „der Lohn von drei Jahren klingelt in meiner Tasche." — „Wieviel ist denn deines Schatzes?" fragte ihn das Männchen. „Wieviel? drei bare Heller, richtig gezählt." — „Höre," sagte der Zwerg, „ich bin ein armer Mann, schenke mir deine drei Heller, denn ich kann nichts mehr arbeiten." Und weil

Atem: „Ich schenke dir dein Leben, höre nur auf zu geigen." Der gute
Knecht ließ sich bewegen, setzte die Geige ab, hing sie wieder um den
Hals und stieg die Leiter herab. Da trat er zu dem Juden, der auf der
Erde lag und nach Atem schnappte, und sagte: „Spitzbube, jetzt gesteh',

wo du das Geld her hast oder ich nehme meine Geige vom Hals und
fange wieder an zu spielen." — „Ich hab's gestohlen, ich hab's gestohlen,"
schrie er, „du aber hast's redlich verdient." Da ließ der Richter den
Juden zum Galgen führen und als einen Dieb aufhängen.

Unlike Emperor Franz Joseph, Lueger liked to ride in autos. During his last years Catholic sisters became part of his entourage. (Courtesy of the Handwritten Documents Collection of the Vienna Municipal Library.)

Under Lueger, municipal funds were used to pay for the
publication of a cheap edition of the writings of Abraham a
Sancta Clara. This Augustinian monk and popular orator
spread anti-Semitism in Lower Austria almost exactly two
centuries before Lueger. Abraham's saying "Trust no fox on
a green heath, and no Jew on his oath," became the title of
an anti-Semitic book for "large and small" during the Hitler
period. This advertisement is from Julius Streicher's Der
Stürmer. (Author's Collection.)

The actress Valerie Gréy, Lueger's rhetoric teacher and confidante. (Courtesy of the Austrian National Library Photograph Collection.)

The portrait artist Marianne Beskiba. (Courtesy of the Historical Museum of the City of Vienna.)

Fortsetzung v. Karte № 2

999.000

HÔTEL · KÖLNER · HOF · NEU · JERUSALEM · AM FRÄNK. JORDAN.

Und das Volk sang Liobesweisen,
Priesen Gott mit Herz u. Hand,
Thaten wie der Herr geheissen,
Zogen ab vom Jordanstrand.
Was der Herr am Wüstensande
Einst versprach, hielt er auch ein:
Schon regiert im deutschen Lande
Neu-Jerusalem am Main

Heil!
Von Neumayer

Beskiba received this postcard from Vice-Mayor Josef
Neumayer. (Courtesy of the Handwritten Documents Collection of the Vienna Municipal Library.)

One of Lueger's correspondents was the popular actress
Hansi Niese, here with Alexander Girardi. Like Hitler,
Lueger was fond of artists. (Author's Collection.)

This waltz was dedicated to "Lueger's Amazons," headed by Emilie Platter. The white carnation was the Christian Social Party flower. (Courtesy of the Music Collection of the Vienna Municipal Library.)

The leaders of the "Lueger Amazons." Revelations of financial malfeasance precipitated the fall of Emilie Platter. (Author's Collection.)

Battle hymn of the "Lueger Amazons." The opening anticipates the Nazi anthem, the "Horst Wessel Lied." (Author's Collection.)

Treuschwur der Christlichsocialen.
Von Dr. Rudolf Hornich.
(Componirt von A. Schwalb.)

Die Fahnen hoch, worauf des Kreuzes Zeichen,
U b dicht zum Schwure schließet uns're Reih'n!
Nicht wollen wir im heil'gen Kampfe weichen,
Wie viele auch der Feinde um uns sei'n!

Dem Vaterlande treu und treu dem Glauben,
Der Väter Sitte und der Väter Recht,
Laßt Bubenspott und Judenhohn nicht rauben,
Was lang gehütet unser alt' Geschlecht!

Es blickt auf uns der Ahnen ernste Reihe;
Was sie vererbt, laßt schirmen uns mit Muth!
Auch uns're Kinder fordern von uns Treue,
Ihr köstlich Erbtheil ruht in uns'rer Hut.

Die Kunst in Gunst, dem Stande seine Würde,
Der Weisheit Ehr', der Arbeit ihren Lohn!
Dem müden Bruder helft bei seiner Bürde,
So wie's gelehret uns der Gottessohn!

Getrost mein Volk, es gilt die höchsten Güter,
Nicht unterliegt die Wahrheit und das Recht!
Wenn alles dich verläßt, lebt dort ihr Hüter,
Zu ihm blick' auf, erlahmst du im Gefecht!

Lueger hoch! Ihm gleicht an Thatkraft Keiner,
Er hält getreue Wacht am Donaustrand.
Von seiner Seite weichen darf nicht Einer,
Uns all' umschlingt ein einzig Bruderband.

Die Fahnen hoch, worauf des Kreuzes Zeichen,
Und dicht zum Schwure schließet uns're Reih'n!
Nicht wollen wir im heil'gen Kampfe weichen,
Sieg oder Tod — der Herr wird Sieg verleih'n!

*Lueger's female supporters caricatured. Lueger as a pilgrim
to Rome. (Courtesy of the Vienna Municipal Library.)*

Der grosse Chinese in der Klimt-Ausstellung.

Chinese: Bei Confuzius und Czin-Czin kann 's ich beschwören,
mir gefallen die Bilder von Klimt.

Many Christian Socials, including Lueger, mistrusted or disliked modern art, symbolized by the works of Gustav Klimt caricatured at bottom left. These two paintings, above and below, Ziegenhirten by Franz Rumpler and Nobelfiaker by Felician Freiherr von Myrbach-Rheinfeld, were more to their taste. (Courtesy of the Vienna Municipal Library.)

Journalist and politician Ernst Vergani. (Author's Collection.)

"Lueger's Streicher," the racist anti-Semite Ernst Schneider.
(Courtesy of the Austrian National Library Photograph
Collection.)

Christian Social politician Hermann Bielohlawek. His proverbial Philistinism was ridiculed by friends and foes alike. Lueger seems to have regarded him as his court jester. (Courtesy of the Austrian National Library Photograph Collection.)

Tolstoi und der kluge Hermann.

Lueger's opponent, the Rabbi Joseph Samuel Bloch. (Author's Collection.)

During a parliamentary session Bielohlawek once referred to Leo Tolstoy as an "old dope." In this Socialist comment, Gessmann is the schoolmaster. This caricature may have been inspired by Wilhelm Busch. (Courtesy of the Austrian National Library.)

~ **Mittel zum Zweck.** ~

(Die zu Studienzwecken gehaltenen Gänfe
auf den Wiener Kliniken werden verschiedenfarbig
angeftrichen, um fie von einnander unterfcheiden
zu fönnen.)

The antivivisection controversy in the provincial diet.
Lueger tells delegate Leopold Steiner that he is painting the
barriers so that he can better differentiate. Laboratory geese
were similarly painted. (Courtesy of the Austrian National
Library.)

Der Dummerer erscheint in der Klinik geschwind
„Sö hörn S' Herr Rektor, oder was Sie sonst sind,
Der Herr Steiner tut Ihnen durch mich dekretieren,
Sie dürfen die Viecher net vivisezieren."

The antivivisection controversy reached campaign proportions. In the following cartoons: 1. Lueger's servant bodyguard Pumera presents doctors of the University of Vienna medical school with Steiner's decree to cease vivisection. 2. The academic senate convenes and decides that theirs are sad times. 3. Even the animals are consulted. Only the ass wants to visit the provincial diet. The rest ask to remain in the clinic. 4. Rector Escherich writes the Christian Socials that "only the ass is against vivisection." But to still their thirst for knowledge, he sends the plague infected "blue" goose. 5. "Enjoy the roast! I hope the ass won't be ashamed to take its place among you." 6. The Christian Socialists ask Lueger for help. Schneider adds his voice to the hue and cry: "I'll no longer tolerate Jewish doctors carving up animals!" 7. Lueger replies: "We have our fire department." So the trucks drive to the university and turn their hoses on the academics. (Lueger had actually thus employed the fire department against the workers of privately owned electric companies earlier that year.) 8. Liberators and liberated celebrate in the rector's hall. At last science is free of animal torturers. The animals rejoice, too: "The devil with all these bacillus theories! There's only one diet, there's only one Vienna!" (Courtesy of the Austrian National Library.)

Es tritt zusammen der akademische Senat,
Hält über die Sache gar hochweisen Rat,
Der Rektor sagt: „Die Zeiten sind trüb,
Die Alma mater dolorosa ist!"

Man bringt auch die Tiere zum Versammlungsort
Und fragt sie: „Wollt Ihr auch wirklich fort!"
Doch nur der Esel, der schreit: „J—a",
Die andern bitten: „Laßt uns da."

Rektor Eiserich schreibt dann voll Hohn:
„Nur der Esel ist gegen die Vivisektion.
Doch nehmt, Euern Wissenshunger zu stillen,
Die ‚blaue' Gans voll Pestbazillen!"

Verspeiset den Braten mit Appetit. —
Auch send ich Euch gleich den Esel mit;
Er wird sich hoffentlich nicht schämen,
In Eurer Mitte Platz zu nehmen!"

„Hilf uns, Lueger, befreien die Viecher,
Nicht fühlen wir uns unseres Lebens mehr sicher;"
Der Schneider schreit noch: Ich werd's net mehr leiden,
Daß jüdische Ärzte die Tiere beschneiden!"

Der Lueger sagt: „Ich bitte sehr,
Wir hab'n ja unsre Feuerwehr."
Es fahren die Wagen auch gleich aus
Und spritzen die Gelehrten hinaus.

Aeskulap   Hygea

D'rauf feiern gleich im Aerztespital   Die Viecher tun ich, wie immer vorbei,
Befreier und Befreite ein Siegesmahl.   Sie grunzen, sie bellen, sie brüllen im Chor:
Jetzt endlich ist die Wissenschaft frei   Zum Teufel mit allen Bazill'n-Theorien,
Von der ganz miserablen Kurpfuscherei.   's gibt nur an Landtag, 's gibt nur a Wien.

A Liberal comment on Lueger's municipal improvement projects. (Courtesy of the Historical Museum of the City of Vienna.)

Lueger "regulates" the electoral bodies. (Courtesy of the Historical Museum of the City of Vienna.)

Die Braven kommen in den Himmel — die Schlimmen in die Hölle.

The apotheosis of Lueger, the damnation of the Socialists.
(Courtesy of the Vienna Municipal Library.)

During his last years in power it was said that no cabinet could be formed without Lueger's approval. (Courtesy of the Vienna Municipal Library.)

"Wil'lem and Lueger shape the century on the chopping block." This prophetic cartoon from 1902 suggests the brutality of the new era and the growing Austro-German ideological affinity. (Courtesy of the Vienna Municipal Library.)

Willem und Lueger

4

The Master Builder: 1897–1910

Das Prinzip der Christlich Sozialen ist nicht: Jedem das Gleiche, sondern
jedem das Seine. . . .
— Hermann Bielohlawek in the
Lower Austrian Diet, January 2, 1907

*T*he inaugural festivities ended, the new mayor set about his tasks as
Vienna's first citizen. Lueger has been consistently honored for his achievements in city improvement, administration, and municipal socialization.
For nearly a century now, biographers from Leopold Tomola to Johannes
Hawlik, who devotes his longest chapter, or nearly twenty-five percent
of his actual text, to Lueger's works as mayor, have stressed the Christian
Social leader's building projects as the true and enduring measure of his
success. Yet few have tried to explore in depth the meaning of his municipal accomplishments beyond their immediate utility,[1] and even fewer if
any have inquired more deeply into the spirit that informed his undertakings. However, his achievements are more significant for their direction
than their usefulness, as this chapter is intended to demonstrate. This
chapter also touches on a Lueger attempt — more symbolic than real in its

effect — to perpetuate his name beyond the confines of Austria. This some-what belated, amateurish, and unsuccessful diplomatic gambit suggests the negative effect he might have had on imperial foreign policy had he become Archduke Franz Ferdinand's prime minister, as the archduke intended, once he had succeeded Franz Joseph as emperor.

The longer Lueger remained in office the more holding power and exercising it became ends in themselves. His building projects expressed this as well as their serving the more obvious practical functions. Such undertakings as the second spring mountain reservoir, which had long interested Lueger, and the expanded central cemetery continued Liberal construction tradition, but have been largely ignored as such by Lueger's biographers. Yet there *was* something new about Lueger's building projects. Unlike his predecessors, Lueger made sure that he would be remembered as their sole author, and thus immortalized. (The Lueger Memorial Church in the Central Cemetery, which can be seen from far and near, is another example.) They thus became a more personalized political expression than the constructs of his predecessors. The new century on which Lueger left his imprint would see many similar endeavors, some of them on a national level in states unborn in Lueger's time.

According to the Lueger biographical tradition, the mayor's municipal achievements were a "breakthrough to Christian Social reform," motivated by his selfless love for his native city.[2] Somewhat ironically, even Lueger's erstwhile opponents, the Socialists, have helped perpetuate this interpretation. In 1926 an imposing bronze statue of the Christian Social leader was erected in Vienna's first district in a square honoring his name. At that time Lueger's former opponent, the Social Democrat mayor, Karl Seitz, honored the Christian Social leader as a pioneer in municipal socialization.[3] Such has been his consistent image.

A description and analysis of some of Lueger's more openly, ideologically oriented endeavors will form a portion of chapter seven. However, mention should here be made of some of his important public works as such, to establish a basis for the long-range evaluation of his effect in this one area of endeavor, and to examine the extent to which they continued or departed from earlier Liberal efforts.[4] A description of Lueger the "builder" is intended to prepare in part for an assessment of the man and his influence more comprehensively than his biographers have until now presented.

Karl Renner, an important figure in early Austrian socialism, called attention in his memoirs to the lack of intellectual and ideological content in Lueger's speeches.[5] Elsewhere, he asserted that Christian Social economics, and by implication Lueger's own concepts in this area, were so primitive that elementary instruction was required. This Renner tried to provide, pedantically, during a provincial diet session shortly before Lueger's death.[6] Renner's innovation might have been useful at an earlier date, for, to be sure, Lueger did not develop or try to implement original systematic economic or political theories. Yet, his posthumous reputation as a far-sighted political and economic practitioner, whose municipal socialization and construction projects are the tangible evidence of his theories, has been proclaimed by his biographers, who have seen brilliant foresight instead of the common sense, instinct for political survival, energy, and experience that were probably at work. Lueger not only learned from the example of larger municipal projects begun by Liberal predecessors, but also profited from prior Liberal decisions to proceed with the modernization and improvement of the city. Moreover, he was well aware of the trans-European trend toward municipal socialization. It will be remembered that greater Vienna, the most important arena of Lueger's activities, was created during the Liberal era. A general European upswing after nearly a quarter century's depression also contributed to the success of Lueger's undertakings. As an initiator and continuer of public works, Lueger was probably less a "true genius as a municipal politician," less "the man between the times"[7] than a man at the right time, and one who was very much aware of Roman and Viennese traditions in this area. Despite their history of achievements, as builders and innovators, the Liberals had run out of steam. This was now to be provided by the Christian Socials, whose dynamic spokesman, Lueger, articulated the ambitions and implemented the desires of interest groups that had come to political consciousness, but that had been neglected or ignored by the Liberals. The tradition was there—at least in part—for Lueger to pick up and carry on without any inventiveness.

Yet in theory Lueger was at a disadvantage before the more industrially alert Socialists, who predictably, if not mechanically, explained Vienna's and Austria's woes as a result of the economic contradictions inherent in capitalism. During Lueger's early years as mayor, such jeremiads had little effect on his popularity or on the achievement of his goals. Though his politics were sometimes inconsistent, and often betrayed transparent opportunism, he usually succeeded in courting first one group or faction, then another, to win a point, consolidate a gain, or achieve an immediate advantage. Where these tactics failed, the tendency of others to abase themselves before the power he symbolized or actually commanded, even where no threat to use it existed, usually carried the day for him.[8] He was, after all, the mayor of the royal and imperial residential city, a fact he increasingly emphasized during his later years. The dignity of this posi-

tion, and his forensic ability to impress the wavering, on which he probably calculated, were enough to awe all but the most fearless or recalcitrant.

Nonetheless, long years of experience had imparted to him a sound
practical, if not theoretical, grasp of the more material problems that confronted Vienna as a modernizing metropolis. As an avid reader of the
popular press and probably also of some of the more specialized journals,
Lueger was no stranger to prevailing socioeconomic theories, or at least
to notions about their practical implementation. With the passing years
he seems to have perceived the need to integrate Vienna more carefully
as a corporate entity, socially, economically, and culturally, as well as
politically. In this way he parted company with his Liberal predecessors,
many of whom were successful entrepreneurs, and who had been content
to run the city as a business operation, but without much regard for the
long-term effects of their politics. At points in his career Lueger grasped
the political importance of urban environments in achieving community.
His insight was probably gained through his experience as a municipal
councillor, as well as through his theoretical university training to be an
administrator and jurist, which doubtlessly acquainted him with the social
implications of administrative policies. But he also believed that the
municipality should stimulate business. After six years in office, he announced to the municipal council: "If anyone promotes industry, it is the
municipality of Vienna. . . . The building of the gas and electric works
and other great undertakings prove that it is solely the community which
in an energetic way, and not just in mere words, endeavors to promote
industry by diverting millions to it."[9]

Because of his posthumous reputation as a great leader with the common touch, it is ironic that Lueger was less successful toward the end of
his mayoralty in handling some of the more unruly municipal personnel
and in checking the growth of rivalries within his party. Lueger's declining
health probably played a role here. Yet, the rivalries served his immediate
personal ends, for his own hand was strengthened as an arbiter. But the
long-term effects of rule by personal style rather than system were dis-
astrous for the party. Lueger's death in 1910 left a vacuum at the center
of power that was never adequately filled. Probably this was as he had
wanted it; there were to be no rivals to his fame.

As a Christian Social, Lueger was narrowly protectionist in his economic outlook. His policies were aimed at fostering the prosperity of German Austrians, to him the fundamental imperial nationality. A secondary
goal was to promote the success of the Slovenes and Bohemians who settled in German Austria, and especially in Vienna. They were the backbone
of the metropolitan work force. The main thing, he said, was that they

spent their money there. Municipal building projects would provide the wherewithal, Vienna would be economically rejuvenated, and he believed that the benefits would flow to the rest of the empire.

He rejected some entire nationalities as useless in promoting Vienna's prosperity. In one Landtag session he criticized the importation of Italians, because they were hardworking, but too thrifty. Viennese workers should be hired before others, even if their labor was more expensive, because they at least would spend and in so doing help revive trade and commerce.[10] But the Italian worker

> eats nothing, drinks nothing, he doesn't need anything, he lives only on polenta and when he does spend a little money, he spends it on the lottery, that is his only passion [amusement]. . . . The Italian worker doesn't need clothing, or shoes either, and I believe an Italian worker wears the shoes and clothing he is born with for the rest of his life [lively amusement], at least until now I haven't seen him change [renewed amusement].[11]

Public works that took a long time to complete were no misfortune, Lueger added, and it therefore followed that interim unemployment was to be avoided. To its credit, St. Stephen's Cathedral had taken "more than a century" to complete. A whole school of stonemasons developed as a result, which contributed to the "honor and fame of the fatherland."[12] During the same diet session Lueger advocated direct negotiations between consumer and producer, whether they were the state or municipality and the tradesman, or worker and tradesman. Intermediaries and subcontractors were a deeply rooted evil and should be eliminated. Later during his mayoralty, the Socialists tried to embarrass him by pointing out that he had resorted to intermediaries, created holding companies and the like, to achieve some of his goals. But Lueger was not to be embarrassed: the achievement was the thing, the means counted for less, or sometimes for nothing at all.

Complaints about rising food costs mounted during Lueger's mayoralty. To help combat this problem, private and socialist consumer cooperatives were founded, thus continuing a movement that had begun in 1864 during the Liberal era. The multiplication of such cooperatives, however, was an implicit criticism of Lueger's failure to cut food costs, something he and other Christian Social leaders had indicated they would do by eliminating middlemen. A city brewery and slaughterhouse were created during the Lueger era, but they antagonized some of his supporters, the *Greissler*, or grocers, in the process.[13] Meat cutters grumbled about a municipal slaughterhouse from 1905 on. One of Lueger's formerly staunch supporters, a municipal councillor and evidently prosperous butcher, Georg

Hütter, introduced many interpellations and proposals criticizing the city slaughterhouse. Lueger treated Hütter like a spoiled and privileged underling whose objections were unworthy of serious consideration, one of his favorite tactics. He mocked the suggestion that Hütter was badly off: "Just look how poor . . . Hütter is starving [lively amusement] just see how he looks. The poor man has only three riding horses, only three, and the others have none. . . . It's simply terrible how the man is starving and robbed of everything. [Amusement] I want to help him through the municipal slaughterhouse, but . . . he can't even take that. . . ."[14] But despite the mayor's witticisms, general objections to rising prices, and the objections of his party members to consumer cooperatives, the municipal slaughterhouse and brewery continued. Lueger was unsuccessful in halting the price spiral or in checking the growth of cooperatives. From a low point of 239 in 1890, they climbed to 1,469 in 1913, having nearly doubled since 1900.[15] No significant economic improvement of Vienna's lower and middle classes took place during Lueger's regime. In 1910 nearly eighty-three percent of Vienna's working population earned less than twelve hundred Kronen, and was therefore exempt from paying income taxes.[16] Although the existence of the Viennese laborer had improved over the past two generations, his life was still a struggle for existence. The financial foundation of Vienna's working population, two-thirds of which consisted of workers, day laborers, and domestic servants, remained extremely weak while that of most of the tax-paying middle class was little stronger.[17] Before becoming mayor, Lueger's radical-sounding economic politics had been enthusiastically applauded by those dissatisfied with their material lot, who probably found his diatribes against "intermediaries" plausible, especially against shadowy Jewish figures and similarly mysterious or otherwise dimly understood forces. These could easily be blamed for economic woes and many surely believed that Lueger would change all of this. After more than a decade of Christian Socialism it is doubtful that the same malcontents would have applauded Lueger's speeches of the mid-1890s. Yet it seemed as though no one could replace Lueger as mayor, so effective were the party publicists on his behalf, and so skillful was he at keeping possible rivals for his mantle divided and at odds. Lueger became a fixture in Viennese life thanks to his tireless politicking and ubiquitous presence at public functions and honorary ceremonies. The Christian Socials maintained their power by restricting the franchise, corrupt machine politics, and Lueger's dynamic personality. So firm was their grip on Vienna after 1895 that it became impossible to dislodge them until after World War I and the introduction of more equitable voting laws. With the parliamentary elections of 1907, however, Socialist gains confronted the Christian

Socials with a serious challenge. By then Lueger's health was rapidly declining. The days of his unchallenged power and that of his party in the national arena were numbered.

The municipal gasworks project had been started in October 1896. A year later in parliament Lueger made his remarks about this project a focus of anti-Semitism. Answering critics that a Jewish company was among those supplying pipes for the new gas company, he said that it was "sad . . . that things [had] gone so far that we can't finish our labors without the Jews." But he then added with a demagogic flourish: "We are not to blame, we fight for the liberation of the people from the power . . . of the big Jews, and, gentlemen, you will see that the first battle that we in Vienna have to fight is against the English Gas Company, and that we must win."[18]

If the construction of the gasworks was the opening barrage in Lueger's action against "Jewish financial interests" and "foreign influences" in Austrian life, additional salvoes in the municipalization engagement were the building of the electric works and the city takeover of the transportation system. The three private companies that provided the city with electricity were bought out, though not without a lengthy and occasionally acrimonious competition for customers between the city and the private owners.[19] Technological problems were fewer, because equipment did not have to be replaced, as with the aging gas lines and inadequate lighting fixtures.

Vienna had received its first gasworks in 1828;[20] the English Imperial Continental Gas Association had supplied gas from 1843,[21] and some of the original equipment was still in use when the Christian Socials came to power. But the first electric plant went into operation in 1889, making modernization unnecessary.[22] As with the gasworks, the electric plants were supposed to operate at a profit, and therefore to furnish additional revenues to the municipality.[23] Only secondarily and romantically was the city's illumination meant to bathe "the most beautiful and busiest squares and streets, above all the Ringstrasse . . . in the brilliance of numerous arc lamps, an enchanting vista."[24] Lueger's lack of romanticism, his ruthlessness in eliminating the private electric companies, was revealed in 1903 when he ordered municipal firemen to turn their hoses on workers from private companies who were engaged in unauthorized excavations.[25] By 1908 the private companies had been liquidated, though the complete municipalization of the electric works was not achieved until August 1, 1914.[26] Vienna's upper classes profited most from the electrification. In 1913 the most desirable districts possessed the most electric lights per residence. The most poorly illuminated dwellings were in areas whose laborer residents doubtless could not afford the rates.[27]

Hand in glove with the electrification of houses and office buildings went the electrification of the trams. Here, Vienna had been overtaken by Budapest, which had begun an electric tram system in 1889. Lueger was determined that the imperial capital would remain second to none in transportation, and especially not to Budapest, the actual and symbolic capital of his most implacable enemy. There was a need for public transportation improvement in Vienna. Horse-drawn trams, operated by the Vienna Tramway Company, were inadequate in every respect, overcrowded, inefficiently run, incapable of meeting the demands of a modern metropolis. But the city's omnibuses, also horse-drawn, were even worse. "'These forlorn old vehicles, lumbering, dirty, musty, unspeakable, seem to be the dubious offspring of an alliance between a rural diligence and a decayed berlin [sic].'"[28]

Lueger's interest in the tramway problem,[29] and particularly in the tramway employees as an important source of political support, because of their necessity to the operation of the city, went back to his days as a municipal councillor. He had championed their interest, and they responded by voting for the Christian Socials.[30] On at least one occasion, Lueger had assigned an even higher priority to tramway personnel problems than to ideological considerations. Even after he had become an outspoken anti-Semite, he defended a Jewish tramway employee—an early instance of Lueger's use of the "honorary Aryan"—who had been fired by the Vienna Tramway Company for publicly urging the firm to contribute to the employee pension fund.[31] When, two months after he took office, the tramway employees went on strike, Lueger supported them.

After much public debate, the Vienna Tramway Company was liquidated and replaced by a new privately owned operation organized by the Berlin firm of Siemens und Halske. Yet, when the personnel contracts were drawn up, tramway workers were denied important benefits and guarantees. Siemens was not obligated to employ former Vienna Tramway personnel. Nor were concrete provisions made for minimum wages, length of workday, or the amount of retirement benefits.[32] Such deficiencies were later partly corrected, but the price was increased fares and paternalistic policies on Lueger's part toward tram employees, who were expected to regard him as the proprietor of the municipal establishment that they were to serve loyally, efficiently, and without hesitation.[33]

Lueger's opponents pointed out that the Christian Socials were reneging on campaign promises to "socialize" municipal services by allowing Siemens und Halske, a private company, to run the city's transportation system. This was a valid criticism, for in effect Lueger was merely exchanging one privately run operation for another. One possible reason for this was political: in 1898, when tram negotiations were being worked out, the building of the gasworks was still in progress and not scheduled for completion for another twelve months. To have undertaken a second "municipal socialization" project simultaneously, rather than leaving the modernization and running of the trams to Siemens und Halske, would have doubled the risk of public dissatisfaction had plans gone awry, for both services were widely used.[34] The Christian Socials were still relatively new in office and could ill afford major defeats.

Another possible reason for delaying socialization of the trams was the practical consideration of returning a portion of the anticipated profit from the tramway operation to its German creditors the Deutsche Bank. Lueger had declared that the city had no intention of purchasing Vienna Tramway Company shares. The result was a sharp decline in stock prices. At that moment the Deutsche Bank, acting as Lueger's deputy, had bought the shares, thus eliminating the control of a private Viennese bank, the Reitzes Gesellschaft, over the Vienna Tramway Company. The city's credit rating rose with the purchase of the shares, and Lueger obtained further financial support. He boasted of this in a municipal council meeting as an "Aryan" triumph, for the Reitzes Gesellschaft was owned by Jews.[35] This was pure demagogy.

Lueger's partnership with the Deutsche Bank had begun in 1896. The Christian Socials had been refused credit for the building of the gasworks then by both foreign and domestic banks, doubtless because Vienna was heavily indebted and had a low credit rating. (For years Lueger had sharply criticized the Liberals for their spending, but he incurred greater indebtedness by initiating the gasworks even before he became mayor.) These factors, rather than a "Jewish plot" to defeat Lueger's efforts at reform, as his partisans claimed, were almost certainly to blame for the refusals.[36] Georg Siemens, director of the Deutsche Bank and Siemens und Halske, no doubt perceived the profitability of loaning money to Vienna with one hand and supplying it with equipment for the future electric works with the other.[37] Strohbach was an experienced businessman and handled the stock purchase negotiations. Lacking experience in this sort of financial dealing, Lueger had reason to be cautious and also to watch his own party members, because corruption among the Christian Socials was not uncommon.[38] Here, Lueger's behavior suggested that he had learned important lessons from his earlier conflicts with Felder and venal Liberals.

The Deutsche Bank affiliation with the Vienna tramway operation proved to be anything but happy.[39] Investment returns were smaller than had been anticipated[40] and personnel problems continued.[41] When the city took over the operation of all but a few minor lines on July 1, 1903, there was general relief among the business partners. In evaluating Vienna's public transportation system during the Lueger years, praise for its modernity and such special features as tourist tram excursions[42] should be balanced against fruitless demands by municipal councillors for reduced workers' fares and unheeded appeals to eliminate increased Sunday tariffs, as evidently pertained in Berlin.[43] Such futile demands, however, did not prevent Lueger's government from issuing free or reduced fare tickets to nuns, priests, monks, and evidently to editors of the *Reichspost* and *Deutsches Volksblatt*.[44] Whatever the final judgment, the growth of the city's public transportation net and improved capacity were impressive. In 1899 Siemens und Halske had taken over a network of eighty-four kilometers. By 1913 the city was operating a network of 265 kilometers, the most extensive of any city in the world.[45] The annual number of passengers between 1903 and 1913 had more than doubled from 158 million to 323 million.[46] Looking back from the vantage point of 1913 to the days before Lueger attacked the tramway problem, the average Viennese who depended on municipal transportation had good reason to be happy.

In their excellent political history of Vienna, Seliger and Ucakar have called attention to the spurious designation of "socialism" as applied to the communalization of Vienna's public utilities under Lueger. Although communalization did begin during the Lueger era, neither as a minority oppositional party nor as the leaders of the municipality were the Christian Socials authentically anticapitalist.[47] Here, Lueger was consistent. Although he had attacked big business in parliament and was cheered for this reason by some,[48] he had also qualified his anticapitalism as early as 1889, at the Second Katholikentag, for the benefit of party members who were real estate owners or shareholders, and doubtless also for his own benefit because he needed their support. As mayor, and with the need to attract capital for his sizeable municipal projects, he not only distinguished between "good" and "bad" capital, but in 1903 went so far as to portray Vienna as a haven for investors:

> But you won't have noticed opposition in principle from me toward capital. So long as capital does what it is intended to do: to serve as a tool for the attainment of great advantages for one or the other, for the worker, too, etc., to that extent capital is good. But when it is used to subjugate all others, the state, the country, the city, to get all of labor in its power, then capital must be decisively opposed. But we thereby scare off only disreputable capital; honorable capital can come to Vienna any time; it will always find a protected place here and will also receive sufficient support.[49]

In his inaugural speech Lueger had stated that he hoped the city's revenues would be enriched through income from municipalized utilities. And he probably hoped that they as well would provide money for the salaries of loyal Christian Social officials and patronize workers in newly created jobs. But significantly, Vienna's chief source of income continued to be derived from taxes and payments on municipal debts, as during the Liberal era.[50] Though the yield from municipal utilities increased from 7.9 percent to 14.5 percent between 1895 and 1913,[51] it still took third place after debt payments. This was probably a good deal less than Lueger had hoped for, especially if he had pinned his hopes on Mandl's optimistic prediction of the 1870s.[52] All the same, and despite the continuing need to rely on traditional sources of revenue, the Christian Socials under whatever name departed significantly from Liberal policies of private ownership by initiating municipal proprietorship of utilities and transportation.[53]

Yet another project of longstanding interest to Lueger — one might say that it became the nearest thing to an obsession — was the construction of a second mountain spring reservoir. This has been celebrated by Lueger partisans as his "greatest work."[54] It was an immense project and took more than ten years to construct. The single-mindedness with which he pursued this goal suggests something more than, or perhaps besides, the selfless desire to serve his native city, attributed to him by most of his biographers. Lueger's determination to realize this goal bordered on fanaticism. The leader of the Vienna anti-Semites even publicly praised Baron Albert Rothschild in February 1902 as "one of the best Viennese and a true cavalier" for allowing the city to use his land without remuneration.[55] Lueger was subsequently photographed in the Rothschild equipage.

A few months before the cornerstone was laid he tried to win the support of the municipal council. Vienna's existing water supply, he argued, was inadequate, for aesthetic as well as human needs. Reminding his listeners of the city's magnificent fountains, Lueger complained that they seldom produced water, "and when it is to be seen, it is so trifling that the '*Männeken Piss*' in Brussels looks like an abundantly flowing current."[56] Though the owner of the necessary spring and surrounding lands had placed his property at "a rather high price," Lueger reminded his listeners of the Roman king who had wished to purchase nine books from the sybil. When the king complained that the price was too high, the sybil threw three books into the fire. She then demanded the original price for the remaining six, and when the king refused again, she threw another three books into the flames. The king ended by paying the original price for the last three books. "If we don't accept this offer today," Lueger allegorized, "we'll be much worse off than the Roman king with his books."[57] His training in Latin and its associations were seldom far from his mind. There was a strong element of Caesarism in Lueger's personality, and his determination to complete this understaking was galvanized by anxiety lest another rob him of the distinction of achieving a memorial of classical Roman dimensions and of Roman inspiration.[58] His admirer Hitler would have understood this.

If Lueger's urgency to complete this task betrayed an anxiety, this for once was well-founded. He did not live to see the completion of the Second Spring Mountain Reservoir, which was dedicated in December 1910, nine months after his death. The construction of the pipelines for the new reservoir obviated negotiations with private owners for the purchase of existing equipment, as had been so with the first two projects. In excavating for the reservoir pipes Lueger started from scratch. In the early 1890s he had stressed that in "all projects for the completion of Vienna's water supply . . . the water supply of the municipal area is exclusively the province of the municipality and may not be placed in private hands. . . . Even if the transport of water to Vienna is provided through private sources, the delivery of water to consumers may take place only through the municipality."[59] The new reservoir would have fulfilled Lueger's hopes by nearly doubling the water supply in 1911, and increased it even more the following year.[60] Yet here, as with electrification, there was to be no "socialization" of consumption during the Lueger years, rather just the opposite. Between 1900 and 1910 affluent districts privately increased their water consumption at a more rapid rate than the poorer ones.[61] So far as water consumption went, "the Liberal tradition of social discrimination was sharpened" under the Lueger regime, rather than merely continued.[62]

Lueger's various municipalization projects brought him into conflict not only with Socialists and Liberals, who objected to the cost[63] and the draconian methods by which he forced through the necessary legislation, but also with members of his own party. The latter feared that the increased numbers of municipal employees would pose problems of political control, fears which in some cases later proved to be justified.[64] If Lueger pinned his main hopes for increasing the city's revenue on income from the new gasworks and electric plant, additional municipalization schemes such as a city brewery,[65] livestock delivery agency, and slaughterhouse[66] were intended as much to create political capital as to augment Vienna's income.[67] But these latter projects created more problems than they solved. The brewery ran at a deficit,[68] while the slaughterhouse, which as we have already seen alienated some of Lueger's staunchest supporters, failed to achieve its objective and lower prices.[69] In addition, all three enterprises posed special problems for the party leader, who had to be increasingly careful as the Christian Socials extended their influence, not to seem to favor his urban constituents over his agrarian supporters. Despite his caution and a warning in his last will and testament not to allow the party to favor one class or interest group over another, a dichotomy between urban and agrarian Christian Socials continued to develop. During the First Republic, the agrarian interest got the upper hand.

Lueger's biographers have pointed with pride to the creation, renovation, or expansion of more than 100 schools during his mayoralty.[70] Lueger's educational policies deserve a separate treatment (see chapter seven), but a few words about the school buildings are in order. During a Landtag session, he had indicated the centrality of schools as well as the importance of religion in them, using a significant metaphor:

> There can hardly be anything more lovely and better than the new school buildings of the City of Vienna. We are building veritable palaces in the former suburbs, because we are proceeding on the assumption that the school should be a shrine for children, and are therefore of the opinion that a splendid home in the school should be offered, too, for poor children.[71]

Lueger knew the political value of children.

Biographers such as Kuppe and Soukup have suggested that the schools built during Lueger's mayoralty provide a fitting monument to his greatness, an appropriate symbol for his love of education.

> Above all, promoting and developing the school system were dear to the mayor as the chairman of the Viennese district school council. He considered school not merely a place for the inculcation of knowledge, but principally an institution which existed to serve religious, moral, and fatherland-*völkisch* education. . . . The school buildings of the mayor . . . were the most newly equipped *Volk* and *Bürgerschule* palaces which he had built in open and airy locations, removed from the noise and dust of the metropolis. The friendly façades, adorned with meaningful sculptures and reliefs, attracted . . . the children. And the interior design, spacious classrooms, physics labs, drawing and exercise rooms, vocational training areas for boys, dining rooms and kitchens, also school gardens, playgrounds and gyms, made the children feel at home in the school.[72]

Kuppe's laudatory remarks about Lueger's schools have been echoed by most of his biographers, particularly since World War II, though little has been said since 1945 about the ideological implications of Christian Social pedagogy.

The mayor's autocratic, if not dictatorial, and discriminatory policy toward non-Christian Social teachers is likewise usually passed over in silence.[73] Before 1914, at least, Christian Social publicists were much less reticent about such matters.[74] And they were also outspoken about teaching methodology and curriculum. As the conquerors of the Liberals, they postulated that the rights over education were theirs as part of the spoils of victory. With Lueger as chairman of the Vienna District School Council and with Christian Social majorities in the local and Lower Austrian school councils,[75] the ruling party made and enforced its educational policies to suit itself. Although there can be little doubt that Lueger's new and renovated schools provided pleasant and agreeable surroundings for Vienna's children, the direction and nature of the educational process were another matter.

His own attitude reflected what would now be tagged the "mortar and bricks" philosophy of education. The physical creation of the structure was an end in itself; the difficult feat had been to initiate the necessary legislation, round up the appropriate money, and attend to the details. Schooling itself should be conducted along "traditional" lines. On October 15, 1908, at the dedication of the 100th school constructed during the Christian Social regime, he exclaimed: "A hundred buildings! That's a city in itself! If we put the buildings together, many would declare them one of the most important and beautiful cities."[76] Lueger's remark concealed one of the less positive aspects of his schools. For by this time, it had become apparent that, operationally speaking, the upper and middle classes had once again been better served than the workers. Generally, districts with large worker populations sent their children to schools with higher pupil-to-teacher ratios.[77]

Apart from such construction projects and the municipalization of utilities, however, Lueger has also been applauded for making Vienna a more hygienic city. Although it is true that the private and street sewage systems increased by more than sixty percent between 1896 and 1913,[78] the decision to extend these systems had been made during the Liberal era. This was part of a larger plan to improve facilities in the imperial capital, to be undertaken at the imperial, provincial, and municipal levels.[79] Moreover, at least some evidence suggests that while sewage systems in middle- and upper-class residential areas improved markedly during Lueger's mayoralty, systems in the poorer districts remained primitive.[80] No *Putzteufel* when it came to the hygiene of open-air markets — in a municipal council meeting Lueger responded to a complaint about a noisome market that he suspected it had been that way for some time, but it now stank only because he was mayor — he was also less than fanatical about the need to maintain strict hygienic standards for individual refuse disposal. To a suggestion by one of his party members that those who dropped orange peels in the street should be arrested for endangering the lives and limbs of others, Lueger replied: "Those who walk in the streets should watch . . . where they step. That's why our Lord gave them eyes; it won't do to imprison a child because he throws away orange peels. Anyway, there's a difference between orange peels and dust; oranges are a very healthy food, but dust is very unhealthy!"[81]

During Lueger's mayoralty, projects apart, a growth in Vienna's labor force took place.[82] Between 1897 and 1910, the number of municipal workers and employees increased from 4,760 to 10,449.[83] To assist in the apportioning of jobs, a labor exchange was created in 1898. This branch of the municipal government had had a predecessor in the Liberal Union for Labor Exchange. During the Lueger years, 546,459 jobs for males were posted and 647,369 for females, plus 18,632 for teachers of either sex.[84] Lueger denied charges by Socialists that the labor exchange was administered according to party considerations, but nonetheless insisted that it remain in Christian Social hands.[85]

The labor exchange was highly political in apportioning jobs. Lueger himself stated that its purpose was "to break the 'terrorism' of the Social-Democratic leaders." "If the Social Democrats stayed away from the municipal labor exchange, so much the better for the Christian Social workers."[86]

Before 1897 Lueger had courted unfranchised workers as a source of potential support. Once in office, however, he made it plain that municipal workers who supported rival parties risked losing their jobs. Some were fired for just that reason. Lueger justified his actions: "A mayor . . . who maintains order cannot tolerate such conditions under any circumstances whatsoever."[87] Lueger's remark was cheered by the majority Christian Socials in the municipal council, thus underlining the subservience that came increasingly to characterize their behavior, and which Lueger seems to have actively encouraged.

One of the few Christian Socials who did not always submit to Lueger and retained an independence of action throughout Lueger's rule and beyond was Leopold Kunschak.[88] A former saddlemaker's apprentice, Kunschak was one of the most versatile and talented organizers of the younger generation of Christian Socials, possibly the most versatile and talented after Lueger himself, even though he lacked the mayor's educational advantages. Kunschak's first contribution was to organize a Christian Social Workers' Association during the 1890s. He thus filled an important need among the Catholic working class. From about 1880 on, the social question, which centered on the proliferation of the urban poor in the most demoralizing conditions, had been conspicuously neglected by the higher Austrian clergy.[89] Content to minister to the needs of the upper classes, the clerical aristocracy, with few exceptions, left the proletariat to the Social Democrats. Though Pope Leo XIII's May 1891 encyclical *Rerum Novarum* marked the formal interposition of the church in the social question, the higher Austrian clergy either continued to remain indifferent or contented themselves with promoting nonpolitical prayer societies for workers. Political activism among clergymen was frowned on and helps explain why Lueger's early supporters among the lower clergy found themselves in disfavor with their superiors.[90] The princes of the church also objected to welfare operations by secular organizations, believing that this activity usurped Christian charity or interfered with the divine scheme of things. With these attitudes prevailing among the Austrian church leaders, it is hardly surprising that Social Democrats found Lueger's party wanting in Christian charity toward the poor. While Lueger boasted of his achievements in the area of welfare,[91] one of his opponents retorted, probably without exaggeration, that the municipal administration "deals with the disabled poor as annoying nuisances, and lets these unfortunates feel full hatred through its functionaries. . . . In the district poor institutes . . . the poor are not infrequently regarded 'as the monstrosities of mankind.'"[92]

Yet Kunschak was different in some respects from the run-of-the-mill party functionary. Despite the opposition of some party members, who feared that the Christian Social Workers' Association might provide a cover for Social Democratic spies, intensify class distinctions within the party, and further diminish the influence of the lower middle class,[93] Kunschak's association was born in 1892. Recognizing the need for a mass circulation Catholic workers' newspaper, he founded the *Freiheit* in 1895, serving as dispatcher, administrator, and chief editor. A sample reading of this paper reveals the priorities of the Christian Social labor wing. Reports about the formation of new chapters of the Workers' Association, with their quasi-religious, quasi-military ceremonials, were interspersed with anti-Semitic and anti-Socialist polemics. In 1900 *Freiheit* was renamed the *Christlichsoziale Arbeiterzeitung*. By 1908 it was being printed in editions of twenty thousand.[94]

Kunschak had been attracted by Lueger during the early 1890s, and a "close and intimate relationship" developed that lasted until Lueger's death.[95] Lueger had heard Kunschak speak at an anti-Semitic outing organized by Ernst Vergani,[96] and was apparently so favorably impressed with the young apprentice that he immediately invited him to his law office. There Kunschak was overwhelmed by Lueger,[97] and he stated that their subsequent friendship affected his personal and political growth.[98] While Lueger's response to Kunschak is unknown, the advantages of cultivating an able and loyal young supporter who might challenge the Social Democrats, and perhaps even make inroads in their burgeoning membership, must have seemed obvious. For even at that early point in the development of the Christian Social party, the limits of its appeal were becoming apparent. A wider and more heterogeneous base of support was needed if the party was to flourish and to extend its influence. Moreover, by the early 1890s Lueger's role as the sometime friend of the Social Democrats was rapidly coming to an end.[99] His alignment with political Catholicism made the possibility of reconciliation with Social Democracy increasingly remote. Perhaps he recalled August Bebel's contrasting of Catholicism and Marxist Socialism with fire and water.[100] Before all else, Lueger aimed to build a mass party with himself at its head. This ambition both monitored and censored his priorities, in accepting or rejecting options that furthered this goal.

While Kunschak may have been at first flattered by the attention of Lueger, who by the mid-1890s had become an enormously popular, if local, Viennese cult figure, the younger man became increasingly disenchanted with his hero and the party, once Lueger had become mayor. As the undisputed leader of the Christian Socials, mayor of the imperial capital, and master of a commanding majority in the municipal council and provincial diet, Lueger disdained bargaining with his own party members. His will was to be obeyed, his wishes, wherever possible, to be anticipated and granted. This went for Kunschak, too, whose Workers' Association, which was always largely dependent on the party, was looked down on as socially inferior by many of the lower-middle-class rank and file. To them Kunschak had become too independent, and his organization a potential threat as a power within a power. Markör Nagorzansky, a Lueger sycophant who preached subordination of the workers to the lower middle class, founded a rival Christian Social labor group, at the possible instigation of Lueger and Gessmann.[101] Lueger's nomination of Nagorzansky in 1900 as an electoral candidate led to a serious quarrel between Lueger and Kunschak in the Rathaus. Enraged that the Workers' Association refused to endorse Nagorzansky, Lueger flew at Kunschak with clenched fists, shouting that he refused to take lessons "in his house" about whom to nominate, and that Kunschak could leave if he didn't like it.[102] Kunschak left, accompanied by a delegation from the Workers' Association. After a fruitless attempt at reconciliation during which Lueger became even more excited than at the earlier interview, Kunschak and his followers drafted an ultimatum unanimously threatening to resign their party functions en masse "unless the conflict was satisfactorily resolved at once."[103] Realizing that a public quarrel with the popular and able Kunschak might prove disadvantageous, Lueger managed to clear up their differences, but on his own terms, and not before Kunschak had been denied an interview. Kunschak, who had destroyed his large portrait of Lueger after the quarrel, was persuaded by his mother to submit to the mayor, for "Lueger is always Lueger, and you are only Kunschak."[104]

Thereafter, Lueger respected Kunschak, not only for the independence and skill of his leadership of the Workers' Association, but also for his forensic talent. After a municipal council debate with the Social Democrat Franz Schuhmeier,[105] Lueger expressed "the warmest thanks for the manner and way" in which Kunschak had refuted Schuhmeier, and said he would see to it that Kunschak's speech was "printed and distributed in hundreds and thousands of copies."[106] Of Kunschak's continuing loyalty to the party there can be no doubt. In 1907 a Social Democratic municipal councillor charged that Kunschak helped ensure the proper political orientation among municipal employees by assisting in the firing of Socialist tram workers.[107] Kunschak continued to hold important local, provincial, and national positions. At the time of his death in 1953 he was president of the Austrian Nationalrat, the nation's highest elective assembly. Recalling the scornful attitude of some of the party rank and file toward him and the Workers' Association, it is ironic that it may well have been his efforts that saved the Christian Socials from dissolution following Lueger's death in 1910.[108]

Kunschak demonstrated courage of a sort by criticizing the municipal and national governments for failing to provide adequate wages for city employees and housing for workers,[109] if one considers the jealousy with which Lueger guarded his leadership prerogatives. But he also showed himself to be an apt and willing pupil of Lueger in his anti-Semitic techniques. Kunschak continued to attack "Jewish big business" after Lueger had fallen silent on this subject.[110] He also opposed the granting of asylum to Jewish refugees following World War I, thus recalling Lueger's earlier support for Schönerer's anti-Jewish immigration bill.[111] Kunschak's politics were characterized by outspoken anti-Semitism throughout his career.[112]

The Lueger-Kunschak dispute reveals the underlying tensions, rivalries, and fractiousness that typified much of the inner party workings during the Lueger era. Such divisions benefited Lueger up to a point, for he could usually resolve the problems if he chose to do so, thereby enjoying and profiting from the role of the paternalistic arbiter. If he selected the other alternative, his pitting one group or individual against another prevented undesirable concentrations of power, and usually weakened both sides. An incident such as the Kunschak-Nagorzansky dispute, for which Lueger was probably at least partly to blame, tells much about his managerial style, the negative consequences of which were an inevitable lack of coordination, a loss of unity and purpose, let alone further rivalry and mistrust. Early in his career as a Liberal, Lueger had sometimes successfully practiced this tactic of divide and conquer. As mayor and party leader, he applied the same technique to augment his own power. Such machinations became an end in themselves and made it virtually certain that he could have neither a strong-minded, nor an independent, successor.

Apart from his personal style, however, some aspects of Lueger's politics between 1897 and 1910 must be described. During this period the effect of his declining health on his career cannot be dismissed. As the man who came to control majorities in the municipal council, provincial diet, and parliament, he was in his day unique among Austrian politicians of the constitutional era. Yet the burden of office began to tell, and though Christian Social electoral victories continued to mount and Lueger's honors multiplied, his health declined. Long years of campaigning and the endless speechmaking and travel they entailed, often under the most difficult circumstances, took their toll. The effects of nephritis, diabetes, and uremia, for which there were then no known cures or effective treatments, necessitated frequent and often extended vacations away from Vienna beginning in 1906.[113] These Lueger could sometimes turn to his and to the party's advantage, though his absences probably did nothing to stimulate the independence of other party members. From May 1907 his eyesight was impaired to the extent that newspapers and correspondence had to be read to him, and interpellations and proposals that he once read for himself had to be read for him at council and diet sessions.[114] A white runner was installed from his apartment in the town hall so that he could make his way without assistance. Lueger's failing health was exploited by his party in various ways, and not only by his enemies. Many used his health as a means of deflecting criticism of the man. Thus, Schuhmeier once remonstrated that this alone prevented a more vigorous criticism of Christian Social politics. Yet until ill health and the arrogance of power separated him from his early and staunchest supporters, Lueger never neglected the rank and file.[115]

Lueger campaigned for the last time in district elections during the autumn of 1909 and appeared in the municipal council and diet until about a month before his death. Intrigues over the succession had been fostered indirectly by Lueger himself through his steadfast refusal to allow any inner party group to challenge his own authority, and through his treatment of leaders such as Kunschak, whom he may have regarded as a potential rival. Nothing was more certain to provoke Lueger's wrath than a show of independence if this ran counter to his will. This authoritarianism and outright jealousy of power were probably rooted in his upbringing and reinforced by his formal education. His lengthy political apprenticeship confirmed these tendencies. Many of his attitudes and the resulting policies seem similarly rooted in earlier stages of his career. The actual possession and exercise of power for their own sake did not much affect his basic outlook on matters about which he had long held firm opinions and for which he was obviously prepared to alter his position, if circumstances required him to do so. Yet, if anything, his will to achieve goals became all the more patent from 1897; Lueger was usually prepared to take the necessary steps.

Thus, between 1897 and 1910 as Lueger's health gradually worsened, his politics as such revealed fewer innovations than the novel methods he sometimes employed to attain his ends. But even the methods may in some cases have been practical applications of earlier theories or lessons. For example, many years before, while at the university, Lueger had learned how the Romans had reaped benefits by practicing economic imperialism on client states.[116] As an imperial politician himself, he may well have recalled this lesson and tried to translate theory into practice by exploiting trade relations with neighboring states. In one instance, Lueger's gambit was preceded by yet another attack on Hungary and the Judeo-Magyars. During his last years these were the principal targets of his abuse for being the alleged chief beneficiaries of the Ausgleich. Hungary was not as well off as Lueger would have his listeners believe. In fact, Hungary was a poor country. It has been estimated that on the eve of World War I, Hungary's total national wealth was scarcely more than half of Austria's, "whose population was only about 20 percent larger; and Austria itself was poor by West European standards, not to speak of American."[117] During a demagogic display in parliament in 1906, Lueger went so far as to ask Franz Joseph if he was willing to assume responsibility for precipitating the seemingly impending destruction of the empire by allowing Hungary to employ an independent customs' tariff.[118]

Where Lueger subsequently departed from his usual Magyar-baiting was in trying to embarrass Hungary by following up his parliamentary attack with a visit to Bucharest. There he was officially to participate in a Rumanian triple jubilee at which Austria had a pavilion. Less officially, Lueger also tried to pave the way for expanded trade relations with Rumania at Hungary's expense.[119] Lueger was very much an economic imperialist. He welcomed the annexation of Bosnia-Herzogovina in 1908, to provide another market for Austrian goods. (He and Mandl had favored the occupation in 1878 for the same reasons.)[119] However, in 1906, his visit to Bucharest also implied a gesture of anti-Magyar, anti-Semitic solidarity with Rumania, whose leaders had for years criticized the treatment of Rumanians in the Hungarian crown lands. Yet at least one Rumanian economic commentator viewed Lueger's visit with justifiable skepticism, if not outright suspicion. Was he perhaps trying to sell old wine in new bottles, or perhaps more wine, and thereby expand the existing market at Rumania's expense at that? For more than thirty years Rumania had been "the tributaries of Austria and those who have profited by it have been the Hungarians. In Hungary much progress has been made, thanks to the Austrian markets; Rumania has even lost what it had before, always accepting the goods not only from Vienna, but also those sent from Pest, which impeded Rumanian industry."[120] Although it was all well and good for Lueger to have been feted, to have had a street named after him, and to have been received by King Carol, "one thing is certain . . . that Rumania will not agree to any meeting with Austria before finding out how her government has settled its economic and trade agreements with Hungary, or if she will insert a clause in these agreements that will be to [Rumania's] advantage. Otherwise, no agreement is possible."[121] Whatever Lueger's true motives for visiting Bucharest, he succeeded again in outraging the Hungarians and in disquieting governmental moderates even before his departure from Vienna. Lueger's opponents had suspected that his visit concealed another, agitational purpose. But his Rumanian visit is also interesting for the light it throws on his indifference to diplomatic convention and unconcern for any discomfiture he might have caused in ruling circles. Or perhaps by 1906, after ten years of power, he had become merely arrogant, and had visited Bucharest as an egotistical and agitational gesture.[122] Here, as with other of Lueger's actions, several interpretations are possible. In any case, the monarchy had had an alliance with Rumania since 1883,[123] and friendly relations existed between the two, at least officially. Formal trade agreements had also been concluded. Lueger's visit, therefore, was viewed by the Socialists as a publicity stunt to gratify his enormous ego and enhance still further his equally enormous popular image.[124] Others, perceiving it as an anti-Hungarian gesture, thought it risked disrupting imperial economic unity by trying to expand Austria's shrinking markets in the Balkans. Disruption of this sort was something "no serious economist or responsible politician would have dreamed of."[125]

A proper assessment of the effect of Lueger's politics during his lifetime, and beyond, requires a look at the growth in Christian Social strength from 1896 to 1910, and the effects of this growth on Lueger. Responding again, perhaps, to the theoretical training of his university years, Lueger thought of himself as both the repository of powers and the transmitter of mandates of a still higher authority. He doubtlessly believed himself to be a worthy intermediary, and that the many honors heaped on him were no more than the just rewards of his labors. He requested and received the distinction of "excellency" to precede his name, because this permitted him to occupy a prominent position when he dined at court. Lueger said that this was also "'an honor for the city of Vienna.'"[126] He said he thought it was better to see his picture rather than someone else's in public school offices. He was untroubled by what anyone might think, he added, because everyone who knew him realized that he was "completely devoid of any personal vanity, and avoid[ed] certain accolades rather than seeking them."[127] Perhaps it was in this frame of mind that the mayor agreed to have the square before the town hall named "Dr. Karl Lueger Platz," thus sharing with Kaiser Wilhelm II the distinction of being the only living man to have had a Viennese street or square named after himself.[128] In later years his official pronouncements were often prefaced with "from my position as mayor of the imperial capital and residence . . . ," as if to suggest that the exercise of his official duties added luster to the center of empire.

Lueger could not have been unaffected by the fact that the Christian Socials had become the leading party in the Landtag as early as 1896. By 1902 this lead had increased to a two-thirds majority, and by 1908 to nearly three-quarters, thus assuring Lueger's party of automatic passage of legislation. The Christian Socials were increasingly supported by the representatives of small- and middle-farm holders. Lueger had won agricultural support away from the Liberals as early as 1896.

In the municipal council, which the Christian Socials had controlled from 1896 as well, Lueger's party also went from strength to strength. A measure of its domination, and of Lueger's popularity, may be seen in the results of his seventh election to mayor. On March 31, 1909, Lueger was reelected for another six years, winning an overwhelming 130 votes. The remaining twenty ballots were left blank.[129] His speech of acceptance was more subdued than at the time of his sixth election in 1903. Then, still in good health, the demagogic aspect of his personality was very much in evidence, as he proclaimed himself an agitator who would always oppose "the enemies of [his] fatherland Austria, [and the] enemies of the Christian people."[130] The completion or progress of such major municipal building projects as the gas and electric works, and the overwhelming Christian Social victory in the provincial diet elections a few months before, had made him seem invincible. These tangible achievements lent substance to his claim that Vienna was an island of the fortunate, at least for prosperous Christian Socials.[131] Among Lueger's occasional admirers, few then recognized that "it took Liberalism . . . 30 years to degenerate from a party of freedom and progress to a party of servile *Hofrats* and reactionary informers — Lueger and his followers achieved that in less than three."[132]

Since 1907 the Christian Socials had commanded a parliamentary majority, having forged an alliance with the Catholic Conservatives, and Lueger spoke with the assurance that there were no effective challengers to his own, or to his party's, authority. But the weaknesses of one-man rule and the corruption of power had also begun to tell. Although complaints about Lueger's authoritarianism and bullying tactics were not unheard before 1903[133] and could have given him pause before the Landtag victory of 1902, he brooked no resistance thereafter. Lueger was in the habit of commanding silence when he spoke.[134] After all, municipal councillors had elected him mayor because of his energy and ruthlessness; why should he conceal these qualities? The chief target of his animosity, the Social Democrats, felt the effects of Lueger's rule and recognized his ability to destroy them had he but the power. In 1904 he stated in parliament: "[The Social Democrats] are the inner enemy [of the state] and must be fought. The army is there to protect the life and property of citizens against certain turbulent elements. If the military were placed at my disposal, I would know how to use it."[135]

After 1904, however, events had begun to overtake the Christian Socials as well. The municipal brewery and slaughterhouse ran at continuing deficits, thereby giving the Socialists anti-Lueger ammunition. The mayor himself was involved in new anti-Socialist, anti-Semitic incidents, thereby prompting renewed criticism that he was trying to divert attention from more pressing issues, such as the rise in consumer prices. And Lueger's health began a steady decline. By 1907 it was impossible for him to campaign for the crucial parliamentary elections that ushered in universal manhood suffrage. As a result, the Socialist became the second most popular party in parliament.

But despite Lueger's political losses, the man's prestige and personal popularity continued to grow. Was the party leader, whose own honesty was above question, to blame for the corruption of other Christian Socials? Had he but known of the abuses being committed in his name. . . . The pretender to the throne, Franz Ferdinand, welcomed him into the Belvedere Circle. Lueger was to be the new emperor's first choice as prime minister,[136] though it is doubtful that he would have accepted the honor, even had he been able to do so. "I'll not enter the ministry," he had said following the 1907 elections. "I shall very happily remain mayor of Vienna, and am here . . . a completely independent man."[137] As mayor and party leader, Lueger realized that he enjoyed unusual power and a freedom of action denied ministerial appointees whose tenure of office depended on the favor of the emperor. Lueger was sure of himself with the electorate, less so with a royal protector, especially Franz Joseph. To have gambled his political fate on the whim of a single individual would have meant to embrace an earlier form of patronage alien to his professional development and nature. Lueger was the product and agent of a developing mass politics, which however imperfect and incomplete was a major factor in his career and personal fate.

Although some might blame Lueger's declining health for the irregularities of other Christian Socials, continuing Christian Social electoral victories gave rise to additional charges of balloting corruption. Lueger could not ignore this issue. Though he acknowledged some irregularities, he blamed these on inaccurate voting lists, which were impossible to keep up to date. Elections had been run as honestly as possible, he insisted, and any infringements were negligible.[138] Privately, however, Lueger responded differently. When a Socialist municipal councillor documented electoral illegality, Lueger said he would redress the issue, but would deny any malfeasance in public if word leaked out.[139] But Lueger could afford to be generous.

The Christian Socials had ensured that the voting laws guaranteed their party continued success. By 1900 the position of the Christian Socials in Viennese politics was so strong that it seemed virtually impregnable. A new municipal electoral law created a fourth curia, yet excluded from voting in municipal council elections anyone who had not lived in Vienna without interruption for at least three years.[140] Lueger had insisted on this residency clause, which he had wanted to hold at five years, because he probably realized that this would eliminate thousands of transient laborers who had more to gain from supporting the Socialists. Responding to growing demand for wider suffrage during a city council meeting in March 1899, Lueger had suggested that the curial system be abolished and mandates be distributed according to the size of the population.[141] But in return, he insisted on the five-year residence as a franchise requirement. He and his supporters realized full well that most workers, regardless of how long they had lived in Vienna, occasionally moved out of the city for a month or more on jobs, and would therefore be disqualified from voting.

Lueger's proposal required the support of the provincial diet and the approval of the emperor. A few days later while Lueger was visiting Rome for an audience with the pope, Strohbach introduced the draft of Lueger's proposal in the diet. An electoral reform committee was formed under

Magistrat director, Richard Weiskirchner, who soon let it be known that the government would not accept the new proposal. In mid-April, Ernst Schneider moved that the committee instruct the municipal council to revise the proposal in such a way that the curial system be preserved, and that "'the demand for a universal franchise be met.'"[142] Lueger's original proposal was "swept under the table," but since he was in Rome at the time he appeared to bear no responsibility. This was no doubt the way he and the other Christian Social leaders had planned it.

A new proposal creating a fourth curia with twenty mandates, one per district, but retaining the earlier three with forty-six mandates each, was passed by the diet towards the end of May. The Christian Socials had set the clock ahead fifteen minutes, opened the session early, and forced through the proposal before the opposition could organize or the workers could protest as they had done earlier before the town hall.[143]

Although Lueger might pose as the supporter of universal manhood suffrage, he realized that the imperial government would never grant approval for this measure, at least not in 1900. It took the 1905 revolution in Russia for Czar Nicholas II to grant a duma and additional concessions. These developments, as well as threatening worker demonstrations in Vienna, Prague, and other industrial centers of the Habsburg Empire, moved Franz Joseph to action. He granted universal manhood suffrage to the Austrian and Hungarian parliaments in 1907, but "not to the Austrian *Landtage* or the Hungarian counties."[144]

Between 1899 and 1900 the Socialists, who had agitated for the reduction of the residency voting requirement to six months, staged massive demonstrations in protest, all to no avail. Despite universal manhood suffrage for imperial elections from 1907, Vienna retained a curial system for municipal elections that disqualified one-third of the male residents over twenty-four years old as late as 1912, and women were denied the vote altogether.[145] Thus the first three privileged curias continued to elect 138 municipal councillors, and the fourth curia from 1900 sent but twenty municipal councillors to the town hall. Lueger was no doubt disappointed that the residency requirement had been established at three, instead of five years, but he said he was happy that "the German character of . . . Vienna" would be preserved by the new law.[146] Here he referred to the undesirability of enfranchising itinerant Slavic workers — particularly if the Slavs supported the Socialists.

Yet another development that strengthened Lueger's power was the creation of a municipal statute affecting the city council. As the leader of the Christian Social opposition in 1890, Lueger had attacked the city council because it was controlled by the Liberals. However, once in office as mayor, Lueger reversed his earlier position and here as elsewhere revealed himself as the true heir of the very Liberals he had ousted. Under Lueger the city council (Stadtrat) was not only preserved, but its appointive powers, and his as a member, were also extended.[147]

In December 1909, three months before Lueger's death, Franz Schuhmeier summarized the effects of nearly fourteen years of Christian Social rule on Viennese government. By then the municipal council existed largely to synchronize the decisions of the city council and the Christian Social Bürgerclub. Lueger's party had made the municipal council an assembly mainly designed to perpetuate his own control and that of his party: "The result is, therefore, that while one party in Vienna commanding 110,936 voters, holds 135 mandates, the other party with over 98,000 voters in Vienna, has only seven mandates."[148]

At the height of Lueger's power as mayor a few years before, a foreign observer described some other aspects of the imperial capital that have been ignored by Lueger's biographers who have emphasized instead his public works achievements. While Vienna was architecturally splendid[149] and great wealth was contained in the museums, palaces and churches,

> the purses of the great majority of the Viennese are light indeed. The visitor to Vienna might spend many weeks in the capital and arrive at the conviction that here, at least, sordid poverty was entirely unknown. He would have seen nothing to lead him to suspect its existence in the stately splendour of the crowded streets, inhabited by millionaire bankers and financiers. But, nevertheless, in the back alleys of the city he might have found many thousands who earn their daily bread in 'sweating dens,' and whose wages hardly suffice to keep body and soul together. The pressure of this grinding poverty naturally falls most heavily upon women. For them, fourpence a day for eighteen hours' labour is no unusual remuneration. I could give endless examples of the terrible amount of distress and suffering endured in silence in Vienna. I will only mention one typical case, which was reported in the Viennese press as nothing in any way remarkable. A workman, who had unintentionally killed a comrade in a quarrel, was sentenced to a short term of imprisonment, after which he was to pay compensation to the widow of the victim. The compensation was fixed at a penny a day, as he was able to prove that, though a vigorous and hard working man, the total of his possible earnings would certainly not enable him to exceed that amount. The widow, we are told, accepted the judge's award with tears of gratitude. A penny a day, she affirmed, added to her own earnings, would enable her to keep her children from actual starvation![150]

Despite Lueger's boasts about Christian Social achievements in welfare, no significant improvement in the condition of the poor came about. Such improvement could not have been possible without far-reaching changes. New voting laws, decent worker housing, and more equitable wage distribution would prove necessary. The continuing influence of entrenched interest groups in the Christian Social party, Lueger's defense of these groups, or his acquiescence in their politics, as well as his concentration on public works that benefited his constituents, made such changes impossible.

Lueger's clearly symbolic fascination with politically useful projects again focuses the observer's eye on his centerless, drifting, style. His construction of a huge political apparatus was in a sense equivalent to some of his public works. Both seem directed more toward self-gratification than meeting concrete social needs. The complexity of his attitude and policies toward the Jews reveals a similarly centerless drift with nonetheless grotesque consequences.

5

Running with the Hares,
Hunting with the Hounds

So far as his anti-Semitism goes, Lueger became milder after his in-
auguration, and his verbal sallies against political dissidents more
measured, more statesmanlike.

—Johannes Hawlik, *Der Bürgerkaiser*

[C]lerical anti-Semitism, which prevailed mainly in the Austro-
Hungarian Empire . . . must be regarded as a forerunner of the
biological-racialist anti-Semitism that the Nazis were to perfect; it
represents a long-standing, sinister tradition from which Adolf Hitler
demonstrably was unable, and indeed unwilling, to escape.

—Gerald Fleming, *Hitler and the Final Solution*

No single aspect of Karl Lueger's career has roused more controversy
than his anti-Semitism. There are two poles of opinion about Lueger as
anti-Semite and little neutral ground in between. For a century now, Lueger
has often been attacked as one of the principal instigators of political
anti-Semitism on the one hand, or defended as an actual friend of the Jews
on the other. Somewhat incongruously, those belonging to the latter camp
have occasionally suggested that Lueger's anti-Semitism was justified.[1] His
defenders have included Austrian Jews, such as Arthur Schnitzler and
Stefan Zweig, prominent literary figures of Vienna's high culture during
the early years of the twentieth century, and his more recent Austrian
biographers. In the other camp, post World War II historians, such as
P. G. J. Pulzer and Carl E. Schorske, have seen Lueger as an important
progenitor of modern political anti-Semitism and as a protofascist.[2] At

the heart of the issue since 1945 has been the question whether Lueger influenced the developing ideology of Adolf Hitler, and thus contributed to the preparation for the Holocaust. Hitler praised Lueger in *Mein Kampf,* during his World War II "table talks," and elsewhere.[3] Although critical of Lueger's peculiar variety of anti-Semitism, Hitler nonetheless lauded him as a statesman, suggesting that he may have owed the Schönerian racial focus of his own anti-Semitism to the rejection of Lueger's alternative brand.

The reluctance of Lueger's recent Austrian biographers to confront his — and his nation's — anti-Semitism becomes understandable within the framework of recent events. In a country where seventy-five years after Lueger's death and forty years after the end of World War II, an S.S. war criminal was welcomed by a minister of defense; where during the same year the interment of the remains of an alleged victim of a medieval ritual murder became the center of a national controversy; where later the same year a bomb destroyed a Jewish shop in Vienna's second district, the former Jewish ghetto, as during Lueger's mayoralty;[4] and where as late as 1986 a slogan from *Mein Kampf* graced a World War II memorial in a building of the University of Vienna — in such a country it is scarcely surprising that Lueger's anti-Semitism is considered to be of "distinctly secondary importance" in most Austrian Lueger biographies. Those of us who lived in Austria during the 1986 national presidential campaign in which Kurt Waldheim was elected, and who have followed the series of anti-Semitic incidents that ensued, know that anti-Semitism continues to thrive in Austria and that "the Lueger tradition" has emerged again to reveal the power of the past over the present.

Until the early 1980s, some Anglo historians held that while Lueger had dampened his anti-Semitism after becoming mayor, "the widespread acceptance of mild, almost incidental, anti-Semitic opinions"[5] was an element in the climate that nurtured Nazi barbarism. However, in 1981 John W. Boyer challenged some aspects of the prevailing opinion about Lueger's anti-Semitism and his influence on Hitler. Specifically, Boyer denies as false Hitler's "perception of Lueger as a dictatorial, charismatic *Führer*-type."[6] Boyer also asserts that "Lueger never disliked Jews personally," that "after 1897 . . . he frequently encountered and occasionally even befriended influential and wealthy Jews," that he "wore his professed antisemitism lightly and . . . used it principally in the realm of public propaganda."[7] Lueger, Boyer adds, dealt with Jews "with sobriety and respect."[8] When questioned about unfair personnel practices in the treatment of Jewish municipal employees, "Lueger declared that all personnel matters were a question for the Stadtrat [city council] and that, personally, he had

adopted a neutral stance on the issue."[9] "In his parliamentary speeches,"
Boyer continues, "Lueger was surprisingly sparing in his use of the anti-
semitic issue. Usually only an adverse turn in political events or a vital
tactical manoeuvre which required an antisemitic 'cover' would motivate
Lueger to bother with the Jewish issue. Beyond this, he confined his antisemitism to occasional jokes, innuendoes, personal slanders and comic
interludes."[10] In this lighthearted vein, "Lueger's prejudices were cultural
and class-oriented, but not racial."[11] Though Boyer admits that Lueger
once "commented that, personally speaking, he believed that Austrian
Jews should be deprived of their voting rights," this "statement was a
palpable lie, . . . intended to protect his flanks [to refute charges] that
Lueger was 'going soft' on the antisemitic issue."[12] Boyer adds that Lueger
"could hate Jews for the tendency to create a culturally pluralistic society
and for their often superior educational and intellectual backgrounds. . . .
[but he] could not help but respect them since they *were* well-educated
and talented, especially in light of the fact that many Austrian Jews had
risen from petit-bourgeois social disabilities to achieve through their own
energies bourgeois prominence, a pattern of social mobility quite similar
to Lueger's own."[13] Within the larger European context, "in light of the
enormous fund of protests that European Liberalism was 'dead' or that it
had somehow 'failed', men were forced to experiment with new modes of
political behaviour and new ideological conceptions to fill the civic cultural void."[14] In a word, Boyer's arguments bring Lueger's anti-Semitism
into the same ultimate pragmatism which, Boyer suggests, marks Lueger's
political personality — as another technique rather than a principle.

In some respects, Boyer's article elaborated on conclusions in his
monograph on Viennese radicalism. Building on Boyer's assertions in
both works, Robert Wistrich has suggested in writing about the ambiguities
of Lueger's position that Lueger "partially succeeded in taming and domes-
ticating Viennese antisemitism with a heavy dose of Austrian *Gemüt-
lichkeit.*"[15] In another work Wistrich has stated that Lueger "the anti-
Semitic dragon-slayer of Austro-liberalism became, in the twilight of his
career, the conciliatory elder statesman of Habsburg loyalism and the civic-
minded architect of Viennese 'municipal socialism.'"[16] Still more recently,
Leon Poliakov in *The History of Anti-Semitism* flatly states that "the enthusiastic tribute that Hitler paid [Lueger] in *Mein Kampf* does not seem
justified, for the Jews did not suffer under his administration," and Steven
Beller adds that "Lueger was not a serious antisemite."[17]

No group of writers has been more fully in agreement with the assess-
ments of Boyer, Wistrich, Poliakov, and Beller than most Lueger biographers since 1945. One post–1945 biographer virtually ignored Lueger's anti-

Semitism altogether. This was Rudolf Kuppe, whose 1947 biography is a model of tactful historical reconstruction. Gone were the references to Lueger as a champion of "Aryan interests" that featured prominently in his 1933 biography. Gone, too, were the often lengthy quotations from Lueger's outspokenly anti-Jewish speeches. Another postwar Austrian biographer who has more to say about Lueger's anti-Semitism, but who nonetheless largely exonerates the mayor and party leader from preparing for the Nazi era, is Kurt Skalnik: "Dr. Karl Lueger is exonerated by the judgment of history. In 1880, 1890, 1900, life still proceeded along such a well-defined order, that one could afford to play with anti-Semitism without destroying human morality and descending into a demonic underworld."[18] More recently, Johannes Hawlik has sketched the cultural-political environment of Lueger's anti-Semitism in one of the shortest, yet most digressive chapters, of a 1985 biography commemorating the seventy-fifth anniversary of Lueger's death. Hawlik does not completely dismiss the possibility of Lueger having influenced Hitler, but he nonetheless provides "a tiny defense" for Lueger's anti-Semitism: "Under the influence of the Enlightenment . . . and considering the belief in progress during the nineteenth century, no one, not even the most virulent anti-Semite, conceived as possible a regression to the barbarism of the Middle Ages (in the grand style of the twentieth century) as Hitler's Final Solution."[19]

Even Hawlik's "tiny defense" seems overstated, despite his qualification. In his futuristic work *Aus dem Jahr 1920* (1900), Josef Scheicher, the Christian Social politician and publicist priest, did "conceive as possible" the partial extermination of Austrian Jewry.[20] Moreover, in December 1902, shortly before the Christmas recess, Hermann Bielohlawek, during a municipal council session presided over by Lueger, called for the destruction of the Jews and stated "that the Viennese population . . . has as its program: the eradication (*Ausmerzung*) of Jewry. From that we shall not depart."[21] Bielohlawek's speech was received with "lively applause" and he was congratulated from all sides. Furthermore, another Christian Social, Ernst Schneider, predicted in 1901 a coming time when Jews would be "killed and burned. In Rumania, they're starting already to drive the Jews out, and with us, it will get to the point that we'll drive these parasites out of the country, which they only ravage."[22]

Boyer further refers to "the . . . limitations of [Lueger's] power," that even "had he wished to eliminate all discrimination against the Jews, the more antisemitic sub-elite of the party would have expected some concessions."[23] It is the central argument of this chapter, and of other portions of this book, that far from "wish[ing] to eliminate all discrimination against the Jews," through his continuing and malicious recourse to provocative

174

anti-Semitism, and his overt or covert support for anti-Semitic legislation and other actively discriminatory measures, Lueger ensured the continuation and intensification of anti-Semitism as a central feature of Christian Social politics throughout his mayoralty—and beyond. And only the limitations imposed on his power by the imperial authority and his own declining health prevented a potentially more violent expression of anti-Semitism. It was the imperial legal qualification on his power and its enforcement in some cases, rather than any charitable attitude on the part of Lueger and his supporters toward the Jews, that prevented them from "suffer[ing] extensive material or cultural deprivations from Christian Social rule." Lueger made anti-Semitism respectable, and in so doing made it more dangerous.[24] After Lueger's death, younger Christian Social politicians carried on his anti-Semitism in "the tradition of the Christian Social party." Toward the end of the First Republic they established a clerical fascist dictatorship. "Antisemitism flourished in the First Austrian Republic. . . . Austrian antisemites may have been even more vicious toward the Jews in the 1930s than were their counterparts in Germany."[25] The roots of this variety of anti-Semitism were nurtured during the Lueger era.

Anti-Semitism was a constant instrument of Lueger's politics from 1887 until he became too ill to campaign. While his remarks were sometimes moderated in the public forums, anti-Jewish slurs remained frequent in his speeches to local constituencies. And, though anti-Semitism had penetrated the thinking of the highest officialdom by the time of Lueger's mayoralty, and was therefore not new (Kielmansegg referred to Gessmann as "an out and out *Judenstämmling* [Jew], with all the characteristic qualities, especially the intense acquisitive sense of this race"),[26] under Lueger it became more comprehensive and more insidiously pervasive, in all aspects of cultural, social, and political life, than ever before. It remained an open feature of public life until 1945, and has continued if in sometimes more concealed or hypocritical forms. Although some Viennese refer to Schönerer as the forerunner of Nazism and deplore his crude racist anti-Semitism, much as some Germans deplore that of Julius Streicher, Lueger is usually absolved by such Viennese from having contributed to the rise of Hitler. For them, Lueger remains "the respectable anti-Semite."

When Lueger himself failed to initiate direct anti-Semitism, it was usually instigated by other Christian Social leaders vying for his favor, a dependent group most of whom proved incapable of functioning politically once he was out of the picture. To them Lueger was a sort of ultimate ideological authority for anti-Semitism, but not intimately involved in the details. "Lueger knew what he wanted, and everyone who knew him, knew it too," as Rudolf Spitzer observed in his 1988 Lueger study.[27] Lueger was capable of hating, and probably did "hate Jews for the tendency to create a culturally pluralistic society, and for their often superior educational and intellectual backgrounds," as Boyer has put it; and there is little countervailing or contravening evidence to the speculation that he balanced this animosity with respect for their "education" and "talent." Just the opposite seems to have been so. His stance goes beyond both political expediency and a theoretical preference for cultural unity. Lueger defended the most rabid Christian Social anti-Semites, such as Father Joseph Deckert and Ernst Schneider. The mayor awarded a medal to Deckert, and silenced Liberal protests in parliament against Schneider, "the conscience of the Christian people," according to Lueger, when Schneider proposed "that a special police force supervise the Jews around Easter time" to prevent ritual murders.[28]

In the light of continuing Austrian anti-Semitism, it is not surprising that Austrian views of Lueger remain substantially unchanged, and that recently there has even been a return to some of the earlier prewar emphases in Hawlik's biography. But the picture of Lueger as a man who despite appearances liked Jews or was at least indifferent, of Lueger the benign, of Lueger the closet philo-Semite, distorts and obscures his role and that of his party in the development of twentieth-century anti-Semitism and the violent form it took. Lueger's anti-Semitism in reality assumed several ominous if expedient shapes. His public remarks and the implications of his policies sometimes pointed to a racial bias, Boyer notwithstanding,[29] but these were not the only indications of his attitudes.

Although it may be true, as Robert Wistrich has pointed out, that "pre-1914 Christian-Social agitation . . . first synthesized hatred of socialists and Jews in Austria,"[30] Lueger also, if in less original fashion, routinely linked anti-Semitism with hatred of Liberalism, Hungarians, and Freemasons. But in all these hateful chimeras, "the Jew" was primary and constant: thus, *Judensozi, Judeoliberalismus, Judeo-Magyar, Judenfreimaurer.* Lueger also added another amalgam to the spurious alloys of anti-Semitism to describe Jewish journalists, *papierene Juden.*[31] Toward this latter group, and especially the journalists of the Liberal press, Lueger directed his most implacable anti-Semitism. Even Kielmansegg, who denied that Lueger was authentically anti-Semitic, conceded that the mayor's anti-Semitism did extend to the offices of the *Neue Freie Presse* in the Fichtegasse,[32] — Lueger admitted this — thereby suggesting Lueger's insight on the importance of propaganda and mind control.

Lueger made extreme and damaging anti-Jewish remarks before and after he became mayor. Thus, for example, in 1894 during a parliamentary session, he corrected a Liberal delegate, Heinrich Popper. Lueger denied having said at a mass meeting that it was immaterial to him whether one shot or hanged Jews. "Beheaded!" Lueger corrected the speaker.[33] And before and after he became mayor, Lueger asserted in parliament that Jewish sects practiced ritual murder.[34] Although Lueger's statements are remarkable in themselves, it is important to bear in mind their larger context as well. When he made them, European attention was occupied by the Dreyfus affair, and at the same time, a kind of ritual murder hysteria swept over parts of eastern Europe. On one occasion, a Frenchman was mistakenly assaulted as a Jew by a group of brick makers who thought he wanted to draw blood from their children.[35] Referring to the Dreyfus affair, Lueger told an electoral meeting in 1895 that the eyes of the French had been opened, "and even they will one day realize that the Jew has no fatherland and therefore knows no fatherland."[36]

For much of his later career, from the mid-1890s until at least as late as 1907, Lueger attacked Jews in the university. Thus, for example, in 1899 he claimed in the Lower Austrian Diet that "Rumanian and Galician Jews . . . had reduced the Vienna medical school to a level that could not be thought of as lower."[37] It should be noted that Lueger's and his party's anti-Semitism was not confined solely to verbal abuse. The Lueger regime tried to instill anti-Semitism in the youth by appropriating municipal funds for, and facilitating the printing and distribution of, *Wiener Kinder* in Vienna's elementary schools. This outspokenly Christian Social and occasionally anti-Semitic children's periodical was printed by Vice Mayor Heinrich Hierhammer. Its contributors included Richard von Kralik and Josef Scheicher.[38] (See illustrations.)

Under Lueger, Jewish representatives to elective bodies controlled by the Christian Socials and presided over by him were insulted and sometimes intimidated, usually without his saying a word. In fact, Lueger occasionally defended the insulter. When on rare occasions Gentiles objected to Christian Social behavior, they received the same abuse as the Jews. Lueger's government discriminated against the hiring and promotion of Jewish municipal employees, and sometimes fired Jewish teachers. During his mayoralty Lueger himself was directly involved in anti-Semitic incidents and scandals.

Considering the long history of anti-Semitism in Austria, it is perhaps more, rather than less, surprising that Lueger did not become an outspoken anti-Semite before he did. Opportunism was doubtless a factor here, but Lueger's had been a deeply traditional upbringing and home environment. Among most Austrian Catholics, the Jew was the eternal alien. Though guaranteed religious equality by law, the Jews of Lueger's time were regarded by Catholic Austrians as nonetheless unequal, a group apart, "un-

German," even racially separate, by extremists. Yet Austrians who thought this way were not necessarily active anti-Semites. Lueger surely realized this. Some of his more offhanded remarks about Jews betrayed a popular and more general habit of thought, rather than cunning political calculation. Thus Jews might be tolerated or not, as circumstances and the mood dictated. This outlook had its roots in medieval and baroque times, when earlier Habsburg rulers had exploited or persecuted or merely tolerated Jews, as they saw fit. But there were other, more modern aspects to Lueger's anti-Semitism, such as his occasional racism, sometimes distinguishing as he did between Aryans and Jews. Moreover, his stated wish on one occasion that Jews be "weeded out" of the university medical faculty anticipates the euphemistic language which would later be used by others to conceal the more violent practices of totalitarianism.

If Lueger's anti-Semitism before his mayoralty reflected his ruthless drive for power, his continuing anti-Jewish agitation and anti-Semitism from 1897 betrayed criminal irresponsibility, because his pronouncements and actions carried the authority of official sanction and the party he led continued until 1907 to extend its power and thus its anti-Semitism into regional and national politics. The context of his remarks and actions are significant. This was the Europe of the Dreyfus affair, an affair used by Lueger and his followers after 1897 to incite hatred. Ritual murder cases were a continuing feature of late Habsburg history, and the authenticity of ritual murder had been endorsed by the mayor and party leader himself. Twelve ritual murder trials took place in the Habsburg Empire between 1867 and 1914, and a pogrom in Galicia in 1898, a pogrom so violent that a general revolt threatened and martial law had to be declared. The physical safety of Jews in the multinational realm, at least the safety of lower-class Jews, was not as secure as Stefan Zweig has implied, and there are recorded instances of anti-Semitic violence during Lueger's mayoralty.[39] Lueger and some of his lieutenants routinely exploited anti-Jewish developments in neighboring countries for whatever advantage they might afford. Actual restraint, or the threat of restraint by the imperial government, limited violence against Jews by the mayor and his followers. There were also the subtler restraints imposed by nearly a century of peace. The aggressions released by World War I would destroy not only traditional obedience to higher authority as well as the traditional authority itself, but also loosen customary moral inhibitions. The postwar increase in violence was an escalation of what had formerly been merely verbal hostility; anti-Semites of the 1920s did not have to create any new arguments because these had already been legitimized by Lueger and the Christian Social party.

Lueger's brand of anti-Semitism had been at least partly anticipated. Almost precisely two centuries earlier, Abraham a Sancta Clara (1644–1709), an Augustinian monk, mastered "the complex instrument of mass appeal"[40] as no one else in Germany or Austria was to do until Lueger. A violent, though never opportunistic, anti-Semite unlike Lueger, Abraham nonetheless "responded to the pressure of the masses," and "became . . . one of the chief carriers to spread [hatred of the Jews] in his century."[41] Although the origins of Lueger's anti-Semitism are obscure — there is no indication that he was influenced by Abraham — anti-Semitism had reappeared with periodical intensity in Austria during times of crisis. This recurring aspect of Austrian anti-Semitism sometimes also emerged in Lueger's behavior in times of crisis, thereby indicating that here he was completely traditional.

Richard S. Levy has suggested that a distinction between anti-Jewish sentiments and anti-Semitism ought to be drawn to clarify Lueger's significance:

The first is endemic in Austria and Europe in general; the second is a new phenomenon of the late 1870s, and, even though it feeds off tradition, it entails actions either directly against Jews or the exploitation of anti-Jewish sentiment for other political ends. The difference between action and sentiment is the difference between traditional suspicion, contempt, or hatred of Jews and antisemitism, the political harnessing and on-going cultivation of that feeling. The former can issue in an occasional pogrom, an occasional tract, or the retention of legal discrimination; the latter can result in genocide. Lueger was an anti-Semite, not just a Jew-hater. His massive influence on Austrian politics has to do with . . . the entrance of antisemitism into the political culture of Austrian life. It becomes a permanent institution embodied in parties, propaganda societies, its own press. In the modern era it always entails a broader world-view and sees the Jewish question as insoluble unless other grievous problems are also faced — liberalism, socialism, constitutionalism, vivisection, the gold standard, etc. Once its political potential has been demonstrated and after a certain point it possesses a dynamic and rationale of its own; it can be relied upon to produce a certain kind of support for political ventures from the socially threatened.[42]

Although Lueger's university years marked the zenith of prosperous Liberalism and neo-Enlightenment influence, following the Austro-Prussian War of 1866, Pan-German members of at least one student fraternity attributed "Austrian patriotism to the dominance of 'oriental elements' — that is, Jews."[43] Anti-Semitism spread and intensified during the hard times following the crash of 1873.

Ignaz Mandl had employed anti-Semitism during an 1877 election

campaign and Lueger had been praised by the anti-Semite Karl von Zerboni following the Fogerty affair of 1882. For the next few years, Lueger
was evidently uncertain about supporting the anti-Semites.[44] In 1886 in
the municipal council he praised a Jew, Adolf Fischhof, one of the famous
revolutionary leaders of 1848. "No one of the gentlemen here in this hall
can hold a candle to him and no one alive can compare to his political
past, service to the city of Vienna and to his integrity.'"[45] However, in 1887
Lueger placed himself squarely on the side of the anti-Semites by supporting Schönerer's anti-immigration bill in parliament. As Lueger drew closer
to the clericals, the frequency and intensity of his anti-Semitic remarks
increased. In February 1889 he broke with Mandl. A few months later,
he was receiving advice from an anti-Liberal about how to achieve the
maximum anti-Semitic effect in Northern Bohemia when he delivered a
speech there on September first.[46] By the following year the anti-Semitism
that was to be significant in Lueger's rise and would mark significant aspects of his politics for the duration of his career had become a feature
of his public personality.

Already he had coined the word "Judeo-Magyar," which won him thousands of votes. As time passed, Lueger's anti-Semitism assumed a more
threatening form than name-calling. During the centennial of the French
Revolution in 1889, the Panama Canal scandal broke in France. Sensa-
tional revelations about bribery and corruption among the highest officials, and about Jewish middlemen, were given prominent coverage in Viennese papers. Lueger was doubtlessly referring to this in parliament when,
during a lengthy anti-Semitic speech in February 1890,[47] he stated that "if
revolution should break out in France, not the archbishop of Paris, and
no longer poor monks would be shot, but it would become unpleasant
for other people."[48] Lueger was to perfect this sort of thinly veiled anti-
Jewish threat over the next fifteen years.

During the 1890s Lueger and his party also attacked the alleged preponderance of Jews in some professions,[49] and particularly in the university medical school.[50] One of the few to oppose this aspect of anti-Semitism
was the rabbi Dr. Joseph Samuel Bloch. A parliamentary representative
from Galicia, Bloch had exposed both the fraudulence of *Der Talmudjude*,
a book that "sought to prove the depravity of the Jews by means of ex-
tracts from the Talmud,"[51] and of its author, Canon August Rohling, who
claimed expertise as a specialist on Judaism. In 1891 in parliament, Bloch
also exposed the hypocrisy of Karl Türk, the German Nationalist who,
together with his family, had been treated by a Jewish doctor after Türk
had delivered an anti-Semitic diatribe. And during the same session, Bloch

called Lueger's attention to the upsetting effects of anti-Semitism on children, an outcome that Lueger denied, for he claimed that children didn't attend "our meetings." Bloch also asserted that Christian children had on two occasions struck out the eyes of Jewish students and had been sentenced by the court.[52]

Anticipating Nazi rhetoric, Lueger accused Jews of being "the destructive element" in every country: "Whenever a state has allowed the Jews to become powerful, the state has soon collapsed, while in those states where they understood enough to isolate the Jews, the monarchical principle was saved, the people were saved from many things they would otherwise have suffered."[53] This unoriginal aspect of Lueger's anti-Semitism — it was common practice of anti-Semites to accuse Jews thus — remained relatively constant, though he sometimes moderated his words after he became mayor. If Jews wanted to live among non-Jews, they had to subordinate themselves. He stressed this in a speech to his inner-city constituents in 1905.[54] In the relatively early phase of his parliamentary career (1892), Lueger had stated that the Jew was behind all that was negative in modern life. For Lueger, the Jew alone ruled; for the Jew alone was there prosperity.[55]

In the early 1890s, Lueger also attacked Austrian schools as a training ground for Jewish professionals. Accordingly, the "Jewish Liberal" teacher, as well as the "Jewish press," were the most dangerous enemies within the later Jewish menace, not only because of their secular and anti-Catholic bias, but also because they allegedly served the implicitly alien Jewish nation.[56] Whether they were "concealed" as members of the Liberal German School Association (Deutscher Schulverein) or occupied chairs at the university (almost no Jews had chairs at the university), Jewish educators were singled out, as individuals and as a group, as special targets of Christian Social gibes. This aspect of his anti-Semitism, like the Jewish subordination theme, also remained constant. Although he sometimes trimmed his sails to obtain Jewish financial backing for one of his municipal building projects, sought the counsel of baptized Jewish financial advisers, such as August Lohnstein of the Länderbank, or even praised Baron Albert Rothschild after he had granted the city a free right-of-way through his property for water lines, Lueger never altered his opposition to Jews in Austrian education. A public statement to this effect in November 1907 involved him in the last anti-Semitic controversy of his career, the Wahrmund affair.

No other aspect of Lueger's anti-Semitism resulted in more protracted or acrimonious disputes, for some of his adversaries, who often were not Jews, numbered among the empire's most articulate people. They defended their positions with skill, carried the battle into the Christian Social camp, and exposed Lueger and his party for the unscrupulous manipulators they were. But the reasoned and often trenchant replies of oppositional intellectuals had little apparent effect on Lueger or on any of his followers, who continued to use anti-Semitism much as before, probably reckoning this as no more than another aspect of maintaining and extending their power. Only Lueger, and probably also Gessmann among the party hierarchy, may have grasped the potentialities of modern political propaganda inherent in their insistence on party, faith, and sometimes also on race, as prerequisites for teaching, and for other appointments.

Lueger understood the importance of education as a means to advancement and to control. He owed his first rise in no small measure to academic excellence, after all, and later to having applied his knowledge, though this was tempered by experience, a pragmatic knack, and often by intuitive understanding. And he had most certainly studied the Liberal management of teaching appointments in Vienna's elementary and secondary schools, and was thus prepared to refine such management techniques once power was his.[57] During his mayoralty campaign in the mid-1890s, Lueger gave a foretaste of what was to come. The specific target of this Christian Social attack was Hermann Nothnagel, a famous physician and teacher on the university medical staff. Though a non-Jew, Nothnagel was hated by leading Christian Socials, and especially by Lueger, because he was a prominent defender of Jews. Nothnagel had probably become a marked man as early as 1891 when he declared "at the opening meeting of the Society to Combat Antisemitism . . . that antisemitism was a disgrace and that its consequences were degeneration and barbarism."[58] Both the name Nothnagel and the physical appearance of this Prussian lent themselves to the ridicule of his enemies. The name translates as "makeshift," "stopgap," or "emergency hook," and his appearance was described by an astute observer. This was Sigmund Freud, who would abandon abstinence from tobacco when Emperor Franz Joseph refused to sanction Lueger's election to mayor, and "smoke . . . a cigar to celebrate."[59] Freud characterized Nothnagel as "a germanic caveman, . . . completely fair hair, head, cheeks, neck, eyebrows, all covered with hair and hardly any difference in color between skin and hair. Two enormous warts, one on the cheek and one on the bridge of the nose; no great beauty, but certainly unusual."[60] Nothnagel remained a favorite target of Christian Social abuse. Lueger once implied in the provincial diet that only Nothnagel's greed for profit made him oppose the moving of the clinics to the city's outskirts, because he could reach patients more swiftly in the center.[61] On another occasion, Lueger withheld from Liberals the use of municipal assembly halls and schools for lectures, because they refused to "abandon" the lackey of the Jews Nothnagel. Lueger demanded that all speakers and lecture topics be approved by the Christian Social–controlled city council. Though Nothnagel had never even delivered lectures to this group of Liberals, their leaders refused to negotiate on the issue of censorship in any case, and requested Lueger to reconsider his decision on the use of the halls. After all, he controlled the city council. Smiling, Lueger replied: "In all legal and technical-administrative matters, I am the cleverer, and allow no one else to intervene. But so far as anti-Semitism goes, any old hand is as clever as I, or cleverer!" In this way the Liberals were refused the use of the halls.[62] At the time of Nothnagels' death in 1905, Lueger's first vice mayor, Josef Neumayer, who the same year was quoted in the municipal council as saying that "so far as he was concerned, all Jews could be burned alive,"[63] remarked to Lueger that "we need not react to other 'great' events [Nothnagel, etc.]."[64]

The occasion for Lueger's 1895 attack on Nothnagel was provided during a budgetary debate in the provincial diet over the amount of support to be given to the university medical schools. Following anti-Semitic slurs on university educators by Josef Gregorig,[65] Lueger's supporters received a rebuff they long remembered.[66] The remarkable feature of this incident was that the Jews were eloquently defended by Laurenz Müllner, a Catholic priest, who was at the same time chancellor of the University of Vienna. Also remarkable was the fact that Müllner's speech was extemporaneous. On January 4, 1895 Müllner, a well-known teacher in his own right, lived up to his title of *Rector Magnificus* as well. Gregorig had ridiculed the university as "Jew-infested." Punning on Nothnagel's name, Gregorig added: "Only yesterday I read that once again a new . . . Jewish professor had just been appointed, and if you look at the whole business out there, you'll see how the holy halls have been transformed into a mumblatorium on an emergency hook [*"in ein an einem Nothnagel hängendes Mauscholeum"*].[67]

While Gregorig's remarks elicited mirth and applause from the anti-Semites, Müllner castigated him in his retort for making unsubstantiated generalizations and insulting the university and individual faculty members. Even professional educators could no longer generalize about individual disciplines as Gregorig had done, Müllner added. There was no longer such a thing as "a *doctor universalis*":

Study itself makes one modest . . . , and I expected here, least of all, to hear it flatly stated . . . that we have retrogressed. . . . A colleague was specifically named, Professor Nothnagel. . . . I don't know what connection delegate Gregorig has to natural science. (Boisterous amusement.) [Gregorig was a shirt maker.] But if he has such a connection, I recommend an easier book to read, though I think he may have a little trouble studying it, and this is . . . the physiological psychology of Wundt. There, he can orientate himself, perhaps, about what is thought of Professor Nothnagel. . . . Furthermore, . . . I would like to say something as a Catholic scholar. I believe Dante was perhaps a Christian. I ask only that you examine his 'Divine Comedy' and read Dante's remarks about a Semite, about Averoës. Dante's was a great spirit and Thomas Aquinas was a man of high nobility, and also a saint; the tone of such men's remarks, even about Jewish scholars, is completely different, even where agreement is impossible. Every year I necessarily refute Spinoza, but I say it here . . . that though I refute his system, I bow nonetheless before that great spirit and before that noble man.[68]

Müllner's words only irritated the anti-Semites. Lueger, who twice interrupted Müllner, and who was obviously stung by his remarks, revealed his racism and the "differential" aspect of his anti-Semitism by discounting Spinoza — for whom Lueger said he also had "great respect" — as a typical Jew. Spinoza, Lueger informed his listeners, had been persecuted by his coreligionists and racial comrades, not by Christians. That, he added, was something "a priest of the Catholic religion should and must know."[69] The noble Jews had all vanished and those who remained were the ones Lueger fought. He implied that as a Catholic priest Müllner was a traitor for having defended them. Lueger's words were cheered by his followers. Ernst Schneider interjected that Müllner was an "honorary rabbi" and that he should get circumcised.[70]

Having rejected humanistic considerations, Lueger suggested that the only values that truly counted were the ones that served palpable political goals, in this case to be determined by himself, and without reference to earlier mores or ethical considerations. And the tone of Lueger's remarks and the responses of his supporters suggested that the values themselves, which reflected a spontaneity, would be determined by an irrational interaction between speaker and audience. Lueger the "artist and . . . actor . . . unknowingly [fell] more and more into the mental attitude of the audience in the galleries," as Bloch observed.[71]

Such an interactive politics may have contributed to another significant anti-Semitic incident, again an attack on the Jewish members of the medical faculty, in 1903. In any case, Lueger's behavior in 1903 revealed that his demagogy remained undiminished. Moreover, the Christian Socials then tried to extend their control over Vienna's hospitals, Kielmansegg's realm. In 1903, as in 1895, the budget was under debate. For some two weeks before the incident, Lueger's party in the provincial diet had been attacking the ostensible failure of primary schools to deliver the educational goods. One of the central figures in the new incident was Hermann Bielohlawek, a merchant and something of a court jester among the Christian Socials, who flaunted his ignorance and Philistinism. According to Bielohlawek, students often left the schools with their heads stuffed full of useless knowledge and as ignorant of basic reading and arithmetic skills as when they had arrived. The fortunate ones received a more useful education only after they reached the university.[72] As they had for some years, the Christian Socials also criticized modern education for undermining religious faith. Bielohlawek implicated the Jews in the process, making it clear that his party did not oppose them because of their religion. Instead, he shared with Schönerer the viewpoint that the race itself was at fault.[73] In referring to the recent Hilsner ritual murder trial in Bohemia and the Dreyfus affair, Bielohlawek aroused "lively applause and amusement" when he announced that deporting one Jew to Devil's Island where Dreyfus had been imprisoned was insufficient; only after all Jews had been sent there would "there be quiet in our fatherland Austria."[74] In a subsequent diet session, Leopold Steiner, one of Lueger's closest friends, criticized the hospitals by painting the horrors of vivisection practices at the university anatomical institutes, to the growing indignation of his listeners. Steiner demanded that the government enforce an earlier decree prescribing control measures.[75] He then described various malpractices against hospital patients by implicitly Jewish doctors, concluding that vivisection was responsible for inuring the doctors to patients' suffering. Only when administrative officials had replaced the doctors as leaders of the hospitals would such abuses cease."[76] It seemed clear which party would provide the administrative officials, at least to Kielmansegg, who opposed Steiner's criticism by correcting technical points and suggesting that some aspects of it were exaggerated.[77]

Steiner's vivisection criticism rallied the Christian Socials to his support. Josef Scheicher said that he wished Steiner's proposal had included a demand for the abolition of vivisection "once and for all,"[78] but the university chancellor, Ritter von Escherich, was indignant "over the grave insults" leveled at "the entire medical faculty and the medical profession."[79] This in turn elicited a Christian Social interpellation that included quotations from a 1902 pamphlet *Murder in the Service of Science* by Dr. Paul Förster. A party anti-Semite in Germany who held a Ph.D., Förster luridly depicted the horrors of vivisection on man and animals.[80] The interpellation ended with a demand for the abolition of vivisection and the "strict surveillance of all hospitals," and, in particular, those that predominantly treated the poor.[81] On October 28 the diet was the scene of Christian Social attempts to hinder the promotion of a Jewish doctor over his "more deserving" Christian compatriots, and of further revelations about vivisection and medical malpractice allegedly perpetrated by Jewish doctors. With the support of anti-Semitic shouts of other Christian Socials, Steiner denounced as mendacious and distorted the reports of "the Viennese Jewish press" about the vivisection affair, the diet, and its individual members.[82] Two days later, Lueger delivered a speech in support of a motion of urgency begun by himself and signed by other leading Christian Socials. In the motion he rejected as "insolent" a declaration of the university medical college faculty protesting the interference of the diet in the vivisection matter, and its meddling in the affairs of the medical institute.[83] Denying that either the medical college or the doctors' profession had been attacked, Lueger stated that the entire incident had been blown out of proportion so that "certain men and animal knackers can act as though they alone were the doctors. The college of professors," he added, "should look to itself, and rather endeavor to weed out certain elements from the doctor's profession which only injure it, so that finally, a Christian conviction will return to these circles."[84]

Lueger's words were cheered as usual in Christian Social assemblies, and subsequent speakers supported his remarks. When they had finished, Lueger summarized his thoughts on the vivisection issue by remarking that it was the duty of the diet to protect poor people in the hospitals from vivisection. The doctors placed too much trust in scientific progress by "so-called graduate doctors who learned in the medical faculty." Great progress in medicine, Lueger assured his listeners, "had actually been made by laymen," just as progress in legal education had usually been achieved by the laity. When torture was abolished, this had been due to someone who had possessed "no more than a warm heart for mankind." Scholars should practice modesty. "If a scholar is so haughty that he says that no one else has anything to say [interjection: Then he's certainly a Jew!] then I say: my dear scholar, if you can make a blade of grass one day that a cow can eat [amusement] then I'll take my hat off to you; but so long as you are unable, then you're a quack like the rest of us [amusement]."[85] Lueger concluded by adding an amendment to his motion that all the "proposals, inquiries and debates" about the issue at hand were to be printed and distributed among the people, thus suggesting his appreciation of the value of this topic as agitation. His original motion and amendment were unanimously approved and Lueger was heartily applauded, cheered, and congratulated for many minutes after his speech.

In two succeeding sessions Kielmansegg and the Socialist Karl Seitz voiced the opinions of moderates who must have been appalled at the spectacle of the mayor of Vienna and leader of what was rapidly becoming the leading imperial party denigrating scholars, celebrating amateurs, and calling for the "weeding out [of] certain elements from the doctor's profession," by which Lueger had meant the Jews. The satirists and caricaturists had a field day. (See illustrations.) Kielmansegg made the important points that most of the abuses cited in the pamphlet *Murder in the Service of Science* referred to foreign incidents, and that considering the many patients treated each year, often with complicated diseases, complaints about malpractice were negligible. The reputation of Vienna's hospitals was deservedly high and would remain that way as long as they were under his jurisdiction. While Kielmansegg was applauded and congratulated by many for seeming to uphold the majority opinion,[86] Seitz, who spoke the following day, was heckled by Gessmann, Bielohlawek, and Lueger for defending vivisection.[87] The great physician Billroth, Seitz reminded his listeners, could never have performed his miraculous operations had he not first experimented on thousands of animals.[88] Moreover, the patients who had experienced successful operations owed their recovery in no small measure to the thousands who had lain on the operating table before them.[89] The real reason the Christian Socials had provoked this incident, Seitz added, was that rich Jews, who were symbolized by the learned doctors, were the most dangerous enemies of the Christian Socials.[90] Bielohlawek, who spoke after Seitz, questioned whether the Christian Socials had agitated against science or the doctors at all, but Lueger agreed with Seitz that the whole issue revolved around the Jewish question. In speaking thus Lueger gave form to the incoherent anxieties of his followers, and possibly also to his own subconscious fears. In any case, Lueger's words distilled his feelings about Jews in higher education and revealed dissatisfaction with Vienna's hospitals as he alleged they were controlled by the Jews:

When at last Jewish corpses are dissected, perhaps the doctors will then learn still more than they can from dissecting ours. . . . The medical school in Vienna won world fame at a time when only Christian professors . . . a Skoda, Oppolzer, or however they were called, laid the foundation for the medical school's fame of the university of Vienna. But as soon as the Jews got in, the fame of this school in Vienna sank low [cry: So it is!] and when the accusation is made that we're opponents of science, then I say, no, we're not opponents of science, but we do oppose science being misused merely for the advantage of isolated dissolute, brutish, and brutalized individuals.

The medical school will only thrive again and the hospitals once more become places of refuge, whether for rich or poor, when the principle — out with the Jews from the university and the hospitals — is enforced, so that we Christians can be humanely treated [hearty applause].[91]

Despite Lueger's continuing demagogic sallies, the furor over the hospitals gradually subsided, and the whole incident served more to reinforce the image of Lueger and the Christian Socials as Philistines, rather than as anti-Semites, at least among the Liberal cartoonists. (See illustration.) Karl Kraus saw both aspects. He commented that the Liberal dialectic had given place to the Christian Social, and that the new tone was doubtless worse. Uglier and lower than flaunting education, as the Liberals had done, was flaunting snobbery over ignorance. To be a leader of the people in the Luegerian sense meant opening the floodgates to mass instincts and inundating defenseless culture. Two Christian Social program points had emerged from the affair: "The Jews should have anatomical equality the same as Christians, that is, should be dissected as well as Christians; but while preparing them for equality as objects of medical study, they should lose their equality as subjects of medical study, be driven from the university and the hospitals."[92]

By 1903 Lueger usually had the last word on political matters in Vienna, and thus it was with the hospital affair, though this particular utterance carried an unintentionally ironic ring. When later in November, during a municipal council session, a Christian Social, Karl Glössl, described the traffic in human skeletons of poor Catholics between the hospitals and private purchasers, thus depriving the deceased of Christian burials, Lueger agreed with Glössl that it was "downright depressing. . . . I certainly have nothing against it that corpses serve learning. . . . But if that is right, and if that is so important, then all men should participate: the rich with the poor, the Jews with the Christians. Justice for all! [Lively applause.]."[93]

Unlike the Lueger-Müllner exchange of 1895 or the hospital incident of October–November 1903, the Wahrmund affair four years later was triggered neither by a budgetary debate nor a legislative conflict, but by a Lueger welcoming speech. Privately, he claimed that his remarks had been prompted by the desire to please the many priests attending the Sixth Katholikentag in November 1907 whom he greeted in his official position as mayor.[94] Publicly, he insisted that he had been misunderstood, that his words had been directed against nationalistic violence in the universities.[95] Yet, Lueger's remarks may not have been as extemporaneous as he would have liked some to believe. As early as July 22, 1907, Reichsrat member Ernst Count Sylva-Tarouca informed Lueger that Cardinal Gruscha had inquired whether Tarouca would organize the Katholikentag, "since this was the wish of the Austrian episcopacy." Gruscha "intended to precede [the meeting] with a collective pastoral epistle against the *Los-von-Rom* Movement and the anti-dynastic and anti-Austrian tendencies of the radicals." Tarouca expressly requested Lueger's support and advice "in this affair," which he had already mentioned to him the preceding winter.[96] Whatever the true inspiration for his remarks, in the furor that followed, the anti-Semitism of his Katholikentag speech was largely obscured in a larger controversy over secular versus religious education.[97] During his welcome, Lueger had stated that much had been achieved in the Viennese schools, secular and religious teaching had been successfully integrated. And yet, another great task remained, "the conquering . . . of the university." No longer should the universities be a seedbed for revolution, upheaval, and atheism, no longer should teachers have to be armed with clubs and whips to impart knowledge, as he had read in the papers that it was necessary for them to do: "But there will be a hard struggle. So long as it is possible that among eight newly appointed professors there are seven Jews [indignation], a great struggle must follow until we have come so far that among eight appointed professors there are seven Christians. [Applause.] I don't believe that any of us will slacken."[98] Socialists, Liberals, members of smaller parties and their respective presses, and prestigious scholars such as Friedrich Jodl and Ernst Mach censured or ridiculed Lueger's remarks, Mach stating that Lueger wanted to turn the clock back to the fourteenth century,[99] and that he had no desire to share the fate of such a people and country. Yet, the indignation of the university faculty and that of Lueger's other critics provided but a foretaste of what was to come.

On January 18, 1908, Ludwig Wahrmund, professor of ecclesiastical law at the University of Innsbruck, delivered a lecture in the large municipal hall in Innsbruck, subsequently published as "Catholic Weltanschauung and Free Science."[100] He repeated the lecture in Salzburg. The thrust of Wahrmund's remarks had been anticipated by his earlier criticism of the discrepancies between church dogma and modern scientific inquiry. This had already roused the ire of local church leaders and university administrators, but his most recent attack was the last straw. Wahrmund's lecture was confiscated in many places by the government, and the controversy over clerical or secular education, which had been raging in Austria for many years, erupted anew, spilling over into political life once more. In the Tirol, a long-standing feud between the Christian Socials and Catholic Conservatives prompted the Conservatives to distinguish between Catholics and Christian Socials "in religious respects."[101] In Graz student violence reached such proportions that the university had to be closed for the summer, an action repeated in Innsbruck when Wahrmund returned from a short trip.[102] At length, Wahrmund was transferred to Prague. He secretly signed an agreement accepting an annual ten thousand Kronen research sabbatical from the government for up to two years, and an annual pension of two thousand Kronen should he choose to retire thereafter. By agreeing, Wahrmund thus removed himself from the political scene, for the terms of the new arrangement leaked out and discredited him. Though he soon relinquished the honoraria, he was in any case deprived of a university platform for his agitation.

The Wahrmund affair had at least two significant aftereffects. In the autumn of 1908 Freiherr von Beck resigned as prime minister, in part because he had lost the support of Archduke Franz Ferdinand, who thought Beck had "let Wahrmund down too lightly."[103] In the literary realm, the Wahrmund affair helped inspire Arthur Schnitzler's play *Professor Bernhardi*, which characterized the ignoble actions of some of the principal actors in the original affair.

Lueger, who by 1907 could do no wrong, at least in the opinion of Christian Social publicists and apparently also in the eyes of the archduke,[104] emerged with his reputation enhanced as a defender of Catholic education. At the height of the affair, he was kept posted by Alfred Ebenhoch, the minister of agriculture, who seemed both casual and irritated by it all. To him, the affair was a cloud in the sky that would soon pass away; "Wahrmund on every corner. . . . How will it end? It drives one crazy."[105]

Two weeks after Lueger's remarks, a minor Christian Social paper, the *Badener und Mödlinger Bezirksnachrichten*, published "the authentic meaning" of Lueger's speech, at least as it was intended to be understood by the party rank and file. The editor of this political weekly, Hans Arnold Schwer, one of the younger generation of Christian Socials, was municipal councillor, sometime playwright,[106] and vigorous defender of "Christian culture." He had also had a somewhat minor, if vociferous, role in the Hilsner case, having written a polemic intended to silence the demands of Thomas Masaryk for Hilsner's retrial. Schwer claimed that Hilsner had murdered not one, but two Christian girls.[107] In a front-page *Bezirksnachrichten* article, "A Jewish Trick," such issues as educational philosophy, freedom of speech among educators, and the threat to freedom of scientific inquiry were subordinated to the "threatening character of the progressive Jewish infestation among university professors." According to the article, Lueger "had emphasized nothing other than what he had had to emphasize in his entire anti-Semitic past." The *Bezirksnachrichten* implied that Germans should maintain unity in the face of Jewish attempts to sow dissent.[108]

In the municipal council, Lueger brushed aside objections from the Socialists that he had exceeded his authority by welcoming the clerical parties at the Katholikentag in his official position as mayor. The Socialists asserted that Lueger had not spoken for "many thousands of Viennese who did not belong to the clerical party, but who, in opposition to the tendencies represented at the Katholikentag, were deeply disquieted by the serious threat to the development of the entire culture." Ridiculing the author of this challenge, Lueger asserted that there were "many things" outside the official statutes that he was obliged to do as mayor. Had he not attended this Catholic occasion in which "cardinals, archbishops and bishops had participated," he would have been "a coward," and betrayed his Catholicism as well. He had greeted the participants in the name of the majority Catholic population as "a courteous mayor of Vienna, the imperial capital and residence," and would continue to do so whether the Socialists liked it or not.[109]

The Müllner-Lueger exchange, Vienna hospital incident, and Wahrmund affair revealed Lueger's anti-Semitism toward Jews in higher education. Other, more casually anti-Semitic remarks underlined his fundamental assumptions about the extent to which Jews were to be tolerated, in which areas of endeavor, and in what capacities. Lueger stated that he respected pious Jews[110] and Hermann Bielohlawek subsequently added that he respected the religion but despised the race.[111] However, Lueger's distinction suggests that he was less tolerant of Jews who were inconspicuous about their religion. He was suspicious of those who tried partly to assimilate. Individuals with semi-Jewish parentage who had become baptized Christians and staunch Catholics, such as Vice Mayor Josef Porzer, or those of partly Jewish descent, such as Gessmann, but whose Catholicism was beyond question, were awarded Lueger's toleration. He needed such men regardless of their heritage because of their ability, and particularly Gessmann, who was a gifted and ruthless organizer. However, Lueger became uneasy when identities were blurred, whether culturally, religiously, or racially. "Authenticity" was the thing.[112] Lueger wanted to know whether someone was a *Mandl oder ein Weibl* (man or a woman). Blurred identities created uncertainties and impaired his apparent need to categorize, to place people and things and qualities in "proper" relationships and order. This need, which may have developed during his upbringing, when social hierarchy was much clearer and more distinct than it would be in the changing, dynamic society of fin de siècle Austria, was reinforced by his formal education, profession, and experience: he was, after all, a lawyer and insisted on legalistic categories if the need presented itself. Lueger's insistence on clear-cut distinctions, particularly as they affected the Jews, was shared by other prominent Christian Socials. This insistence sometimes manifested itself as hostility, which suggests the nature of the obstacle that impeded Jewish advancement in late imperial Austria and thereafter. Christian Social leaders rejected Jews for allegedly lacking intrinsic qualities believed to be possessed by "Christians" or, to some Christian Socials, possessed by "Aryans."[113] Dynastic loyalism, anti-liberalism, and clericalism were defenses for some, to preserve a stable, traditional order. Jews who could assimilate and become "hidden foes" stood for the opposite.

And yet, despite his open or veiled anti-Semitism, some Jews defended Lueger and his administration, fearing, perhaps, that worse was to come once he departed the scene. This impression is conveyed by an anonymous and ungrammatical letter to Lueger from a "good patriotic Hungarian Jew" who, though he was an opponent of the mayor "on principle," nonetheless admired his "administrative talent." The letter contained a home remedy and was evidently received by Lueger while he was on one of his periodic cures:

> I convey the feelings of all Israelite Hungarian Jews when I wish you complete recovery and still more decades at the helm of the imperial city of Vienna as mayor.—I have the conviction that Austrian Jews also think this way, for if someone like Bilohlawek [sic] comes to power, then woe to Israel in Vienna.[114]

Here again, Lueger was different things to different people, and sometimes had it both ways.

When it came to discriminating against Jews in cultural matters, Lueger was notably less successful than in the professional realm. Although the Christian Socials might withhold promotions from deserving Jewish teachers and municipal officials, and thus immediately achieve the desired effect, Lueger learned early in his mayoralty that cultural anti-Semitism — the exclusion of Jews from cultural affairs organized or run by the Christian Social municipal government — posed thorny problems. Other party members were slower to understand these problems and continued to pursue ineffectual cultural policies long after these had been discredited or had failed altogether. The fact that they could continue to do so without Lueger's interference suggests his increasing caution toward cultural anti-Semitism, or perhaps his growing indifference, or an expression of the divergent tendencies among the ruling party that appear to have become more frequent as Lueger's health deteriorated. In any event, Lueger's control over the Christian Socials was never perfect, and the party machine sometimes functioned most inefficiently, if at all.[115] The "Aryan Theater" fiasco illustrates several such failures.

This theater was in part a result of attempts by Adam Müller-Guttenbrunn, a writer and unsuccessful theater director, to make good his earlier failure, while at the same time trying to revive a more traditional Germanic culture. According to Müller-Guttenbrunn, German cultural decline in Austria had been precipitated by Jewish literary predominance. Another impetus toward the creation of the theater was the desire for quick profits, the speculation by private citizens that their investments in the theater at a favorable rate of interest would be speedily rewarded. Still another impetus was the desire by outlying district residents to create a major "suburban" theater, for most of the principal playhouses were in the first district.

Both Müller-Guttenbrunn and the theater enthusiasts revealed their anti-Semitism by excluding Jews as actors or playwrights from the new undertaking. They thereby probably hoped to capitalize on the prevailing anti-Jewish feelings of the Christian Socials and German Nationalists. Things went wrong from the start. Intended as an important event in the fiftieth anniversary celebration of Franz Joseph's ascension to the throne, the opening of the "Aryan Theater," or Kaiserjubiläums-Stadttheater as it was more formally called, was clouded by the recent assassination of Empress Elisabeth. Lueger had shown interest in a popular and implicitly anti-Semitic theater project as early as 1890.[116] Although he had been a member of the Jubiläums Theater Association since 1896,[117] he criticized the opening night play, Heinrich von Kleist's *Die Hermannsschlacht*, a classical "Aryan work" by an "Aryan playwright," in the thinking of Müller-Guttenbrunn. At a banquet after the premiere Lueger told the guests that a play in which a wench threw her lover to a bear did not correspond to the tastes of the Viennese, that they did not want "a disgraceful play" like Kleist's *Hermannsschlacht*.[118] Lueger's words were ridiculed from Vienna to Königsberg as proof of Christian Social philistinism. Although the mayor and party leader was much more cautious thereafter in his remarks about theater matters, he still continued for a time openly to defend the enterprise. During the following summer, for example, he boasted before an assembly of the Christian Social Workers' Association that his party had created its "own theater . . . to which . . . Christian men can go and take their families, without fearing that the ears of their poor children will be dirtied by smut,"[119] as he implied they were dirtied in theaters operated by Jews.

Lueger's biographer Hawlik has pointed out that Jewish actors sometimes participated in Jubiläumstheater productions and that some Jubiläumstheater works were written by Jews.[120] Whenever it became known that Jews were overtly or covertly participating in Aryan Theater productions, anti-Semitic papers would invariably call Müller-Guttenbrunn to task. Such incidents were comparatively few during his administration, and the toleration of Jewish collaboration may well have been calculated by Müller-Guttenbrunn to soften Jewish hostility toward himself, particularly after it became apparent that the party theater was failing.[121] The abandonment of the "Aryan clause" occurred during the administration of his successor, Rainer Simons, but only over the strident objections of some Christian Socials. Anti-Jewish plays were, however, performed under Müller-Guttenbrunn, thereby achieving one of the party's central ideological purposes. Such works included *Der Rechtschaffene,* about the Offenheim corruption trial of the 1870s; *Helden der Feder,* depicting Jewish influence-peddling in the Viennese literary world; *Eigenthum,* portraying the victim of Jewish financial machinations; and a mutilated version of *The Merchant of Venice.* These efforts were intended to proclaim the beliefs of Aryan Theater supporters, though they failed for artistic and other reasons. *The Merchant of Venice,* an early production, enjoyed the greatest agitational success of the four but was in all other ways fully unsuccessful. It created a cause célèbre and anticipated a similar agitational use of this work in Nazi Vienna. (See illustrations.)[122]

The timing of Müller-Guttenbrunn's version in October 1899 was a happy coincidence for the anti-Semites, taking place as it did a month after the second conviction of Alfred Dreyfus for treason. This development no doubt intensified the critical controversy surrounding the play, for public opinion had become polarized: the Liberals condemned the injustice of the verdict in France; the anti-Semites unanimously approved.[123] Lueger and many other leading Christian Socials attended a performance. One Christian Social observer remarked "that such a play would doubtless make a more powerful impression than an electoral meeting," while a Liberal commented on the barbarousness of the audience, which "behaved as though . . . Hilsner . . . had been playing Shylock."[124]

The Merchant of Venice might soon have disappeared from the critical scene had not a reviewer from the *Wiener Volksbothe,* a small Christian Social paper that catered to the janitorial mind, mistakenly hailed Grillparzer as the author. This blunder prompted a sardonic letter to the *Volksbothe* from an unknown writer signing himself "William Shakespeare," who demanded that his authorship be acknowledged. The *Volksbothe* promptly did so, and apologized for its error, adding that no "Freemason like Grillparzer [could have written] a play [of such obvious anti-Semitic tendencies.] Grillparzer's body must, no doubt, [have been spinning] in its grave, but would now [come to rest in] its original position . . . , because Mr. Shakespeare had so promptly corrected the *Volksbothe.* The publication of his letter had thus squared accounts."[125]

Responding to the original *Volksbothe* blunder, a Social Democratic critic "rejoiced . . . that the anti-Semitic and anti-English movement had been strong enough to refute the Jewish lies about Shakespeare being the author of the *Merchant.*"[126] Word of the *Volksbothe* blunder spread as far as England, prompting the *Manchester Guardian* to observe with disdain that Johann König, the editor of the Viennese paper, "was a Christian Social member of a school board 'entrusted with the education of hundreds of children.'"[127] A Liberal paper provided the last well-aimed shot in the affair, with a telling revelation of the disgust many felt over the prostitution of art for party purposes and over the attempt to capitalize on contemporary hatred. The deeper meaning of the play had been obscured. Shakespeare's Shylock had been cheated of his justice

> through bad sophistry. Although that justice may be reprehensible, the wrong done him is even more egregious. This old, greedy, hate-filled Shylock who insists upon his bond, who rejects three and even ten times his money and remorselessly covets that overdue pound of flesh, this dogged struggler for his justice — what sort of an idealist is he compared to the 'pedlars' who scorn him and applaud the trampling of his justice as a victory of the good cause![128]

There was no reply from the Christian Socials to this comment. So far as they were concerned, "the quality of mercy" toward the Jews was always strained.

Müller-Guttenbrunn and others involved in the Aryan theatrical venture were dissatisfied with the "mildness" of his anti-Jewish productions. Accordingly, he tried to stage more venomously antagonistic plays. However, such out-and-out anti-Semitic works as *Harte Hände, Söhne Israels,* and *Die Büsserin,* all of which pointed forward to one of the most violent Nazi films, *Jud Süss,* were forbidden by the censor. A residue of restraint, it seems, existed at some governmental levels, at least before World War I. Not to be put off by official prohibition, Müller-Guttenbrunn published the first two works out of his own pocket and distributed thousands of copies. (See illustration.) He was convinced of the ineffectiveness of other anti-Semitic plays by such writers as Ernst Vergani and Jörg Lanz von Liebenfels, evidently one of Hitler's early intellectual mentors, lamenting to Vergani that his play was too honestly objective, and that objectivity was "our old illness," by which Müller-Guttenbrunn probably meant that the play was not anti-Semitic enough.[129] In his last effort as a racist director, Müller-Guttenbrunn proved with *Athara,* depicting the failure of intermarriage, the truth of Jorge Luis Borges's aphorism that "censorship is the mother of the metaphor." In any case, Müller-Guttenbrunn's dissemination of the forbidden plays won him the support of some of the more extreme Christian Social anti-Semites in the provincial diet and was remembered by them as one of his better achievements when he resigned in October 1903 shortly before he went bankrupt.[130]

In the autumn of 1903 during the demise of the Aryan Theater, some Christian Socials proposed the creation of a literary prize of two thousand Kronen to be awarded to an Austrian writer of "Aryan origin" for "an artistically important dramatic work."[131] Such a prize was created and conferred several times during Lueger's mayoralty, on Meinrad Sadil, for example, a Benedictine monk, two of whose plays had been produced in the Aryan Theater, and on Karl Domanig and Eduard Hlatky, among others.[132] That these last two recipients were Lueger partisans and members of Richard von Kralik's circle vindicated an earlier Socialist observation that Christian Social measures to promote Aryan culture had fostered a second literary clique no lovelier than its Liberal counterpart.[133] In this way, even after five years of artistic mediocrity and cultural-political fiascoes, Müller-Guttenbrunn's ideas not only continued to win at least tacit support among some Christian Socials, but also found welcome implementation. A cartoon in the racially anti-Semitic *Kikeriki* commented on the literary prize proposal (see illustration), and afforded a "psychogram" of the prize's authors. In this supposedly complimentary cartoon, a well-dressed Weiskirchner, who became the last Christian Social mayor of Vienna between 1912 and 1919, and Sturm, another anti-Semitic member of the Landtag, are shown trying to free Pegasus,[134] the emblem of artistic inspiration, from a chariot representing the adverse Jewish influence over art and culture. Classical imagery is thus juxtaposed with the symbol of anti-Semitic racism in a blend of antique and contemporary. If one recalls Lueger's classical references and elegant taste in clothing, one can see that in some respects this cartoon reflects his cultural predilections and racial prejudices, as well as those of Sturm and Weiskirchner.

Though Lueger became steadily disenchanted with the Aryan Theater, Müller-Guttenbrunn continued to pursue his ideological convictions till the end. For those who had followed the development of the theater and knew about Müller-Guttenbrunn's racist preoccupations, the underlying intent of *Athara* would have been clear enough. It was well received by the critics. After his bankruptcy, Müller-Guttenbrunn took to reflecting on his recent cultural failure. In one article he proclaimed himself the prophet of a new sociopolitical salvation, whose messiah had perhaps already been born, but who had not yet spoken.[135] He then turned to writing novels. Among them was the anti-Semitic *Gärungen Klärungen*. Both the article and the novel were written under the pseudonym of Franz Josef Gerhold. Müller-Guttenbrunn's career evinced a Péguyian blend of mysticism and cultural politics. Lueger was quintessentially political, by contrast, and far more practical. He never lost sight of the political cost of more adventurist cultural programs. Referring to the theater, he somewhat diffidently warned Müller-Guttenbrunn's successor to look at that bed before he lay down in it, and not to "be surprised if the fleas bite you."[136] This bon mot revealed another facet of Lueger's personality: his refusal to allow himself to be humiliated by failure, at least in public. This tendency, along with his apparently total indifference to contradictory behavior, was demonstrated on many an occasion. Once, for example, Lueger had delivered an anti-Semitic speech in the Leopoldstadt. A few days later at a reception he offered his hand to Alfred Stern, the chairman of the Israelite Religious Community. Stern refused to shake hands with Lueger unless he took back his anti-Semitic remarks. "But you'll still give me your hand," said Lueger, jokingly. When Stern refused to extend his hand, Lueger simply moved on, joking all the while.[137]

Some larger European developments should be sketched in to provide a working context for Lueger's anti-Semitism. Although 1903 had been a quiet year for the great powers of central and eastern Europe, the calm was deceptive and soon to be shattered with far-reaching effects. In February 1904 war broke out between Russia and Japan. Russian politics were transformed, not only because of the defeats suffered by that country, but also as a result of social and economic disruptions that culminated in an unsuccessful revolution the following year. These developments affected events in Austria-Hungary as well. Franz Joseph, seeing the riots and strikes in Russia, and further disruption in major Habsburg industrial centers, had ordered his ministers to prepare legislation granting universal manhood suffrage. Well did he recall the Revolution of 1848, which had brought him to power, and he was wise to have feared the 1905 specter of the earlier upheaval, which this time could have cost him his power.[138] Granting the vote to the workers was intended to forestall this, just as the creation of a duma in Russia by Czar Nicholas II was carried out as a concession for much the same reason.

Alert to the consequences of the franchise reform, which meant a drastic increase in the number of worker voters, the Christian Socials responded with their usual demagogic agitation, blaming Austria's ills on the insidious influence of "Jewish Social Democracy," much as they had blamed "Jewish Liberals" for the woes of the Viennese lower middle class in the 1890s. Here, as before, the Jew remained the constant target. However, a more strident note, and in a more threatening key, resonated through their agitation, because of the revolutionary activity in Russia and the racial tone of the czarist response. There, too, Jews were being blamed for Russia's various ills, but with more immediate and destructive results. Czarist-sponsored pogroms, carried out by bands of thugs known as the "Black Hundreds," terrorized thousands.[139] Many fled and sought refuge in other countries.

Austrian anti-Semites warned of anarchy in the Habsburg Empire should the "Jewish Social Democrats" get the upper hand, in some cases applauding the activities of the "Black Hundreds," and agitating to close Austrian borders to Russian Jews. They were seen literally as the carriers of disease, for a cholera epidemic raged across Russia in the summer of 1905, and less objectively as the carriers of revolutionary contagion, for it seems unlikely that the average person who had escaped from one revolutionary situation with little more than his life would have sought another in a country that served as a haven. Although Lueger took no definite stand on the Russian disorders until late in 1905, waiting as usual for the optimum moment, his feelings could easily be inferred. Earlier that summer he had responded to an inquiry in the municipal council about the effectiveness of border and hostel controls affecting "certain immigrants," by promising to caution the appropriate authorities to be especially watchful. When Franz Schuhmeier questioned Lueger's use of the phrase "certain immigrants," the mayor replied, "I used the same term [as in the inquiry]; I know that the Jews are meant thereby [Amusement.]."[140]

Yet another contemporary development should also be outlined, insofar as it, too, perpetuated ill feeling between Lueger and the Jewish community. This was the longstanding Christian Social agitation against ritual slaughter,[141] which peaked during 1905, a most turbulent year in several ways. Sometimes linked to agitation for the municipal slaughterhouse,[142] demands for prohibition of kosher butchering were ultimately defeated, though not before a lengthy struggle in the municipal council, diet, and even parliament.[143] The defeat of the Christian Socials meant that the rights of a religious minority had been upheld as previously guaranteed by the law.[144] This reaffirmation, however, did little to improve relations between Lueger's party and the Jews.

In the lurid fantasies of some of Lueger's more macabre followers, ritual slaughter was inextricably linked to ritual murder. One anti-Semitic cartoonist even pictured Lueger as the possible victim of such a kosher plot. (See illustration.) By the end of 1905, caricatures of ritual slaughter, ritual murder, and violent Russian revolutionary Jews had merged in a gory synthesis. The Jew, in various guises, thus continued to be the exclusive target of hate, though in a still more protean form than when Lueger had identified him as a *Judeo-Magyar*, *Judenliberaler*, and *Judenfreimaurer*. Intentional or not, such agitation within the context of 1905 events could have led to violence. The *way* Jews were perceived changed drastically in the eyes of an increasing number of Viennese during Lueger's day, through such anti-Semitic caricatures as were appearing in periodicals like *Kikeriki* and *Figaro*.[145]

Lueger himself embodied the wishes of the extremists, often focusing their hatreds and articulating their destructive desires on such occasions as an electoral assembly in December 1905. The tone of the assembly had been set throughout the autumn by a series of sometimes violent Socialist demonstrations for the universal franchise. These reached a grand finale on November 28, when 250,000 Socialists paraded before parliament, this time peaceably, for five hours. The Christian Socials used these occasions as fresh justifications for anti-Semitic agitation. Lueger and other party leaders singled out "Jewish Social Democracy" for the injuries inflicted on those it had ostensibly led astray. Lueger indicated that the Jews among the Social Democrats were cowards: during a demonstration in Vienna, early in November, at the decisive moment the Jewish majority had withdrawn. Harm had befallen only their Christian followers, Ernst Schneider added.[146] For the remainder of the month the Christian Socials continued to denounce "Jewish-incited turbulence" in cities across the empire. The climax of Christian Social agitation came on December 4 during a Lueger speech in Primmer's Hall, Zum Franz Josefsland. As he was speaking, Lueger uttered what was arguably the most sharply worded warning he had delivered to the Vienna Jewish community since he had become mayor eight years before. He admonished the Jews of Vienna that if they supported the Social Democrats, "the same thing could perhaps happen as in Russia."

Yet, even this admonition had been anticipated in April of the same year when he had told the Jews that if they "want to live among us . . . [they] must modestly take the place that the Lord and history have reserved for them." In December, however, he went much further. Lueger had been preceded on the rostrum by other speakers, one of whom equated "good Austrians and good Christians" with "good anti-Semites." Pointing out that government authorization for Lueger's sixtieth birthday celebration had been withheld in 1904, though the Social Democrats had been granted permission to demonstrate all the while, another speaker implied that the government favored the Socialists over the Christian Socials. Unless Socialist agitation among the youth was halted, he added, the morale of the army would be undermined and the troops would mutiny, as they had in Russia.[147] Perhaps Dr. Lueger would rouse the Christian Socials of Vienna and Lower Austria, and then the government would realize that other, "more commanding" classes than the Social Democrats would have a say in things.[148]

The tone of the meeting thus having been established, Lueger mounted the speaker's podium. During the first part of his speech, he justified his position on a five-year residency requirement in Vienna for the proposed universal franchise, insisting somewhat ingenuously that such a demand did not amount to withholding the franchise. Native Viennese had the right "to determine their own fate," he stated, and transients should be excluded from voting. No Bohemian who had lived in the capital for a few months should become a Viennese, he added. At length, Lueger spoke of the recent Socialist demonstrations in the empire and the need "from our side" to create order. One cause of the fear of violence in Austria had arisen out of the czarist October Manifesto, which had created a duma, and only recently had it occurred to some Russians that the turbulence in their country was a result of Jewish revolutionary agitation. As a result, "so-called . . . Jewish persecutions" had ensued, and papers all over the world had demanded protection for Russian Jews. Liberating "certain people" was "an ideal" only when it came to liberating them from the czar, but not "from the tyrants and the revolutionary elements." And then Lueger stated:

> I especially warn . . . the Jews in Vienna not to go as far as their co-religionists in Russia, and not to admit the Social Democratic revolutionaries. I warn the Jews, most expressly; for the same thing could perhaps happen as in Russia. We in Vienna are anti-Semites, but are certainly not inclined to murder and violence. But if the Jews should threaten our fatherland, then we will show no mercy. I wanted to warn of these sad possibilities.[149] [Emphasis in original.]

Lueger's remarks were frequently interrupted by cheers and lengthy applause, and when he had finished, minutes passed before the concluding speaker could be heard. His words seem to have produced a cathartic effect on his followers. Three days later, Liberals and Socialists attacked Lueger's speech in two interpellations during a municipal council session. "It would be a sad thing, if the security of an individual and/or property depended on political confession or on the grace of the lord mayor," said one; Lueger's speech amounted to "legally prohibited incitement against a religious community," added another.[150] Indignant at having been challenged, Lueger denied that the interpellations belonged within the competence of the municipal council at all, since he had spoken on December 4 "in [his] capacity as a diet representative." Lueger claimed he was accountable only to those municipal councillors who had voted for him; no one else had the right to criticize him. "I am responsible to my electors alone."[151] He then added that he had only permitted the interpellations to be read because he wanted to show how his opponents fought against him, so that all could see "how personal and political hate were joined in distorting everything."[152] Lueger defended his allegation that the Jews had aligned themselves with the Social Democrats. When he looked at the leaders of the Social Democratic party he could plainly see

> as must anyone admit who was halfway able to distinguish races, that the leaders of Social Democracy were almost exclusively Jewish. [Lively applause.] It may well be that one or the other of the gentlemen is baptized . . . but it's certain that many are absolutely authentic Jews, and also that the one who is supposed to be baptized—Dr. Adler—is certainly recognizable to anyone as a Jew.[153]

During his remarks, Lueger identified as almost exclusively Jewish the leaders of the Russian revolution, which was closely connected with the recent turbulence in Vienna, and he presented himself as a patriot willing to defend his country if it was threatened. His speech had been "completely correct," he insisted, but now it was being used against him to start "a highly unfair campaign." He ridiculed those who had begged the prime minister for protection from Dr. Lueger:

> I can only say to you: rarely is there a party, in which the mildest, by far the mildest, is the leader. Here in the representative body of the community of Vienna, justice rules for all. [Applause.] For the Jews, too. If a decision had to be made, I never asked for a baptismal certificate; never have I distinguished between Christian and Jew, and because I . . . have appealed to the Jews not to tie themselves to a revolutionary and turbulent party; for that, all of a sudden, a clamor is raised against me.[154]

Ignoring the question of a Liberal municipal councillor, Donat Zifferer, about who decided whether or not Austria was threatened, Lueger denied ever having committed injustice toward any Jew, "never in my whole life," a statement that was palpably false, as some of the municipal councillors must have known. Lueger then claimed to have protected Jews "very often . . . often against the will of my party. That's the truth about me and you know it, too, and should have considered that, before directing such interpellations at me."[155]

Though Lueger was cheered as usual at the conclusion of his remarks, his opponents did not soon forget his December 4 speech.[156] Moreover, his subsequent qualifications and defensive tone suggest that he suspected he had gone further than political prudence dictated.[157] His pulling back was something even a hate-filled anti-Semitic article on the front page of the *Reichspost* could not conceal, and the Jews were warned by this paper in much the same tone as they had been in Lueger's original speech.[158] Some days later in a municipal council session, one of Lueger's old acquaintances, the Liberal Ferdinand Klebinder, tried a partial explanation of the man whom he had known for "about 40 years."[159] But the more Klebinder tried to conciliate, the more hostile other councillors became. Lueger had "spoken to us from the heart! It was high time that he spoke!" interjected one; "The Jews robbed us blind!" shouted another.[160] Another councillor, Viktor Silberer, summed up the feelings of the Christian Social majority: "One thing is clear: we have led a struggle against the Jews, and we shall lead it as long as God grants us life; so that in Vienna Christianity remains at the helm, so that the Christian people is master in its own house, and not foreign, alien Jews."[161] Lueger had attracted many with such attitudes.

Despite what had appeared to be another anti-Semitic propagandistic victory for Lueger and his party early in December, the winners of the contest of autumn 1905 were the Socialists, though this would not become apparent until the next parliamentary elections in the spring of 1907. Socialist gains at that time surprised even Lueger. His plan had been to discredit the Socialists, but this had not to his consternation even slowed them. However, one or two things should have become apparent in 1905 to everyone. As Lueger approached the end of his career, his response to Socialist agitation had become mechanical. This suggests that he was beginning to lose touch with the lower classes — their lack of representation, adequate housing, or a living wage for many workers. But perhaps by this time, after nearly ten years of power, he had grown indifferent to many immediate problems. He was more confident than ever of his popularity. What did he care if Jews were offended by his remarks? By that time, by frequent application, anti-Semitism had been "normalized" as an agitational weapon, made "respectable," thanks to him. And yet, the double-edged nature of his tactics was plain: Lueger dared not challenge the imperial government and risk intervention by further incitement. Imperial Austria was not imperial Russia. Although the czar followed the advice of his anti-Semitic advisers, with whose opinions he always agreed, Franz Joseph was not an anti-Semite, at least in his official position. The emperor was the real bulwark against extreme anti-Semitism. Lueger knew this.[162]

Lueger's remarks were often if not characteristically anti-Semitic. Another instance of anti-Semitism can be seen in an exchange with the Habsburg ambassador to Bucharest, János Markgraf von Pallavicini, where Lueger imputes a general cowardice to Jews. In the autumn of 1907 in a Christian Social–controlled parliament, Lueger informed the representatives that he had corrected Pallavicini about the number of Magyars in Bucharest. When Pallavicini had expressed concern about the possible effects of a more pro-Rumanian orientation by Austria, namely, that this would result in a bloodbath in Bucharest because of the many Magyars living there, Lueger had replied: "But excellency, . . . how can you say that; there are very few Magyars in Bucharest; there are Hungarian Jews in Bucharest [amusement], and they—you can rest assured—will not spill their blood [renewed amusement]; before that happens, they'll run a little further, where perhaps they will be protected against bloodshed."[163]

But Lueger's anti-Semitism reached well beyond general cultural matters, personal slurs, demagoguery, opposition to kosher slaughter, and attacks on alleged Jewish hegemony in universities. In at least one area his anti-Semitism had more concrete objects. To be a Jew and a municipal official during the Lueger era was to be at a distinct disadvantage. Complaints that promotion of deserving and sometimes senior Jewish officials was being denied cropped up throughout his regime.[164] Boyer balances Lueger's policy in personnel matters against those of his predecessors: "in fairness to the Christian Socials . . . even under the Liberal regime before 1895 the number of Jews appointed to important positions in the Magistrat was very low. The antisemites simply made a virtue out of the Liberals' vice."[165] Evasive irony aside, however, Ludwig Klaar, a Viennese district chief medical officer during the Lueger era, was acutely aware that he had been discriminated against, when without real reasons, he was refused a promotion to the city medical department. Klaar would not have considered such a policy to be a virtue at all. On June 25, 1907, the Liberal municipal councillor Oskar Hein was convinced that Klaar, "who has for some time performed the relevant functions to everyone's satisfaction, though recommended by his colleagues, was not promoted because of his Jewish origins. Instead, the position went to a medical officer junior to him, who, however, is the fortunate holder of two papal decorations."[166]

When confronted with the complaint, Lueger resorted to a familiar tactic: he appealed to irrelevant procedure. He declared that he was unaccountable, for he had been absent when the promotion had been discussed. He therefore "refuse[d] to accept any responsibility whatsoever." He had "nothing to justify as [he had been] absolutely innocent of the whole affair." After a five-year effort Klaar was eventually promoted in 1912 and thus "achieved the dignities he had wanted and deserved."[167] But this did not take place until two years after the real roadblock had been removed by death, and then only after the intervention of three leading Christian Socials, including a priest. In 1907, unable to intervene directly against Klaar, Lueger had chosen "to manipulate . . . from behind the scene."[168]

Lueger was perfectly willing to appear to cooperate with Jews, as circumstances required. He sometimes tolerated baptized Jews who had attained wealth and power, such as Rudolf Sieghart, who denied that Lueger was an anti-Semite, and August Lohnstein. But Lueger warned his followers to be watchful: though Jews might appear to be Christians by attending church, they were still Jews, and therefore not to be trusted. And though an evidently cordial relationship existed between him and August Lohnstein,[169] Lueger categorically denied as false the assertion that Lohnstein was his adviser during a municipal council session; yet later, during the same interview, he hinted that he had been less than truthful in his denial.[170] When it was no longer possible to deny Jewish financial support for his municipal projects, Lueger dismissed and doubtless perplexed Liberal and Socialist criticism, stating that he was happy that his opponents were vexed that he had "obtained the money this way."[171] Both Lueger as mayor and the Christian Socials happily embraced bequests from Jewish organizations and individuals. It was frequently stipulated by the donors that such bequests were to be bestowed on the municipality, or to charitable organizations and private persons, regardless of religious affiliation, to be determined by the leaders of the ruling party.[172]

In late October 1909 Lueger appeared at a mass rally, evidently for the last time. Both he and Kunschak spoke in Vienna's thirteenth district. Though Lueger's anti-Semitism was implicit—he remarked that he stood by his old principles as a "good German, good Christian, ever and evermore"—[173] Kunschak fulminated against the Jews much as had his mentor years before, blaming them for sowing nationalistic strife. He became vitriolic in condemning the "Jewish press." At another meeting, Kunschak ended an anti-Semitic harrangue with the words: "Always and forever true to our German people, and battle Jewry till destruction! [Thunderous applause.]"[174]

At a provincial diet session chaired by Lueger the following February, 1910, only a few weeks before his death, anti-Semitic interjections by Bielohlawek and other Christian Socials about alleged Jewish economic hegemony in Hungary prompted an irritated response from Karl Renner: "I can't seem to drive it out of your heads; everywhere you see only Jews. You're so Jew-infested that you see Jews everywhere as an alcoholic can see only mice. You fail to see the great national economic facts and the determining factors!"[175] Renner's words characterize Christian Social anti-Semitism at the time of Lueger's death—they saw only Jews. His admonition points to the growing imbalance and distortion of reality among Lueger's followers. The party leader had both fostered and fed the delusions of the rank and file in what was a spiral of mutual reinforcement.

It remains in this overview of Lueger's anti-Semitism to glance at its effect on subsequent politics. Some of his biographers even after 1945 argue that it was minimal. Prominent Austrian Jews are cited in support of their position. Although it cannot be denied that such authors as Arthur Schnitzler and Stefan Zweig largely discounted accusations of anti-Semitism against Lueger, the weight of their opinion must await a full appraisal of the depth of their knowledge of Lueger's politics. Schnitzler and Zweig were members of Vienna's Jewish upper middle class who liked to think of themselves as assimilated, so secure that they could never be expelled. Such persons are often out of touch with the harsher realities of everyday politics and sometimes deny them, even when presented objective facts. This is a recurrent Austrian tendency. Schnitzler, who died in 1931, was spared witnessing the complete destruction of the world he had known, and of which he had been so penetrating a critic. Zweig was less fortunate. He committed suicide in 1942, mourning the loss of "the world of yesterday."

Another such Jewish writer is the Socialist Friedrich Austerlitz. Although he was not from the upper middle class, he likewise dismissed Lueger as a serious anti-Semite. To him, Lueger "was a man who had not invented antisemitism but merely had given it political expression, in order to ventilate and exploit mass grievances against liberal hegemony, which in Vienna had acquired an unmistakably Jewish flavor in the late nineteenth century."[176] Austerlitz, like other Austrian Socialists of his time, dismissed anti-Semitism as "'the Socialism of fools,'"[177] and may have felt that in time those afflicted would come to their senses. This has not happened. And it should have been plain to Austerlitz that far from abandoning anti-Semitism once the Liberals had been defeated, Lueger continued to exploit it, especially against the Socialists. Like Schnitzler, Austerlitz died in 1931, and was likewise spared final disillusionment. All three writers viewed the past from the vantage point of the barbarism of the 1920s and 1930s. Lueger naturally looked "minor league" in comparison. At the time of his death, Viennese Jewish papers divided roughly along class lines: bourgeois journalists tended to minimize Lueger's effect as anti-Semite; proletarians saw him as an opportunist who tolerated Jews only when it was advantageous for him to do so.

Some Jewish politicians have qualified their criticism of Lueger's anti-Semitism. Joseph Samuel Bloch, for one, struck a psychological note and stated that "Dr. Lueger was pious in the same sense as he was anti-semitic. Personally, it was not of much account, but it was useful."[178] Yet one might temper Bloch's opinion with his general statement that "towards the end of our life . . . [one] remembers the peaceful and happy hours only, and with growing years they shine in growing radiance whereas every thing [*sic*] sad and melancholy gradually sinks into oblivion, as if covered by a grey veil."[179] This general qualification balances his other judgments about Lueger's anti-Semitism. Another Jewish politician, Josef Redlich, defended Lueger's anti-Semitism and praised him for stimulating a "new and healthy" Austrian patriotism. Redlich, who never adjusted his imperial outlook to the Republic, died in 1936, two years before the Anschluss. And yet another Jewish politician, Sigmund Mayer, surprisingly condemned Lueger, not for being an anti-Semite, but for not being one "in reality."[180] Mayer seems to have disapproved of Lueger's apparent want of sincerity on any level of this topic.

In evaluating such mild opinions about Lueger's anti-Semitism, it is well to recall that the Vienna of Lueger's day was also the Vienna of Otto Weininger, Arthur Trebitsch, and other problematic self-hating Jews, some of whom saw in Lueger and the Christian Socials a welcome counterbalance to the predominating Jewish cultural influence. Extremists such as Weininger evinced the "Hermann Levi syndrome": they would bear any insult, suffer any indignity, and in Weininger's case, commit suicide, to be purged of their Jewishness.[181]

Theodor Herzl was still another kind of man, though he, too, had been an extreme assimilationist at one time, and dreamed of leading a mass conversion of Vienna's Jews in St. Stephen's Cathedral. During Lueger's campaign for the mayoralty, Herzl saw Lueger outside a polling place and may thereby have grasped something of his true significance: "A man next to me said with tender warmth but in a quiet voice: 'That is our Führer!' Actually, these words showed me more than all declamation and abuse how deeply anti-Semitism is rooted in the hearts of these people."[182]

It may be true, as Boyer asserts, that Lueger's "political mode . . . was baroque."[183] Even if this is interpreted to mean freewheeling and eclectic, something more must be added: Lueger's supple responsiveness to the crowd and its passions and his willingness to swim in such perilous seas. In a word, pointedly, a distinction must be drawn between psychologizing his behavior and its hard reality. One judges a tree by the fruit it bears. It may well be that Lueger was even worse than an anti-Semite, that, given world enough and time, the rest of humanity would have been next. Such psychological questions may be interesting, but they remain academic in the arena of politics and people who die.

Did Lueger himself believe his anti-Jewish remarks? We may never know. Over forty years after Lueger's death the last imperial finance minister, Alexander Spitzmüller, asserted that Lueger told him in April 1909 that anti-Semitism was a good means to get ahead in politics, but once one was on top, it was of no further use; it was "the sport of the rabble."[184] If Lueger made this statement, it was shortly after having been elected mayor for the seventh time, after having received the most overwhelming vote of confidence in his career. He could afford to be generous, though such statements cost him little and had no effect on the Jews. There was a reflexive quality about all of Lueger's behavior—more than a touch of what J. P. Stern has called "total immanence." When Lueger delivered an anti-Semitic diatribe, no one may have believed "in anything; or rather, . . . few if any believe[d] in the man before them but all . . . fully believe[d] in the image they [had] created."[185] No matter what he said, the public Lueger, the one that counts, did appeal to his listeners' "readiness to take part in the religious image-making, to connive at his self-dramatization as a messianic figure."[186]

In one respect Lueger was consistently laudatory toward the Jews. Before and after he became mayor, he praised them for preserving the appearance and sanctity of their ancestors' graves,[187] and he added that he wished the Christians would be inspired with a similar spirit. In Vienna's otherwise carefully groomed Central Cemetery, dominated by the Lueger Memorial Church, the large old Jewish section is now overgrown and untended.

6

The Lueger Gretl

He is the darling of the women's world, he wins them all over, because
he never compromised himself. That a man of such qualifications in his
youth planned to become a priest, as he assured me, is not surprising.
　　　—Franz Stauracz, *Dr. Karl Lueger, Zehn Jahre Bürgermeister*

[Lueger and Liechtenstein] have succeeded . . . in convincing their
country-women that the fate of Austria is in their hands. The Empire is
lost, they tell them, unless the Jews be driven forth, and it is the women
of Austria alone who can drive them forth! They have convinced
them . . . that they have a mission, and women are never so happy as
when playing the missionary.
　　　—*The World*, London, December 31, 1902

The Christian Viennese Women's League is one of the most powerful
weapons of the Christian Social party, and the Social Democrats feel it,
too.
　　　—Lueger to the Women's League of Brigittenau, October 19, 1902

*T*he term *Lueger Gretl*, a reference by members of the Social Democratic women's auxiliary to Lueger's female supporters, caricatured a popular turn-of-the-century cliché. "Gretl" was the idealized Teutonic woman,
the exemplar of Lueger's loudly Germanic supporters, even though many
of them were Czechs or of Czech descent. In a composite image, Gretl
was blue of eye and fair of hair, coiled in braids over her ears, dressed
in a plain, dark-colored, ankle-length skirt, white blouse, rose-embroidered
vest, and wearing black suede shoes with silver buckles. She was believed
to embody the essence of *volkstümlich* domestic virtues. According to one
who knew Lueger well,

> [Lueger] calculated on the instincts of the *Volk* soul, and his clever mind soon
> discovered the sensitive spot on which to concentrate his efforts. He attracted

women, appealed to their domesticity, to religion, to the education of children; first, he unctuously depicted how man degenerated amidst the present conditions, then heaven was painted in the rosiest colors. . . . He flattered women by suggesting their incomparable power over their husbands – "A clever woman can do anything, can have her will everywhere; simply influence the men, then it will work." Thus the women . . . were driven into a veritable frenzy of joy. Countless meetings took place and as the pièce de résistance, 'He' appeared, greeted with frenetic applause.

He knew his "harem" well, as he scornfully referred to the feminine hangers-on, and said what was expected of him. An incomparable paroxysm seized the people; meetings followed one another, festive events, homages for the man of the people, every possible honor; one crowded and bumped oneself raw just to snatch Lueger's handshake. Yes, when Lueger was refused the mayoralty by His Majesty, the crowd was furious. I believe these stormy times were the most brilliant in Lueger's career.[1]

With these words, Marianne Beskiba, Lueger's mistress and confidante of fifteen years, described his effect on the masses. Among his many admirers, the Christliche Wiener Frauenbund, or Christian Viennese Women's League, was arguably the most enthusiastic and best organized party group during the first ten years of his mayoralty.[2] "Lueger's Amazons," "the Lueger Garde," or the "Lueger Gretl," as they were variously called, whipped up preelection enthusiasm for *der schöne Karl*, raised money for the party through door-to-door canvassing, often contributing from their own meager savings, urged their men to vote for Lueger and his candidates, and agitated as political shock troops. Inverting the usual scornful cry "Lueger's Amazons!" the mayor once exclaimed: "If you are the mayor's Amazons, you are the bravest of all, for the Amazons were also very brave. Now then, good luck, my Amazons, in this new year!"[3]

Lueger's attention to his female supporters was effective. By 1902 politics among Vienna's women had contributed to a profound transformation, according to a contemporary foreign observer:

The great ladies of Vienna certainly owe Dr. Lueger a debt of gratitude if for nothing but that he has provided them with a new and very keen interest in life. Until he took them in hand they cared no more for politics than they did for bygone fashions, and would as soon have thought of paying a visit to the Bourse as to the Reichsrath. . . . They had not . . . a single thought in their heads beyond pleasure. . . . Things have changed since then, however, thanks to Dr. Lueger. At the present time there are no keener politicians in Europe than the ladies of Vienna, and none who wield more influence. Of this the result of the recent elections in Lower Austria is a proof. Had it not been for the help they gave them, never would the Anti-Semite leaders have been able to sweep all before them in the fashion they did.[4]

At the time of Lueger's death, one of his oldest and most implacable journalistic enemies, the *Wiener Sonn- und Montags-Zeitung,* attributed his success without qualification to the Frauenbund. "It was they who decided the men to side with Lueger, it was they who became the prophets of *der schöne Karl.* Never has a tribune fought with more clever means. The Christian Social Women's League, scorned by their opponents, penetrated the families, moved from home to home, and through their words he became a brilliant leader."[5]

Attributing Lueger's good political fortune solely to female enthusiasm, as the preceding observers did, would be inadequate and unsatisfactory. Yet, to slight his appeal to women and their assistance to his cause would be to ignore their considerable role in his career, their part in spreading Christian Social doctrines — and particularly Lueger-style anti-Semitism — among the young, and to underestimate him as a Viennese phenomenon. According to one Viennese politician, a successful mayor of Vienna must be *fesch* — dashing — before all else,[6] and Lueger fulfilled this requirement.

Another Viennese politician, one of Lueger's close collaborators, and later third vice-mayor, Heinrich Hierhammer, recalled the mayor's conviction that it was impossible to overestimate the importance of women "in all areas of public life."[7] Lueger's authentic feelings about women in politics — that women were to provide active support for him but not to have an active voice in politics — did not matter. He was candid about this to his women and denied that he intended to "conquer great political rights" for them.[8] His aim was to alert women to their agitational and economic power, and to bring this power to bear for the advantage of the ruling party. "The haves and the have-nots" became a frequent theme in his speeches to the Amazons, who cheered him on, and tried to play their part in the extension and consolidation of Christian Socialism. In Lueger's public and private life, women were considerable, with the public, political aspect emerging dominant. Though the main purpose of this chapter, therefore, is to describe the political activities of Lueger's female supporters, mention will also be made of the role of women in his private life, for the light it sheds on his personality and on his political development. In fact, Lueger may possibly have owed the refinement of one of his most important professional skills, his mastery of rhetoric, to a female teacher.

The most tangible evidence of his popularity among Vienna's women was attested by the very existence of the Women's League, which was formally created two weeks before Franz Joseph sanctioned Lueger's fifth election in April 1897. However, well-organized groups of Lueger's female supporters had campaigned from 1895, and women had assisted politically as early as his first parliamentary campaign in 1885.[9] John Boyer has aptly indicated the novelty of the Christian Social concentration "on bourgeois females" during Lueger's electoral campaign. One of the chief purposes of such attentions was to organize

> an effective boycott of Jewish merchants in retribution for the alleged influence of the Jewish community in preventing Lueger's confirmation. Previous attempts at a *Kauft nur bei Christen* [Buy only from Christians] campaign organized by the "Christian Family" associations had met with marginal success at best, but contemporary reports from late 1895 indicated that this time the party's boycott was seriously injuring a number of Jewish-owned businesses. . . . Most important, Lueger was setting his female cadres up to play a shadow role to the Social Democrats. Several of the women's rallies got out of hand, and angry women marched from the rallies in small groups screaming at passersby and local shopkeepers, some of them Jewish. The party elite would never have tolerated this kind of behavior from its male voters, but covertly encouraged such street and sidewalk rowdiness from the females. . . . The police were totally baffled by these disturbances and felt uncertain how to deal with them: they were hardly riots in any conventional sense of the word, but small groups of angry women marching down the sidewalks swinging umbrellas and chanting "Hoch Lueger!" were hardly to be tolerated. The dramatic entrance of the Christian Social women on the political scene was intended by Lueger and Gessmann to suggest to the government that the antisemites could also bring the women out onto the streets if they so desired.[10]

The Christian Social women added considerable luster to Lueger's aura. By the end of his first term in office in 1903 the mayor's enemies considered his power to have grown so great through the efforts of his female supporters that the Rathaus was dubbed the *"Luegeria."* The Christian Socials expected their women to further common party goals with vigor, and they complied enthusiastically, sometimes using unorthodox methods. At an outing in Semmering, a chartered train carrying a contingent of the Frauenbund halted in a station beside another train occupied by a Socialist educational club. Initial bantering through open windows gave way to taunts and shouts of "Phooey Lueger!" Angered, the Christian Social ladies raised their skirts and displayed their backsides to the Socialists. Indignant reports in the Socialist papers ridiculed "the Christian women who always said so much about morals and morality. A worker's wife would never do such a thing even in a conjugal bed room."[11]

In reporting the ceremonies that formally founded the Women's League in March 1897, the *Reichspost* enumerated the major purposes of the organization. The Lueger Gretl were intended to preserve family and religion against the attacks of the Socialists, to keep the Christian, and explicitly German, home free of Jewish newspapers, and to educate their children within the Christian church.[12] These themes recurred more or less regularly in Lueger's speeches to his Frauenbund chapters.

The following year the Women's League expanded into an active vocal role in foreign politics. With the connivance of Lueger in February 1898, the Amazon Corps massed in the *Volkshalle* of the town hall to oppose five hundred female Viennese Dreyfusards, who had sent a declaration of solidarity to Dreyfus's prominent defender, Emile Zola. The specific targets of the Women's League included Viennese Jewry and the "notorious" five hundred "girls of Vienna."[13] Anti-Dreyfusard protests were frequently staged for the next several years, and the Frauenbund remained implacably against Dreyfus for the duration of the affair and thereafter. In 1906 League spokesmen attributed Dreyfus's pardon to the influence of the Alliance Israélite Universelle.[14] Another foreign political interest of the Frauenbund was the Boer War. At a Christmas rally of the Frauenbund in the Volkshalle, league president Emilie Platter informed her listeners that "the sons of the so-called Liberals of Britain . . . lock poor women and children in a kind of prison, in the notorious concentration camps." Women, and especially children, were dying by the hundreds, perhaps by the design of their captors. Such deeds were condemned as "a disgrace for Europe," and the members of the Viennese Women's League were called on to join their sisters in the German Reich in protesting this development.[15]

The elusive Emilie Platter was a shadowy figure in Lueger's party, as befit her actual role in Christian Social politics. She was one of those early Christian Socials who enjoyed brief notoriety during the palmy days of Lueger's popularity and then vanished without an apparent trace.[16] Her rapid rise and fall can be explained within the context of Lueger's career. Emilie was a native of Brandenburg and the wife of the Christian Social municipal councillor Hugo Platter, a postal official. Beskiba describes her simply as "an educated, plain, older woman."[17] (See illustrations.) Kielmansegg was more blunt and cynical and implied that her political activity stemmed from transparent opportunism. He was also contemptuous of this glittering parvenue and her special offices. With heavy sarcasm, he referred to the occasion when he had had the honor of making the acquaintance of "the great speaker and President of the Central Committee of the Christian Social Viennese Women's League."[18] But despite her apparent defects, Platter must have had considerable energy and organizing talent to preside over the creation of many Frauenbund chapters, to supervise their activities, meetings, and excursions to sometimes distant areas, and to participate in them for ten years.

The chief organ of the Women's League was the *Österreichische Frauen-Zeitung*,[19] published by Franz Klier, a former *Reichspost* editor who, as well as Lueger, took credit for creating the Frauenbund.[20] While secretary of the League, Klier's dogmatism and commercial-mindedness angered many members who gave freely of their time and talents without pay. Klier had many enemies and did enjoy Platter's support, but did not long survive her resignation in the spring of 1906, and soon thereafter fell out of active politics.[21] The *Frauen-Zeitung* was antifeminist, in the sense that it discouraged the political and social independence for women advocated by some Liberals and Socialists. Parents were urged by the *Frauen-Zeitung* to educate their daughters to be selfless, obedient, contented, willing to make sacrifices, and in general to be self-effacing.[22] The reticence of the Lueger Garde toward female emancipation was criticized by Austrian feminists, particularly the Socialists. In addition, the *Documente der Frauen,* one of whose publishers was Rosa Mayreder, censored the Frauenbund for failing from her point of view to represent women's true economic and social interests. The *Österreichische Frauen-Zeitung* was accused of playing on its readers' lowest instincts and trying to spread clerical and anti-Semitic hegemony through feminine influence throughout the nation.[23] If the boasts of the *Frauen-Zeitung* are any indication, such charges were accurate, for by June 1902 Platter presided over Frauenbund chapters from Troppau to Triest,[24] and hoped that an all-embracing national Christian Social Women's League would soon flourish. Four years later the Frauenbund numbered twenty thousand members.[25] The Lueger Garde ceased as a separate entity toward the end of 1907, having been the last to join a larger national Catholic women's organization.[26] By that time the Christian Socials had merged with the Catholic Conservatives to become the strongest party in parliament, and the type of feminine activist support that had until now been vital in Lueger's earlier successes at last receded in importance, at least in the minds of the party leaders.

Centralized control over Lueger's women emanated from the Frauenbund organization. Emilie Platter was assisted by two vice presidents, Theresia Ruzizka and Karoline Brskowsky.[27] Divided within districts into local branches, or *Ortsgruppen,* local branches were administered by a chairwoman, deputy, secretary, cashier, advisory council, and committee.[28]

The creation of Catholic women's organizations in Germany and France was greeted with approval by the *Frauen-Zeitung* as implicit victories for the anti-Semitic cause. Foreign Catholic women's activities were also occasionally reported in the *Frauen-Zeitung.* Klier implied that the credit for new foreign women's leagues was his. He had founded the original

Frauenbund, after all, though he added that "the Viennese women can be proud . . . not to have worked in vain."[29]

Though the formation of the League had been approved by Kielmansegg for promoting exclusively charitable activities, the potential for political activity was apparent from the very beginning. According to Beskiba, Lueger's

> mere appearance at a meeting got the belligerent ladies in the required mood and, while the *"schöne Karl"* provided the listeners with his suggestions from the podium in a racy, bantering way, he understood with juristic cunning how to touch on political themes, without in the least damaging the letter of the league statutes.— He succeeded in getting around the directives of the statutes with admirable, incontestable cleverness. . . . Every seat was fought for, no distance was too far for the enthusiastic admirer, no weather too foul. The crowd queued before the hall doors long before the opening. Lucky was the girl permitted to place a white carnation [the Christian Social flower] in the buttonhole of one of the honored, especially 'our' Lueger! The chosen palpitated with enchantment for three days thereafter.[30]

So well-known was the effect of Lueger's appearances on his female admirers that a feminist critic satirized one of his euphoric admirers: "You just can't believe how such a meeting affects your heart and mind. Lueger and the Prince [Alois Liechtenstein], and all the other gentlemen; they're tremendously intelligent and well-read. My heart simply flutters when I hear all the intelligent things they talk about."[31] But there was another, less happy aspect to Frauenbund ceremonies. The frequent ceremonial consecration of Women's League standards anticipated the panoply of subsequent totalitarian ritual:

> Each of the local branches was distinguished by a standard: these standards with all the festive splendor were very costly; the individual local branches participated at every conceivable consecration of the colors in order to bring together as many flag precincts as possible. If one of the members of the League died, the appropriate local branch provided escort for the coffin beneath the flower-bedecked flag and a funeral wreath at least as far as the church.[32]

When Lueger was reelected mayor in 1903, "delegations from all the Viennese branches with their flags and standards" assembled in the festive hall of the town hall to participate in his oath-taking.[33] The appearance of the League presidium, together with all the chairwomen of the local chapters, was described by the *Frauen-Zeitung* as merely fulfilling "an act of gratitude to the lord mayor who [had] supported the Christian Viennese Women's League from the beginning through his good will in counsel and deed."[34]

The emergence of political potential from an originally religious ceremony was probably nursed by Lueger's personal perceptions and ambitions. Although the theoretical social role of women had prompted many books and articles by Lorenz von Stein, Lueger applied theory to reality and mobilized women politically rather than intellectually. Stein's books had emphasized the centrality of the wife and mother as economic and social harmonizers, and his articles appeared in the *Wiener Abendpost* when Lueger was an avid reader of the Vienna press. Lueger may also have realized the political importance of women through his study of the Revolution of 1848. In any case, theory and practice emerged during the early 1880s when he met Valerie Gréy, an actress, theater director, and rhetoric teacher. Her highly individualistic behavior made her in some ways an embodiment of Steinian theory in practice, and she may have caused Lueger to ponder the political potential of women. She herself was sensitively attuned to politics and specialized in providing rhetoric lessons to politicians. Her pupils included Pernerstorfer, Kronawetter, and Lueger.[35] Gréy may have been the first woman outside Lueger's family[36] to have taken an active interest in his politics — the Ur-Lueger-Gretl — and he once asked her to intervene with an editor who criticized his and Mandl's abuse of democracy by involving themselves with anti-Semites. Because she helped shape his literary and cultural tastes,[37] and was herself engaged in the same social and cultural life of the imperial capital as Lueger, her background and their friendship are important.

Before their meeting, Gréy had already had an unusual, if not raffish, career. Lueger first met her as one of his legal clients, during one of her entanglements over her alleged "systematic thefts" of other theater directors' plays. Legal problems may have caused her to leave Vienna for a time in the summer of 1882.[38] Divorced with two daughters, Valerie was probably born Jewish — she was born Caroline Valerie Loewey in Pest — though she was not practicing Judaism when she married one of Lueger's former legal colleagues, Eduard Franz Stipek, in 1888.[39] *Evangelisch* is entered beside her name in the Protestant marriage register. Her birth date is uncertain, one source stating that she was born in 1842, two years before Lueger, another in 1845.[40] Gréy was attracted to the theater at an early age. When but five years old, she made her stage debut in Budapest with the famous actor Adolf von Sonnenfels.[41]

Her father, the fortress commandant at Komorn, and mother objected and went so far as to burn her cherished edition of Schiller.[42] But Gréy continued her theatrical career. She toured Europe, became the first dramatic female lead of a German language troupe in St. Petersburg,[43] and later, apparently in 1880,[44] founded a theater that bore her name in Vienna's first district. Gréy was proud of her productions, actors, and actresses. She liked to point out that some who later attained fame had first appeared in her productions.[45] At the age of eighty, she was celebrated as Vienna's oldest actress; and her motto, "macht nichts" ("who cares?"), written on the back of a photo to one of her admirers,[46] suggests her lifelong insouciance and indifference to decorum.

Gréy came along at the right time for Lueger, particularly when he was breaking away from the ruling Liberal party but had not yet found his own way, and when he was uncertain about many things, perhaps even about his own future in politics. In 1881 Lueger served as legal counsel to her theater.[47] His first surviving letter to her is dated June 10, 1882, after he had left the Liberal party. Its style is informal and plunges the reader into the middle of one of Gréy's protracted legal struggles.[48] Their correspondence must have lasted for at least a few years. Only one of her letters to him survives from March 1882.[49] Brief and ungrammatical, it comments on the Fogerty affair. However, some three dozen of Lueger's letters to Gréy tell of mutual friends and encounters and comment on miscellaneous social, cultural, and political matters. Although there are significant gaps in the correspondence, particularly between July 1882 and December 1883, as well as between May and December 1884, the letters nonetheless provide at least a partial portrait of the developing politician. Lueger appears at his most engagingly human. He displays wit, humor, and an interest in art and letters. He is occasionally ironic toward his friends, and particularly toward Gréy. Failing once to see her at her home as they had apparently agreed to do, he relates the circumstances of his visit, and then leaves it to her "well-developed legal judgment, honed by so many court cases," to determine whether he is "liable for prosecution."[50] On another occasion, he teases her about an evidently broken relationship with an editor of one of Vienna's most influential papers (the *Neues Wiener Tagblatt*): "What have you actually done . . . to have turned a heart once filled with love? Or have you perhaps done *nothing*? What is it that has transformed this love sick Seladon [sic] into a raging enemy?"[51]

Lueger's feelings toward Gréy grew increasingly tender. Thus in May 1884 he refers to an invitation she had extended for him to visit her for a few days in the country, but regrets that he cannot accept because of "business and public profession."[52] The following year, as their relationship grew closer, Lueger accepted her invitation to a supper and returned her invitation a few days later. He was hopeful that Grey would visit him, mentions gifts from her, and wishes "my Valerie would find the peaceful haven where she could securely dock her life's ship."[53]

In his memoirs, Joseph Samuel Bloch stated that Lueger "met with truest friendship, purest devotion, greatest self-abnegation from Jews," that he took advice from them, that he "dined and slept with Jews."[54] The possibility that Grey was Jewish and that she and Lueger were close leads one to wonder if Bloch's comment included her. Although it is difficult to say with any certainty whether Lueger was in love with her, many years after he had died Grey claimed that he had once come close to marrying her, but that her response "Dear friend, you are married to politics and have no time for a wife!" ended the matter.[55] This was supposed to have taken place in 1885, the year Lueger was first elected to parliament, when he complained that "to say I am healthy would be self-deception. Mine is a life of continuous tumult and the consequences are gradual."[56] In further support of Grey's recollections, Lueger's letters do convey the impression of occasionally hectic activity through apologies for broken engagements and invitations declined. Once, when he invited her to share supper, his invitation was accompanied by a request for "some instruction."[57] In this way he may have tried to combine business with pleasure, but business may well have been the more important. This invitation was extended during Lueger's first parliamentary campaign when his need for "some instruction," presumably in rhetoric, was at its height. Business before pleasure. Again, in April 1885, he asked her to undertake a diplomatic mission to the editor and publisher Theodor Hertzka, whose *Wiener Allgemeine Zeitung* had criticized Lueger's and Mandl's "misuse of democracy" in flirting with guildsmen and anti-Semites.[58] And yet, perhaps it was Valerie Grey, a divorcée with two children in difficult circumstances, rather than Lueger, who wanted to marry and thereby gain the security of a more established existence. Suddenly after his election to parliament he had become a man with a political future. Had Lueger learned at that time about Grey's possibly Jewish origins? In another letter from this time he was cryptic in mentioning that he had done "a very foolish thing" in letting her read an anonymous and now lost letter to him:

> Why do you cry, dear Madam? Does this change anything? No. Do you perhaps think that my judgment, my viewpoint will be influenced? Surely you don't believe this. So, kindly let the world write and say what it will. You and I can't change their opinions and we must bear this like an inevitable fate.
>
> Console yourself, dear Madam! We are not the first and won't be the last to whom things of that kind happen.[59]

Had someone, perhaps another politician, threatened to disclose their relationship at the time of Lueger's flirtation with anti-Semitism? By 1885, for at least two years, Leopold Hollomay, an outspoken anti-Semite who was jealous of Ignaz Mandl for religious as well as for other reasons,[60] had tried to isolate Lueger from his mentor.[61] It seems doubtful that a man like Hollomay whose reaction to Mandl was extreme, according to Lueger,[62] would have been more charitable toward Gréy, especially if he had known that she might be Jewish. In his letter to her Lueger implied that his "judgment" and "viewpoint," possibly toward Gréy, would remain uninfluenced, in any case. But his correspondence ended, perhaps for good, the following month, nonetheless. Possibly he had had second thoughts. Though he was not to become openly anti-Semitic until 1889 and his final break with Mandl, they had already quarreled several times by 1885. Lueger may have thought it prudent to avoid entangling alliances.

Lueger's final letter to Gréy in an unknown hand but signed by him was written in August 1896 when he was the most popular anti-Semite in Austria, first vice-mayor and anticipating the great prize. The official tone of the letter betrays no trace of the warmth of their former friendship. By 1896 the priorities of power had separated him from many of his friends, their more humanizing values, and the influences of his youth.

August 22, 1896

Dear Madam,

In reply to your letter of the eighth of the month, permit me to inform you that you can speak to me Wednesday of next week at 9 or 9:15 A.M. in the town hall.

Respectfully yours,

Dr. Lueger[63]

On the face of it, his letter tells us that a resumption of their earlier friendship may have become impossible, though it may be that because he did not write the letter, a more official tone was required.

Besides her talents as actress and theater director, Gréy was also a writer. Her 1894 novel *Paula* and four-act drama *Helene* of 1903 are melodramatic pieces full of betrayals, duels, and suicides. A similar sensationalism characterizes many of her stage productions. No roman à clef, *Paula* nonetheless provides sympathetic portraits of its heroine and a distinguished older man, *der Sanitätsrath*. One again is led to speculate if both figures may have been modeled in part on herself and Lueger. Gréy's writings reveal a preference for older, benign, paternal men — increasingly, the public image of Lueger. It is perhaps not without significance in this respect that she divorced her second husband who was several years her junior in 1909 after twenty-one years of marriage.[64] By this time she had written more plays, one of which, *Der Schlierach Lois*, enjoyed modest success.

Lueger apparently preferred artistic types in women like Gréy to the more stolid, and, one suspects, stodgy wives of some of the municipal councillors and leading Christian Socials, with whom he nonetheless frequently shared vacations and outings. Was he merely performing a duty in this regard, or did his behavior reflect a dualism in his personality? Perhaps he wanted the best of both worlds. His domestic regimen, sternly administered by his older sister Hildegard,[65] provided stability in a schedule that was otherwise erratic, and a life that was frequently turbulent in the extreme, to include "boisterous" electoral meetings and at least one assassination attempt.[66] Considering the unhealthy conditions, the hectic pace, and the many smoke-filled halls in which his politicking was carried out at all hours, it is surprising that his health held up as long as it did, yet it was diabetes and the complications stemming from it that did him in. Though he thrived on turbulence, notwithstanding his protestations to the contrary, even he was aware of its potential cost.

Another woman who figured prominently in Lueger's life was the portrait painter Marianne Beskiba. She was an energetic organizer for Lueger's cause and for a short while a Frauenbund chapter secretary as well.[67] Beskiba is the sole Lueger Gretl to have recorded her impressions of the mayor and party leader in her memoirs. In some respects the picture she presents of herself is the very opposite of the more optimistic and enterprising Gréy. This is not surprising, for Lueger, after a liaison lasting from 1894 to 1909, discarded her as a mistress, even though their relationship was at one point close enough, as she claims, to prompt his promise of marriage. In all significant ways the relationship ended in her complete disappointment. She is vague about some details, but her memoirs are nonetheless a detailed if often spiteful, morose, and occasionally hysterical catalog of Lueger's flaws. Yet for all its limitations and the caution with which one must treat her assertions, hers is a valuable record, for its content reveals the expedience of Lueger's politics. It unknowingly hints, further, at the dangers of unrestrained ambition, especially when it is accompanied by the rapid and unimpeded increase in power growing out of repeated Christian Social victories. Her descriptions of Lueger's relationships with other party members make it apparent that his sense of responsibility to those who served him, or who served in the name of the party, did not figure high on his list of priorities.

Beskiba's observation that he lived "only for struggle, for restless activity," betrays an essential Faustianism. "I believe that this man had set absolutely no tangible goal. He strove only forward, always further and further, as far as human possibility permitted."[68] On an entirely different, though nonetheless personal, note Beskiba's memoirs record some of Lueger's habits and preferences. They detail his tastes in food and drink, his delight in solid bourgeois fare—he once went on for several pages in a private letter about dumplings—his love for roasts, Pilsner, apple strudel, but also for a more esoteric and expensive cuisine, for caviar, crabs, game birds, the finest wines and champagnes.[69] A heavy smoker from his youth onward, Lueger blamed his palsied hands on nicotine. As honors were heaped on him, he began to dress accordingly, gradually assuming the role of a leading dignitary, elegant in appearance, and usually restrained in his public, if not always in his private, dealings with imperial officials. It was said during his last years that so great had his power become that no prime minister could be appointed without Lueger's approval. Beskiba states:

> If Lueger did not assume the rank of a prime minister, his will nonetheless reigned in government circles. I vividly remember his vehemence when the Bienerth Ministry took over the helm. It came to the formation of a cabinet. Gessmann was dismissed as Minister of Public Works; I remarked to the mayor that not a single, actual member of his party now possessed a portfolio. Suddenly his extinguished eyes flashed like lightning, he struck the table with his fist and thundered:
> "I'll teach Bienerth; he'll do as I want!"
> A few days later Dr. Weiskirchner was Minister of Trade. He always received his instructions from Lueger, as did almost all ministers, including Bienerth, who were dependent on the mayor in a certain way.[70]

Though Lueger displayed a weakness for jewelry in his later years, the golden cuff links, watch chain, and stickpins he wore were almost all exclusively presents from others.[71] For Lueger did not enjoy spending his own money. In fact, he was actually parsimonious to the extent that he caused Beskiba embarrassment in restaurants by checking the bill with painstaking care.[72] When she once took him to task for this, he admitted that she was right, then remarked that he had acquired this trait from his mother who had had to struggle to make ends meet for her family.[73] It was too late to change, he shrugged.

Beskiba's description of Lueger's striking physical appearance—the noble head, penetrating eyes, one of which turned out somewhat and lent irony to his remarks, if he so chose, thick dark hair, full gray beard and pert nose — is like those of others. But she adds something more. Closeup, his face was weather-beaten and betrayed many wrinkles, an aspect captured by few photographs or paintings.[74] The doubleness of his character may thus have found its mirror, and the defects of the man gradually became apparent to her. This was something that neither the elegance of his attire nor the dignities of office could conceal, at least from Beskiba's critical eye.

Lueger's continuing contacts with other members of the Women's League and gossip about his and Beskiba's liaison were a constant source of irritation to her. In one of the few of his surviving letters and a note — he demanded that she burn the letters and he then extinguished the ashes with champagne[75] — Lueger tells her to ignore the others, and to let "such talk in one ear and out the other."[76] "Since when do you study the Odyssey? There aren't any sirens or Circe here; there are only old women, and I can say with Napoleon: Millennia look down on me."[77]

Lueger had realized when he became mayor that with the kind of power he wielded wealth was superfluous — might even have become a burden. Accordingly, he relinquished half of his salary, a fact noted by his earlier biographers who wished to contrast Christian Social "frugality" with Liberal "extravagance."[78] Yet, there is no denying that in contrast with many other Christian Socials, Lueger was honest in his personal financial dealings. According to Beskiba again, he was more troubled than angered by the dishonesty of other party members.[79] He sometimes tried to conceal their thefts, perhaps, even by covering them from his own funds. When Beskiba remonstrated that this only encouraged further larceny, and that he should make an example of one of the felons instead, Lueger responded: "That won't do! I must maintain the integrity of the party at any price."[80] Preserving appearances for political purposes rather than confronting unpleasant realities and trying to change them was the important thing here, as well as elsewhere. Political success clearly outweighed personal morality.

Lueger could be the cultivated gentleman. His knowledge of geology impressed her.[81] He held forth on this subject during an excursion, though he realized that the others who accompanied them neither understood what he was talking about nor cared. "Buffaloes," he whispered to her.[82] Beskiba also describes how he was moved by scenic beauty, relating how a waterfall had inspired him to write a poem during his student years.[83] Lueger's youth shows a normal if unexceptional romanticism. Conventional, too, were his superstitions, and his melodramatic observation to her that a plunge into the turbulent falls they were overlooking would result in instantaneous death.[84]

Beskiba believed that Lueger's recurring illness and the intrigues of her enemies prevented them from marrying and destroyed their friendship. She once threatened to kill herself as her uncle and three aunts actually had in 1894, the year when she and Lueger had begun their correspondence. Through the years Lueger remained adamant on marriage: he was already too old, too ill, the other party members would make fun of him.[85] Estrangement and recrimination eventually followed. Beskiba uses purple prose to describe their final break in November 1909. She had received a commission to paint Lueger's portrait and visited him in the Rathaus. When she rejected his advances, he became enraged:

> He staggered, a terrible change suddenly came over him. His face became pale as a corpse, his eyes started out of their sockets, foam rose on his blue lips. With unbelievable strength he threw me to the floor, howling: "canaille! canaille!" Then, scolding and cursing, he pushed me to the door.
>
> I attempted to moderate:
>
> "Remember, it's All Souls' Day! Are you crazy? The poor souls will avenge me."
>
> "The poor souls can . . ." he hissed like a madman.
>
> Those waiting in the adjoining room for an audience certainly must have heard Lueger's wild shouting. Now he stood framed in the door, pale as death, with trembling lips, his body trembling. I embraced him with a last, long, painful look.[86]

In 1911, the year after Lueger died, Beskiba failed in a suicide attempt. She survived in poverty and obscurity until her death at the age of sixty-five in 1934, the same year that Grey died.

Although Lueger's liaisons were evidently a source of gossip, the press was silent about his loves during his lifetime. This was an era when prominent and powerful public figures, living ones, at least, could have no sex life. One suspects that mutual courtesy among "gentlemen" precluded public airing of such matters. However, Lueger's "escapades" with the Women's League — for so they were treated by Socialist satirists — were more ridiculous than prurient in the eyes of his foes. His "antics" were fair game for enemy journalists and became a rich theme for comedy. Lueger's refusal to marry Beskiba may have indirectly proved the effectiveness of such satire, may have betrayed his anxiety that a domesticated Lueger would have become absurd, or at least have lost a mythical, bigger-than-life dimension. He had long been considered Vienna's most eligible but elusive bachelor, the darling of his female followers, and as usual had exploited his permanent and increasingly geriatric eligibility as a marketable political commodity. This suggests that he was at least dimly aware of the sexual dimension of Christian Social support, something that would have been lost had he married. (Hitler was certainly aware of this dimension in his own career and gave it as a reason for not marrying.)

Lueger's sex appeal was the theme of several hilarious satires by the Socialist Emil Kralik, better known by his pseudonym "Habakuk."[87] In an *Arbeiter Zeitung* column "Der Genosse aus Wildwest," Kralik regularly parodied the Frauenbund, presided over by the fictitious Frau Zwozerl. In a typical episode, "Sezession," Frauenbund members are eagerly anticipating the Fasching season with its parties and balls, which will provide the opportunity to dance with Lueger. However, their enthusiasm is dampened when they learn that a Christian Social conclave has decided that Lueger will not attend any festivities that season, for these would be injurious to his health. Substitutes for the mayor are considered — Prince Liechtenstein, too dull; Prior Rudolf Graf Mels-Colloredo, Lueger's rival at one time for the affections of the Amazons[88] — and rejected. "A ball without *der schöne Karl,*" decides a Gretl, "is like a head without hair, or teeth without a mouth." After various solutions to the problem have been considered and rejected, the members revolt against Zwozerl to form their own separate Frauenbund chapters, as the meeting collapses in anarchy and chaos.[89]

In thus satirizing Lueger's appeal, Kralik isolated the central and original purpose of the Women's League: to translate Lueger's appeal into political power. *Frauen-Zeitung* topics suggest additional priorities and other major objectives. These were often reported by the *Reichspost, Volksblatt,* and other major and minor Christian Social papers, as the Frauenbund attracted increasing attention and assumed more significance. To read the *Österreichische Frauen-Zeitung* is to enter the domestic world of the Christian Social rank and file of Lueger's time, or perhaps better, to visit the imaginary domestic environment of party journalists. The official organ of the Lueger Gretl was pious to the point of sanctimoniousness. Originally subtitled *Zeitschrift für die christliche Frauenwelt* (Periodical for the Christian Women's World), the *Frauen-Zeitung* eventually styled iself as an exclusively Catholic journal. In fact, "Catholic" came to be substituted for "Christian" in the subtitle. The *Frauen-Zeitung* regularly reported Vatican developments in the "Römischer Brief" column, carried accounts of *Ortsgruppen* meetings in which Lueger's speeches were featured, favorably contrasted the Christian *Weltanschauung* with the evils of Liberalism, Socialism, and anarchy, and was outspoken in its support of the existing male-dominated social structure. Such events as the assassinations of the Empress Elisabeth and of King Umberto of Italy were cited as implicit or transparent proof of Jewish plots to destroy the established social order.[90] For, above all else, the *Frauen-Zeitung* was outspokenly and implacably anti-Jewish. The anti-Semitism of this weekly periodical assumed various forms and was frequently racist, distinguishing between "Aryans" and "Jews" as between good and bad. A special feature included advice about how to educate children into anti-Semitism.[91]

Like Lueger, Klier insisted that neither the *Frauen-Zeitung* nor the Frauenbund advocated religious anti-Semitism, because there could be legal action on the grounds of infringement on the rights of legal religious equality. They were, after all, "Christians" in their beliefs and practices. "But Christian love should not . . . mean that one feels love only for another kind, for a race that thinks differently, so that this suppresses the love for one's own people."[92] Lueger put it another way: in allocating brotherly love among various categories of non-Germans, Jews ranked last. His remark was greeted with "great amusement and stormy applause" by a Frauenbund gathering.[93]

The *Frauen-Zeitung* was patently sympathetic toward foreign racism, whether directed against Jews, blacks, or orientals. Thus, for example, Klier's paper reported that "the southern states of the North American Union form a front against the Negro-friendliness of President Roosevelt and threaten violence if he sends them black officials. That may not be 'human'—but perhaps they have a Negro Question, as elsewhere—a Jewish Question."[94] A great novelty for the *Frauen-Zeitung* was the speech of an American Negro woman, delivered "in a broken German-American dialect" to a Berlin Women's Congress. The tone of the article was partly incredulous, suggesting that the reporter was amazed that a black could communicate in German at all, partly snide and condescending. The journalist wondered if the speaker would have received the same enthusiastic applause in her native land as in "reactionary and medieval . . . Europe."[95]

Lueger was touted by the *Frauen-Zeitung* as the high priest of anti-Semitism and from all reports lived up to his image.[96] It therefore naturally followed that his wisdom on this subject was prominently featured.[97] In 1903 a Lueger quotation framed in an ornate rectangle created the impression of an aphorism: "The anti-Semitism of modern times is not the disgrace of the nineteenth century, but one of its greatest achievements. Is it not then actually glorious and honorable to provide for its issue? Do we not fulfill this task in the grandest manner when we protect our children and children's children from disgraceful subjugation?"[98] Lueger was certain to receive enthusiastic endorsement from his female followers when he expressed the expected opinions on topical anti-Semitism. For example, in

November 1900 such papers as the *Reichspost* and the *Deutsches Volksblatt* ran front-page polemics against a Jewish shoemaker's apprentice, Leopold Hilsner, who, it later emerged, had twice been falsely convicted for a ritual murder.[99] Lueger told his followers of Mödling, a Viennese suburb, that the complicity of Hilsner and other Jews in the crime was "very unpleasant" for the Jewish community, but he further implied that Jewish unity precluded them from admitting Hilsner's guilt. Lueger suggested that Jewish solidarity be countered with Christian solidarity, that Christians remain unwavering in their belief in Hilsner's culpability.[100]

One of Lueger's anti-Semitic speeches was treated as a major policy statement by the *Frauen-Zeitung*. His remarks were delivered to the Ortsgruppe Eggenburg during a 1905 Christian Social Party Day. His statements are worth repeating because they again reveal that Lueger, the anti-Jewish agitator, was still active at this relatively late date in his career. More significant, they also provide insights into his thinking about his own importance as an anti-Semitic politician. Lueger said he was happy to note that "times . . . had improved": when he had first appeared in Eggenburg, it had been impossible to speak negatively about Jews without embarrassment. But since then, things had changed, thank God. When he had first tried to criticize the activities of Jews, the responsible official tried to cancel the meeting. Only the intervention of a local churchman had saved the official from the crowd. Now one could speak about the Jewish population without having charges filed against him. "I don't want to deliver a very anti-Semitic speech; I regret that I didn't bring my friend Schneider; he would have seized the opportunity to deliver such a speech." Lueger said he thought that the Frauenbund owed its existence to the breakthrough of the anti-Semitic idea in troubled times. He admitted that the Jews still controlled finance, but added that thanks to the municipalization of Vienna's utilities, he had weakened their grip somewhat. The price of meat was high because Jews were the middlemen between the producer and consumer; farmers' wives should therefore be particularly careful not to patronize Jewish shops; women should be especially watchful about Jewish peddlers and warn their husbands not to patronize them, because in so doing, the entire Christian people was injured. Lueger then departed from his usual anti-Semitic opinions by remarking that Jews had started to attend churches in Vienna so that others would refuse to believe that they were still Jews. But Christians should not be fooled. Whenever Christianity was attacked, Jews and their helpers, the Social Democrats, were always the aggressors. He thus suggested his underlying racist intent: once a Jew, always a Jew. More than forty years ago, he continued, the German poet Dingelstedt had warned that Christians should beware of being confined to ghettos by the Jews. This could soon come about, he admonished, but if his listeners helped, together with their men, things would soon improve. Lueger was convinced that the Frauenbund would do its share. All must assist in liberating the Christian people from its chains.[101]

In touching on the need for economic boycott, one of the favorite themes of Frauenbund speakers, Lueger also suggested the most important purpose of the league, apart from his own political advantage,[102] and the related aspect of political agitation for the Christian Socials. Readers of the *Frauen-Zeitung* were politically provided with lists of "acceptable" Christian merchants and warned away from specifically Jewish-owned stores and shops.[103] "Buy Only from Christians!" readers were exhorted from the paper's masthead, though evidently without much success. Four years after the founding of the league, the *Frauen-Zeitung* published an article "Where Do Christians Buy?" in which it was concluded that Jewish shops were being patronized more than ever, in fact, ninety percent of the time. Though various explanations were offered, the official organ of the Lueger Gretl could do little more than repeat threadbare slogans and advise readers to patronize the advertisers in Christian papers, and before all others, those in the *Frauen-Zeitung*.[104]

For at least one Lueger Garde leader, boycotting Jewish businesses was intended to achieve another purpose besides that of merely weakening the alleged Semitic economic grip on Vienna and Austria. A more novel aim was announced by Vice President Theresia Ruzizka shortly before Christmas in 1899. She informed her listeners that women might be instrumental in solving the Jewish question where men had failed: "If the *Reichsrath*, provincial diet, and municipal council did nothing, women knew how to help. If they purchased no more from the *Herren* Hebrews, then they would be forced to emigrate. The Christian Yule festivities would be desecrated if a present bought from a Jew lay beneath the Christmas tree," she warned.[105] In thus postulating the emigration of the Jews, Ruzizka anticipated the central theme of Josef Scheicher's *Aus dem Jahre 1920*, which was endorsed by Platter shortly after its appearance a few months later.[106] Ruzizka's remarks were followed by those of Ernst Schneider, who was admired by Beskiba for his "integrity."[107] Schneider suggested that Christians maintained a more closely cooperative and loving relationship in their marriages than Jews. Jewish husbands looked on their wives as mere tools for reproduction, Schneider assured his listeners.[108]

"The enlightened *Führer* of the Christian people of the *Ostmark*," as Platter referred to Lueger,[109] told his listeners during an *Ortsgruppe* meeting in Vienna's seventeenth district to fulfill the familial tasks "which our Lord determined." The Christian Socials were helping to further this goal by trying to enable the Christian woman to get out of the factory and back to the home. The Christian wife had been called to educate the children:

> Where she is missing, the children will not be educated as they should be. It is sad to see the kind of institutions we have to replace the mother: crèches, day nurseries, then come kindergartens and then school itself. The child is not at home, it is turned over to strangers, because the mother must go to work in the factory. That is a misfortune for human society. . . . There are professions enough where the woman, as a consequence of her physical and intellectual condition, will find a place, but where the man belongs, the man should work, and the woman should preserve and educate the family; that is the only correct standpoint of the Christian Social Party. The women who follow us understand and approve this standpoint. Now the elections are coming again and you have the duty to agitate always and everywhere.[110]

Lueger's opinions were endorsed and elaborated on by a contributor to the *Frauen-Zeitung* who suggested that Christian women were already "a little bit emancipated." Had they not united and commenced activity in an area that had until now been exclusively the preserve of men, the political area? The Lord rejoiced over such emancipation, for women had not cooked the worse for it, nor neglected their domestic labors. And this sort of emancipation had brought glorious victory. However, the type of emancipation sought by American women, who wanted to become judges, mayors, and the like betrayed feminine dignity. Women might become doctors, though, especially if they worked beside their husbands, or writers — Baroness Ebner-Eschenbach provided a case in point — but the choices were clearly circumscribed. If women desired emancipation within the prescribed professions, their efforts were enthusiastically endorsed.[111]

Lueger's educational notions were predictably applauded by the Frauenbund, which deplored the Freie Schule movement, the inclusion of Social Democrats and Pan-German Nationalists on public school faculties, and the contact between Christian and Jewish children. The *Frauen-Zeitung* reported on erring teachers who instructed their students about evolution, and editorialized by including strong doses of fundamentalism and Christian moral teachings. In one series, "The Christian Weltanschauung," Count Josef Ledochowski condemned Freemasonry, "the embodiment of Liberalism," for undermining religion in public life and fomenting godlessness.[112] The emancipation of women was one of the main goals of the Freemasons, the product of the destruction of ecclesiastical authority in the school and home, he asserted.[113] In subsequent installments Kant and Lombroso were attacked,[114] Darwin's theories were condemned as false in their entirety, and the authenticity and credibility of the origin of man according to the Holy Scriptures were defended.[115]

The *Frauen-Zeitung* agitated for the Aryan Theater, urging its readers to attend such ideologically loaded works as the anti-Semitic *Der Recht-schaffene* and the mutilated *Merchant of Venice*. After the mass attendance of a Frauenbund contingent at the latter play, a *Frauen-Zeitung* reporter commented that the evening had been a revelation "for many a doubting soul." Both the "meaning and the importance of the play were fully comprehended by . . . more than 800 women. The applause at the right places said this."[116] However, lapsed party theater protégés were dealt with harshly. The playwright Rudolf Hawel had achieved his first notable success at the Aryan Theater with *Mutter Sorge*. But when he deserted to the Christian Social opposition and created a satire on the ruling party, *Die Politiker*, he was condemned as a traitor.[117]

In artistic matters in general, the Frauenbund shared Lueger's tastes, whether consciously imitating the Master or not. It was ironic that Lueger, who together with municipal councillor Rufus Mayreder had "won approval for the permit to construct the new Secession building"[118] shortly after he had become mayor, later expressed disapproval of the movement to Beskiba,[119] and added his name to a list of Christian Socials who opposed the purchase of Gustav Klimt's *Die Medicin*.[120] Scandalized by the Secessionist art movement, a *Frauen-Zeitung* art critic reflected that the new art had been spawned by the same environment as the Panama scandal and Dreyfus affair:

> Whoever has not lost all feeling of shame and self-respect will find it impossible to approve this development which was slowly prepared through the influence of Freemasonry. They know very well that poison is not simply served up in bitter doses, but sweetened, and little by little. With its first appearance, this art consisted of ludicrous, often insane caricatures, portraying men and objects in unthinkable forms and colors, and one smiled over it! For to paint women and men with blue or green hair is simply unnatural, and yet the Secession gloried in the "ever natural." . . . I heard . . . the remark of a gentleman from abroad, that he thought the Secession exhibit flouted all morals, and regretted having made the journey to Vienna. And yet this exhibit was attended by a great many *women* and *girls*! The children and youth must be subjected to evil influence first in order to prepare fertile soil for every perniciousness.[121]

The underlying homiletic and authoritarian tone of such commentary was typical of the official Frauenbund outlook and of Christian Socialism during the Lueger period in general. Attacks on aesthetic relativism and moral didacticism were also common, and such teachings were often pessimistic in the extreme.[122] Admonitions were offered more often than practical solutions or suggestions for improvement. Sometimes the hope was expressd that "Christian virtues" would ultimately triumph over the godless machinations of "Jewish" Liberalism and its equally "Jewish" hand-maidens, Freemasonry and Social Democracy.[123] Sustained complaint about deficiencies at all levels of society was the norm for the *Frauen-Zeitung*.[124] Its journalists were cultural pessimists. Articles from this paper assumed a threatened and embattled readership; it was implied that be-tween the readership and social, political, and cultural disaster stood only Lueger and his chief lieutenants, Liechtenstein, Gessmann, Schneider, and Bielohlawek, who were frequent celebrities at league meetings. Thus Frauen-bund members received little cheer or cause for rejoicing from the *Frauen-Zeitung* beyond an attempt to portray a sense of community in the meetings of Lueger's followers. Humor, as such, was sometimes of the *Schadenfreude* variety. On one occasion the members were to be titillated by an anecdote about a Hungarian official being buzzed by a swarm of black and yellow wasps — the Habsburg colors.[125]

Immorality was an indelible characteristic of the Jewish race, the *Frauen-Zeitung* preached. An especially acute danger, therefore, was posed for German Christian girls by Jewish employers, for the possibility of ra-cial pollution was ever present. In a feature article, readers learned of the thwarted attempt by a Jewish official to seduce a fifteen-year-old orphan who worked as a house servant. The official was reportedly tried, con-victed, and sentenced to four months imprisonment. The article concluded that such crimes deserved "severe punishment."[126] A racial threat of a dif-ferent sort was identified by Pastor Josef Dittrich, an experienced Chris-tian Social agitator, who warned the women in Lueger's home district of Margareten that a Japanese victory over Russia in the new war in the Far East would soon make "the competition of the yellow race perceptible in all areas."[127] As Christians, Dittrich told the Frauenbund, they had no choice but to support the Russians. The *Frauen-Zeitung* lamented continu-ing Russian defeats and blamed them on Jewish anarchists and nihilists. Frauenbund speakers at *Ortsgruppen* meetings were praised for having identified Russia as "the only great nation which publicly fought and restricted the Jews."[128] In the eyes of Klier's paper, the Japanese came to pose a threat to "Christian Europe," economically, racially, and culturally, second only to that of the Jews.[129]

The Lueger Gretl gradually declined in importance as the Christian Socials consolidated their hold on Viennese and Lower Austrian politics. The most valuable political function of these women was tactically agita-tional, and toward the end of Lueger's life, they became superfluous. Petty rivalries and internecine struggles were symptomatic of this decline. Yet the actual dissolution of the league was accelerated by the fall of Platter and Klier. The fortunes of the Frauenbund, an inner party group, were in part tied to the fortunes of its leaders. The organization and its fate may thus be seen as a microcosm of the Christian Social party, although the larger entity, at least, survived Lueger for another generation.

As early as the Rathaus Christmas celebration of 1903, Lueger had hinted that there was dissension within Frauenbund ranks. But he quickly reassured his listeners that he would continue to support the league as before, emphasizing that he would not try to supplant the existing organization by creating alternative women's groups in some districts to circumvent the difficulties, as some had perhaps speculated. He proclaimed "the *Bund* an important part of the organization of the Christian people"; and he remained "always ready . . . to intervene decisively," if necessary. If here and there "things . . . that are not pleasant" had appeared, it was better "to pass over them lightly."[130] Although he remained vague about the unpleasantries, Beskiba suggests that Platter's unflagging support of Klier, who was "hated by almost all the women,"[131] led to her fall and to his. Platter loaned Klier money from Frauenbund funds on at least three occasions. His failure to repay them in their entirety was the evident source of rumors and criticism of her leadership.[132]

Toward the end of April 1906, Platter resigned as president of the Frauenbund "for purely personal reasons."[133] She had refused to run for reelection and was succeeded by Marie Porzer, the wife of the second vice-mayor.[134] Though rumors of financial mismanagement involving Platter and Klier never came to formal charges, anxieties that they might prompted a statement from her in the *Frauen-Zeitung* six months after her resignation. The wording and tone of her denial, in which she asserted that she was "pure and blameless in every connection, also as *wife* and mother,"[135] was in keeping with the ideal, if not always the reality, of the stereotypical Lueger woman.

Platter's statement appeared less than a month before the *Frauen-Zeitung* ceased publication in November 1906. Frauenbund meetings continued into the next year until the league merged with the larger Austrian national Catholic women's organization. Reports of such meetings in smaller, more local papers were perfunctory and dwelled on past achievements, particularly those in which Lueger had been prominent, but could no longer be because of declining health. In this way, his name continued to be linked to the Frauenbund and the seeds of legend were sown. It is tempting to speculate that the vitality of the league reflected that of the party leader. In any case, the Frauenbund was most vigorous during the early years of Lueger's mayoralty, when his more spectacular municipal building achievements were accompanied by equally spectacular electoral successes, when the force of his personality was strongest, and when he was most effectively able to resolve differences within party ranks. Victories at the polls were measurably assisted by Lueger's women, who embodied a new style, more personal agitation, and who carried the Christian Social message into the home as no other group had done before them. Thanks to them, and to the *Österreichische Frauen-Zeitung,* Lueger and Christian Socialism came to be seen as an established class and were associated with traditional values opposing the forces of anarchy and godless materialism personified by the Socialists. Through the *Frauen-Zeitung,* Christian Socialism became further identified with Christianity, law and order, Germanic idealism, and morality. These connections remained in the minds of many. But the *Frauen-Zeitung* also joined these values to anti-Semitism. Such ideas, disseminated by this and other papers, and by the women they represented, took root in many families, a fertile area for subsequent growth.

Hermann Nothnagel. When prominent non-Jews such as the surgeon Hermann Nothnagel and University of Vienna Rector Laurenz Müllner (shown on the following page) condemned anti-Semitism, they earned the undying hatred of Lueger and his party. (Author's Collection.)

PROF. DR. LAURENZ MÜLLNER,
Rector Magnificus der Wiener Universität.

*Laurenz Müllner. (Courtesy of the Austrian National
Library Photograph Collection.)*

*Lueger's early political mentor Ignaz Mandl, whose party
was probably the first to use anti-Semitism in a Viennese
electoral campaign in 1877. (Author's Collection.)*

Der Judenliberalismus glaubt, er fährt infolge der Nichtbestätigung **Lueger's** in den Himmel,

During Lueger's career political anti-Semitism assumed these graphic forms and became widespread. The caricature above and the three that follow appeared in the autumn of 1895 when Lueger's third election to mayor failed to receive the necessary sanction from Franz Joseph. The anti-Semitic Kikeriki *depicted inflated Jewish hopes dashed, attempted Jewish accommodation to Lueger, and Lueger as a Christian martyr. After discrimination against Jews on religious grounds had been prohibited by law, anti-Semitism found expression in racism. (Courtesy of the Vienna Municipal Library).*

Gratulationskour beim neugewählten Bürgermeister.

Eine Neuerung.

Die Bürgermeister von Wien erhalten als Amts-Ehrenzeichen, wenn sie judenliberal sind: **die goldene Kette,**

wenn sie christlich-sozial sind: **die Dornenkrone.**

Wahrscheinlich leiden sie an Mahleria.

Kikeriki: Sie, Herr Wachmann, was sind denn das für Hütten?
Wachmann: Das sind die Monumente für den Direktor Mahler und Hofrat Wetschl.

The above two cartoons show Gustav Mahler as a target of
Kikeriki. (Courtesy of the Vienna Municipal Library.)

When playwright Arthur Schnitzler received the Bauernfeld
Literary Prize, the Minister of Education Hartel was pilloried
as a lackey of the Jews. (Courtesy of the Vienna Municipal
Library.)

Iſrael jammert über den chriſtlichen Ritualmord an Dreyfus und verlangt neuerlich die Antiprieſung der franzöſiſchen Generale und Heiligſprechung aller Drei- und Vierfüßler.

Kikeriki *was not the only Viennese anti-Semitic tabloid. Theodor Taube's* Figaro *commented sardonically on the "Christian ritual murder of Dreyfus." One of Taube's anti-Semitic plays,* Der Rechtschaffene, *was produced with scant success on the party stage. (Courtesy of the Vienna Municipal Library.)*

Kikeriki!

Nr. 89. 5. November 1903. **Humoristisch-politisches Volksblatt.** Postsparkassa-Konto Nr. 801.189. Telephon-Nr. 3942. **43. Jahrgang.**

Alle Rechte für Illustrationen und Artikel vorbehalten.

Neuestes.

Zu den zahlreichen, den Österreichern und Ungarn gemeinsamen Angelegenheiten ist eine neue hinzugekommen: die gemeinsamen Ungelegenheiten.

Der Woeikl und der Zein haben ihre Landtagsmandate zurückgelegt, da ihr Freimut zu ihrer Wehmut in keinem Verhältnisse mehr steht.

Genosse Schuhmeier hat das Pendel in der Rotunde, das schwingt, ohne „gebutscht" zu werden, wegen Erwerbstörung geklagt.

Die durch das Gastspiel der Frau Jarno-Niese eingeleitete Fusion des Jubiläumstheaters mit dem Josefstädter gilt als bevorstehend.

In Mazedonien sollen alle Mörder — mit Ausnahme der Selbstmörder — amnestiert werden.

Das neue ungarische Ministerium ist bis zum Schlusse des Blattes noch nicht gestürzt worden.

Der mazedonische Aufstand droht zu erlöschen, da es im ganzen Lande keinen Christen mehr zu ermorden gibt.

Die Landesjudenschaft Niederösterreichs hat gegen die Eröffnung der Kaltwasserheilanstalt am Handelskai wegen Gefährdung der öffentlichen Sicherheit Protest erhoben.

Der Fürst von Bulgarien will den Entente-Mächten eine lange Nase machen.

Dann ade!

(Nach bekannter Melodie.)

Wenn Jud' Jarnos Zoten Kunstschwein
Zwischen „Hahnwirt" und „Grundstein"
Immer schmutz'ger weitergrunzt;
Wenn bei Währing das Theater
Simonistisch ein beschnatter
Jude neuhebräisch punzt:
Dann ade, ade, ade! Dann ade, ade, ade!
Dann ade! Schatz, lebe wohl!

Wenn für grimme Ungarnhasser
Übers schmale Leithawasser
Nach Canossa geht der Weg;
Wenn in Post noch alle Neune
Stehen fest im Glorienscheine,
Für Cis' Ohnmacht als Beleg:
Dann ade, ade, ade! Dann ade, ade, ade!
Dann ade! Schatz, lebe wohl!

Wenn der Mahler nicht mehr rappelt,
Im Orchester nicht mehr zappelt,
Daß ein'm Hör'n und Seh'n vergeht;
Wenn der Wetschl mit Courage
Selbst sich reduziert die Gage,
Weil er so schon auf sich steht:
Dann ade, ade, ade! Dann ade, ade, ade!
Dann ade! Schatz, lebe wohl!

Wenn auf Universitäten
Die Karnikel sind von Nöten,
Daß der Jud' sie lebend spickt;
Wenn in solchen armen Hirnen
Von gelehrten Geisteswaserln
Wird das Heil der Welt erblickt:
Dann ade, ade, ade! Dann ade, ade, ade!
Dann ade! Schatz, lebe wohl!

Die Befreiung des Pegasus.

Provincial delegates Sturm and Weiskirchner free Pegasus from the Jewish cultural yoke. Austrian school children learned Friedrich Schiller's poem Pegasus im Joche. The racist anti-Semitism is a post-classical addition. (Courtesy of the Vienna Municipal Library.)

Lueger as the possible victim of a kosher plot. (Courtesy of the Vienna Municipal Library.)

In the eyes of Austrian anti-Semites, the Jews were responsible for the 1905 Russian revolution. (Courtesy of the Vienna Municipal Library.)

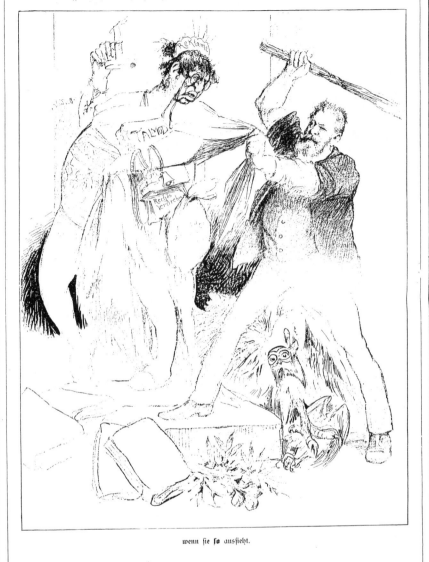

"Dr. Lueger is actually a bitter opponent of science, if it looks like this." A comment on the Wahrmund Affair. (Courtesy of the Vienna Municipal Library.)

Nr. 25   Wien, 26. März 1908.   **Humoristisch-politisches Volksblatt.**   Telephon Nr. 218/IV.   **48. Jahrgang.**

Gegründet von G. F. Berg.

Alle Rechte für Illustrationen und Artikel vorbehalten.

Neuestes.

Die diesjährige Märzfeier wurde in der üblichen Weise zu der üblichen Zeit an den üblichen Orten von den üblichen Personen abgehalten und von der gewissen Presse mit den üblichen Worten und Bemerkungen begleitet. Der christliche Teil der Bevölkerung verhielt sich ruhig und trachtete seinerseits alle — — „Üblichkeiten" niederzukämpfen.

Um noch im Jubiläumsjahr den Bau der neuen Hofburg fertigzustellen zu können, wurde soeben der bei der Karlskirchen-Renovierung beschäftigte Maurer an den Franzensring kommandiert.

Der Ring des Saturn ist unsichtbar geworden, weil er ihn bei der allgemeinen Teuerung hat — versetzen müssen.

Trotz der „Erleichterung" für die Maturanten wiegen die Schulpakel noch immer ihre zwölf Kilo!

Operettenkonflikt.

Bravo, bravo, Bosniak!
Bist ein Mann doch von Geschmack.
Also nicht vergebens gab
für dich aus sein Geld der Schwab.
Und du zeigst doch eine Spur
Der gepriesenen Kultur,
Höher als ganz Wien du stehst,
Weil die „Witwe" du verschmähst.

Bravo, bravo, Herzegowzen
Die durchaus ihr nicht so oft seh'n
Wollt die Hanna Glawari
Wie der Rest der Monarchie.
Auf dem ganzen Kontinent
Das vernünftige Element
Seid nur ihr, denn ihr allein
Fielt nicht auf den Blödsinn 'rein.

Aber leider, Bosniaken,
Hat die Sache einen Hacken.
Denn noch schlechter ist, was jetzt
An der „Witwe" Stell' ihr setzt,
Wenn ein Hoch ihr tausendtönig
Peter bringt, dem Schmierenkönig.
Dieser König und sein Prinz
Sind die übelste Provinz.

Den Geschmack daran, Großserben,
Muß man schleunig euch verderben,
Vorbereiten eine nette,
Zwar nicht neue „Operette".
Denkt ihr noch des alten Strauß,
Aufgeführt bei euch zu Haus'?!
Sagt, ob dieser euch genüg'?
Wollt ihr einen „lust'gen Krieg"?

Anläßlich der Verurteilung

eines Richters wunderte sich der Staatsanwalt darüber, daß der Betreffende so lange im Amte belassen worden sei, obwohl seine ganze Umgebung ihn als alten Teppen erkannt habe. — Wenn alle jene Vorgesetzten, die von ihren Untergebenen (natürlich unter sich) „senile Blödlinge" genannt werden, pensioniert oder kassiert würden, dann sähe es mit dem Avancement in Oesterreich besser aus!

Tragikomische Situation.

Der **Wahrmund** im **Lügenmaul.**

Punning on Wahrmund's name "true mouth," Kikeriki identified a tragicomical situation: "Wahrmund in a lying snout" — that of the Jewish press. (Courtesy of the Vienna Municipal Library.)

„Ich bin kein Judenfresser!"

Kikeriki: Wahr is! Mir schmecken s' a net! Aber i bitt', steht das im **alten** oder im **neuen** Katechismus?

Erscheint jeden Donnerstag und Sonntag
und kostet solo Wien, Provinz und Ausland vierteljährig mit
portofreier Zusendung 4 Kronen.
Abonnements ins Ausland werden bei den betreffenden
Postämtern unter unserer Post-Nr. 3833 angenommen.
Buchdruckerei Fritz Gabriel Ilger & Comp. (verantw. Leiter: Joh. Schröder).

Sprechstunden des Eigentümers
Fritz Gabriel Ilger
Mittwoch und Samstag von 12 bis 2 Uhr mittags.
Redaktion und Administration:
1., Grünangergasse Nr. 6.

When for tactical reasons, or to avoid the charge from imperial authorities that he was discriminating against the Jewish minority whose rights he was duty-bound to respect, Lueger denied that he was an anti-Semite, Kikeriki called him to task. (Courtesy of the Vienna Municipal Library.)

The Liberals saw such incidents as evidence of Lueger's opportunism. Here, he attends a seder. (Courtesy of the Historical Museum of the City of Vienna.)

The following eight caricatures depict the swindling of Galician peasants by Jewish travel agents. After the peasants have departed from Oświęcim, better known today as Auschwitz, the Jews confiscate the peasants' property and divide the spoils. The ruined peasants return, inform the authorities, and the Jews are arrested and jailed. The seventh picture parodies Jan Matejko's painting Rejtan before the Sejm *(a reproduction of which directly follows). These eight originally tinted caricatures were part of Lueger's collection of anti-Semitica. (Courtesy of the Historical Museum of the City of Vienna.)*

Lueger presents the officers of the anti-Semitic German-Austrian Writers' Association to Emperor Franz Joseph. (Courtesy of the Austrian National Library Photograph Collection.)

Ritual murder and politics. Both before and after he was elected mayor, Lueger stated in parliament that he believed the Jews practiced ritual murder and referred to the legend of Anderl von Rinn, a Tirolean saga. In 1985 the interment of Anderl's remains triggered a national cause célèbre in Austria, and controversy over Anderl continues. (Author's Collection.)

Raimund-Theater.

„Die luftige Witwe" zieht ein. Draußen steht die Volksmuse als „traurige Waife".

The downcast Germanic Volksmuse stands aside as the implicitly Jewish theatrical spirit, symbolized by The Merry Widow, surges into a former "German theater." Though some of his party members were outspokenly opposed to this particular operetta for anti-Semitic reasons—one of its librettists was of Jewish descent—Lueger had little to say about it, doubtless because of his earlier gaffes over the party theater. Ironically, The Merry Widow was one of Hitler's favorite operettas, and the Viennese actress Rosa Albach-Retty recalled that Hitler tried out for the chorus. (Courtesy of the Vienna Municipal Library.)

ZUM
BLEIBENDEN GEDÄCHTNIS
AN DAS FÜNFZIGJÄHRIGE
REGIERUNGS-JUBILÄUM
S.ᵉ MAJESTÄT DES KAISERS
FRANZ·JOSEF·I·
ERRICHTETEN ZWEITAUSEND
WIENER·FAMILIEN·IM·
VEREINE·MIT·DER·
GEMEINDE·WIEN·
·DIESES·
·VOLKSSCHAUSPIELHAUS·
ALS·EINE·PFLEGESTÄTTE·
·DEUTSCHER·KUNST·

This tablet dedicated the Kaiserjubiläums-Stadttheater as a place of "German art." More than an expression of nationalism in an intensely nationalistic era, the plays of the Jubiläums Theater were originally intended to challenge the "Jewish influence" in Vienna's theater world. (Author's Collection.)

Moſche. Sarah. Rabb. Sender. Peſcha. ⸬ Abraham. Gode. Michel. Zipa.

1. Actſchluß.

Conclusion of Act I, Söhne Israels. Though this racist anti-Semitic play was forbidden to be performed on the party theater stage by the imperial censor, director Adam Müller-Guttenbrunn paid for its publication and distributed it and another such play in thousands of copies. (Courtesy of the Theater Collection of the Austrian National Library.)

The actor Leopold Nowak played Shylock in the first *Jubiläums Theater* version of Shakespeare's Merchant of Venice. *The purpose of this production was transparently political and appeared shortly after Alfred Dreyfus's second conviction for treason in 1899. (Courtesy of the Theater Collection of the Austrian National Library.)*

Another transparently political version of The Merchant *appeared in Nazi Vienna in 1943. Werner Krauss (right) played Shylock. (Courtesy of the Theater Collection of the Austrian National Library.)*

Nazi Propaganda Minister Goebbels was inspired to make a major anti-Semitic film with Lueger and Georg Ritter von Schönerer as the heroes. Wien 1910, directed by E.W. Emo, was the result. The above and the following four illustrations are stills from the film. The plot centers on a dying Lueger's attempts to save the city's finances from a Liberal take-over. Lueger explains the individual emblems of his mayor's chain of office to local children: "In the second district . . . there is a lot of . . . heavy Jewish money, and with that go envy, greed, hate, and all the seven deadly sins." When Schönerer visits Lueger shortly thereafter, the mayor begs him to protect his life's work. The film's subplot centers on the conflict between the Liberal leader and his son, who goes over to Lueger. In the municipal council, the son causes a major anti-Semitic incident by assaulting Viktor Adler, who has jeered at Lueger. Following Socialist revelations about Lueger's love life, Adler's editorial office is wrecked by the Christian Socials. Wien 1910 starred major actors Rudolf Forster as Lueger, Heinrich George as Schönerer, Lil Dagover as Lueger's lover, Carl Kuhlmann as Lechner senior, O. W. Fischer as his son, and Herbert Hübner as Viktor Adler. (Courtesy of the Austrian Film Archive.)

Lueger im Himmel.

Petrus (zu den Engeln): Kinder, räumt 's schön z'samm', der Wiener Bürgermeister hat immer viel auf Ordnung g'halten!

Already a legend at the time of his death, Lueger was assured of a prominent place in the memory of the Viennese and in heaven, at least according to party cartoonists. St. Peter tells the angels to tidy up, because the mayor of Vienna always prized order. (Author's Collection.)

Lueger in the 1980s. (Author's Collection.)

7

Lueger and the
"Gelatin Intelligentsia"

I have begun to cleanse the schools of Vienna, and I have carried this
out rather well, thank God.
                    —Lueger to the municipal council, *December 20, 1904*

I believe that many . . . who are . . . our opponents will agree with me
when I say that the teachers who instruct our children must be of good
Austrian, good German, and Christian disposition. (Applause.) Others
cannot and will not be tolerated.
                    —Lueger to the Landtag, *December 22, 1904*

*I*n describing his style, which "always bore the marks of a certain grace,"
Carl Schorske remarks that Lueger "belonged to the strange silent community of understanding that subsisted in Vienna between the decaying
nobility and the depressed 'little man'—what Hermann Broch called the
'gelatin democracy' of Vienna's gay apocalypse" (*Fin-De-Siècle Vienna*,
136). My term "gelatin intelligentsia" thus derives from "gelatin democracy," and in this chapter epitomizes those who rejected aspects of Liberal
aesthetics and values in an attempt to reinforce more traditional petit
bourgeois social and cultural mores. In so doing, the gelatin intelligentsia
paradoxically helped inspire and contributed importantly to the development in Austria of a counterculture.

Born of the "dissonance between emotion and scientific rationality,"
in Hannah Hickman's phrase, gelatin intelligentsia signifies a group of

Lueger supporters personified by his chief lieutenants and younger generation subleaders. Although often imprecise or inarticulate about their values, or in some cases only dimly aware of them, such persons increasingly tended to embrace tangible, materialistic, and often quantifiable goals — necessarily so, perhaps — to which they gave their own meanings. Lueger was their mentor, and he saw to it that party values were upheld and spread in the public schools under Christian Social control.

More specifically, the gelatin intelligentsia rejected the aesthetics of Viennese Liberal high culture because they were too cosmopolitan, too abstract, often totally incomprehensible. This high culture was far removed from the sentimental, völkisch-nationalistic, and religiously oriented values of traditional petit bourgeois Lower Austrian Catholicism. Believing that theirs was a distinct and separate culture from Liberal "modernism," and separate also from the high culture of the aristocracy, the gelatin intelligentsia remained "traditional." It also occasionally promoted a technology whose very lack of qualities, whose neutrality, lent itself to whatever purpose its users desired. Lueger's municipal gasworks, trams, and electricity plant reflect admiration for modern technology. While acknowledging the significance of such creations and his technocratic attitude in a larger progression toward "reactionary modernism," this chapter will deal less with the concrete manifestations of such technology and its meaning than with Lueger's and his followers' attitudes toward the political uses of culture and education, and the employment thereof. The fruit of Lueger's cultural politics became apparent in the next generation and beyond.

By the end of the nineteenth century, traditional Lower Austrian cultural values had grown brittle. The culture itself, as it found expression among Lueger's lower-middle-class followers, had begun to show the effects of its own collective expediency, an attitude their response to his leadership sanctioned and accelerated. As their disregard for cultural restraints increased, the moral underpinning which once, if however imperfectly, supported an earlier traditionalism, weakened and gave way. The final result was a nihilism that proved fatal to civilized values and practices in Austria. The baleful effect of Lueger's cultural politics is perceptible in that country even today.

When it came to culture, Lueger was never totally abstract or theoretical or, for that matter, totally pragmatic, but truly expedient. Lueger's cultural politics, however, had theoretical foundation. During his university years, he had studied the effect of "reciprocal intellectual forces" on individual "intellectual development."[1] "The intellectual life is free," he learned from Lorenz von Stein, and it was "the task of the mind" to "renew . . . the entire intellectual life in each individual existence."[2] This was the educational process and was "as old as the world." Yet individual intellectual freedom also poses a problem, according to Stein, because intellectual life and intellectual renewal necessarily became the objects of "state activity": since the state made the rules governing education, "education . . . [was] an absolute process."[3] In a student essay, Lueger wrote that the protection of the "individual in the social situation is obviously the responsibility of the human community, since the protection of the same is in everyone's interest. Only the human community in its entirety, i.e., the state, can guarantee this protection." The state's sole purpose, then, was "to protect [only] the existing society."[4]

Lueger took these views seriously. As mayor, he distinguished between the individual and the larger community in his policies, but despite his university essay, the individual came to assume a distinctly secondary importance, though Christian Socials enjoyed a great advantage over members of rival parties. Lueger behaved as an all-powerful mediator, paternalistic, if not increasingly authoritarian, though he sometimes also masked his power and methods for tactical reasons by claiming to be of secondary importance in the city council or the party. In no area were his theoretical beliefs and the policies that stemmed from them more in evidence than in the administration of cultural and educational matters. Of all the leading Christian Socials, he sensed most keenly the possibilities of controlling people through ideas, and promoted his ideas, particularly in school matters. To Lueger, strong traditionalist that he was, the general principles of education and culture were self-evident, and he tried to ensure that such principles were effectively implemented. Lueger's attitudes toward elementary education were consistent: children must be raised as good Catholics, good Austrians, and obedient citizens who were vividly aware of the superiority of Germanic civilization. That the realization of these goals could lead to anti-Semitism becomes clear in his remarks and in the attitudes and practices of Christian Social teachers. Lueger rejected or tried to silence the educators whose views differed from his. His dogmatism in this area, as well as his general understanding of culture, inevitably generated controversy before and after he became mayor. As one might expect, he publicly rejected freethinking secularism. Toward Pan-German Nationalist teachers, he displayed implacable enmity. The beliefs of this Protestant group, which was implicitly pro-Prussian, though its supporters in the monarchy were Habsburg subjects, were antithetical to Austrian political Catholicism on one hand and to the multinationalism of Austria-Hungary on the other, both of whose principles Lueger aimed to uphold.[5] This frequently created conflicts, for as a staunch Austro-German, Lueger had difficulty in resolving his own firm nationalism and its public expression with the no less firm nationalism of Czechs in Vienna, an increasingly important and volatile element in the city's population. Though he posed as a friend of the "Bohemians," avoiding confrontation with them or with any other Slavic group in the capital, Lueger continued to believe that the Austro-Germans were the superior nationality and should control municipal and imperial politics.

John Boyer has called attention to the "ambivalence" of "Lueger and other Christian Social politicians" toward "the upper bourgeois intellectual elite," adding that the Christian Socials desired to associate with them on the one hand but "resent[ed] their attainments" on the other.[6] This suggests an uncertainty, if not a conflict, of values among the Christian Socials. Yet, as Lueger grew older, such a conflict resolved itself; and he gradually abandoned the university aspiration to emulate the "upper bourgeois intellectual elite." Instead, he embraced Christian Social values, which had more in common with his early domestic environment. The traditional lower-middle-class culture returned as a counterculture to oppose the dominance of Viennese high culture by Jews. Though he revealed classical taste in art from time to time, Lueger was essentially mired in popular culture, a resentful response to the esoteric trend of modern art, which was shared by his admirer Hitler. Lueger used counterculture to criticize Enlightenment doctrines of moral progress and faith in human equality. Yet, he respected the rationalism that made technological progress possible. The mature Lueger upheld *Biedermeier* values, and with them, the repressive traditionalism of the *Vormärz*. He regressed even further and began to admire the Middle Ages, showing the influence of Vogelsang and Schindler.

In 1890, a month after the death of Vogelsang, Lueger told the provincial diet that more had been done for art in Vienna during the Middle Ages than at present, when parvenu stockbrokers were spoiling the plastic and dramatic arts, destroying "the [*Biedermeier*] comedy and the farce . . . and they have made a miserable caricature of the former happy and easygoing life of the common people in Vienna."[7] Ten years later he remarked during a municipal council session: "People scold a lot about past times . . . about the Middle Ages, about the conditions of the so-called Dark Ages when the great hat covered the sun, etc. [an allusion to the large hats worn by priests], but I can tell you one thing, among the people, there never were such sad conditions as there are now in the time of the Enlightenment."[8]

Toward the end of his career, yet another cultural impulse engaged Lueger. He supported attempts to blend classical Greek culture, early Germanic mythology, and Christianity. Such endeavors took the form of a Viennese Hall of Fame on one of the city's outlying hills. This structure was to be both a kind of acropolis with adornments inspired by Christian and pagan German motifs and a Valhalla,[9] a museum and a living monument to the city, which would also be a recreation park.[10] Lueger's efforts were discouraged by Archbishop Simon Aichner, who requested the mayor to desist from planning a "heathen cultural place" as a cornerstone of Christianity, which "hinders the good success of the Catholic missions in Central Africa and elsewhere."[11] Lueger's indifference to Aichner's letter and his proceeding with the project suggest that the archbishop's plea fell on deaf ears. The one constant and distinguishing feature of Lueger's mature cultural viewpoint was his nostalgia and his idealization of antiquity. About this he was outspoken.

In the manner of his expression, if not in some of his views, Lueger came to resemble Eduard Pötzl's satirical character "Herr von Nigerl," a self-confident arch-Viennese *Hausmeister* who blustered before questions he could not answer. Thus, in one of his many escapades, "der Herr von Nigerl" as "Timon of Vienna" acts like Shakespeare's misanthrope and blusters away his ignorance of the newly completed *Hof- und Burgtheater*, the national court theater.[12] Though Lueger's want of knowledge never fell to the level of Herr von Nigerl's, the mayor's occasionally dogmatic reassertion of earlier cultural values suggests the gradual disappearance of his youthful intellectual eclecticism. And as the years passed, the more Liberal concepts that he had entertained during his student days disappeared.[13] His political importance and its force in cultural matters made this a significant change.

In referring to Lueger's anti-Semitism and in trying to explain his popularity, Joseph Samuel Bloch also touched on a larger cultural-political phenomenon that Lueger both reflected and exploited:

> Men had revelled in humanity in the eighteenth century, [in] the age of enlightenment; love of mankind was the word of the day; was the topic of every conversation, the theme of all political pamphlets, was preached from the pulpit in churches, from the desk in Parliament, and in all public assemblies, till one got sick of it, and nerves were utterly deadened to such feelings; the reaction came at last, they longed for contrasting spiritual food, and hatred in all its various shapes, as religious hatred, racial hatred and hatred of caste became a necessity, gratified spiritual desires, and he who touched on such subjects was cheered and had won the willing ears of the masses.[14]

Although many may have longed for "hatred in all its various shapes," the vestigial influence of enlightenment theory at first remained evident in some of Lueger's proposals. Thus, at the beginning of his mayoralty, humanistic Lueger had criticized the bad effects of industrialism on Vienna and sought support for public recreation areas. His appeal was rational, addressing as it did the need to reverse environmental destruction, and visionary as well, for it painted pictures of better and happier surroundings. However, his vision was also political. By converting some areas of the city into parks, he created green areas, and thus removed the possibility that cheap municipal housing might be built on such lands. Any threat to the income of the landlords who were among his most important supporters was thereby also removed.[15] His motives in this respect had been transparent to Kielmansegg from the days of the Fogerty affair in the early 1880s, when Lueger opposed the building of an overhead railway. This "superbly designed project," in the view of the governor,[16] Lueger publicly opposed "because of . . . technical details." But privately and candidly, Lueger admitted to Kielmansegg that he represented the landlords who constituted eighty percent of the municipal council. If the railway were constructed, cheaper housing would become available in the outlying areas and the rents in the inner city would fall.[17] He exerted himself to prevent this: "To dramatize the issue, he and his lower-middle-class, property-owning followers constructed a mock-up of a viaduct resting on iron pillars on the Schwarzenberg Platz in the middle of Vienna to suggest that the proposed project would ruin the city's skyline and endanger property values. He thus pioneered in a political aesthetics and also tapped economic anxieties."[18]

In his inaugural address as mayor fifteen years later, Lueger deemed it an obligation to create more parks, and proceeded to do so. His environmental "prescience" has become legendary and his efforts have been praised by his biographers, and not a few of his foes.[19] But as usual there was a coincidence of political and altruistic motives. Shortly before Lueger's death, one foreign observer commented that if one could look into the mayor's soul to determine his priorities, he believed Lueger would choose flowers in all the windows rather than cheap meat in Viennese homes, "food for the eyes and the soul" rather than for the stomach.[20] However, one of Lueger's opponents criticized the neglect of worker districts in the larger effort at beautification. More than ten years after Lueger took office, Franz Schuhmeier pointed out that the flowers that decorated the Ringstrasse did little to alleviate the misery of the workers. Where they lived, the air was bad and the streets turned into quagmires when it rained. The ubiquitous plaques honoring Lueger's horticultural triumphs, Schuhmeier added, achieved an effect opposite to what was intended when they appeared wherever a new sapling had been planted and a handful of grass seed had been sown.[21] Schuhmeier had a point. Lueger's thirst for honors and commemoration became so well known that when an elephant was born at Schönbrunn Zoo, a wit suggested that a tablet immortalize the event: "Born during the Mayoralty of Karl Lueger."[22]

Lueger's stated desire to preserve and maintain the landmarks of Vienna and Lower Austria sometimes stimulated demagogic excess. For example, he once suggested that St. Stephen's Cathedral was an exclusively Christian property. He thereby denied not only a rival politician's assertions that this landmark belonged to Austrian society as a whole, but he also implicitly excluded Jews as a part of the cultural, and larger social, community.[23] The idea that St. Stephen's belonged to all Lueger deemed "laughable." Such remarks were telling. As often as not, his words bespoke his anti-Semitism as well as his cultural nationalism. In this case, he belligerently added that good Catholics and good Protestants would know how to defend their "religion" and "nation" if they were threatened.[24]

Lueger's cultural politics were not confined merely to creating recreational areas and preserving or defending landmarks or monuments from real or imaginary foes. He and his intelligentsia actively promoted "indigenous art" in several forms. They subsidized the anti-Semitic German-Austrian Writers' Association[25] (see illustration), greeting its creation as "a release from a nightmare that burdened the breast of every truly German-feeling friend of literature."[26] They also made repeated efforts to promote the writing of "artistically important dramatic work[s]" by "Lower Austrian writers, who through their Aryan lineage are qualified to create authentic indigenous popular art."[27] They emphasized their determination by requesting imperial approval for the funding of a two thousand-Gulden annual prize. Although such steps did not get very far, the Christian Social–controlled diet did win approval for a subsidy to support the implicitly anti-Semitic Association of Catholic Writers of Austria.[28] Interest in Christian-German dramaturgy was intensified by the Aryan Theater project, which, though a failure, nonetheless stimulated further efforts to build a similar stage in the third district. Before the Aryan Theater collapsed, one municipal councillor stressed that the same principles should be upheld by creating the third district playhouse, so that "German . . . Aryan art again prevails."[29] After its failure, anti-Semites contented themselves by inserting a clause in the organizational statutes of the new theater, which was never built, to prevent Jewish children from receiving any of the four hundred free tickets that were to be distributed during school vacations.[30] Only after this provision had been ridiculed by Liberal and Socialist municipal councillors was it omitted.[31]

Many Christian Social municipal councillors agreed that any theater on which they had any influence should achieve an educational, if not an ideological, goal. This held true even after Müller-Guttenbrunn's failure.

One of their spokesmen, Johann Laux, a priest and declared racial anti-Semite,[32] demanded to know why the municipal theater, which had been pledged to promote German plays, to uphold and cultivate Christian German values, was being given over to productions of *The Merry Widow,* "the favorite of our Jewry," and Ludwig Anzengruber's *Kreuzelschreiber,* a play of pronounced anti-Catholic tendencies.[33] Lueger, who had become increasingly prudent about theatrical pronouncements following the *Hermannsschlacht* incident, pleaded that he was too busy to take a more active part in such matters:

> I myself have no influence at all on the plays performed there. To be honest, gentlemen, I don't meddle in this affair; I have so much to do with beef, so much with coal, that I just cannot trouble over plays. The report of the Magistrat has been submitted to me, will soon be taken care of, and, if the gentlemen wish, I shall report on it in the plenum of the municipal council. (Municipal councillor Schuhmeier: Municipal council theatrical censorship!) Silence, please, you should have had your fun by now. [Amusement.][34]

Laux's opposition to Anzengruber's play echoed an earlier difference of opinion among the higher and lower clergy over cultural matters. In 1901 a request for money for an Anzengruber monument triggered a debate in the municipal council. While Theodor Wähner, the editor of the *Deutsche Zeitung,* the official mouthpiece of Lueger's party, defended Anzengruber as one of the most important German and Viennese poets of the nineteenth century, Canon Anton Schöpfleuthner, the master of St. Stephen's, critized Anzengruber's *Der Pfarrer von Kirchfeld.* In this work, Schöpfleuthner pointed out, the title character forbids his flock to attend the kind of meetings the Christian Socials had been organizing by the hundreds during the past years, calling such meetings "a suicidal movement."[35] The canon had thus isolated one aspect of Anzengruber's work that may have been objectionable to some of the more militant Christian Socials, but there was another, even stronger reason for his objections that remained unspoken. This particular play, which also criticized conservative tendencies within the church, was a favorite among the lower clergy in Vienna, and they had applauded its performance in the Aryan Theater.[36] Any attempt to honor Anzengruber, who had been just as critical about the shortcomings of the upper Catholic clergy as he had been about secular failings, was bound to irritate someone like Schöpfleuthner. Lueger himself avoided a confrontation with his party members on this and like issues, or was otherwise evasive, preferring to postpone decisions that might antagonize one or another party faction. This Fabian tactic stood him in excellent stead.

In the light of Christian Social efforts to subsidize Aryan authors, it was inevitable that the honoring of a Jewish dramatist with an "Aryan literary award"—at least as far as the Christian Socials were concerned—would provoke a fight. This occurred in March 1903 when Arthur Schnitzler received the two-thousand-Gulden Bauernfeld Prize for his one-act play cycle *Lebendige Stunden*. In parliament Pattai submitted an inquiry to the minister of culture and education, Wilhelm Ritter von Hartel, requesting an explanation for the decision, for Pattai had been part of the committee who had made this award. Giving the prize to Schnitzler injured "the rights of the non-Jewish writers' world," Pattai stated, because it violated "the meaning and purpose of the bequest."[37] Foreigners would be misled by receiving the impression that German literature in Austria was being written almost exclusively by Jews, an impression strengthened by the fact that this prize had been awarded to Jews in the past. Moreover, the quality of their works "was the lowest possible." The Bauernfeld Foundation had not originally been intended "to promote the dissemination of the Semitic spirit in literature," Pattai concluded, "which often enough . . . so grossly injures the moral and aesthetic feeling of the indigenous population of Austria."[38] Pattai's inquiry once again revealed the anti-Semitic arguments of the Christian Social intelligentsia against other contemporary literary developments. Their opposition emerged, not only in parliamentary inquiries, municipal council interpellations and debates, cartoons, feuilletons and reviews of works by Jewish authors, but sometimes also in criticism of such non-Jews as Sardou and Ibsen, whose works were held to embody "the Jewish spirit."[39] A Landtag representative from Floridsdorf, Alfred Knotz, once rejoiced during a session that Vienna possessed at least one theater "where Jewish authors, where Zola, Dumas, Sardou, Ibsen are not performed."[40]

Another facet of the Christian Social distaste for what they called modern was their tendency to think allegorically. If Lueger and other Christian Social leaders revealed any overtly cultural-political preferences, these were directed toward new plays with whose historical heroes they could readily and easily identify.[41] In this respect Lueger was like Hitler, Stalin, and Mussolini, all of whom enjoyed historical allegorical theater. Mussolini wrote a play *Cavour*, which was performed in wartime Berlin. For his part, Lueger enjoyed the 1899 play *Konrad Vorlauf* by a municipal official, Wolfgang Madjera. In this uninspired work, "false perspectives abound[ed]," and subordinate developments assumed paramount importance; "crucial events [took] place between the acts and had to be explained later—" according to one reviewer from the clerical paper *Das Vaterland*.[42] Despite its artistic shortcomings, it was cheered by Lueger. The play's hero was an early fifteenth-century Viennese mayor named Vorlauf. When he tried to mediate between rebellious workers and aristocratic rivals, Vorlauf exclaimed, "He who wants to understand the people must listen to them." At this speech Lueger shouted "bravo!"—perhaps with a touch of cynical irony—[43] from the municipal loge. From Lueger's point of view, "the play offered everything a Viennese could want: the tribute to a great son from his city, fealty toward an ancestral ruler, an outstanding sense of justice, and parallels to the present times 'since the mayor today also has to keep a stiff upper lip on all occasions.'"[44] The Socialists were less complimentary, seeing in *Vorlauf* "an apotheosis of the Lueger regime and derision of the working class."[45]

Vorlauf, as part of the permanent Aryan Theater repertoire, was to have begun a series of historical epics. Each year, such works were to have been performed on October 3, the emperor's name day. But lack of success of this play augured ill for similar future efforts. It was replaced after nine performances, possibly at the insistence of the court, which may have considered the drama subversive, for the historical Vorlauf had been executed for treasonable opposition to the ruling family. Yet, the following year another historical play was performed. *Der Dorflump von Dellach* by Hans Arnold Schwer revealed "the bloodless dramatics of [the *Volksblatt's*] ritual murder editor," in the words of the *Arbeiter Zeitung*.[46] This drama was even less financially successful than its precedessor, and a quarrel developed between Müller-Guttenbrunn and Schwer, each blaming the other for the failure.

Continuing disagreement among the Christian Socials about precisely what constituted acceptable dramatic fare doomed subsequent efforts. One faction thought religious allegories should take precedence; another argued that the age cried out for secular themes.[47] A similar conflict underlay some of the disagreements within the party itself. Interestingly enough, the party theater's most popular work was *Quo Vadis?*, a dramatization of Henryk Sienkiewicz's novel about first-century Christianity. This play enjoyed a run of 100 performances by the spring of 1903. *Quo Vadis?* doubtless appealed to the party theater public for several reasons, including its sensationalism, muted sexuality, religiosity, and fundamentalism. Most critics recognized the play's blatant propagandistic intent. While the Christian Socials celebrated a glorification of Christianity, and the failure thus "of fifty years of Jewish agitation," a critic for a Jewish working-class paper "thought he had been transported into the midst of a . . . Christian Social meeting resounding with anti-Jewish agitation." He suggested thereby that anti-Semitic "propaganda had passed from proclaiming to acting out fantasies."[48]

In a letter fifteen years after Lueger's death, Wolfgang Madjera complained that "Aryans of all party persuasions" had been principally responsible for the failure of the party theater.[49] Moreover, he predicted that "German narrow-mindedness" rather than "the malice of the Jews" would defeat "Christian-German culture in Austria." His criticism could serve as a summation of the entire literary-theatrical endeavor of the Christian Social intelligentsia. Lueger himself became impatient though gradually indifferent to the theater as an ideological instrument, if he had ever thought it would work in the first place. Other Christian Socials, however, continued to back this avenue of influence as second only in importance to the press in disseminating ideas.[50] Attending to the city's affairs, harmonizing the factions within the party, and caring for his own declining health took more and more of Lueger's time. Experiments in cultural politics like the Aryan Theater episode were left increasingly to subordinates. Even without the theater, however, Lueger's cultural opinions owned their own force, not only because of his position, but also because of the great personal popularity and respect he commanded. Moreover, as far as play selection went, some Lueger supporters tried to please him by providing the kind of fare they thought he would like.

Lueger's cultural politics was always subtly "interactive." For example Müller-Guttenbrunn evidently tried to accommodate Lueger's dramatic and musical preferences as well as his own in developing the Aryan Theater repertoire. This shows up in the five-year performance record of the party theater.[51] Lueger had indicated the broad outlines of his taste *docere et delectare*—a very ancient position—following the premiere of *Die Hermannsschlacht:*

> The true Viennese always mixes seriousness and levity, laughter and tears. Every Strauss and Lanner waltz laughs and cries at the same time, as do Schubert's dances. Even the greatest Viennese vernacular poet, Ferdinand Raimund, could laugh and cry at the same time, as well as perhaps the greatest poet of all times, Shakespeare. We have to try to produce the right mélange. At this we Viennese are past masters.[52]

Some of the more popular actors, writers, singers, and musicians[53] realized that they had a friend in the mayor. Accordingly, he was named an honorary member of various musical and theatrical groups, including the Österreichischer Bühnenverein. Occasionally they sought his intervention in professional and political matters as well. For example, the popular actress Hansi Niese, who received gifts from Lueger, requested help in obtaining a building permit for the Theater in der Josefsstadt, managed by her husband.[54] And the populist writer Peter Rosegger, who stated that both he and Lueger strove for similar goals, though they pursued different paths,[55] encouraged Lueger's support for a German language school in a border area.[56]

For all his traditionalism, however, Lueger was thoroughly "modern" in his close acquaintance with artists and entertainers; he enjoyed mingling with them as an equal rather than seeing himself as their patron and therefore avoiding them because they were socially inferior. This began in his early professional years and may, as with Valerie Gréy, have had a formative influence on him. Lueger's close association with the world of art and acting, however, indicates a subtle change in key. He may have intended to facilitate a newer and different kind of social integration through his public friendships and contacts, which would be watched by many. Clearly, something that extended beyond class considerations and that was ideologically modern informed his behavior. As party leader and mayor he knew well that his political behavior provided a model. Yet, it is impossible to determine whether politics was always foremost in his mind as the following incident reveals. He once defended his decision to honor the popular folk singer, Franz Fischer, on his fiftieth birthday, and before the celebrated geologist Eduard Suess on his seventy-fifth. However, because Suess was a Liberal, a question about Lueger's authentic motives necessarily remains.[57] In any case, his decision here says something at least about his topical priorities.

One of the most "Viennese" of all Lueger's characteristics, his love of music, and particularly of Austrian regional music, was probably inherited from his mother.[58] He supported many musical ensembles in word and deed from his early years, and religious musical groups were voted subventions by the municipal council once he became mayor.[59] Yet even this culturally respectable activity at times took on a more immediately political, or ideological, tinge in his hands. Lueger sometimes made political capital out of everyone's love of music. In 1885, for example, at the time of his calculated support for Schönerer, Lueger drafted a speech welcoming members of a German-Nationalistic singing group, the Wiener Liedertafel, of which he was an honorary member. On this occasion, he praised the "preservative qualities" of the German *Lied,* asserting that "as long as a people remembers its songs, it cannot perish."[60] Later as mayor, his politicization of music was more subtly directed, not only because of Christian Social support for the church and its music, but also because of anti-Semitic attacks on "Jewish influence" in the arts. Socialist and Liberal criticism of Christian Social allocations for "Christian art and science" added fuel to the fire.[61]

In late May 1909 Lueger's remarks at the Haydn centennial celebration in Eisenstadt created a considerable to-do, and not only among the musicians. The special significance of this incident grew out of the fact that Lueger attended the Haydn ceremony both in his official position as first citizen of the royal and imperial capital, something he stressed, and as the host of an international musicians' congress. As such, his very presence carried obvious weight, and anything he said or did would obviously be widely reported — and was. Lueger showed his characteristic vanity when, irritated that he had been relegated to the fifth or sixth place among the dignitaries slated to place wreaths on Haydn's grave, he refused to yield pride of place to anyone. On the arm of a nun, Sister Mathilda, because he was practically blind at this time, a symptom of his diabetes, he made his way to the head of the procession.[62] Ever since the emperor's refusal to sanction his elections, Lueger had been sensitive to questions of protocol and official procedure, something his assistants occasionally learned to their cost.[63] On one occasion the mayor angrily complained to Prince Rudolf von Liechtenstein about being turned away from a memorial service for the Archduchess Elisabeth and made to "pass all the rows of people, . . . which must have appeared as if I had wanted to force my way unauthorized into the funeral service."[64] During the ceremonies at Haydn's grave side, Lueger triggered another anti-Hungarian incident when he praised Haydn, who was buried in what the mayor considered to be Hungarian soil, as "a faithful German and good Austrian," the composer of "the holy national anthem that is here disdained." Then he declined an invitation from Prince Esterhazy to attend a "pious ceremony," because "the Austrian national hymn was not permitted to be played."[65] Though the *Reichspost* praised the cathartic effect of Lueger's remarks as something that had needed to be said in the face of continuing Magyar "provocations,"[66] other papers were less pleased.

The *Arbeiter Zeitung* ridiculed Lueger, for he had also revealed his ignorance of musical theory during a short speech on the same occasion.[67] The *Neue Freie Presse* criticized the "polemical character" of his words.[68] Apart from his obvious pique, it is difficult to escape the impression that Lueger's remarks were inspired only by disappointment over an error in protocol. The Haydn celebration incident suggests as much about his motivations as it does about his patriotism assumed by his earlier biographers to have inspired such remarks. In any case, Haydn's greatness as a composer assumed a secondary importance.

Lueger tried writing poetry, though the single surviving example is doggerel. He nonetheless enjoyed the couplets of popular Viennese folksingers, though he sometimes used them to make a political point. Richard Waldemar, a celebrated comedian as well, provided Lueger with the basis for a political comparison. The mayor told the municipal council how Waldemar sang about the perpetual construction that went on in Vienna's streets. First came the pavement breaker, then the ditchdigger, then the gas pipe layer, and others. And when their work had been completed, they started all over again on another corner. Lueger used Waldemar's song to criticize the request of a group of teachers for a raise. He said that if he agreed to raise the salaries of one category of teachers, others would soon flock to him with the same request.[69]

On another occasion during a Landtag session, Lueger had patronizingly quoted some verse that he evidently thought had been written by a Liberal, without realizing that the true author was Heine. This provided the *Neue Freie Presse* with the opportunity to ridicule Lueger's ignorance. Karl Kraus related the incident in *Die Fackel*, and then recalled that a cultural editor of Vienna's principal paper had committed a worse error four years previously. Kraus asked: "And now I ask who is more worthy of scorn: an assembly speaker who, in the intellectual smoke of party politics does not recognize Heine, or a high-brow paper, professionally oozing education and progress, that ridicules Schiller's verses as a dilettante attempt in its literary section."[70]

Lueger's artistic traditionalism and growing dislike of the Secessionist movement — *l'art juif* in the words of Theodor Kornke, a lawyer, municipal councillor, and outspoken defender of "Christian Social aesthetics"[71] — were revealed in his preferences for painting and sculpture. According to Beskiba, he had a good eye but he understood nothing of painting.[72] Yet, Lueger's opinions about the arts achieved a notoriety or fame, depending on the cultural political camp one belonged to. One of his traditionalist pronouncements even acquired an aphoristic renown among his followers. According to Kornke, at the unveiling of a monument of an architect "of the old school," Lueger stated: "Today, where ugliness is made a principle, we must doubly honor men who have created beauty for us."[73] On another occasion, Lueger told Christian Social artist Josef Engelhart that the main thing was that people immediately recognized what a monument was supposed to represent: "Only then can people be interested in it and happy, and the human purpose is thereby achieved as well as the artistic."[74] For Lueger, the artist must thus accommodate himself to the traditional function of art (and to the stupidity of his audience, he might have added), rather than express himself. Stylistically speaking, he felt the *Biedermeier* period was an ideal. He therefore praised Ferdinand Georg Waldmüller as "perhaps Vienna's greatest painter," and reckoned it as "an honor" that the municipality had acquired his paintings wherever possible.[75]

In 1901 Lueger and other leading Christian Socials created an annual twenty thousand-Gulden prize to promote "indigenous art" in Lower Austria, and thereby tried to revitalize this aspect of culture much as Müller-Guttenbrunn had tried to revitalize the Austrian theater by producing early nineteenth-century plays.[76] However, in this instance, anti-Semitism did not assume the same importance as with the Christian Social–initiated literary prize, when the "indigenous art" clause made the anti-Jewishness of the proposal transparent, probably because there were few Jewish artists.[77] Art prize money was spent to purchase the paintings of such artists as Carl Freiherr von Merode, Franz Rumpler, Johann Victor Krämer, Robert Russ, Josef Jungwirth—"really pretty pictures" instead of "a lot of Secessionist pictures," in the words of Liechtenstein[78]—and also of Ernst Stöhr, Felician von Myrbach, and Rudolf Ribarz. (See illustrations.) Liechtenstein was unintentionally ironic, for Stöhr, Krämer, and Myrbach were prominent members of the Secession.

Controversy surrounded the building of a museum to house the paintings. The Christian Socials sometimes sided with the Liberals in support of one architect's designs; at other times they condemned the entire modernist movement, for which Josef Hoffmann, the architect, was occasionally blamed for the worst excesses.[79] Kornke once quoted Hoffmann as saying that if one did not hurry through Vienna's streets one would "die of shame and pain," because of the "lack of sensitivity, and barbarism of our buildings," such as the town hall and parliament.[80] Christian Social indignation at such statements indicates something more than mere Philistine disapproval. Kornke and other like-minded Christian Socials considered the ideas, opinions, and especially the designs of Hoffmann as attacks on the existing social order, because they opposed established beliefs—a Steinian idea.

Lueger and his followers announced their intention to rehabilitate society, and part of their program turned on renewing the aesthetic, artistic traditions of the past. In contrast with this artistic emphasis, however, their attitude toward technology looked to the present; indeed, it anticipated that of Hitler. Here, and importantly, Lueger and some of his henchmen were somewhat unusual among the era's anti-Semites. "We live in a time of express train speed, of electric speed," said the mayor.[81] During a Landtag debate with Viktor Adler, Lueger praised the technology of the fin de siècle. This as well as Christian Social dynamism, he implied, had made possible great achievements in communal politics. Though the Liberals had the same possibility, the Christian Socials were cleverer and had better understood how to exploit their opportunity.[82] A further indication of Lueger's embracing modern technology was the creation of eight mayoral fellowships for students of the Technical University in Vienna.[83] In 1903 Schwer and other municipal councillors proposed that Vienna participate in the St. Louis World's Fair of 1904, to refute the lies of the *Neue Freie Presse* and "the international Jewish press about the Habsburg imperial capital." Specifically, the Americans were to be shown the results of the Christian Social influence on Vienna of the past few years, "a triumph of our technicians."[84] Perhaps it was not entirely coincidental that some of the most virulently anti-Semitic Christian Socials, including Bielohlawek, Anton Baumann, and Schneider—significantly enough, a mechanic[85]—supported increased aid to technological development. This group proposed an aviation prize of thirty thousand Gulden "for successful flight achievements by native Austrians."[86] To them, machines were simpler and easier to understand than modern art and the impulses that lay behind it. This group living in a period of accelerating change and conflicting values perhaps believed that modern technology in time would of itself solve the problems of modernism.

Yet, the rejection of some aspects of modernist culture may also have been due in part to the nonpolitical thinking of the Secessionists themselves, as Carl Schorske has pointed out. They "had set out to regenerate Austria by creating a whole *Kunstvolk*" but had ignored the political implications of their actions in a highly politicized society. By 1908 Gustav Klimt petulantly complained that "public life was predominantly preoccupied with economic and political matters."[87] To Josef Hoffmann, social questions were "for the politicians to solve," such problems were "not the concern of artists."[88] Lueger would probably have agreed, though he also grasped the social and cultural dimensions of his politics and those of technology.

Despite the vehemence and occasional venom of the debates over art and architecture, Lueger demonstrated rough jocularity, if not common sense, in artistic matters. By ridiculing the prudishness of some of his party members, he helped restore balance. After a postal official municipal councillor had repeatedly objected to a proposed monument, an allegory including a nude woman (see illustration), Lueger said that "the fear of a naked woman was terrible," and added that he would write to the pope and ask him to close the Vatican art collection because it contained too many nudes.[89] On another occasion he defended a church mural design of Alfred Roller against the criticism of clergymen that it was too sensuous and therefore inappropriate for a church. Lueger, who had just returned from a visit to Italy and was filled with impressions of Rome, indicated the boldness of Michelangelo and other artists of similar stature in their religious art: "The popes themselves ordered and approved of it." This time, however, he was challenged by an irate clergyman: "Bosh! . . . these popes are roasting in hell, too!" The design was changed.[90]

The proverbial Philistinism of Christian Social Hermann Bielohlawek at least once surprised even Lueger. Or perhaps it would be more accurate to say that Bielohlawek's lack of Philistinism on this occasion elicited Lueger's irony, for he was used to Bielohlawek's antagonism toward those of artistic temperament. When Bielohlawek proposed a "monumental colossal fountain" to celebrate the sixtieth anniversary of Franz Joseph's reign, Lueger said he never knew that "Bielohlawek was such a great friend of art."[91] Bielohlawek had acquired his reputation because of an incident in parliament. Exasperated over the many books introduced as evidence by a Social Democrat, Leo Verkauf, Bielohlawek had exclaimed: "Another book! I've lost my appetite!"[92] His words were variously quoted, or misquoted, by the foes of the ruling party to ridicule the Christian Socials' lack of cultural values and antipathy toward education.[93] Though Bielohlawek sometimes capitalized on his reputation for Philistinism to good effect,[94] he did, however, defend some Secessionist creations, such as the Postsparkasse (Postal Savings Bank) and Kirche am Steinhof, which were distasteful to other Christian Socials.[95] On at least one occasion, he even praised the Secessionists for introducing a new furniture style; significantly, however, this had led to the creation of new jobs for cabinetmakers.[96] But Bielohlawek's qualified approval of some Secessionist products may have been motivated by sycophancy, because the structures had been designed by Otto Wagner, an established architect, and evidently a friend of Lueger. Bielohlawek and Robert Pattai found qualified praise for the Secession,[97] but they also appear to have mistrusted this movement, thus reflecting aspects of the more general animosity of the anti-Semites toward cultural modernism reflected in such publications as the *Deutsches Volksblatt* and *Kikeriki*. (See illustrations.)

Although Lueger openly relished defending tradition, he was inconsistent in his attitude about the preservation of historical sites. He was also cynical about the would-be protectors of architectural monuments. He and Otto Wagner dismissed efforts to preserve an eighteenth-century war ministry, an important part of an architectural ensemble and a valuable structure in itself, Wagner referring to it as an "old box."[98] In an article in the *Wiener Illustrierte Extrablatt*, Wagner added that "we live for the living and not for the dead. If men want to see the dead, they should go to a museum. We want to live in a modern city that satisfies all the appropriate aesthetic and hygenic requirements."[99] In this sense, he and Lueger existed "to get rid of the past and to get things done."[100] But Lueger defended the preservation of the Florianikirche, a structure linked with his youth for which he evidently had a sentimental attachment, as he did for the Karlskirche in which he was christened and after whose patron saint, Karl Borromäus, he had been named.[101]

Lueger revealed healthy practicality, as well as impatience and skepticism, when the regulation of the Wien River was delayed because of the dilatoriness of sculptors. He was dismissive, too, about the stone carvings that were to adorn the walls containing the river:

> Gentlemen: I have reviewed the matter and am convinced that we won't finish this year . . . if it continues like this; that is my opinion. I am convinced that all the things yet to be done are not for the sake of beauty. For instance, a few carved crocodiles are supposed to be added — and the unfinished keystones are already there — and be adorned with an iron neckband [amusement], with a ribbon over it, and its head must naturally be pointed down, in order to symbolize the harnessed force of the old Wien River. In the middle of the keystone is a human face with its mouth wide open from which a fountain of water should gush; then, there are a few places for elephants . . . [amusement], which are also supposed to gush water. I won't concern myself with these things any further; instead, I took my, that is, your garden director with me, and told him: study the matter, beautify it, after all, why has our Lord created climbing plants? [amusement.] Plant as many as possible; and in the few ponds, whose purpose eludes everybody, include a few flowers, as well. The Viennese will be tremendously pleased with the whole thing, and we'll finally be done with it. I was told that carving these animals — the crocodiles — will cost 50,000 Gulden. [Hear! Hear!] That's pure madness, such bad business. Please take note of this. I shall endeavor to bring this affair to an end.[102]

Lueger participated in artistic occasions, sometimes revealing his tastes for adornment and his religiosity through casual remarks during formal ceremonies. Less than a year before his death, at a celebration honoring the winners of a window decoration contest, he stated:

> I admire all that artists create; I am happy when new façades arise — if they are not all too Secessionistic — I admire the works of engineers, builders, and architects, but what our Lord has created and still creates, all of our artists cannot attain. Therefore, artistic works must be completed by natural adornment. The cultivation of flowers and plants is . . . an indication of how far the culture of a city has developed. The decoration of houses and public parks brings joy to the hearts of the people and gives the whole city a happy appearance.[103]

In cultural and social matters, Lueger was occasionally flippant or vulgar or both. He once wished the leaders of an architectural congress good luck in selecting a meeting place, because "Viennese women were 'well built.'"[104] In a similar vein, the mayor addressed the question of medical care for schoolchildren as follows: "[I am] afraid that now and again a school doctor [will] be found, who examined the Viennese girls a bit too closely!"[105] And here, according to one who knew Lueger and the times, was the secret of his success with many. While European officialdom during the early years of the century abounded with frock-coated dignitaries like himself, he alone often spoke impromptu and said what was on his mind[106] and probably also on the minds of many of his listeners.

Usually cautious about taking sides in his party on cultural matters, by the end of his career Lueger avoided aesthetic debates as much as possible and public confrontations between rival artists and architects altogether. During one of his last municipal council sessions, he promised to facilitate an inquiry about the design of the municipal museum, but then facetiously added that he would not attend any meeting "of these experts" because he feared for his "physical safety."[107] In speaking thus, Lueger suggested that he was less anxious about charges of Philistinism from his rivals than antagonizing one or another faction within his party. Lueger's talents as a mediator among the Christian Socials remained unsurpassed, and were doubtless a factor in his calculations on controlling the party. A too smoothly functioning machine was neither desirable nor to be encouraged, for this would have obviated his importance as peacemaker. However, preserving the appearance of consensus and serenity among the Christian Socials exacted its price, as did maintaining the outwardly attractive appearance of the inner city. After his death events would prove that divisions among the Christian Socials were at least as formidable an obstacle to effective party functioning as challenges from the Socialists and that external adornment of Vienna's center counted for less than the discontent of ill-housed and underrepresented workers.

Lueger's nationalism became a factor in his cultural politics because of his emphasis on maintaining the "essential German character" of Vienna.[108] This aspect of his politics explains his appointing elementary and secondary school teachers who were loyal to the party and to his own notions of patriotism. Yet his nationalistic policies had to be applied with a measure of caution, not only because of the multinational character of the capital and his duty as mayor to administer impartially, but also because there were many non-Germans among his supporters, particularly Czechs or those of Czech descent.[109] Lueger early mastered the vital political skill of being all things to all people, for example, of being "Karl Lueger" to his German-minded supporters and "Karel Luegera" to the Czechs.[110] His success in this respect was attested in March 1908 at the time of one of his periodic illnesses, when a group of German tradesmen, lawyers, officials, and hoteliers from Silesia and Moravia solicited his support. This group felt that the imperial capital lacked "an organization which promotes an up-to-date development of the national ideas of German Viennese and the application of their *völkisch*-legal ideas in a strictly national sense."[111] By contrast, Czech cultural and economic institutions seemed to be flourishing in Vienna, and the petitioners included a front-page article from a widely read German-language paper *Silesia* to prove their point.

The Silesians and Moravians hoped that the condition of Lueger's health would permit him to reply. The few words scribbled on this document suggest Lueger's answer: "Be reassured, so long as I am mayor of Vienna, the city will preserve its German character."[112] Perhaps Lueger's petitioners were ignorant of his expressions of tolerance toward the Czechs, or that he had on at least one occasion expressed unwillingness to involve himself in "political quarrels" between Slavs and Silesians.[113] But Lueger's oft-quoted statement "Leave my Bohemian in peace . . . I'm on the best of terms with him"[114] did not prevent Hermann Bielohlawek, who boasted that his own speech betrayed no trace of Czech accent, from emphasizing that "we Christian Socials are Germans through and through."[115] Nor did Lueger hesitate to say that as long as he was mayor "not a word of Czech would be spoken" in the municipal council, nor could he imagine that any other mayor of Vienna would behave differently.[116] Lueger's insistence on German in the Rathaus and as a language of instruction in the schools became famous, and some of his supporters once even proposed that a clause be inserted in advertisements for teachers' positions that only those of "German descent and of German attitude" (*deutscher Gesinnung*) would be considered for employment.[117]

Lueger's nationalism was played out against a background of growing tension and violence among the Habsburg peoples. In 1908 the annexation of Bosnia and Herzogovina by Austria-Hungary nearly caused an armed conflict with Serbia. The following year, Lueger tacitly supported the granting of subventions to German schools in Slavic areas, though possibly as much for economic as for nationalistic reasons, for it was argued that the cultural loss of German-speaking regions would lead to their loss as markets.[118] Yet, despite his outspoken nationalism, Lueger did not object to the continuation of Czech cultural practices in Vienna. Doubtless he realized it would have been impolitic to do so. "As late as 1934 there were still 50,000 Czechs in Vienna (with their own primary schools)" and "the Czech community . . . retained a distinct subculture of its own . . . in defiance of and quite apart from the Viennese milieu."[119] However, Lueger did draw the line when it came to cooperating with Czechs from rival parties. Rather an alliance "with Liberals of the German nation than with Liberals of the Czech nation," he remarked, thereby revealing another nuance of his fundamental Austro-Germanism.[120] Even toward the Magyars he occasionally revealed his differentiating tendencies, distinguishing between Hungarian Christians and the "unprincipled bands of Jewish and

Freemasonic exploiters," who, according to him, remained Austria's most implacable foes.[121]

Lueger's single most important effect on cultural politics took place in primary and secondary education. From his earliest years as a municipal councillor he had demonstrated interest in educational matters.[122] Later, during his first campaign for parliament in 1885, a local teacher advised him to stress his accountability to win the election, and promised him seventy votes as well.[123] Both votes and advice seem to have stood him in good stead. Ironically, however, Lueger's role in educational politics once he had become mayor was fully authoritarian. The basic freedoms, freedom of expression, freedom of inquiry, and political freedom were denied teachers throughout his mayoralty and beyond. Teachers were officials, according to Lueger's follower, Gregorig, and as such were obliged to obey orders.[124] Thus did the Christian Socials and Lueger give accountability to supporters among the teaching profession.

The narrowing of Lueger's views on the degree of freedom admissible in education mirrors the decline of Liberal influence in Vienna's public schools and the reestablishment of clerical control.[125] Clerical as opposed to secular education was a thorny issue in Austria. In 1855 the Concordat between Austria and the Holy See provided for the reestablishment of far-reaching ecclesiastical authority over many phases of public schooling. However, in 1869 the so-called Reich primary school law, or Reichsvolksschulgesetz, in effect reestablished secular dominion over all but religious teaching in the public schools.[126] This law reflecting Liberal views was deeply resented by the conservative Pope Pius IX, who denounced it and refused to recognize its validity. Yet another major phase of the struggle developed in 1883. An amendment to the Reichsvolksschulgesetz included the provision that public school directors must have the same religious belief as most of their students and be able to hold religious instruction. This amendment led to still another rapprochement between church and school. But from 1883 the schools became the focus of increasingly politicized power struggles between clerical and secular educators, coinciding with the decline of Liberal power and the rise of radical parties, Lueger's among them. The Christian Socials controlled the Vienna District School Council, which Lueger headed, and governed hiring, firing, and promotions.[127] In 1903 he remarked during a Landtag session:

I have already repeatedly declared that I get along with the *Reichsvolksschulgesetz* in Vienna very well, very well, excellently! I have already regulated everything in Vienna [amusement] and if the [imperial] authorities had a little more courage [exclamation: So it is!], if they didn't crawl in fear before the Social Democrats and Schönerians, in all of Austria everything would have been regulated long ago. [Applause.]

One needs no change in the *Reichsvolksschulgesetz*, one needs only an energetic hand, guided by a head that knows what it wants, that directs the hand and does what is right and good for the people. [Applause.][128]

Persistent and determined efforts in the representative bodies by Liechtenstein, Ebenhoch, and Vergani, among others, to reverse the liberalizing efforts of post-1867 educational reforms were supported by the Katholischer Schulverein under the protection of Franz Ferdinand.[129] The Schulverein, which received financial support from the representative bodies controlled by the Christian Socials, became an important center of resistance to educational Liberalism. Vice-Mayor Josef Porzer, one of the Schulverein's most tireless exponents, called it "the organ and mouthpiece of the entire Catholic movement in Austria."[130] An attack on the Liberal educational reforms by Prince Liechtenstein in 1888, a proposal to reduce mandatory schooling from eight to six years, and to limit subjects to religion, writing, reading, and mathematics elicited criticism from the eighteen-year-old Karl Seitz, who had just completed his teacher-training education. This incident bears retelling because it anticipates, in its characteristics, Seitz's opposition to Lueger's educational policies, which were much the same as Liechtenstein's. Seitz, who describes the incident in an unpublished memoir,[131] had been named to deliver a student speech of thanks at commencement ceremonies. After doing so, he referred to Liechtenstein's proposal, which would have eliminated instruction in natural history, physics, geography, and history, as "a disgraceful law," and promised that if it were passed the younger teachers would oppose it with unimaginable unity of purpose and strength. Seitz called his words a slap in the face to visiting dignitaries, including some clerical officials. Though the school director held his concluding speech as planned, he withheld Seitz's teaching certificate. The incident was reported in the papers, became an issue in the provincial diet, and a complaint was lodged with the Statthalterei. After receiving advice and the assistance of Dr. Moritz Weitlof, a parliamentary delegate and president of the Liberal Deutscher Schulverein, Seitz was granted his certificate, though with a low grade in morals. He ends his account: "The Liberals at that time were still really freethinking people."[132]

A far different outlook prevailed under Lueger. His words "I'll make the school laws myself"[133] summarize his general authoritarianism, if not his specific attitudes toward the schools during his mayoralty, and the authoritarianism of Christian Social school officials. Before 1897 Lueger said that the Christian Socials had opposed the abuse of schools for political purposes[134] and that he was the friend of teachers in defending those of them who supported the Christian Socials against professional discrimination by the Liberals.[135] But once in office he behaved toward Socialists, German Nationalists, and sometimes also toward Jews[136] as had the Liberals toward the Christian Socials. It was, in fact, over the question of promoting a Jewish teacher that Lueger may have uttered the reply that subsequently came to be remembered as his most notorious quotation: "I decide who is a Jew!" According to Oskar Hein:

> Once a deputation from the teachers' association in the second district had asked me to intervene with the mayor concerning the advancement of a Jewish temporary assistant teacher who had been there a decade. Dr. Lueger, to whom I had mentioned the matter, told me: "You are also a politician. You know that we must accommodate the party to which we owe everything." I responded that the party owed more to Dr. Lueger than he did to the party. Dr. Lueger explained that he realized that these poor teachers were being unfairly treated, but that he could not prevail on the party in this matter. When I doubted this, he responded with a genuine Lueger witticism: "In those things in which I am smarter than others, I always succeed, but what a Jew is, everyone knows as well as I." After repeated urgings, I finally received the promise that the city council would successively appoint the assistant teachers. This promise was loyally kept.[137]

Under Lueger, the struggle in the schools reached a new intensity, and education became more politicized than ever. The Liberal Deutscher Schulverein was refused municipal subsidy.[138] Teachers who held views contrary to those of the ruling party and who were active politically often received formal reprimands, were sometimes fired, or when this proved impossible because the teacher had tenure, were denied promotions,[139] often in complete disregard for considerations of seniority or merit. When charged with unfairness in such instances, the mayor claimed that he could not influence the city council, which was responsible for such decisions. Such an assertion is difficult to accept as true, for the city council was made up entirely of Christian Socials and Lueger was the chairman — not known for brooking opposition if he wanted his way. He flatly stated that he would "not promote professed Social Democrats and Schönerians."[140] His attitude in this regard became so well known that Viktor Adler once told a Landtag session how the mayor invited all new and probationary teachers to the town hall and asked them to give him their word that they were neither Social Democrats nor German Nationalists, something Lueger later admitted. However, he added that although not obliged to answer, if they refused they would not be hired.[141]

In January 1898, early in his mayoralty, Lueger stated his views about education during a Landtag session. These are important enough to treat in some detail, because they indicate what he and the Christian Socials were after. Lueger's words also revealed much about himself. Though he acknowledged the rights of teachers to express their opinions freely, the mayor added that the school neither could nor should become the "arena of political dispute." Refuting the argument of Ferdinand Kronawetter that a teacher was "nothing more than . . . another worker," Lueger said that it was not as though a teacher were a shoemaker whom he would patronize whether he were a Socialist or Christian Social, and that the sole criterion for judgment should be whether the shoe fit.[142] "We don't leave a pair of boots with the teacher, but . . . our children to be educated, and here we do have the right to ask: what sort of education do you mean, what sort of ideas do you have, and how will you use them? (Dr. Kronawetter: The Social Democrats have them, too! — Dr. Gessmann: But we're the majority! And we won't permit Social Democrats in the schools!)"[143]

Lueger then denied that parents and teachers were equal when it came to deciding how children were to be educated. To hearty applause he asserted that parents were far more important in the combination, and that teachers must comply with the wishes of the parents. Lueger denied that his policies were repressive. If a teacher felt that he could not comply with this or that policy, he was free to leave the profession, but as long as he was an educator, he was obliged to comply with the will of the population. This right was not to be infringed upon.[144]

During the remainder of his speech, he defended the right of teachers to speak their opinions freely and openly, but added that this right also imposed a duty to speak "the truth." He implied that because the lies told by Viennese teachers obviated the need to deal with them fairly, school officials were behaving too leniently. Contrary to the assertions of Kronawetter that the Christian Socials wanted to reinstate the inquisition against Protestants and Jews — Schneider had interjected "Bounty for the Jews!" Gregorig shouted Protestants were humans, "We won't burn humans!"[145] — Lueger insisted that his party was impartial to members of all religious groups. But then he added, "If the Jews lived according to the Ten Commandments . . . there wouldn't be any anti-Semitic question at all. . . . We are absolutely tolerant and I have already often said: we fight against intolerance. (So it is!)"[146]

Contrary to popular belief, Lueger continued, Vienna's schools had not attained the acme of perfection. Instruction in German was lacking in thoroughness. Only when an exact knowledge of the mother tongue was achieved could "the national feeling . . . be elevated." The root of

Austria's deficient national pride, to Lueger's way of thinking, lay in the deficiencies of its educational system. Too much time was devoted to play, not enough to preparing children for life's struggle. Yet, when he had spoken of such matters at a recent ceremony for teachers, he had been ridiculed. His detractors, he said, preferred abstract ideas like those in contemporary teachers' periodicals. And what kind of ideas? Hateful abuse of religion, attacks on the clergy and on marriage "the organized form of prostitution. (Hear! — Dr. Gessmann: A female teacher wrote that! An educator of our children!) Gentlemen! A number of teachers hold such views, and you're not surprised when we step forward and say: it can't go on like this! No! Order must prevail, and I hope we'll all do our duty in this regard."[147]

Lueger's words were enthusiastically applauded, and he was roundly congratulated. The response of the Christian Social representatives was predictable, and by this time belonged to a kind of ritual. For years he had elicited the same response by emphasizing nationalism, anti-Semitism, the sanctity of the family and religion, and the need to "regulate" the public schools to suit the ruling party, which, he claimed, represented the authentic wishes of the people. And yet, for sheer effrontery, demagogic opportunism, and hypocrisy, Lueger's speech would have been difficult to match. Remarkable though it was, it deserved something other than enthusiastic applause. The earlier disrupter of Liberal municipal council sessions, though by then the authoritarian boss of a Christian Social majority in both the diet and the council, demanded "order" or, more accurately, *his* order! The member of parliament who had corrected one of his opponents to say that Jews should be beheaded, who said he believed Jewish sects practiced ritual murder, and whose party members shouted that Jews were less than human and should be hunted for bounties proclaimed the utter tolerance of his party. And the consort of Marianne Beskiba castigated those who attacked marriage as an "organized form of prostitution." However, perhaps the most significant part of Lueger's speech was what his words revealed about the change in himself. No longer was the intellectual life free, nor was intellectual self-renewal the task of the mind. The term *education* as he used it had assumed a new meaning. The defender of the free individual's right to determine and define his own education had become its attacker. Lueger had traveled a long way from his student years. But by 1898 he had secured the outspoken support of the majority, commanded by himself, and this had become the most important thing.

Opposition within the representative bodies dominated by the Christian Socials more and more aroused his ire. The participation of Socialist teachers in the Vienna district school council of which he was chairman became a major irritation. When in 1897 two Socialists were elected, Lueger tried for two years to prevent them from assuming their duties. But first two and then four Socialists, Karl Seitz among them, at last joined the council, "the first Social Democrats in a branch of the Vienna municipal administration."[148] Lueger retaliated by firing more recalcitrant teachers. He defended the action of the district school council that had taken the administrative action, for it too often happened in Austria that not enough courage was demonstrated in decisively opposing "certain elements."[149] He told the municipal council:

> I am one of those who will know how to protect the honor of the authority which I represent, and know how to reckon with those who attack this honor. Now you understand me, gentlemen! If I should again have the opportunity to demonstrate my protection of the honor of the district school council, I will do so again. I will not allow certain young men to befoul the district school council in an intolerable manner. [Lengthy applause].[150]

So widespread was the knowledge of Lueger's dictatorial handling of school matters, of his rigid and authoritarian views on education, and so extensive was the discontent among oppositional teachers, even driving some of them to suicide,[151] that Rudolf Hawel dramatized this situation in a semiautobiographical play, *Die Politiker.* Himself a school teacher, Hawel had run afoul of the ruling party for criticizing Vergani's school proposals at a Social Democratic gathering in January 1897.[152] Before writing *Die Politiker,* Hawel had won success as the author of *Mutter Sorge,* the third most successful production of the party theater.[153] However, *Die Politiker* had been rejected by Müller-Guttenbrunn, who feared, probably with good reason, that it would scandalize Aryan playhouse sponsors. The premiere of this work, which cleared the censor only with difficulty,[154] in the Raimund Theater in January 1904 caused a minor sensation as it was. *Die Politiker* was received by Hawel's many colleagues in the audience as a deeply personal statement. Although the Christian Social *Reichspost* greeted the play as the kind of puerile, antireligious and oppositional politics that permeated the pages of the Socialist *Freie Lehrerstimme* of Alexander Täubler,[155] a teachers' periodical, the Liberal *Neue Freie Presse* suggested that *Die Politiker* belonged in the company of Beaumarchais's *Marriage of Figaro,* Schiller's *Die Räuber,* and Anzengruber's *Das vierte Gebot.*[156] All of these works had heralded revolutions, or at least significant changes in society, the *Neue Freie Presse* stated, thereby suggesting that "artists are the antennae of a race." The *Arbeiter Zeitung* gave the play a mixed review.[157]

Die Politiker, which received the two-thousand-Gulden Raimund Prize in June 1904, was a bitter and cynical comment on the politicization of Vienna's education and public life.[158] If the vehement attack of the *Reichspost* on *Die Politiker* is any indication, Hawel's characterizations hit the mark.[159] Trenchant, in any case, was Hawel's criticism of Christian Social influence peddling and nepotism.[160] Most incisive of all, however, was his depiction of a lower-middle-class Viennese society permeated with place seekers and politics. The contempt of one woman for the political ambitions of her husband was reflected in the casual remark of the central character's wife to her brother-in-law: "Are you starting in on politics, too? And all the time I thought you were cleverer."[161]

When in the play Wichmann, the hypocritical though successful municipal councillor, tells Hartner, the leader of the teachers' association, that children should be religiously and practically educated, some members of the audience doubtless recalled the similar views of Lueger. Before representatives of the community and in the provincial diet, Lueger had often made such statements, and sometimes also added that overcrowding of classes did not make effective teaching impossible, as Liberal teachers charged. The mayor claimed that as a primary school student, he had attended a class with 120 other boys, thereby implying that his success had not been impeded by such conditions.[162] Whether the student was properly educated depended solely on the teacher, Lueger insisted. Therefore, the duty of the ruling party was to "reform the schools, so that the children learn something sound, so that they leave the schools . . . thoroughly able to survive life's struggle!"[163] But Lueger overlooked the effect of changes in the social composition of Vienna. Since his youth in the 1850s, a large and increasing proletariat had come into existence by 1900. He ignored this.

During the same session, the mayor remarked that kindergartens and day nurseries could not substitute for maternal affection, which, alas, had become all too rare, because both parents often worked. But he also indicated that the ruling party was taking the problem of child care in hand.[164] Here Lueger anticipated the so-called Christian Social Knaben- and Mädchenhorte, district youth organizations comprised of the children of Christian Socials, which were first created in 1906 in Lueger's former Erdberg constituency. The Knabenhorte were run along strict military and Christian Social political guidelines, and won the admiration of the young Adolf Hitler. According to an early Lueger biographer: "In the boys' schools, Lueger helped to awaken the love of militarism, in the sense that he bestowed his complete sympathy on the Knabenhorte with their military organization and discipline. He gave them esprit de corps and allowed the Hort cadets, the little soldiers, to show their prowess wherever he could."[165]

The leader of the Knabenhorte was Franz Opelt, a reserve army captain, sometime police official, and functionary in the Lower Austrian chamber of commerce and trade.[166] (See illustrations.) Clad in sailor suits, members of the Knabenhorte drilled with miniature rifles, participated in reviews before members of the royal family, and during the sixtieth coronation anniversary celebrations of Franz Joseph, paraded before the emperor himself. So successful an organizer was Opelt that each of Vienna's twenty-one districts eventually received its own Knabenhort. Membership climbed to sixty-eight hundred.[167] In 1907 Opelt created the Association of Military Organized Knabenhorte of Vienna, which served as the nucleus of an empirewide military youth organization under the protectorship of Franz Ferdinand.[168]

Although the purpose of the Knabenhorte was ostensibly altruistic, to prevent the "increasing demoralization and brutalization of the youth," there was no shortage of critics who charged that his militaristic methods defeated the stated purpose of the Knabenhorte. Leopold Tomola, Christian Social municipal councillor, city councillor, and Lueger's earliest biographer, also functioned as a political overseer and mediator for the Knabenhorte,[169] the authority to whom other Christian Socials turned when some of them felt that Opelt's group was obtaining unfair advantages. Thus in 1909 Viktor Silberer implied that the three-year-old organization was receiving an excessively large share of municipal subsidies that were also needed by the Association for the Promotion of the Recreation for Youth, founded during the Liberal era. Should the association be merged with the Knabenhorte? Tomola said no, because the association's purpose was "completely different from that of the Knabenhorte."[170] Lueger was silent during this and other debates over the Knabenhorte, usually preferring either to shelve the issue or, as here, to refer it to the city council, whose proceedings were not made public. When in 1908 Liberal municipal councillor Ferdinand Klebinder complained in an interpellation that "party-political stubbornness and confessional intolerance" prevented the predominantly Jewish second district from receiving its own Knabenhort, Lueger cut short the official reply: "This question will be solved in the general interest," and abruptly proceeded to another item of business.[171] Lueger increasingly preferred to avoid confrontations over outright anti-Jewish discrimination in public education, doubtless because he feared that proof of such discrimination might have prompted imperial intervention.

It seems doubtful at best that Lueger ever accepted Jews as equals among "Christian German Austrians," such as himself. Wily politician that he was, however, the mayor realized that a too blatant display of anti-Semitism in educational matters might impair his relations with powerful, or otherwise influential, Jews, as well as with the Statthalterei, for he was pledged to administer impartially. Again, appearances had to be preserved and his foes deprived of potentially damaging ammunition, so far as this was possible. As early as September 1898, while still posing as the enemy of Jewish capitalism,[172] he avoided taking a personal stand in the municipal council on segregating Jewish children from Christians in the public schools. A city council proposal on this topic, inspired by a decree from the Christian Social–controlled district school council, became a hotly disputed issue, in part because segregation was prohibited by law in public primary schools.[173] Lueger left the explanation and defense of the proposal to other party members; he played impartial mediator. Gessmann, Lueger's right-hand man in educational matters, acted as the chief Christian Social spokesman during a municipal council debate. His anti-Jewish racism was apparent, ironically enough, considering Gessmann's Jewish descent:

> It is unique in the entire development of the history of peoples that a nationality or race . . . which has been dispersed over the entire world for 2000 years, remains unassimilated. [Agreement on the left.] It is not true, gentlemen, that the circumstances are to blame. There have been enough times, when Jewry enjoyed equal rights completely, yes, when it possessed a superior position, and it didn't come to this intermingling, and you can do what you will, it will never come to this intermingling.[174]

Gessmann, whose remarks were interrupted by Christian Social shouts of approval and applause, voiced the true feelings of the majority party councillors—who greeted the school council decree "with animated happiness"—and not a few of the rank and file. On October 5, 1898, the *Reichspost* carried an article on the proposed segregation, which also included a letter from a parent:

> Dr. Lueger knows very well as chairman of the district school council what we want. He has often come to our meetings, even years ago, when we were a very tiny group. Even today my girl cannot rid herself of the Jewish jargon which she picked up in the Leopold school. To be sure, I have no one left in school, but in the interest of others, I desire that the "Reichspost" continues to promote Christian Catholic schools. With that I express the wish of thousands of Christian fathers.[175]

Lueger did know what "thousands of Christians fathers" wanted and capitalized on it for its agitational value. Could he help it if segregation was prohibited by imperial law?[176]

The related issue of discrimination arose a few years later, though this time in a trade school setting. In 1904, during a Landtag session, Ernst

Schneider proposed scholarships for cadets of the Export Academy in Vienna. The proposal included a proviso that applicants "must be members of the Christian faith,"[177] This requirement aroused animated debate, with Schneider, Bielohlawek, Sturm, and other Christian Socials declaiming in the usual direction. Philo-Semitic statements of the Liberal delegate Ritter von Lindheim, who pointed out that the proposal as it stood differentiated between first- and second-class students according to faith, achieved the opposite of what Lindheim had probably intended. His remarks caused Bielohlawek and Sturm to change the wording of the proposal: instead of creating a scholarship for students of "Christian faith," only those of "Aryan extraction" were eligible to apply.[178] Significantly, racial bias here replaced the original religious prejudice.

Lueger was usually successful in deferring action on an unpopular measure, unpopular, that is, with a group he believed he could otherwise control, blaming his inactivity on larger considerations, such as the wishes of his electorate. In this way, he was able to postpone general raises for teachers. To many outspoken complaints about unfairness in the regulation of teachers' salaries after 1904, Lueger stated that it would have been impossible to carry out such a measure without someone remonstrating.[179] He was silent about charges that a younger class of Christian Social teachers had been promoted over their more experienced colleagues. The district school council, acting on the advice of an elected commission, had taken the appropriate measures, the mayor stated. Before the enactment of the regulation, he had tried to intervene in a case where the result of the regulation was perhaps not appropriate. The members of the school council would bear him out that his attempt had been "rather energetic; but I can't know everything, you will understand that." And in particular he couldn't know how the salaries would be regulated. That was the job of the commission. Though he regretted that mistakes had been committed, he believed that it might in time be possible to rectify such errors. For the moment, however, no changes could be made. Complaints must be filed with the provincial school council, the ministry, and so forth. It was not his affair in any case. He had only allowed the matter to be discussed, because so much had already been said about it. A subsequent request for raises for one category of public school teachers was denied by Lueger on the grounds that taxes would have to be raised, something he wished to "avoid as much as possible."[180] He thus revealed a familiar ploy: although chairman of the district school council, he was not responsible for some of its actions, had done his best in isolated instances to rectify possible errors, and so forth. In short, he refused to accept the responsibility for any negative effects of an unpopular measure. His authority as mayor and party leader, the supineness of the Christian Socials, and the weakness and disunity of his opponents in the municipal council were such that he usually got away with such tactics. Thus did Lueger contribute to establishing a tradition of power without accountability, a precedent that was both negative and portentious.

One of Lueger's most enthusiastic supporters in educational matters was the publicist priest Franz Stauracz. Stauracz's attacks on Darwinism reflected a "fundamentalism" in many of Lueger's supporters. In 1897 Stauracz composed a "Darwinistic Teachers' Chorus," which succinctly captured the spirit of the anti-Darwinists:

> Es dröhnt ein Wort mit breitem Schwall
> Herab von den Kathedern all:
> Herr Darwin, du magst ruhig sein,
> Wir treten treu zum Kampfe ein!
> Ob manch' Professor dich verlässt,
> Wir Lehrer stehen felsenfest.
> Ob dein System längst wankt und bricht,
> Wir lassen von dem Utang nicht.
> Uns bleibt die Losung spät und früh:
> Vivat die Affentheorie![181]

As usual in his anti-Darwinist polemics, Stauracz inveighed against Socialists and Liberals, whose press organs, the Socialists' *Arbeiter Zeitung* and the Liberals' *Neue Freie Presse*, he designated as instigators of godless materialism.[182] A recipient of the golden Salvator Medal from the municipal council in 1905 for "his successful meritorious pedagogic activity," Stauracz was later remembered as the man who "roused the parents and all true friends of the people [to] the Liberal cultural danger."[183] Besides writing an early Lueger biography to celebrate the mayor's tenth anniversary in office in 1907, Stauracz also prepared a small abridged edition "for friends of the truth."[184]

Another side of Stauracz's publicist activity was his agitation against the Freie Schule association.[185] This predominantly Socialist-led movement, which was also substantially assisted for a time by Liberals and Freemasons, aimed at the reform of Vienna's schools. The association tried to promote education for the nonprivileged by supporting free education, the creation of nurseries and kindergartens, the abolition of child labor, and by providing funds for needy students.[186] Some of these aims were like, or identical with, those of Lueger and his party, except that they were intended to benefit Socialists. It was therefore natural that the Freie Schule movement would be opposed by the Christian Socials, not only because of its political coloration, but also because the association advocated the complete separation of church and school.[187] The reform of pedagogical methods, which sometimes extended to agitation against corporal punishment of apprentices in trade schools,[188] and agitation for the creation of new schools by the Freie Schule were resisted by the ruling party. The Socialists complained that permission to conduct classes and granting permits to construct buildings were being withheld.[189] Lueger defended Christian Social action in such instances, and added his authority to Christian Social demands in parliament that Catholicism be defended against the threats allegedly posed by Freie Schule supporters.[190] He also upheld the Magistrat against charges of illegal procedures in its dealings with representatives of the Freie Schule. Lueger thus once more reinforced the attitudes and practices of his Liberal predecessors. In the following response of Lueger to a charge of illegality in withholding a building permit to the Freie Schule, there is still an echo of Steinian administrative theory:

> I must . . . say that the allegation against the Magistrat of acting illegally is completely unjustified. Just because the administrative court declared a decision of the building deputation unfounded in the law, it doesn't necessarily follow that the decision in question is an illegal one. There are different opinions; one time this one is right, another time that one. Therefore, one should not use such words as are found in this interpellation.[191]

The founding of the Freie Schule in 1905 was followed by the organization of the anti-Semitic Christian Teachers' Association of Lower Austria two years later. Strife over education intensified and continued until long after Lueger's death. By December 1908 the politicization of Vienna's schools, attacks by supporters of the Christian Teachers' Association on the Freie Schule, and general demoralization among the teachers themselves prompted one of their number, the Liberal Eduard Jordan, who was also a municipal councillor, to remark during a session that he had spent sleepless nights.[192] The anti-Semitism of the clergy was particularly disturbing to him, because their entire worship, their religious rites, as far as he could see, stemmed from the Jews. He thus indicated that in being anti-Semites, the clergy attacked the very roots of its own belief. Whoever called himself a Christian, therefore, could never be an anti-Semite. This held particularly true for teachers, some of whom had flaunted their anti-Semitism. Teachers were the most important element in the school, Jordan asserted. The loveliest and most splendid buildings were completely useless unless someone was there to instruct and to educate, to give himself over to his profession heart and soul. The municipal council might pride itself when teachers unanimously declared that they were happy and content. "That's not possible!" another councillor exclaimed. Not possible? Jordan continued — that was for the teachers to say. And if a municipal administration declared it was impossible to make teachers content when other professional groups were, it might as well announce its bankruptcy.[193]

He had been teaching since the 1870s and had, ran his argument, noticed a change: during the 1870s, never a day passed without parents asking how their child was doing. This no longer happened. There was no enthusiasm for school anymore. What caused this? If his colleagues said that the Liberals were responsible, he could not prevent them. But the Christian Socials were really the guilty ones. One heard little in Christian Social meetings about the importance of the schools or the teachers. For that and for the steadily increasing indolence of the population toward those things, the Christian Socials were to blame. This was damaging. When the Christian Socials meet, they should include the school question on their agenda, and discuss it.[194] Jordan was applauded by his party members. Lueger's intelligentsia remained silent.

There is no doubt that Lueger was keenly attracted to education and its role in society. He was not without keen insight into its subtleties, but characteristically, the direction in which he applied his know-how remains an open question. Improvements, yes; but at what cost and for whom?

8

The Lueger Tradition

Even before Lueger had breathed his last, history began powerfully to
relate and to write the name Lueger and the love the people gave him in
the annals of Vienna and Austria [and] in those of world history.

Truly, a light emanated from him. He belonged to those whom Thomas
Carlyle calls heroes, who, for Julius Langbehn . . . are educators of the
entire people.
        —Eugen Mack, *Dr. Karl Lueger, der Bürgermeister von Wien*

It is not the literal past that rules us, save, possibly, in a biological
sense. It is images of the past. These are often as highly structured and
selective as myths.
        —George Steiner, *In Bluebeard's Castle*

*K*arl Lueger died of the effects of diabetes, nephritis and uremia a
few minutes past 8:00 A.M. on March 10, 1910.[1] His two sisters, some
friends, leading party members, and a handful of church officials and
prominent physicians were in attendance at his bedside in Lueger's Rathaus
apartment. For nearly a month, the Viennese had been prepared for Lueger's death by newspaper reports of his deteriorating condition. Nearly
a million people attended the greatest funeral Vienna had ever witnessed.
In contrast with the mayoralty contest fifteen years before and the imperial
refusal of a public sixtieth birthday celebration in 1904, there was little
public discord surrounding Lueger's funeral. Breaking with court protocol, Franz Joseph and some high aristocrats received the cortege at the
main entrance of St. Stephen's Cathedral. Various foreign dignitaries were
also on hand. Franz Schuhmeier followed closely behind Lueger's casket.

The gathering of high and low to honor the memory of a mayor was unique in the annals of Austria.

One of the few things that marred the occasion for some was the prophetic tone of the funeral oration delivered by Magistrat Director Karl Appel. Anthony Burgess has observed that "the history of our century has shown too much eagerness . . . to hand over the responsibility of moral choice to a charismatic leader."[2] If this is so, Appel's remarks and his subsequent response to criticism suggest that this process was well under way. In his oration, he referred to Lueger as "an emissary selected . . . by a higher power to redeem the sins of a past time, to elevate the trust of the Christian population of Vienna." Alfred Mittler, a liberal municipal councillor, criticized Appel by pointing out that Appel himself had served during the "past time," and that Appel's "confessional agitation" ran counter to the conciliatory spirit of the funeral ceremony. Appel's response was pure Lueger: "'In no way am I responsible to a single municipal councillor, or even to [Mittler's club].'" His reply was cheered by the Christian Social majority in the municipal council.[3]

The costs of Lueger's final illness, funeral, and tomb were paid by the municipality. There were only minor grumblings from his former opponents.[4] For weeks after his death, there was considerable praise for him and for his achievements. Most Austrian and foreign papers lauded the deceased and his communal creations;[5] the *Reichspost* devoted several special issues to his accomplishments. An early attempt to assess Lueger's effect beyond the more obvious centrality of his administrative achievements and to indicate his larger significance was undertaken by Karl Kraus. Quoting Otto Weininger, Kraus suggested that Lueger had been a man whose deeds had resembled genius, but who had lacked the "pure inner greatness" that distinguishes genius.[6] He further implied that Lueger, a great demagogue, had lived "completely in the present," rather than dreaming "of a more beautiful, better future." He also lived for the present without meditating on the past. Transitoriness was a result. Yet, true genius is independent "of [the] concrete-temporal conditions of . . . life," which, however, are essential for generals and politicians.[7]

Kraus, continuing his observations through Weininger, compared politicians to prostitutes. Much "like the great tribune, she believes she brings happiness to everyone . . . she always believes she gives presents to everyone."[8] And everyone believes he "actually benefited," even as Goethe did when he met Napoleon at Erfurt. Great men have limitations, but great tribunes and courtesans are absolutely boundless; they use "the whole world as a decoration to elevate their empirical selves."[9] Geniuses are aware of their gifts and are least dependent on the rabble; not so the tribune. "For the great politician is not only a speculator and a billionaire, but also a minstrel; he is not only a great chess player, but also a great actor; not only a despot, but also curries favor; [and] he not only prostitutes, but he is also the great prostitute himself."[10] Only the rabble is of use to him; he disposes of individualists, if he is unwise, or pretends to value them to disarm them. Great tribunes, as well as great prostitutes, renounce an inner life, and in so doing resemble torches that illuminate only so long as they burn, and then drop out of sight, like meteors, "without meaning and purpose for human wisdom, without leaving behind anything enduring, without eternity—in the meantime the mother and the genius quietly form the future."[11]

Shortly before his death, Lueger awakened from a half slumber and called for his nurse. He thought that a violent hailstorm had broken every pane in Vienna, though not a breath of air had stirred the whole night long. "I dreamt of my mother . . . she was there to bring me out of the storm. . . ."[12] In the end we are all children, Kraus seemed to say.

After the period of mourning had passed, Viennese political life returned to "normal," which was now different. The Christian Socials had lost their most able leader and he was never to be replaced. Lueger's successors lacked the necessary combination of skills, intelligent vigor, ruthlessness, and luck to resolve the internal dissonances and rivalries that now emerged. Another leader with Lueger's uniquely effective, because centerless, centrality was not forthcoming and times had changed. Lueger's longevity in office had only multiplied problems.[13] In 1911 the Christian Socials suffered a major defeat, and the Socialists became the leading party in parliament. Though Lueger's followers retained control of Vienna until 1919, the most important phase of municipalization and municipal construction during the last years of the empire had ended. The next significant phase, the construction of workers' housing on a massive scale during the First Republic, would be undertaken by the Socialists beginning in the early 1920s.

By 1915 the lack of interest in Lueger had become so great that Count Kielmansegg felt he needed to justify a separate Lueger chapter in his memoirs. Despite the personality cult and the monuments, the honors and the titles, the governor came to the unsubtle conclusion that Lueger had not really been the great man and center of events that sycophants and party publicists had tried to make him seem to be. Strategically placed in the imperial government to observe a wide spectrum of developments, of men and events, Kielmansegg was confident that he had been in a position to know. Larger diplomatic crises, the failure of Christian Socialism in checking the growth of Social Democracy, Kielmansegg believed, and the weaknesses of one-man rule had become evident after 1907, during the period of Lueger's declining health. However, as early as 1905 the inadequacy of Lueger's demagogic response to the franchise issue had made the deficiencies of his politics transparent: his mechanical resort to anti-Semitism had then united his foes against him. For the first time, Lueger had qualified his anti-Semitism importantly, and the Socialists had made significant gains in the spring parliamentary elections of 1907. "But in spite of everything, he will be spoken of again,"[14] Kielmansegg added, against his own opinions, and subsequent events have lent his words the quality of prophesy. Kielmansegg suspected that the superficiality and transient nature of much of Lueger's politics may have concealed a more portentious development, though he was uncertain about its true nature. That was to become apparent after World War I.

Thomas Mann has spoken of the "mixture of robust modernity and an affirmative stance toward progress, combined with dreams of the past: a highly technological romanticism," that constituted "the really characteristic and dangerous aspect of National Socialism."[15] Although Lueger's politics and Christian Socialism lacked the consistency of this expression of modern totalitarianism, his attempts to effect an ideological integration of social, cultural, economic, and political elements were important in bridging the earlier, more rationally empirical Liberalism and the post-imperial movements. And, though Lueger was probably not a political romantic in Mann's sense, and certainly not a National Socialist, his values contained the germ of those of his most notorious admirer. Lueger helped ease the transition to modern political irrationalism through his sensitivity to and identification with the inner and unspoken drives of his constituents, and through his ability to translate them into dynamic political forms. This was arguably his most important contribution to late imperial politics and beyond. In these respects, he was perhaps the first important charismatic personality in twentieth-century politics. Yet, Lueger's sensitivities concealed a deeper irresolution of personal values within himself. Viktor Adler sensed this when he told Lueger that the Christian Social leader believed what he said as long as he said it, and something different after he had spoken. In his social legislation, Lueger also anticipated more comprehensive postwar developments. Here, his efforts were likely an expression of the desire to achieve a more thoroughgoing community according to his nostalgic, petit bourgeois notions, a social cohesiveness that he believed was lacking.

By 1910 Lueger had become a legend in Vienna, thanks in no small measure to his flair for the operatic inherited from the "grand" nineteenth century, but owing even more to the efforts of the press. Though his politics had long been censured by Liberals, Socialists, and Pan-Germans, the polemics and anti-Lueger tirades achieved an effect opposite of what had been intended, at least among his followers. Lueger reportage of whatever slant appears to have enhanced rather than diminished his reputation among the Christian Socials, proving again that no publicity is bad publicity. Enemy journalists created a hybrid-Lueger image, part bourgeois-royal, part unscrupulous politician, and part celebrity, while the Christian Social press treated him as a pundit and infallible father figure. His illnesses made marketable copy, especially among the Liberals, whose press reported the progress of Lueger's diseases in prurient detail, much to the disgust of Karl Kraus, but doubtless to the delight of Lueger's enemies.[16] Even Christian Social journalists later provided play-by-play accounts of Lueger's terminal agonies.

Neither the attempts of his foes to discredit him for official negligence[17] nor the revelations of corruption involving some of his closest lieutenants appreciably diminished his immense popularity. In fact, the exposure of Christian Social corruption made Lueger seem to shine by comparison: he retained his reputation for personal integriy. After his death even one of his oldest opponents conceded that "his hands were clean and his pockets empty."[18] Through his persistent political techniques, Lueger revealed an aspect of his temperament that reflected not only habit, but also "deep . . . cultural formation."[19] During Lueger's campaign for the mayoralty when the emperor had refused to sanction his elections, he and his followers had skillfully made the most of his role as martyr, and his popularity had predictably soared. He successfully repeated this tactic in 1904 when imperial authorities refused him a public sixtieth birthday celebration and torchlight parade. They feared clashes between Lueger's followers and the Socialists,[20] and Lueger himself did nothing to lessen their fears. Shortly before his scheduled birthday celebration, he had with more than usual bluntness insulted the Social Democrats and their leaders as "a bunch of scamps" (*lauter Lumpen*). During a subsequent diet session he told the delegates that if he "were master here, there would be absolutely no Social Democrats . . . I would know how to clear these people out, I say that openly!"[21] Those who recalled Lueger's use of municipal firemen to disperse workmen from private electric companies the preceding year required no further proof. In the town hall on his birthday, Lueger crowned his role as martyr with one of his most theatrical gestures. Indignant over the latest imperial "slight," the mayor was loudly cheered when he told his supporters that he would submit to authority "with humility and patience. . . . But I will never forget," a promise that he surely kept.[22]

The Lueger cult that flourished during the First Republic may have sprung up and thrived on its own, but its survival was not left to chance. It was carefully nurtured and tended by his admirers. In some respects the cult flourishes to this day, though the Christian Social party has long faded into history. Not only were many public monuments linked to his name, but major municipal achievements, some of which had their origins in earlier legislative decisions or in the efforts of others, were exclusively attributed to him by the party press, toward further enhancement of his fame. Both Lueger and his lieutenants were quick to point out that such achievements benefited all alike, regardless of party affiliation. What the Christian Socials did not say was that the benefits to nonparty supporters were incidental to the original and more central goals of perpetuating party control over municipal finance through expenditures on new public works and ensuring that predominantly Christian Social districts and interest groups were served first.

Though Lueger's craving for honors and recognition was widely ridiculed during his mayoralty, the jeering ended with his death. It was as though his protracted and much publicized final suffering had expiated the vanity and self-pride that for years had exposed him to derision. Few perceived that the mayor's posthumous fame might have been diminished had his suffering been briefer. In the event, Lueger was mourned less as a great figure than as a symbolical sacrifice for "the good cause."[23] The Lueger tradition has been fed by his biographers and has been given its distinctive shape by them. It has passed through various phases in poetry, song, drama, painting, caricature, novel, and a major Nazi film in 1943. More recently, an interest in the man has been revived in the much visited exhibitions of fin de siècle culture in Vienna, Paris, New York, and Venice. Several of these works will be considered here, not only for what they tell about the man, but also for what they conceal and for what they suggest about his final effect.

In post–World War II biographies, Lueger has come to symbolize socioeconomic achievement, the political arrival of the Viennese lower middle class, municipal reform, and technological progress.[24] The origins of these attitudes may be traced to the earliest Lueger biographies. Two works published during his lifetime within three years of each other already contained the major features of this biographical tradition by hailing his greatness as politician, party leader, and municipal reformer. Their authors were Christian Social publicists Leopold Tomola and Franz Stauracz.

The first work, more a brief biographical *Festschrift* than a single book and "dedicated to all who esteem his energy as a model for emulation," was intended to commemorate Lueger's sixtieth birthday. His behavior at the time — resentful, petulant, and threatening toward the Socialists —

contrasts sharply with Tomola's idealization of the mayor and party leader, who emerges as the leader nonpareil, infused with a quasi-religious sense of mission. So far as Lueger was concerned, Tomola's biography undoubtedly was a consolation prize for the great public triumph he had craved, had doubtless anticipated with relish, and had probably planned in the first place. Yet the *Festschrift* is more revealing from the standpoint of what the Christian Socials wanted posterity to remember about him than accounts of a public celebration likely would have been. When imperial authorities withheld their approval for festivities, Lueger was again denied the deeper psychological confirmation of his social legitimacy, a nagging need throughout his career. And yet, ironically, he was to receive his most enduring "reassurance" from his historical biographers, from Tomola, Stauracz, and subsequent biographers who embellished his legend.

The existence of a publication committee that included some of the leading Christian Socials and the mayor's oldest followers for the first biography suggests that he had a hand in this too. He may have presided over the birth of his own tradition. Some of the anecdotes in Tomola's work, which lend it an authenticity, must have come from Lueger himself, such as his father telling young Karl's first schoolmaster that he had brought him "a little recruit." Some emphases immediately become apparent and suggest Christian Social priorities. Tomola stresses the modernity of Christian Social thinking by focusing on the centrality of technology in their schemes: "the railroads, steam engines, factories and telegraph" that came with the machine age, and the bewilderment of those whose existences had earlier been destroyed for want of education.[25] The Christian Socials were cleverer than their predecessors, Tomola implies, for having placed greater weight on education. This had been anticipated by the love of knowledge Lueger acquired from his selfless parents. This emphasis on young Karl's love of learning could refute the continuing and well-founded charges against Christian Social hostility toward education and public gaffs. Lueger's threats against dissenting teachers shortly before his birthday did nothing to help matters. In fact, by 1904 the Christian Social regimentation of the municipal schools was in full swing, if not already largely completed.[26] Tomola's attempts to portray the ruling party as a promoter of education and defender of knowledge, and thereby to imply that it fostered freedom of inquiry and expression, must have been recognized by many for the pious hypocrisy it was.

In the militantly nationalistic environment of early twentieth-century Austria, no biography of this type could fail to stress Lueger's outspoken patriotism, last of all Tomola's book. His praise for Lueger's zealous love of country established the tone for subsequent hagiographies. According to him, young Karl's loyalty to the crown and sense of tradition had been stimulated by his father's tales of Radetzky's victories in Italy, and, as a nine-year-old boy, by witnessing the arrival of the Empress Elisabeth in Vienna.[27] In 1858 his patriotism had received a further push when he and his Theresianum classmates had attended Radetzky's funeral ceremonies, presided over by Emperor Franz Joseph. However, Tomola departs somewhat from contemporary Christian Social politics, and differs from subsequent Lueger biographies, in praising Franz Joseph's "design for the creation of a great German Reich," which the emperor placed before the other princes in Frankfurt in 1863, though the plan would not have been anti-Habsburg.[28] Lueger was notably cautious about ideas of Greater Germany during his years of power, because he did not want to present Schönerer with any political opportunities.

In reverential tones, Tomola describes Lueger's mission to lead his native city "to genuine, imperishable brilliance . . . and to serve as a shining example for the population of the entire empire, . . . as a model of every civic virtue."[29] In such passages, Tomola implies Lueger's religiosity while underlining his role as a man of destiny. This theme was to be repeated with increasing emphasis until 1945, reaching a crescendo in the film *Wien 1910*, in which it was suggested that Lueger, together with Schönerer, prefigured Hitler.

Tomola is notably silent about Franz Joseph's refusal to sanction Lueger's elections to mayor, handling this as an interlude during which Lueger consolidated his resources before embarking on his municipal improvement program. Lueger's first biographer also ignores his subject's continuing and unresolved tension with high imperial authorities. Embarrassing questions about how Lueger squared the image of loyalty to the ruling house with conflicts between himself and its highest representatives were thereby skirted. The major emphasis of this and of most subsequent biographies falls on his tangible achievements as Bürgermeister. Yet, though Lueger served for another six years, his most significant accomplishments, including the construction of the municipal gasworks, power facilities, most of the schools, and the electrification of the trams, already lay behind him. Although its author could not have realized it at the time, the *Festschrift* already had a valedictory quality about it.

The allusions in Tomola's work to Lueger's "Germanic attributes" and to his paternalism[30] were more strongly emphasized in Franz Stauracz's *Dr. Karl Lueger*, of 1907. Like Tomola, Stauracz also commemorated a Lueger anniversary, in this case, his tenth year as mayor. By this time, however, Lueger's "physical sufferings,"[31] which had necessitated regular summer visits to health spas since 1904, had become chronic. Far more than the *Festschrift*, Stauracz's study amounts to a summing up. It is also more of a full-scale biography, having drawn on reminiscences and articles that appeared at the time of Lueger's sixtieth birthday, that in part were unavailable to Tomola. Through Stauracz, many of the familiar details of the Lueger biographical tradition became more firmly established, and others made their first appearances. For example, where Tomola had been silent about Lueger and anti-Semitism, Stauracz was outspoken, particularly when it came to puffing the Christian Social press as an anti-Liberal, and therefore an anti-Semitic, weapon, something he felt strangely enough that Lueger had neglected.

Stauracz pointed out that the party had generated the press, rather than the other way around. He implied thereby that the party was obligated to support it, adding that Lueger underestimated the power of journalism. This assertion, however, is an oversimplification. It was belied by Lueger's university training, practical political experience and behavior, and by remarks in his correspondence. It may be that in 1907 when the second biography was published, the fortunes of the *Deutsche Zeitung*, the official Christian Social organ, were at a low ebb and that Stauracz despaired of any improvement.[32] Later that year Lueger entrusted the *Deutsche Zeitung* to Friedrich Funder, and the *Reichspost* succeeded the *Deutsche Zeitung* as a reliable and effective mouthpiece.[33]

Stauracz's remarks reflect the factional disputes that became ever more apparent among the Christian Socials as Lueger's physical powers waned. Far from commanding the monolithic loyalties of its members in support of concrete party goals or purposes, Christian Socialism lacked consistency and singleness of purpose and the technology and power to enforce its policies. Lueger and his party operated in a personal context. Christian Socialism owed much of its early dynamism to the dynamism of its leader, as Nazism would to Hitler. "Our program is Dr. Karl Lueger!"[34] summed up the feelings of many and said more than Lueger's followers probably realized. Politics had not yet attained the fully irrational mechanism of a myth-making press, partly at least because Lueger regarded the press as the mere magnification of personal opinions. The kind of personality cult that grew up around Lueger was not yet the full-blown demonic entity of the post-World War I era, but in fact an authentic thing – a real personality cult. As such, it bridged the older tradition and the genuine article of mass politics, in which the leader replaces the personal ruler. One might look at Lueger's power and its rapid disintegration after his death as an exploitation of a psychological reserve, expressed elsewhere in opera. The nineteenth century that shaped Lueger was the century of the personality, of stagnant social forms. Lueger was in part prevented from developing into a Hitler, because, ironically, he was by default still a "person." Lueger inherited a cluster of psychosocial forms from the peak of a humanistic world, through his education and cultural environment. But he was not the same kind of "person" that produced the world he inherited. Yet, at the same time, the forms he acquired and used also inhibited and limited him from becoming a full-blown demonic image like Hitler. In a political sense, Lueger exhausted the supply and force of "person" in public life. That these forms were exhausted is shown by the fact that they could not be exploited again with another pseudo-Lueger.

By including relatively lengthy portions of Lueger speeches with their casually anti-Semitic remarks, which by exclusion mitigate his more radical statements, Stauracz also shows how integral a part of Christian Social doctrine anti-Semitism had become by 1907. Anti-Semitism was a fundamental assumption on which Lueger's and Christian Social politics were based.[35] In this regard, the quiet 1895 remark, cited earlier, of one of Lueger's supporters, "That is our *Führer*," reappeared in Stauracz in a more subtly ominous way. However, in Stauracz's biography, Lueger's anti-Semitism takes on a racist coloration through the inclusion of another remark of Albert Gessmann: when the more radical nationalists fell silent

> *a merger of all Aryans against the common danger of Semitism will be the next consequence* [emphasis in original]. This is necessary and indispensable, if the battle against Jewry is not to come to a standstill.
>
> Nearly a quarter of a century ago on the battlefield of politics, Dr. Lueger kindled the Aryan struggle and won the first victories of the Aryan movement. Today, Vienna and Lower Austria are outspokenly anti-Semitic in their representative bodies.[36]

During the same year Stauracz's Lueger biography appeared, Adolf Hitler became a resident of Vienna, an avid reader of the Christian Social press, and an admirer of Lueger.[37]

Lueger's second biography placed emphasis on his defense of religion in education, as well as on his attempts to eliminate "godless" Social Democrats and "unpatriotic" Pan-German Nationalists as teachers. Lueger was depicted as a shining product of the pre-1855 Konkordatsschule with whose results he "was very contented."[38] Of value to him had been his solid grounding in German language study and acquisition of mathematical skills. It was precisely the deficiencies in these areas of modern schooling that he deplored. Whether this sounded "somewhat medieval" or not, the important thing was that children acquired the proper learning tools to enable them to win life's struggle.[39] By emphasizing these familiar aspects of his politics, Stauracz portrayed Lueger as a consistent champion of education, an important feature of the "Lueger Tradition," which was also repeated by later biographers. The firing and "disciplining" of opposite-minded teachers were also tacitly condoned, and the punitive political measures that the Liberals had employed, as well, were thereby further legitimized by Lueger and the Christian Socials. Stauracz was silent about the Liberal influences in Lueger's education, about any intellectual debt to the utopian Socialists or secular reformers of the early nineteenth century, and about Lueger's republicanism of the university years; he was silent about his university education altogether, except to emphasize the diligence and patriotism during that time that also had been conspicuous throughout his career. By 1907 Lueger's antipathy toward the alleged dereliction of duty on the part of university teachers toward students, which resulted in violence, according to him, and his antipathy toward the "Jew-infested university" itself were presumably too well known to require elaboration. Primary education and educators should be and were being effectively "regulated," and the benefits of Lueger's policies were apparent for all to see.

Stauracz tried to present Lueger as a pragmatic politician, or at least one who had successfully translated Christian theory into practical politics. Thus Vogelsang emerges as Lueger's most important mentor. A result of his contact with Vogelsang and his circle was the introduction of Christianity into modern politics: "Through Dr. Lueger and his party the word Christian again became valid currency."[40] In the context of practical politics, Lueger's earliest and arguably most important mentor, Ignaz Mandl, receives but scant mention and then primarily to link him "to a reckless clique of place-hunters" who doomed "the entire democratic movement."[41] According to Stauracz, Lueger had kept faith with Mandl and Schönerer only "so long as it was compatible with his own honor and the good of the movement."[42] Lueger's behavior toward a former friend on the one hand, and an ally on the other, is thus explained as altruistically motivated, which is in part true, if one includes sacrificing people to an obsession in his definition of altruism.

As could be expected in a commemorative biography, Lueger's activity as communal reformer receives special praise. This most central aspect of the Lueger image initiated by Tomola is much elaborated by Stauracz. His chapter on Lueger as Mayor is nearly twice as long as Tomola's entire *Festschrift*. In addition to detailing the Lueger public works program, the mayor's support for municipal pension funds, insurance companies, savings banks, and various worker benefits are described with a view to disarming Socialist criticism of Lueger's alleged indifference to worker's problems and welfare.[43]

Stauracz's portrait of Lueger as a pious, hardworking, patriotic, selfless, and farsighted leader of the Aryan Christian people remained the standard interpretation for many years. Very few features of this picture were challenged by biographers until after 1945. There seemed little or no need to do so. Although Stauracz's portrait had served the party and continued to satisfy the public need of a hero, it continued to be embellished. Further details were added to the tradition of a wisely virtuous[44] and paternal leader, whose only apparent shortcoming was that he underestimated the power of the press.

Eugen Mack, Lueger's first posthumous biographer,[45] by contrast, sought to remove even this minor blemish by demonstrating the centrality of the press in Lueger's career, or at least in his legendary status. Yet, his copious quotations from Christian Social and other papers show that much of Lueger's fame rested on journalistic endeavor. Mack's interpretation of Lueger's influence was also "great-man history" par excellence:

> In his working program, Lueger carried out three great plans in particular: reconquering Vienna for the Christians, municipalization, that is, the assumption of great undertakings, hitherto operated by large capitalistic companies, by the municipal administration, and directing middle class politics [emphasis in original]. He succeeded. To paraphrase the Dane, Hermann Bang, Vienna lay on a sickbed after the battle of Königgrätz; the fevered imagination of a wounded man unfolded and extended, and signs of illness appeared, such as the stock market crash, bankruptcy, empty dwellings, uninhabited blocks of houses, unemployment and endless charity work. . . . Vienna was reawakened to life [emphasis in original]. . . . There exists a positively fundamental difference between the Vienna before Lueger and 'the three-times expanded, inwardly rejuvenated, strengthened, Christianized Vienna' . . . under Lueger. The brilliant spirit of the mayor gave the Austrian imperial city a thoroughly modern appearance, and its finances another foundation. One can say: Through Lueger Vienna received fresh air, cheap beautiful light, modern streets, cheap transportation, good water, splendid gardens and parks, honest beer, beef and meat prices, good sources of income and that which is the main thing — religion [emphasis in original].[46]

Mack extolled Lueger as a pious, almost saintly figure, who scrupulously observed Catholic religious practices, including fast days, and diligently attended Sunday mass; "amiably tolerant towards every confession [emphasis in original], [he] embodied the tolerance of the Catholic Church."[47] Mack claimed that Lueger was virtually responsible for returning religion to the schools, a nursery "for piety, imperial loyalty, love of fatherland, civic virtue."[48] This had been particularly necessary when "Nietzsche had been able to dare the terrible words that the religion of the cross was a stain on world history."[49] In this way, Mack's biography is an important link in the Lueger tradition. By emphasizing the element of piety, almost holiness, in Lueger's character — *"God was with Lueger"*[50] [emphasis in original] — Mack provided subsequent biographers in Austria with an invaluable instrument. Lueger's holiness could be used to justify his anti-Semitism, opposition to "godless" Socialism, and some aspects of modernism — his opposition to any social, political, or cultural enemy he had chosen to combat and against which his biographers thought a continuing struggle needed to be waged.

The possibilities of using the Lueger tradition in these respects were amply demonstrated in a 1923 biography by Richard Kralik, the first to appear during the interwar period.[51] Kralik tried to draw the strands of Lueger's politics together and to present his career as an expression of contemporary political Catholicism in Austria. More than the life study of a single individual, Kralik intended his work "before all else [to be] *a practical handbook of Christian Social thoughts and pithy sentences*" [emphasis in original].[52] Kralik planned and completed a two-volume work,[53] though only the first part till 1900 was published in 1923. More than a decade had passed since the appearance of Mack's work. A fuller treatment of Lueger's career might have been expected before Kralik's biography under normal circumstances, but the coming of World War I with all the attendant crises, the conflict itself, and the turning of interest from any single person, even Lueger, became inevitable.[54]

However, with the collapse of the empire in 1918 and the ensuing disruption of public life and its loss of social stability, a nostalgia for an earlier, seemingly better and happier era emerged. A hero was needed, someone whose life and works appeared to furnish an exemplar. For Christian Social publicists, Lueger was the only possibility. Since his death, the party had been dogged by scandals within the leadership,[55] electoral defeats, and in 1919 the loss to the Socialists of the municipal government, itself the very citadel of Christian Socialism for nearly a quarter of a century. Kralik's biography established a symptomatic precedent. Whenever times were bad, public or political morality seemed low, or all three, a Lueger study appeared. Kralik's work was succeeded by Rudolf Kuppe's in 1933 during the depths of the Depression, by a second Kuppe biography in 1947 during the aftermath of World War II, and by Johannes Hawlik's study in 1985, the seventy-fifth anniversary of Lueger's death — another time when political scandals and exposures of corruption in high places called in question, for some, the very existence of the Second Republic itself.[56] Lueger biographies appeared at other times, as well, and for other reasons.

The 1920s thus proved to be a major watershed for Lueger studies.

Although his first prewar biographers had emphasized one or another aspect of his career to authenticate his greatness in various yet limited ways, Kralik's effort started a growing tendency to identify Lueger with a larger, more holistic sociopolitical cause, to portray him as the agent of a larger historical process. With the unveiling in September 1926 of a prominent Lueger statue that betrayed both neoclassic and socialist realist stylistic influence, Lueger became the object of a major personality cult in earnest. The unveiling ceremony was a singular event, ranking with the most grandiose spectacles of the Lueger years, such as a children's homage to Emperor Franz Joseph on the occasion of his sixtieth anniversary as reigning monarch in 1908.[57] At the time of the unveiling, a flood of personal reminiscences and articles was published in Viennese papers. Lueger worship had become journalistically fashionable, and his fame as Vienna's greatest mayor has never since been seriously challenged there,[58] even by those who might have been expected to do so. Some prominent Jews and Socialists, such as Mayor Karl Seitz, who delivered a speech at the unveiling, honored his memory.[59] Kralik's biography had helped pave the way for this development by popularizing Lueger anew.

A polymath and "born dictator" who held regular Tuesday evening gatherings for his followers in his villa,[60] Kralik possessed an encyclopedic knowledge of history, literature, music, art, and religion. A great admirer of Richard Wagner and an accomplished musician himself, he was the author of three hundred books, countless articles, critical essays, and plays. In his earlier years, Kralik was frequently embroiled in literary feuds and emerged as the leader of an attempt to purify German literature of "alien" influences. His Lueger biography sought to place his subject in a more detailed historical framework than any of its predecessors. After the opening chapter it declines, alas, into a catalog of Lueger's political appearances beginning in 1889. A former Socialist who became a devout Catholic and an outspoken enemy of Marxism,[61] Kralik blamed the woes of the modern world on the decline of Catholicism since the Middle Ages and the inevitable growth of materialism that flowed from it. This had been accelerated by the French Revolution, he wrote, a catastrophic event, which had fostered the first attempts at "radical revolutionary communism."[62] Hand in glove with this development had come the emancipation of capital and Jewry. Out of this, in turn, Kralik traced the growth of Marxism, which "in contrast to the absolute idealism of Jesus Christ, had built everything on the crassest materialism."[63] But in a Hegelian turn, he added that the emergence of Marxist Socialism had conjured its antithesis in Christian Socialism. Kralik then examined the contributions of the Christian Socials of whom the most important for Lueger's development had been Karl Freiherr von Vogelsang. Yet another important contributor to Lueger's political growth, according to Kralik, had been Schönerer with his ideas of German National anti-Semitism. Yet, Lueger's ideas were stamped by his own powerful individuality.[64] In his approach to his subject, thus, Kralik tried to blend antimaterialism, serious religious thought, and anti-Semitism, all focused in the person of Lueger, the hero. Along these lines this first postwar Lueger biography developed into something more than an implicit attack on Social Democracy and its metaphysical foundations, coming when Christian Social fortunes were at a low ebb.

A critical essay about Lueger by the Liberal journalist Felix Salten appeared the year after Kralik's biography. Anticipating the novelist Theodor Heinrich Mayer in 1927, Salten predicted that Lueger would furnish an apt subject for a fictional work, but that this would have to wait until time had provided "the right distance and the right perspective."[65] Salten and Mayer agreed that "the will of an epoch" had fulfilled itself in Lueger.[66] Mayer's melodramatic *Die letzten Bürger* turgidly depicted Lueger's career, yet added another element (implicit in Kralik) to the tradition: Lueger as harbinger. This view of Lueger became part of the canon in a significant way in Heinrich Schnee's first Lueger biography in 1936, which contains an admiring reference to the mayor by Adolf Hitler. In Mayer's work the fictionalized Lueger, Leopold Brunner, as he slowly dies, realizes his significance:

> "I believe in what was entrusted to me, [and] want to preserve it, until it merges with another of my kind . . . now I know, I shall die and yet never, never be dead!"
> An odd storm tore the clouds to let through a ray of sunshine. It fell on Brunner's face, and the glow within him fused with the sky's brightness into the radiance of the chosen one.[67]

Such a passage recalls a dramatic sequence in the 1925 Sergei Eisenstein film *Potemkin* in which a proletarian mother carrying her dead child up the Odessa Steps is illuminated by a ray of light immediately before her own death. The cinematic possibilities of the Lueger theme were not to be lost on Joseph Goebbels, himself an admirer of *Potemkin.*

The publication of Mayer's work in 1927 coincided with that of Adam Müller-Guttenbrunn's edited diaries by the same publisher.[68] In the diaries, as well as in his posthumous memoirs, Müller-Guttenbrunn from his own perspective characterized the duplicity of the Christian Socials during the Lueger years. He also described in vivid detail the cultural-political fiasco of the party theater, about which Lueger biographers had been and continue to remain silent.

In another medium, that of the popular song, the Lueger tradition gained momentum during the early 1930s. "Der Dr. Lueger hat mir einmal die Hand gereicht," from the 1932 play *Essig und Öl,* acquired local fame through the interpretation of the great Viennese popular actor and singer, Hans Moser. The song is a classic evocation of nostalgia for a bygone era and an apotheosis of the *Greisslerstand,* the small-shop owners who comprised a significant block of Lueger's supporters and who are still a feature of Viennese life. Moser made at least two recordings of the song. The first, a highly emotional rendering in 1934, was followed by a more restrained version some twenty years later. The song's Jewish composer, Robert Katscher, died in exile.[69]

The standard Lueger biography for many years and a codification of the Lueger tradition till 1933 was Rudolf Kuppe's *Karl Lueger und seine Zeit.* It was also the first full and comparatively complete account of Lueger's life at all, and one that sought to interpret his career from the standpoint of a member of the post-Lueger generation.[70] The appearance of Kuppe's study during profound economic, political, and social crises could not have been better timed from the standpoint of those who had experienced prosperity during the late imperial era, who rejected most of the postwar developments, and longed for the earlier period. The author was a *Gymnasium* (high school) teacher and school director, a deeply committed Christian Socialist, and author of a 1926 Lueger memorial *Festschrift.* In his book, Kuppe tried to synthesize much of the known Lueger source material in private and public collections. He also drew on personal reminiscences, anecdotes, and naturally on the perspectives of his own generation. With this in mind, Arthur J. May's dismissive judgment of this biography as "pleasant and diverting glimpses" is unfair and at least partly inaccurate.[71] Much was decidedly *un*pleasant about Kuppe's biography, such as its author's transparent approval of Lueger's anti-Semitism, demagogy, and dictatorial tactics. From another standpoint, the work has serious shortcomings in that it lacks an adequate scholarly apparatus, so that most of the references are impossible to trace. Moreover, Kuppe's reverential handling of his subject precluded any attempt at a balanced evaluation of Lueger's career. Under the politically polarized circumstances in Austria during the early 1930s, such an evaluation would have been difficult in any case. Yet, Kuppe's second Lueger biography in 1947, with the added perspective of another world war, failed to engage even the remote possibility that Lueger's politics had left a negative political inheritance. As with the aftermath of World War I, great historical figures were again needed in Austria to satisfy the desire for earlier grandeur and to legitimize the new politics of the Second Republic. Lueger's image was dusted off and presented again to the public. Almost all the references to his anti-Semitism, a prominent feature of the first effort, were eliminated. In the first of the postwar Lueger life studies, the former mayor and party leader was presented as a municipal innovator and statesman.

But Kuppe's second biography points to something beyond opportunism and toward one of the reasons for the continuation of the Lueger tradition. Lueger had early mastered an art essential to the successful politician during an increasingly democratic era: he could appear to be many things to many people. He succeeded so well that subsequent generations could imbue him with the qualities they wanted him to have according to that part of the man they wanted to see. The biographies of Kuppe and Heinrich Schnee demonstrate that the Lueger tradition was elastic and malleable, and responded to changes in the political climate.

The primary purpose of Schnee's first Lueger biography was far different from Kuppe's. With the attempted overthrow of the Christian Social government by Austrian Nazis in 1934, and the indication thus of Hitler's foreign political direction, it was inevitable that one of the Nazi party faithful would recall Hitler's praise for Lueger in *Mein Kampf* and make the appropriate comparison. Schnee's 1936 *Bürgermeister Karl Lueger: Leben und Wirken eines grossen Deutschen* (Mayor Karl Lueger: Life and Work of a Great German) is introduced by Hitler's reference to Lueger as "the last great German born from the colonial people of the Eastern March (*Ostmark*)." Schnee's fifty-four-page work was based on little if any original research. In fact, a significant part of this biography consists of a lengthy excerpt from one of Lueger's anti-Semitic parliamentary speeches, the same parts, incidentally, that had also been quoted by Kuppe in his 1933 study.[72] Yet, an original feature of Schnee's contribution is its emphasis on such favorite Nazi preoccupations as "blood and soil," "community before self," and the racial nature of anti-Semitism as Schnee saw them reflected in Lueger's politics. Schnee thus added new elements to the Lueger tradition, and he praised Lueger for having anticipated the true bases for the continuing Germanic struggle.[73] His second Lueger biography published in 1960, though more than twice the length of the first, is less original.[74] It reflects post-World War II biographical attempts to diminish the importance of Lueger's anti-Semitism, and therefore to downgrade his ideological connection with Hitler.[75] Schnee's postwar study is largely an account of Lueger's political development and good deeds, with a special emphasis on his Christian Socialism, which was influenced by that of Ketteler and Vogelsang. Although Schnee had praised Lueger in 1936 "as a protagonist of Germanism in the Danube Monarchy, as an upright friend of the German Reich,"[76] he had remained silent in the same work about Lueger's consistent opposition to Pan-German nationalism. However, after 1945 Pan-Germanism fell on hard times, and Schnee related a well-known incident that took place in 1870 when Lueger was evicted from a German national-ist meeting in Vienna for attacking the new Prussian-led Germany.[77] In Schnee's second biography, though, Lueger remains the champion of Ger-manism, as well as a noble and patriotic statesman, "a great figure in our history."[78]

In one of the few references to anti-Semitism in the 1960 study, Schnee makes it clear that Lueger's anti-Jewish diatribes "during his years of strug-gle" did have political significance, though to what extent and about the precise nature of this he remains unclear.[79] And he quickly adds that "Jew-ish authors today are even of the opinion that Lueger's time as mayor of Vienna was a kind of golden age for the Jews."[80] A stronger emphasis on anti-Semitism was apparent in a 1940 novel, *Der Herrgott von Wien*, by Johann Freiner. Unlike Theodor Heinrich Mayer in 1927, Freiner's Nazi-era work made no attempt to conceal the identity of his hero and some of the principal characters by changing their names. Totalitarian states sanc-tion "realism" or "accuracy" in officially approved art, though they are more cavalier about sticking to historical truth, a quality that often enhances, rather than detracts from, propaganda effectiveness.

Der Herrgott von Wien is fictional biography. It was in some ways critical of Lueger — in the same way that Hitler had been critical in *Mein Kampf*. Like Hitler, Freiner indicated that Lueger and the Christian So-cials had failed to appreciate the "authentic" racial basis of anti-Semitism. And like Hitler again, Freiner implied that Lueger had helped perpetuate a flawed social and political system, based on an incorrect appreciation of historical necessity. This system had ended with the Anschluss and the incorporation of Austria into the larger national-racial community of Aryan Germans. In 1940 at the height of German military success, this idea en-joyed wide popularity among supporters of the greater German *Volksge-meinschaft*. Support for this concept was to evaporate as the war widened and the casualties mounted. Freiner also suggested that Lueger's popular success had been eclipsed by the more lasting character of his great public works. Freiner's interpretation was thus technocratic. At last, the novel conveys the impression that "a new creative future" awaited "eternal Vi-enna," thanks to the triumph of National Socialism, and that such crea-tivity had been foreshadowed by Lueger's politics.[81] The monuments dedi-cated to his memory were well deserved.

Lueger's contribution to this future, not to the exclusion of that of Georg Ritter von Schönerer, was the theme of the 1943 film *Wien 1910*. Commenting on its failure as propaganda, Richard S. Levy says that this film "shows . . . the same lack of consistent control or systematic organization to be found in every Nazi endeavor, no matter how seriously taken by the regime."[82] On another level, *Wien 1910* reveals how important the Lueger persona had become in the imagination of the top Nazi leadership. Circumstantial evidence suggests that Goebbels's determination to create this film may have been steeled by Hitler's enthusiasm for Lueger.[83] In any case, *Wien 1910* was one of four anti-Semitic films undertaken by Goebbels in 1939 to demonstrate the possibilities of Nazi cinema. (The others were *Leinen aus Irland, Die Rothschilds,* and *Jud Süss.*) However, production and other difficulties hampered its completion. Some members of the Viennese film colony evidently resisted the creation of *Wien 1910* as it existed in the script of December 1940,[84] but Goebbels remained adamant: "I . . . discussed the critical case of the Lueger film with (Gauleiter) Schirach. In Vienna, there is a radical political clique which wants to destroy this film. I won't let this happen. The film must be made, and then we can decide whether corrections must be made or whether the whole thing should be changed."[85]

Wien 1910 is one of the few attempts to portray an Austrian folk hero in the Nazi cinematic medium.[86] The film is a historic fable from first to last, though it presents "the appearance of accuracy."[87] The plot focuses on a dying Lueger's efforts to foil an attempted Liberal stock exchange maneuver to undermine the value of municipal securities. When word of his impending death reaches his enemies and rivals, only Schönerer refuses to exploit Lueger's misfortune. The mayor and his rival review their differences. Lueger believes that his exercise of power has necessitated compromises from time to time, but Schönerer accuses him of betraying his greatness in so doing. Instead, Lueger should have helped Schönerer clear the way for an all-German empire of world dimensions. The mayor has been too shortsighted, and settled for performing trivial deeds. Lueger replies that, unlike Schönerer, it was not given to him to play the visionary. Each has made a principle of what he has done and both were correct. Lueger ends by begging Schönerer to protect his work, but he has already departed. Though the impression thus created is that he has scorned Lueger, their confrontation has triggered an inner struggle in Schönerer. Respect for Lueger, the man, rather than political differences, ultimately wins out: before the town hall, after the mayor's death is announced, Schönerer doffs his hat with the rest of the respectful mourners.

Wien 1910 contains several anti-Semitic scenes. For example, during a municipal council session in which Lueger defeats the Liberal stock exchange maneuver, the son of the leading Liberal politician is so carried away by Lueger's rhetoric that he strikes the scornful Viktor Adler in the face. The meeting ends in tumult. In another scene, two Jews gloat over a violent confrontation between student supporters of Lueger and Schönerer: "May God preserve our emperor and the idiocy of the goy. As long as they fight among themselves, we are safe. Listen, Ehrenberg. There are two men in Austria-Hungary who could be dangerous to the world—Lueger and Schönerer. God, if there is one, wants them to be enemies. Our luck is almost frightening!"[88] Perhaps the most interesting scene from the standpoint of the filmmaker's attempts[89] to integrate Nazi anti-Semitism into Lueger's cultural politics takes place during the mayor's reception for Viennese orphans.

By 1943 a peculiar blend of politics, religiosity, and culture had become a feature of the Lueger tradition, as in this film. When a boy asks Lueger about the chain of office he is wearing, Lueger removes it and explains its meaning, link by link, emblem by emblem.

> The first and heaviest of all, represents the ruling district, power, and those who wield it. The second, nearly as heavy because it symbolizes the Jewish district, the Leopoldstadt, stands for envy, greed, hatred, and, Lueger adds, "the seven deadly sins" that always adhere to Jewish money. But other links remind one of the world's greatest composers, of Mozart, Schubert, and Beethoven, because their music was born in those districts, and a true Viennese need only strike the appropriate link to unlock their musical essence. At that point the chain slips from his hands to the floor and breaks between the first two links, "between Habsburg and Juda. Schönerer! Schönerer!" he exclaims.[90]

Although this scene is fully fictional, like most others, Lueger's implication that young Viennese must preserve their implicitly Germanic cultural roots does recall some of his actual speeches. In this episode the fictional Lueger merges with the real man in a genuine identity.

Though *Wien 1910* was apparently premiered in Vienna in April 1943,[91] it evidently had few viewers and was then quickly withdrawn. Its screening was subsequently limited to German theaters until after the war.[92] Gerald Herman has plausibly argued that its showing in Austria, and particularly in Vienna, the only place where its full meaning could have been understood, was forbidden because of the fear that it might further stimulate an undesirable regionalism.[93] A year before the completion of *Wien 1910*, the Nazi Sicherheitsdienst (security service) had recommended that another film glorifying Prussian militarism be restricted in its distribution to Reich German theaters, for "any particularized view . . . is to be avoided." Such films stimulated "negative views . . . in the Danube and Alpine regions, where objections to the film's political and historical attitudes are based on a historical, Pan-German point of view."[94] Moreover, *Wien 1910,* if it was to have fulfilled Goebbels's anti-Semitic hopes, had arrived too late to be of much direct agitational value, for most Austrian and German Jews had by this time been rounded up and dispatched to the death camps. Despite the objections to *Wien 1910* and its tardiness, the film nonetheless won the designation "politically and artistically valuable."[95] It thus lived up to Goebbels's official expectations, without, however, fulfilling all his propagandistic hopes. One postwar Lueger biographer, Richard Soukup, who had evidently not seen *Wien 1910,* complained "that it failed in every way from the Austrian standpoint," because the "non-Austrian" author had ignored the "advice of Austrian experts."[96] For that biographer, accuracy of physical detail, such as the fact that the actor Rudolf Forster, who had portrayed Lueger, was taller than the historical figure, assumed a higher priority than confronting any of the larger political or ideological issues that might have been raised by a Nazi film on Lueger.[97]

The first postwar biography to deal with his anti-Semitism pleaded extenuating circumstances. This was Soukup's *Lueger und sein Wien,* published in 1953 by the Austrian Peoples' party, or ÖVP (Österreichische Volkspartei), the successor to the Christian Social Party. Soukup reminded his readers that Lueger's opponents, the big capitalists, were almost entirely Jewish, suggesting thereby that Lueger's opposition had been based on political grounds, rather than on sincere personal convictions. Soukup quoted a passage from Karl Renner's book *Österreich von der Ersten zur Zweiten Republik* to support the argument that during the entire Christian Social era in Vienna, no harm came to a single Jew, and that "the Jewish element in the press, in literature, in theater life, in business life, advanced tremendously, much farther than ever before during the so-called Liberal era."[98] In another part of this book Soukup further quotes Lueger as saying that if the Jews behaved according to the Ten Commandments, as they were duty-bound to do, there would be no question of anti-Semitism.[99] Soukup's biography is a paean of praise to Lueger, eschewing criticism while glorifying past times and the great deeds of a former leader.

In 1954 another biography slightly more critical than its predecessors tried to put Lueger in perspective by placing him "between the times." *Dr. Karl Lueger. Der Mann zwischen den Zeiten* by Kurt Skalnik, a disciple of Friedrich Funder, argued that the Lueger era was a historical apron rather than a closed epoch. Lueger's career, it was suggested, was an intermezzo, thus helping explain his seemingly paradoxical politics and apparently contradictory behavior. Though there were aspects of the old and the new about the Christian Social leader, he nonetheless belonged neither to the nineteenth century nor to the newer one of mass ideologies.

Lueger was always a parliamentarian, "a man of the ballot," Skalnik argued.[100] He added that even a "radical" tactic such as anti-Semitism, if not historically neutral, was harmless when society was regulated by a strong imperial authority.[101] Skalnik here suggested that no one foresaw the genocides of the twentieth century, thereby anticipating Johannes Hawlik's "tiny apology" for Lueger's anti-Semitism in his own 1985 biography.[102] In support of those who had already argued that no harm had come to Jews during the Christian Social era, Skalnik added that so far as anti-Semitism was concerned, "the first of the tribunes" never let the tiller out of his hand.[103] This was the important feature that distinguished him from his more irresponsible successors. Skalnik's argument appeals to those who wish to disassociate Lueger's use of anti-Semitism from the Jewish genocide and who wish to challenge the image of Lueger as a pioneer of the *Ostmark*.

The revival of Lueger's memory was undertaken in earnest during the early 1980s by the resurgent People's party, which lacked an outstanding, or even a picturesque, personality as a leader. Here they were at a disadvantage; the Socialists could point to Bruno Kreisky, who, regardless of what one thought of his politics, had made a name for himself and for his country outside Austria. A charismatic leader, a great Austrian was needed by the conservatives. In February 1983 Lueger was honored in a speech by the ÖVP politician Erhard Busek, who displayed a picture of Lueger prominently on his desk. Busek's remarks inaugurated a Lueger exhibit in Vienna's first district.[104] The following year, the third volume of Helmut Andics's series on Vienna hailed the turn of the century as "the Luegerzeit" in a popular account of the Christian Social era and its effect on the Habsburg capital.[105]

Lueger's renewed popularity, however, came at the same time as a series of exposures of Socialist corruption and declining public morale, and his memory was invoked by conservative politicians as a model of probity, as it had been in the past. However, renewed admiration for Lueger was not confined solely to conservatives. The seventy-fifth anniversary of Lueger's death in 1985 was commemorated by Socialist Mayor Helmut Zilk, who placed a wreath on Lueger's grave in Vienna's Central Cemetery. Officials in the predominantly Socialist Vienna town hall were duly reminded of Lueger's achievements in municipal socialization, though this praise was qualified by the observation that Lueger had hindered the introduction of universal manhood suffrage to perpetuate Christian Social control of the municipal council.[106] However, there were few other qualifications about Lueger that year.[107] He was honored by a room dedicated to his memory in the world-famous Traum und Wirklichkeit (Dream and Reality) exhibition in Vienna's Künstlerhaus, a room somewhat reminiscent of the Dietrich Eckart Zimmer in Hitler's Munich Brown House (Eckart was another of Hitler's mentors)[108] and of the Schönerer exhibit in Vienna during the Hitler era.

Renewed interest in Lueger peaked in the spring of 1985 with the appearance of Johannes Hawlik's *Der Bürgerkaiser Karl Lueger und seine Zeit*, published by the Herold Verlag, founded by Friedrich Funder. A special Lueger photographic exhibit in Vienna's Café Central also opened at about this time. A member of the post-World War II generation, an ÖVP politician, historian, and journalist, Hawlik demonstrated a breadth of knowledge and detachment notably lacking in earlier studies. He also revealed an acquaintance with late nineteenth- and early twentieth-century socioeconomic developments outside Austria that provided a broader context for Lueger's career. Unlike other post-World War II biographers, Hawlik did not ignore or otherwise excuse Lueger from contributing to the rise of political anti-Semitism. He was critical, too, of Lueger's failure to undertake the building of communal housing and of Lueger's excessive reliance on the force of his personality to hold together the disparate elements of his party. And yet, Lueger still emerges as the democratic parliamentarian and pragmatist of earlier biographies, the statesman who correctly gauged and used the possibilities open to him for the good of all, and who used anti-Semitism only as a means to implicitly noble ends. "He was," Hawlik summarizes, "like us all – a man full of flaws and ambiguities. And nonetheless, Vienna is unthinkable without Lueger."[109] Much of Hawlik's book is dedicated to making "Vienna . . . unthinkable without Lueger," while eschewing analysis of his "flaws and ambiguities." Hawlik evokes Lueger's Vienna with descriptions of monuments and some of its more famous architectural landmarks "to fill the . . . memory of the name Dr. Karl Lueger . . . with meaning."[110] In fact, *Der Bürgerkaiser* concludes with the chapter "A Monument for Lueger." This method would doubtless have found favor with the mayor and party leader. Thus, Hawlik has continued to perpetuate the Lueger tradition – at least in part – in a manner begun more than eighty years before by Leopold Tomola with the sixtieth anniversary *Festschrift*.

And while he deplores anti-Semitism, Hawlik nonetheless leaves things up in the air: not only is he uncertain that Lueger was ever really an anti-Semite – Hawlik seems to doubt this – but he also suggests that this most controversial aspect of Lueger's career fades before his more tangible achievements. "Whoever walks with open eyes through Vienna encounters his path everywhere, and realizes that everything he created justifies his oft-repeated formula to plan and work 'for the people, with the people, and through the people,' to create . . . in the few years of fulfillment that were granted to him, for his native city and his country.[111]

Like Freiner, Hawlik's approach to his subject also becomes technocratic; Lueger's works have survived, all controversy becomes secondary and recedes in importance with the passing years. It is said that history, and one might add historians, are "apt to forgive power that claims to be exercised on behalf of future prosperity."[112] A politician's tangible accomplishments may indeed seem more important than the means used to achieve them, but this has not happened in Lueger's case. Hawlik's "Monument for Lueger" is bigger than the man; it overshadows the deeper and more lasting motivations of its subject.

Des Bürgermeisters Lueger Lumpen und Steuerträger by Rudolf Spitzer in 1988 is a more critical study of Lueger than Hawlik's. Comparing and contrasting the claims of Lueger's hagiographers with the ideals and achievements of Austrian Socialists, Spitzer effectively exposes the myth behind much of the Lueger tradition. Spitzer contends that from the 1890s "Lueger can only be understood (from the standpoint) of his incessant dispute with the labor movement," and that both as mayor and oppositional leader he decided the destiny of Vienna for more than twenty years.[113] These assertions may be questioned by some, but Spitzer's work is the first to shed light on the more far-reaching failures of Christian Social politics, and to suggest the importance of subsequent Socialist achievement. Moreover, Spitzer's unflinching delineation of Lueger's anti-Semitism is a courageous act.

In considering the effect of Lueger's career, one estimation stands vindicated by historical developments. In 1905 the historian Richard Charmatz saw in Lueger's politics a symptom of a larger decline. His appraisal in the journal *Deutschland*, containing as it did an indication of where the empire was headed and Lueger's role as harbinger, was somewhat unusual, if not unique, at the height of Lueger's career. Buoyantly optimistic about Lueger, Christian Social publicists at that time practically praised him as divinely inspired, while his journalistic enemies continued to provide trenchant, though somewhat stylized, criticism of Lueger's pretensions, gaffes, and megalomania. The Liberals, Socialists, and Pan-German Nationalists were thus often more amusing than the Christian Socials, but also equally shortsighted about his more comprehensive significance. However, Charmatz saw in Lueger's maneuvering, his denigration of minorities, his continuing need of reassurance (and thus flattery), and his restless desire to monumentalize the symbolical efforts of a declining class — if not even an age — to memorialize itself. To be sure, Lueger's material achievements were real and had immediate social significance and continuing benefit. Yet, one cannot suppress the feeling that the light of his person- ality was lurid and even his victories morbid, because they were conclusions rather than beginnings, that his achievement, to borrow his own classical mode, was Carthaginian. And something without traditional points of reference and restraining authority came to fill the vacuum he could not.

Notes

Introduction

1. I am indebted to Richard S. Levy for this insight.

2. Th. Bogalin, E. Hanisch, W. Huber, Fr. Steinkellner, eds., *Ecclesia Semper Reformanda. Beiträge zur österreichischen Kirchengeschichte im 19. und 20. Jahrhundert* (Vienna and Salzburg, 1985), 315.

3. The remark by Christian Social journalist Franz Klier in 1901 about German anti-Semite Liebermann von Sonnenberg that von Sonnenberg was "no Viennese and no Austrian, and therefore could not understand our feelings," suggests the difficulties that obviated any larger coordination of anti-Semitism. Franz Klier, "Offenes Schreiben an Herrn Max Liebermann v. Sonnenberg," *Österreichische Frauen-Zeitung* (August 4, 1901), 3.

4. Lueger's biographer, Heinrich Schnee, wrote that Lueger and Chamberlain were pioneers of municipal socialization in *Bürgermeister Karl Lueger. Leben und Wirken eines grossen Deutschen* (Paderborn, 1936), 46.

5. Richard S. Geehr, ed., *"I Decide Who Is a Jew!"—The Papers of Dr. Karl Lueger* (Washington, D.C., 1982), 9.

6. Koppel S. Pinson, *Modern Germany* (New York, 1963), 492.

7. John Weiss, *The Fascist Tradition* (New York, 1967), xi, xii.

Chapter 1. The Early Years: 1844–1869

1. Leopold Tomola, *Unser Bürgermeister Dr. Karl Lueger* (Vienna, 1904), 6.

2. Franz Stauracz, *Dr. Karl Lueger. Zehn Jahre Bürgermeister* (Vienna and Leipzig, 1907), 1. This biography of Lueger begins: "To his people Lueger was always that which his name signifies: a Lueger who looks out, looks out at everything that benefits his fatherland, his paternal city."

3. *Stenographische Protokolle über die Sitzungen des Hauses der Abgeordneten des österreichischen Reichsrats im Jahre 1893* (hereafter referred to as *Protokolle*)(March 18, 1893), 10753. See also *Protokolle* (May 25, 1894), 14567.

4. No major anti-Semitic leader has ever escaped this accusation, including Wagner, Marr, Drumont, Hitler, and Eichmann.

5. Bloch was a Jew who publicly fought anti-Semitism. He successfully challenged Canon August Rohling, the author of a scurrilous anti-Semitic work of 1871, *Der Talmudjude*.

6. Joseph Samuel Bloch, *My Reminiscences* (New York, 1973), 228. For information on Albrecht V, see Karl Edward Schimmer, *Alt und Neu Wien*, 2 vols. (Vienna and Leipzig, 1904), 1:375–98.

7. Dr. Heinz Schöny drew up Lueger's family tree. This is included as Appendix I in Geehr, *"I Decide Who Is A Jew!"*

8. Lueger's sister Hildegard possessed a family coat of arms from 1650, when the family lived in Salzburg. Dr. H. H., "Das unzertrennliche Kleeblatt," *Die Volkszeitung* (September 19, 1926), n. p.

9. The *Budweiser Zeitung* picked up on Dr. Bloch's allegation. This was the subject of a sarcastic feuilleton in the anti-Semitic *Volksblatt für Stadt und Land*. See "Die Pest. Nach dem K. von*," (February 27, 1897), 1.

10. Stauracz, *Dr. Karl Lueger*, 1.

11. Rudolf Kuppe, *Karl Lueger und seine Zeit* (Vienna, 1933), 6.

12. Ibid.

13. Grundbuch, Wiener Invalidenhaus, (hereafter referred to as Grundbuch) Heft 21, 154.

14. Ibid. As mayor, Lueger supported efforts to create a monument honoring his father's regiment, which had been renamed the "Freiherr von Hess Regiment No. 49." *Amtsblatt der K.K. Reichshaupt- und Residenzstadt Wien*, (hereafter referred to as *Amtsblatt*) no. 29 (April 10, 1906), 724, 725. See also *Amtsblatt*, no. 75 (September 17, 1907) 2115, 2116.

15. Stauracz, *Dr. Karl Lueger*, 8.

16. Tomola, 10.

17. Grundbuch, 154.

18. Ibid.

19. In her excellent dissertation on Lueger's early political career, Karin Brown writes: "Leopold . . . was fortunate, especially as a newcomer to Vienna where inexpensive housing was desperately scarce, to have decent living quarters provided free of charge as a term of employment." Karin B. Brown, "Karl Lueger as Liberal: Democracy, Municipal Reform, and the Struggle for Power in the Vienna City Council 1875–1882." (Ph.D. diss., City University of New York, 1982), 117.

20. Stauracz, *Dr. Karl Lueger*, 4; Kuppe, *Karl Lueger und seine Zeit*, 9.

21. For example, ibid.

22. The friend was Friedrich Deutsch, a medical student, and with Lueger a member of the "German Academic Reading Society." Deutsch later settled in Moravia, according to the document catalog of the Wiener Städtische Sammlungen, Z[ahl] 841, 1919. Lueger's letters to Deutsch are in Geehr, *"I Decide Who Is a Jew!"*, 31, 33.

23. Marianne Beskiba, *Aus meinen Erinnerungen an Dr. Karl Lueger* (Vienna, 1911), 14, 15.

24. Carl E. Schorske, *Fin-De-Siècle Vienna. Politics and Culture* (New York, 1980), 136. Karin Brown writes:

At home, nothing was spared to assure [*sic*] a proper education for the precocious child, and the entire family, including his mother and two sisters, was enlisted in the all-consuming enterprise of fostering the boy's rise in the world. While his father instilled the discipline and ambition that kept him at the head of his class throughout his school years, Lueger's mother served as devoted accomplice, drilling her son in Latin for hours at a time without understanding a word of the whole tiresome procedure. (118–19)

Quoting Harold Lasswell, John Boyer believes that Lueger's "family may have served . . . as a 'hothouse of ambition,' since Lueger's parents took an extraordinary interest in his academic and professional training, possibly to compensate for their own modest situation." John W. Boyer, *Political Radicalism in Late Imperial Vienna: Origins of the Christian Social Movement 1848–1897* (Chicago and London, 1981), 185.

25. Schorske, 134.

26. Kuppe, *Karl Lueger und seine Zeit*, 10.

27. *Amtsblatt*, no. 100 (December 14, 1900), 2473.

28. He signed his letters to his mother and sisters "Dr. Lueger." See Geehr, *"I Decide Who Is a Jew!"*, 61–63.

29. Stauracz, *Dr. Karl Lueger*, 6.

30. Ibid. At the time of the Anschluss, Hitler made an ostentatious visit to his parents' grave in Leonding-Linz. Like Lueger, Hitler was devoted to his mother. Though both Lueger's and Hitler's relations with their authoritarian fathers at times were strained, both fathers had risen from peasant stock to higher *Mittelstand* status through state service. I wish to thank Professor Richard S. Levy for this thought.

31. Schorske, 134.

32. Ibid. Schorske's source is Schnee, 12. This anecdote, for which there is no source in Schnee, but which was probably taken from an earlier biography by Eugen Mack, who doubtless read the anecdote in the *Reichspost*, may be based on an untraceable verbal quotation, and should therefore be treated with caution. See Eugen Mack, *Dr. Karl Lueger, der Bürgermeister von Wien* (Rottenburg a. Neckar, 1910), 13, and "Lueger Erinnerungen," *Reichspost* (March 10, 1910), 7.

33. Geehr, *"I Decide Who Is a Jew!"*, 300.

34. Johann Freiner, *Der Herrgott von Wien* (Dresden, 1940).

35. Ibid., 47.

36. Kuppe, *Karl Lueger und seine Zeit*, 13.

37. The repression that followed the revolutions of 1848 was a continuation of much that had existed during the *Biedermeier* era, extending as it did to censorship of music and interference in musicians' lives. See Alice M. Hanson, *Musical Life in Biedermeier Vienna* (London, 1985).

38. "Mein Bruder Karl. Aus einem Gespräch mit Fräulein Hildegard Lueger," *Illustriertes Wiener Extrablatt* (September 19, 1926), 3.

39. *Stenographische Protokolle des niederösterreichischen Landtages* (hereafter referred to as *Landtag*) (May 12, 1899), 1068.

40. *Illustriertes Wiener Extrablatt* (September 19, 1926), 3.

41. "Ein Wiener Kind," *Wiener Kinder. Eine Monatsschrift für Wiens deutsche Jugend* (1902), 4.

42. Robert A. Kann, *A History of the Habsburg Empire 1526–1918* (Berkeley, Los Angeles, London, 1974), 372.

43. One of Lueger's enemies, the *Konstitutionelle Vorstadtzeitung*, thought otherwise, later dubbing him "the Cato of Erdberg," but thus all the same suggested the classical effect on Lueger's oratory. Erdberg was a poor area of the third district, which Lueger represented in the municipal council. The above phrase is from Brown, 271. The effects of studying Cicero are described by Felix Somary, the economist and financier, whose Schottengymnasium

education was like Lueger's in its curriculum. Cicero may in fact have inspired Lueger's interest in democratic politics, as well as that in the conflict between justice and power. Somary writes:

> My father took an active interest in my studies, as much as time allowed, and through him history and the old classics came alive. I still remember his remarkable elucidations of Catilina, and should I pass Terni in the car today, I would readily drive up to Amelia with its splendid scenery in order to recall Cicero's *The Defense of Roscius Amerinus* of my father's commentary. How few students understand this book. Most of them struggle with the vocabulary. I spoke Cicero's words over dinner at home. "If my client is condemned, it would be better to live among the wild beasts than to linger on in this swamp of Romulus," and called them unbearable. Whereupon my father answered: "Do you know what it is about? When Sulla administered the proscriptions of the democratic party and every denunciator could be given the property of his enemy, one of his supporters murdered a landowner in Amelia and denounced the landowner's own son as the murderer; and without Cicero's defense the innocent son would have been condemned. Nothing in these words is exaggerated; this language was necessary to counter the wickedness of the time and demonstrates the rare courage of the defender who is usually accused of the opposite." "Something like that is impossible anywhere today," said my mother. "Don't say that," replied my father, "What happened in high Roman civilization can repeat itself now. The struggle between power and justice hasn't been decided yet."

Felix Somary, *Erinnerungen aus meinem Leben* (Zürich, 1959), 21. For details about late-nineteenth-century Schottengymnasium education, see William J. McGrath, *Dionysian Art and Populist Politics in Austria* (New Haven and London, 1974), 27–32 and the sources quoted therein.

44. Even the crudely vituperative Ernst Schneider, "Lueger's Streicher," quoted Latin sayings in his speeches.

45. Karl Wenger, "Lorenz von Stein und die Entwicklung der Verwaltungswissenschaft in Österreich," in Roman Schnur, ed., *Staat und Gesellschaft. Studien über Lorenz von Stein.* (Berlin, 1978), 483.

46. Lueger's cultural politics will be more thoroughly treated in chapter seven.

47. Lueger received his first communion on April 20, 1853. Leopold Kunschak, *Steinchen vom Wege* (Vienna, n. d.), 54.

48. Kurt Skalnik, *Dr. Karl Lueger. Der Mann zwischen den Zeiten* (Vienna, Munich, 1954), 19. Dirk Van Arkel thinks it "likely that he became indifferent to religious questions," though "this does not necessarily mean he lost faith altogether." See Dirk Van Arkel, *Antisemitism in Austria* (Leiden, 1966), 71.

49. Geehr, *"I Decide Who Is a Jew!",* 145. Lueger's early political mentor Ignaz Mandl claimed that, as early as 1873, two years before he was elected to the municipal council, Lueger supported a clerical candidate. *Fortschritt,* July 27, 1883.

50. There is a very large German literature by and about Lorenz von Stein, though much less in English. The best bibliography of his works is included in Werner Schmidt's biography "Lorenz von Stein. Ein Beitrag zur Biographie, zur Geschichte Schleswig-Holsteins und zur Geistesgeschichte des 19. Jahrhunderts," *Jahrbuch der Heimatgemeinschaft des Kreises Eckernförde e. V.,* 14 (Eckernförde, 1956). A comprehensive bibliography of works about Stein is found in Kaethe Mengelberg, *Lorenz von Stein: The History of the Social Movement in France, 1759–1850* (Totowa, N.J., 1964). These two works have been updated by Manfred Hahn, *Bürgerlicher Optimismus im Niedergang* (Munich, 1969); Roman Schnur, ed., *Staat und Gesellschaft. Studien über Lorenz von Stein* (Berlin, 1978); Dirk Blasius and Eckart Pan-

koke, *Lorenz von Stein* (Darmstadt, 1977); and Gundela Lahmer, *Lorenz von Stein. Zur Konstitution des bürgerlichen Bildungswesens* (Frankfurt and New York, 1982).

51. Universitätsnationalien, 1864, 1865, Archive of the University of Vienna. Lueger maintained ties with his alma mater for several years after he had completed his formal study. When at a meeting of student nationalists during the Franco-Prussian War in 1870, he condemned Bismarckian nationalism, he was driven from the hall. See Paul Molisch, *Politische Geschichte der deutschen Hochschulen in Österreich von 1848–1918* (Vienna and Leipzig, 1939), 78–80.

52. A sampling of Lueger's notes and essays from his university years may be found in Geehr, *"I Decide Who Is A Jew!"*, 34–47. A list of Lueger's school notebooks and his instructors is in Appendix II, 353–54.

53. Karl Lueger, "Verwaltungslehre, II. innere Verwalt[un]g nach Vorlesungen von Prof. Dr. [Lorenz] Stein," Handschriftensammlung der städtischen Bibliothek der Stadt Wien, Nachlass Karl Lueger, St.[ädtische] S[amm]l[un]g. Z[ah]l. 1257/12, Box I.

54. Adam Wandruszka and Peter Urbanitsch, eds., *Die Habsburgermonarchie 1848–1918* (Vienna, 1973), I: 609.

55. Alexander Novotny, quoted in Schmidt, 68.

56. Schmidt, 175. In February 1864 Stein saw Austria as the only mediator of the Schleswig-Holstein question with a European perspective. Neither Prussia nor the German Confederation, both parochial powers, could accomplish this task in Stein's view.

57. Andrew G. Whiteside, *The Socialism of Fools* (Berkeley, 1975), 48–51.

58. Schmidt, 77. One of Lueger's student essays evinces concern for "the social question" in Steinian terms. See Geehr, *"I Decide Who Is a Jew!"*, 41–45.

59. "Wiener Tagesbericht," *Neues Wiener Tagblatt* (September 25, 1890), 5.

60. Friedrich Eckstein, *"Alte unnennbare Tage!" Erinnerungen aus siebzig Lehr- und Wanderjahren* (Vienna, Leipzig, and Zürich, 1936), 44.

61. Ibid., 46.

62. Ibid., 47.

63. Schmidt, 74.

64. Ibid., 77.

65. Schnur, ed., 480. Stein influenced such economists and social reformers as Adolph Wagner and Albert Schäffle. He also taught Eugen von Philippovich, one of Lueger's foes.

66. See my translation of Lueger's paper, written as a student, "Is State or Society the More Comprehensive Concept, and How So?" in *"I Decide Who Is a Jew!"*, 44. John Boyer calls attention to Lueger's general adherence to the principles of the *Rechtsstaat* in his dealings with Vienna's Jews. So far as the Jews were concerned, Lueger's theory and practice were often at odds. John W. Boyer, "Karl Lueger and the Viennese Jews," in *The Leo Baeck Institute Year Book* 26 (New York, 1981), 127.

67. Stein's theories about women and the social question appear in two of his earliest publications, *Die Frau, ihre Bildung und Lebensaufgabe* (Dresden, 1851) and *Die wirtschaftliche Erziehung und die Lebensaufgabe der Hausfrau* (Leipzig, 1852). Stein continued to publish books on this topic, succinctly summarizing his thoughts in a series of articles in the *Wiener Abendpost*. Lueger, an inveterate newspaper reader, may well have deepened his earlier perceptions from Stein's lectures through the *Abendpost* series. By the mid-1880s, women had begun to be significant in Lueger's electoral campaigns. For Stein's series, see "Die Frau auf dem Gebiete der socialen Frage," *Beilage zur Wiener Abendpost* (February 25, 1880), 177, 178; (February 26, 1880), 181, 182; (February 27, 1880), 186, 187; (February 28, 1880), 190, 191; (March 1, 1880), 193, 194.

68. Ibid., 182, 194.

69. Beskiba, 24.

70. Maria I. Wittmann, "Die österreichische Frauenstimmrechtsbewegung im Spiegel der Frauenzeitungen. Mit einer einleitenden Darstellung der allgemein österreichischen Wahlbewegung von 1893–1906, im Spiegel der Presse" (Ph.D. diss., University of Vienna, 1950), 61, 62. The governor of Lower Austria, Erich Graf Kielmansegg, indicates that Lueger was probably insincere about wanting female suffrage. See Erich Graf Kielmansegg, *Kaiserhaus, Staatsmänner und Politiker* (Vienna 1966), 386.

71. Lueger's tendency to regard law as something distinctly separate and apart from social and political life may have originally been acquired from his study of Cicero, like some of his early legal concepts. If so, Stein's categorical theories probably reinforced this tendency. See Bruce W. Frier, *The Rise of the Roman Jurists: Studies in Cicero's "pro Caecina"* (Princeton, New Jersey, 1985).

72. But Kuppe mentions a number of Lueger's other teachers. Kuppe, *Karl Lueger und seine Zeit*, 16. Ironically, the liberal opposition held up Steinian concepts to Lueger as a pedagogical model in a parliamentary debate over the international regulation of labor protection. *Protokolle* (April 11, 1889), 12274–76.

73. Johannes Hawlik departs from this earlier publicistic tradition. See his *Der Bürgerkaiser. Karl Lueger und Seine Zeit* (Vienna, Munich, 1985).

74. According to the *Neue Freie Presse*, "he often had the tendency to side with the powerful" (September 24, 1890), 2. Sidney Hook cited Stein's "reactionary tendencies." Sidney Hook, *From Hegel to Marx* (New York, 1950), 199, quoted in Kaethe Mengelberg, "Lorenz von Stein and His Contribution to Historical Sociology," in *Journal of the History of Ideas* 22 (1961), 273.

75. Richard von Kralik emphasized this: "All Christian Social leaders, Lueger, Liechtenstein, etc., repeatedly acknowledged that they were Vogelsang's pupils, that they learned only from him, and through personal teaching, what they tried to put into practice as practical politicians." Richard von Kralik, *Karl Lueger und der christliche Sozialismus* (Vienna, 1923), 23, 24.

76. Some Christian Socials, such as Albert Gessmann and Josef Gregorig, called the Revolution of 1848 a "revolution of Jewry." Lueger added that "the old liberals . . . Jewish liberals . . . have really profited from the movement of the year 1848, all respect." *Amtsblatt*, no. 20 (March 11, 1898), 737–43.

77. Vogelsang himself seems to have considered Stein the least hidebound of the classical university economists, though, and spoke favorably about him. Wiard Klopp, *Leben und Wirken des Sozialpolitikers Karl Freiherrn von Vogelsang* (Vienna, 1930), 311.

78. Wandruszka and Urbanitsch, eds., 609. See also Blasius and Pankoke, 34–45.

79. "[S]killed in business affairs and, at the same time, loyal to the emperor and the State." Victor L. Tapié, *The Rise and Fall of the Habsburg Monarchy* (New York, 1971), 294.

80. Geehr, "*I Decide Who Is a Jew!*", 45. Many years later in parliament, Lueger fervently denied that he had ever been a republican, asserting that he had been a "*Schwarzgelber*," or loyal Habsburg supporter, from his university days. Black and yellow were the traditional colors of the Habsburgs. Whether he recalled his earlier position is uncertain. Lueger was not above denying accusations that were difficult to prove, and did so on many occasions. *Protokolle* (October 2, 1905), 31780.

81. *Landtag* (April 25, 1899), 771.

82. Amartya Sen, "Do Economists Influence the World?" in *The Times Literary Supplement* (December 6, 1985), 1387.

83. Schnur, ed., 480.

84. Schmidt, 108, 109.

85. M. E. Kamp, *Die Theorie der Epochen der öffentlichen Wirtschaft bei Lorenz von Stein* (Bonn, 1950), 17.

86. Ibid., 19, 20.

87. These included Hobbes, Locke, Rousseau, Puffendorf, Leibnitz, Thomasius, Wolff, Kant, Fichte, Bentham, Moser, Montesquieu, Burke, Hugo, Savigny, de Miastre, de Bonald, Lamennais, Schelling, and Hegel. Karl Lueger, "Rechtswissenschaft, nach Vorträgen von Dr. Lorenz Stein," Handschriftensammlung der städtischen Bibliothek der Stadt Wien, Nachlass Karl Lueger, St. Slg. Zl. 1257/12, Box I.

88. As early as 1870 during the defense of his theses, he advocated an active and passive franchise for all adult citizens who could read and write. In this light, his 1875 statement "Oh, I am possibly more of a democrat than anyone," is significant. Quoted in Brown, 122.

89. Lueger, "Rechtswissenschaft." In Blanc's *Organization of Labor,* a work about which Lueger learned through Stein, the following passage was typical:

> Walk through an industrial city at five in the morning and observe the crowd that presses about the entrance to the mills. You will see miserable children, pale, puny, stunted, dull-eyed, livid-cheeked, breathing with difficulty, bent over like old men. Listen to the talk of these children: their hoarse voices [are] hollow, as if muffled by the noxious atmosphere which they breathe in the cotton mills.

(quoted in Ernest John Knapton, *France — An Interpretive History* [New York, 1971], 386).

In the late 1880s, Lueger, in terms that might have been inspired by Blanc, defended Salomon Meisl, a Vienna tramway conductor, who had been fired for allegedly having spoken out at a meeting of tramway employees about the need for company contributions to the pension fund. Lueger urged the elimination of conditions whereby tramway employees might be reduced to beggary and their families made destitute. (Geehr, "*I Decide Who Is a Jew!*", 195–98) Stein had had contact with Blanc and other socialists while he was living in Paris.

90. Lueger's last resting place is a massive tomb within the Gedächtniskirche of the Wiener Zentralfriedhof.

91. *Sätze aus allen Zweigen der Rechts- und Staatswissenschaften, welche nach abgelegten vier strengen Prüfungen zur Erlangung der juridischen Doctorswürde an der k.k. Universität zu Wien, Karl Lueger, Advocaturs-Concipient in Wien, Freitag den 14. Januar 1870, um 12 Uhr Mittag, im k.k. Universitäts-Consistorialsaale öffentlich zu vertheidigen sich erbietet* (Vienna, 1870), n. p.

92. Kuppe, *Karl Lueger und seine Zeit,* 23, 24.

93. Boyer, *Political Radicalism in Late Imperial Vienna,* 187.

94. *Sätze aus allen Zweigen.*

95. Kuppe, *Karl Lueger und seine Zeit,* 18. He was also a member of an apparently democratic student association, "Hilaria." Hawlik, 23.

96. Kuppe, *Karl Lueger und seine Zeit,* 18.

97. Ibid. On the day of Königgraetz, "crying with rage and pain, Lueger cursed Bismarck and Prussiandom" according to Karl's cousin Franz. Quoted in Hawlik, 190.

98. Geehr, "*I Decide Who Is a Jew!*", 31, 32.

99. Ibid., 32, 33.

Chapter 2. The Developing Politician: 1869–1889

1. Details of Lueger's legal apprenticeship are in Geehr, *"I Decide Who Is a Jew!",* 48–50.
2. Stauracz, *Dr. Karl Lueger,* 13.
3. *Amtsblatt,* no. 53 (July 2, 1907), 1474.
4. Stauracz, *Dr. Karl Lueger,* 17.
5. Boyer, *Political Radicalism in Late Imperial Vienna,* 191.
6. Ibid.
7. Richard Soukup, *Lueger und sein Wien* (Vienna, 1953), 122.
8. Brown, 116. "After the revolution of 1848, a city [municipal] council and the mayor selected by it were given extensive authority over the business of the Vienna municipality. Most of the councilmen were elected on a three-class (curial) system, arranged in keeping with taxes paid, and nontaxpayers shared with the rest in choosing a fourth section of the lawmakers. Before assuming the office the mayor had to have the formal approval of the emperor." Arthur J. May, *The Hapsburg Monarchy 1867–1914* (New York, 1968), 309. For details about the Viennese curial system see Maren Seliger and Karl Ucakar, *Wien, Politische Geschichte 1740–1934* 2 vols., (Vienna and Munich, 1985), I: 572 ff., 576 ff.; II: 918 ff., 929 ff., 966.
9. David S. Good questions the traditional view that "the great depression period, 1873–1896, was one of relatively slow growth and sharp cyclic fluctuation compared to the two trend periods on either side." Yet, he concedes that this depression was real in more than an economic sense, that it "destroyed popular faith in liberal ideas and in the business and intellectual elite that espoused them." David S. Good, *The Economic Rise of the Habsburg Empire 1750–1914* (Berkeley, Los Angeles, and London, 1984), 172, 232.
10. Karl Eder, *Der Liberalismus in Altösterreich. Geisteshaltung, Politik und Kultur* (Vienna and Munich, 1955), 218.
11. A sampling of economic statistics for the early years after the crash may be found in Seliger and Ucakar, I: 350.
12. C. A. Macartney, *The Habsburg Empire 1790–1918* (London, 1969), 631, 632.
13. Brown is particularly successful in pointing this out. See Brown, 124.
14. Here, the Liberals had been weakened at the beginning of the decade by Prussian victory over France. See Erich Zöllner, *Geschichte Österreichs* (Munich, 1984), 418.
15. William A. Jenks, *Austria under the Iron Ring 1879–1893* (Charlottesville, Virginia, 1965), 35.
16. Macartney, 631.
17. Vincent J. Knapp, *Austrian Social Democracy 1889–1914* (Washington, DC, 1980), vi.
18. Walter Kleindel, *Österreich. Daten zur Geschichte und Kultur* (Vienna, 1978), 277; Franz Patzer, "Der Wiener Gemeinderat von 1890–1952. Eine parteisoziologische Untersuchung." (unpublished monograph, Vienna, 1952).
19. Brown, 134.
20. Brown writes: "Although the percentage of the population qualified to vote in municipal elections remained very small (the 3.3 percent in 1861 grew to only 5.8 [percent] in 1895), it was this limited electorate that determined the fate of Viennese liberalism and ultimately changed the face of Austrian politics with Karl Lueger's election as mayor of Vienna in 1895" (p. 25). See also Maren Seliger, "Liberale Fraktionen im Wiener Gemeinderat 1861 bis 1895," in *Wien in der Liberalen Ära, Forschungen und Beiträge zur Wiener Stadtgeschichte* (Vienna, 1978), 65.
21. Boyer has indicated Mandl's and Lueger's debt to Wilhelm Neurath, a Viennese

economist. See Boyer, *Political Radicalism in Late Imperial Vienna,* 194. Neurath's theories anticipated Edward Bellamy's best-selling novel of 1888, *Looking Backward.*

Ignaz Mandl deserves more thoroughgoing study as an innovator in political techniques than he has received until now. The scion of a wealthy Hungarian Jewish family, Mandl received his doctor of medicine from the University of Vienna in 1859 but never practiced. On his early career and motivations see Brown, 72–77; Sigmund Mayer, *Die Wiener Juden. Kommerz, Kultur, Politik 1700–1900* (Vienna and Berlin, 1917) 385 n.; *Ein jüdischer Kaufmann 1831 bis 1911. Lebenserinnerungen* (Leipzig, 1911), 252.

22. Schorske, 6.

23. Ibid., 5. See also Eva Holleis, *Die Sozialpolitische Partei. Sozialliberale Bestrebungen in Wien um 1900* (Vienna, 1978), 7. Lueger was later to continue to restrict the franchise to prevent the Socialists from wresting power from the Christian Socials.

24. For Lueger's remarks on the Danube regulation, see *Landtag* (September 23, 1892), 108–12. On the cemeteries, see Max von Millenkovich-Morold, *Vom Abend zum Morgen. Aus dem alten Österreich ins neue Deutschland* (Leipzig, 1940), 225, 226.

25. Cajetan Felder, *Erinnerungen eines Wiener Bürgermeisters* (Vienna, Hannover, and Bern, 1964), 367.

26. Ibid., 364.

27. As late as 1884, six years after he had forced Felder out of office, Lueger could write: "I have never made a secret of my *personal* [emphasis in original] respect for Dr. Felder in spite of my political opposition." See Geehr, *"I Decide Who Is a Jew!",* 129.

28. In a letter to the author, Karin Brown stated that she believed that Lueger became disillusioned with Felder "on closer acquaintance. Felder became for Lueger that power which no longer 'conformed to society.'"

29. The source of this anecdote is Hermann Mauthner, who studied with Lueger. Kuppe, *Karl Lueger und seine Zeit,* 18.

30. Brown, 142.

31. Ibid., 146.

32. Ibid., 150.

33. Ibid., 148.

34. Ibid., 154.

35. Ibid., 119.

36. The trend toward growing isolation among Liberal leaders and the concomitant popular demand for charismatic leaders would become increasingly great. The "little man" never felt truly represented by constitutions and elitist politicians. Hitler never tired of relating his credentials as a little man, the nameless soldier of the war — *das arme Frontschwein* — as a mark of authenticity. See J.P. Stern, *Hitler: The Führer and the People* (Glasgow, 1975), 111, 112. There is more than a hint of popular disaffection with elitist liberalism in a handwritten poem from 1878, enclosed in an election ballot, which Lueger saved. It was evidently by one of his constituents:

> Let them grumble, let them rage;
> Let them quarrel about nothing;
> We, we fight to live.

> With much sound and little substance,
> Only caring for their own well-being,
> That's all they do and want.

When will peace come back again?
Will justice ever be prized again?
Can one still harbor such wishes?

Yes, when passions are defeated,
When everyone is given his due.
Then happiness and prosperity will return.

See Geehr, *"I Decide Who Is a Jew!"*, 298.

37. Heinrich Brunner, *Grundzüge der deutschen Rechtsgeschichte* (Leipzig, 1910), 18, 19.

38. Lueger was particularly sensitive to charges that he was a *Streber*, or hustler. He often denied that he was, maintaining, rather, that he fought "for the people and against their enemies." Geehr, *"I Decide Who Is a Jew!"*, 188.

39. Felder, 216. In an unpublished addendum, *Infamien des Dr. Johann Nep. Prix. Meine Rechtfertigung. Katzenpfoten*, Felder continued in much the same vein, belittling Mandl and Lueger's efforts to root out corruption that neither he nor a dozen members of a special commission could find. Handschriftensammlung der Wiener Stadtbibliothek.

40. Brown, 162.

41. On Kirschlehner, see also Sigmund Mayer, *Ein jüdischer Kaufmann*, 252. Mayer incorrectly identifies Kirschlehner as "Kirchmayr."

42. Brown, 162. Lueger's version of these events may be found in Geehr, *"I Decide Who Is a Jew!"*, 112–15.

43. Brown, 163.

44. Ibid. Lueger's drafts of these motions are in Geehr, *"I Decide Who Is a Jew!"*, 106, 107.

45. Brown, 164.

46. Ibid.

47. Ibid., 166.

48. Geehr, *"I Decide Who Is a Jew!"*, 107, 108.

49. Ibid., 109.

50. Karl Lueger, *Verwaltungslehre II. innere Verwaltg, nach Vorlesungen von Dr. Stein*, Nachlass Karl Lueger, St. Slg. Zl. 1257/12, Box I.

51. Brown, 189n. 159.

52. Ibid., 168.

53. Ibid., 168, 169.

54. Geehr, *"I Decide Who Is a Jew!"*, 125.

55. Brown, 169.

56. Ibid.

57. Brown writes: "For a young man of Lueger's temperament, accustomed from childhood to affection, praise, and reward for concentrated effort, who had also committed his personal and political aspirations to a plan of action that had badly misfired, the foregoing events may well have engendered a deep personal crisis" (170).

58. Felder, 250, 251.

59. Ibid., 216.

60. Geehr, *"I Decide Who Is a Jew!"*, 110, 111. Though a draft letter to the Lower Austrian court, this document probably reflects Lueger's true feelings.

61. Brown, 173.

62. *Landtag* (February 27, 1893), 317.

63. Geehr, *"I Decide Who Is a Jew!"*, 193, 194.

64. Brown, 173, 174.

65. A description of this area is contained in Brown, 76.
66. Ibid., 177.
67. Ibid., 178.
68. Ibid., 193.
69. Ibid.
70. Lueger's version is summarized in Geehr, *"I Decide Who Is a Jew!"*, 122–25.
71. Brown, 194.
72. Ibid., 195.
73. Ibid.
74. Ibid., 196.
75. Felder's memoirs quote various responses to rumors of his resignation. See 259–62.
76. The original core of the city grew from 632,127 in 1869 to 725,658 in 1880, while the outlying districts, which were incorporated in 1890, grew from 335,437 to 385,363 during the same period. Reinhard E. Petermann, *Wien im Zeitalter Kaiser Franz Josephs I* (Vienna, 1913), 143.
77. Sigmund Mayer, *Die Wiener Juden,* 385, n.
78. Brown, 197.
79. Ibid., 197, 198.
80. Felder, 264.
81. Ibid.
82. Brown, 199.
83. Ibid., 202. Lueger seems to have nurtured this myth himself, or at least to have become attached to the notion that he championed the "little man" from the time of this election. See Geehr, *"I Decide Who Is a Jew!"*, 298.
84. Brown, 202.
85. Ibid., 204.
86. Friedrich Heer once told me that an elderly passenger on a Viennese tram complained about the weather, and then added, in all seriousness, that such inclement conditions would never have been tolerated under Lueger.
87. Brown, 208.
88. Ibid., 210.
89. Ibid., 211.
90. Quoted in Brown, 212.
91. Even Kuppe, arguably Lueger's most partisan biographer, concedes that "the constant attacks of the anti-Semitic *'Bürgerklub'* [Lueger's political club] on the one-sided and arbitrary conduct of business in the town hall increased the job-weariness (*Amtsmüdigkeit*) of Mayor Dr. Prix." Kuppe, *Karl Lueger und seine Zeit,* 331.
92. Brown, 213.
93. Ibid., 214.
94. Until 1890 there existed a tariff barrier enclosing Vienna's inner nine districts. Those who lived within the confines of the barrier had to pay a food consumption tax. See Rudolf Kuppe, *Dr. Karl Lueger. Persönlichkeit und Wirken* (Vienna, 1947), 94–96.
95. Brown, 218. In 1908 Social Democratic municipal councillor Ludwig Wutschel reminded Lueger of his words of July 8, 1878, during a trial in which Lueger had presumably defended a Social Democrat: "The improvement of social conditions is a goal of every reasonable man, for everyone feels that the present social conditions are not the final and best that can be achieved. . . . The ideal will never be achieved, but to strive for the ideal is possible. And the Social Democratic party does that" (*Amtsblatt,* no. 102 [December 22, 1908], 3030).
96. Brown, 224.

97. A contemporary cartoon depicts police chasing two thieves who are safely concealed in "the light of a municipal gas lantern." Ibid.

98. Lueger's views on this are contained in Geehr, "I Decide Who Is a Jew!", 164, 165.

99. Lueger and Mandl at one point thought that attempts to commemorate this anniversary were inadequate. See Geehr, "I Decide Who Is a Jew!", 251.

100. Brown, 241n. 160.

101. These are described in Brown, 256.

102. Ibid., 259.

103. Ibid.

104. Ibid., 260.

105. Ibid., 244.

106. Ibid., 263.

107. Brown has incorrectly identified Ritter von Kronenfels as the Governor of Lower Austria. See Brown, 265, 266.

108. For details, see Geehr, "I Decide Who Is a Jew!", 167–73.

109. Ibid., 166, 167.

110. Ibid., 300–4.

111. Boyer, Political Radicalism in Late Imperial Vienna, 202, 203.

112. See Brown, 269, 270; and Geehr, "I Decide Who Is a Jew!", 174–85.

113. It will be remembered that Lueger subsequently claimed to have left "the old Liberal Party in . . . 1876." However, this was more to indicate his economic disenchantment than to mean that he established a new party. Landtag (February 27, 1893), 317.

114. The fine was remitted to an appellate court.

115. Geehr, "I Decide Who Is a Jew!", 187.

116. Ibid., 187, 188.

117. Quoted in Brown, 271.

118. Vienna Municipal Library Handwritten Documents Collection, I.N. 45721. Hereafter, documents from this collection are referred to by their I.N. number.

119. Whiteside, 86.

120. Erika Weinzierl, "Antisemitismus in der österreichischen Literatur 1900–1938," in Mitteilungen des österreichischen Staatsarchivs (Vol. 20, 1967), 356.

121. Some of the pioneers of this literary movement are mentioned in Nagl et al., Deutsch-Österreichische Literaturgeschichte (Vienna, 1930), III: 350, 766. For discussions of parallel developments in Germany see Ernest K. Bramsted, Aristocracy and the Middle-Classes in Germany (Chicago, 1964) and George L. Mosse, The Crisis of German Ideology (New York, 1964).

122. Nagl et al., III: 767, 768.

123. Ibid., 769. On Giskra, see Kielmansegg, 199–204.

124. B. Aba, Moderne Grössen (Vienna, 1883), I: 21.

125. Ibid., II: 58, 59.

126. The Statthalter of Lower Austria, Kielmansegg, wrote that Lueger won thousands of voters through the use of this term alone. Kielmansegg, 401.

127. These include Der Mord in der Judenstadt (1873) and Das Kruzifix der Juden (1873). During the early 1890s Wiesinger publicly argued that the racial anti-Semitism of the German radicals should be suppressed and replaced by a "finer and more moral" variety. Nagl et al., III: 264. On Wiesinger, see Nagl et al., III: 263–67.

128. Boyer is uncertain about "how serious Lueger was in joining Fischhof," but Lueger's dedication to the older man seems hardly in doubt. At an assembly Lueger physically

shielded Fischhof. Boyer, *Political Radicalism in Late Imperial Vienna,* 210; Sigmund Mayer, *Ein jüdischer Kaufmann,* 296.

129. Ernst R. Rutkowski, "Die revolutionäre Bewegung und die inneren Verhältnisse des Zarenreichs von 1877 bis 1884 im Urteil österreich-ungarischer Diplomaten," in *Mitteilungen des österreichen Staatsarchivs* (1955), 437n. 359. The *Freiheit* subscriber list was classified information.

130. On the social radicalism of this era in Austria, see Jenks, *Austria under the Iron Ring,* 158–78. According to Richard S. Levy, Most was an infamous character who was thrown out of the Socialist Workers' party in Germany because of his anarchism. He took a predictably radical line regarding Adolf Stöcker's attempt to win over workers in Berlin. See Franz Mehring, *Geschichte der deutschen Sozialdemokratie,* 2 vols. (Berlin, 1960).

131. Geehr, "*I Decide Who Is a Jew!*", 203.

132. Gessmann's description of his first meeting with Lueger on an excursion during the summer of 1878 is quoted in Kuppe, *Karl Lueger und seine Zeit,* 73. It seems doubtful, however, that Gessmann then recognized in Lueger "the appointed leader in the struggle against Liberalism," for Lueger had no intention of overthrowing the Liberals at that time. Brown, 284.

133. Friedrich Funder, *Vom Gestern ins Heute* (Vienna and Munich, 1953), 268. Kielmansegg goes even farther than Funder that there "was actually no inner bond between them," "actually, both disliked one another." Kielmansegg, 416.

134. Kuppe indicates that Mandl was jealous of Gessmann, which may well have been true. Kuppe, *Karl Lueger und seine Zeit,* 78.

135. For Felder's ironic response to this rupture, see Felder, 298.

136. I.N. 40901.

137. The school issue is treated on pp. 285–97.

138. An anti-Semite lithographer, Leopold Hollomay, wrote a letter to Lueger at this time in which he scorned Mandl as an opportunist whose actions were governed by his allegiance to "his Semitic people." I.N. 40933.

139. This letter is included in its entirety in Geehr, "*I Decide Who Is a Jew!*", 131, 132.

140. "Dr. Ignaz Mandl," in *Neue Freie Presse* (May 5, 1907), 11.

141. Geehr, "*I Decide Who Is a Jew!*", 129.

142. Felder, 298, 300.

143. Kuppe, *Karl Lueger und seine Zeit,* 101; Stauracz, *Dr. Karl Lueger,* 24.

144. My account is based on Whiteside, 107–12.

145. Ibid., 107.

146. Ibid., 108. Whiteside writes: "Democrats of all orientations had been demanding nationalization of all railroads for over ten years. The German radicals argued that a profitable line that charged notoriously high rates and had a stranglehold on the economic development of the empire should not be turned back to capitalist exploitation" (107). Why Lueger and Schönerer invoked Bismarck's name is unclear.

147. Geehr, "*I Decide Who Is a Jew!*", 281, 282.

148. Whiteside, 108.

149. Ibid., 111.

150. Ibid., 112.

151. Skalnik, 44. According to Skalnik's categories, most of the new voters were small tradesmen and nearly a third were private officials. For the electoral structure of Cisleithanian Austria, see Kann, *A History of the Habsburg Empire 1526–1918,* 424 ff. Cisleithania was the "Austrian" half of the dual Monarchy, and included, in addition to Austrian Germans, some Italians and various Slavic groups. See Macartney, map 5, 572, 573.

152. On Steudel, see Brown, 77, 78; and Felder, 162, 163.

153. See Geehr, *"I Decide Who Is a Jew!"*, 145. Heinrich Friedjung asserted that Mandl, rather than Lueger, developed the most important of Lueger's program points. F., "Ein Vorspiel zu den Reichsrathswahlen," in *Deutsche Wochenschrift* (March 15, 1885), 5, 6.

154. See Geehr, *"I Decide Who Is a Jew!"*, 87, 140, 141. Despite the activity of the campaign, Lueger evidently had time to take a vacation to Sicily from about May 15 till the latter part of May, thus attesting the difference between electoral campaigns a century ago and now. He refers to this trip in a letter to Valerie Gréy. "Unbekannte Lueger-Briefe an eine Wiener Dame," in *Neues Wiener Journal* (September 19, 1926), 6.

155. For a sampling of documents attesting Lueger's activities during this campaign, see Geehr, *"I Decide Who Is a Jew!"*, 141–54. An idea of his demagogic style may be gleaned from a draft speech on pp. 151–54.

156. Boyer, *Political Radicalism in Late Imperial Vienna*, 213, 214.

157. Ibid., 214.

158. Ibid., 211.

159. Lueger's program, delivered as a speech, is in Kuppe, *Karl Lueger und seine Zeit*, 123–27. Lueger's handwritten draft, which prefigured the speech, is in Geehr, *"I Decide Who Is a Jew!"*, 142–44.

160. Boyer states, rather baldly, that "after 1886 Lueger made no mention of universal suffrage" (*Political Radicalism in Late Imperial Vienna*, 212). He did mention it several times in public forums, but more and more the concept of universal suffrage came to have strings attached. After he became mayor, Lueger argued that to have the vote, adult males should have lived in Vienna for at least five years without interruption.

161. Kuppe, *Karl Lueger und seine Zeit*, 125. Lueger was probably referring to the social turbulence of the preceding year. See Jenks, *Austria under the Iron Ring*, 160, 161.

162. Boyer, *Political Radicalism in Late Imperial Vienna*, 212.

163. Kuppe, *Karl Lueger und seine Zeit*, 126.

164. The creation of greater Vienna is a case in point. See Kielmansegg, 383, 384.

165. Boyer provides details, *Political Radicalism in Late Imperial Vienna*, 213.

166. Kleindel, 281.

167. Whiteside, 119.

168. Ibid., 120. Whiteside calls this "the most extreme anti-Semitic bill ever proposed in Austria, [Schönerer's] so-called Chinese Bill, which he claimed was analogous to the United States Congress's exclusion of Oriental immigrants."

169. *Protokolle* (October 19, 1886), 3900.

170. Boyer, *Political Radicalism in Late Imperial Vienna*, 215. Boyer adds:

But Lueger could not be certain how long this kind of tenuous relationship would last. To prevent internecine warfare, he proposed a temporary antisemitic-Democratic coalition for the 1886 Council elections. Rather than merely voting for each other's candidates, various Democratic and antisemitic district associations agreed in February 1886 to run a common slate of candidates. The goal of this strategy was to prevent confusion in the minds of the newly enfranchised 5fl. voters, who were participating for the first time in municipal elections.

171. See Geehr, *"I Decide Who Is a Jew!"*, 46, 47.

172. *Protokolle* (October 19, 1886), 3900.

173. Gerhard Silberbauer, *Österreichs Katholiken und die Arbeiterfrage* (Graz, 1966), 63.

174. This was a *Standesvertretung*. Silberbauer, 64.

175. Jenks, *Austria under the Iron Ring*, 13.

176. Ibid., 153.

177. Boyer calls attention to Lueger's refusal "to support [the accident insurance legislation] extension to workers in the craft industries or on the farms" (*Political Radicalism in Late Imperial Vienna*, 214).

178. See Lueger's letter in Geehr, *"I Decide Who Is a Jew!"*, 193, 194.

179. Kuppe, *Karl Lueger und seine Zeit*, 142.

180. Boyer argues that this June 1887 speech, rather than the better-known one of September, deserves the designation of "Lueger's 'first antisemitic address'" (*Political Radicalism in Late Imperial Vienna*, 216). In noting the Liberal press's denunciation of Lueger as an anti-Semite, after he had supported Schönerer's exclusion bill, Boyer states that "Lueger was simply buying time for his own uncertainty" (216).

181. Peter G. J. Pulzer, *The Rise of Political Anti-Semitism in Germany and Austria* (New York, London, and Sydney, 1964), 173.

182. My account is based on Boyer, *Political Radicalism in Late Imperial Vienna*, 218, 219.

183. Whiteside, 146.

184. I.N. 41559.

185. Ibid.

186. Boyer, *Political Radicalism in Late Imperial Vienna*, 220.

187. Kuppe, *Karl Lueger und seine Zeit*, 167.

188. This incident is described in Whiteside, 132–37.

189. Macartney states that "Francis Joseph is said to have been especially wounded by Schönerer's having voted against the Army estimates on the ground that world power position was a luxury which a rotten edifice like Austria could not afford" (655n.2).

190. Whiteside, 143.

191. *Protokolle*, (March 20, 1888), 7393.

192. Lueger's correspondence to Vogelsang may be found in Geehr, *"I Decide Who Is a Jew!"*, 225–45.

193. Ibid., 229.

194. Ibid., 244, 245.

195. Ibid., 221–23.

196. Ibid., 221.

197. Ibid., 223.

198. Johann Christoph Allmayer-Beck, *Vogelsang. Vom Feudalismus zur Volksbewegung* (Vienna, 1952), 105.

199. Seliger and Ucakar, II: 721.

200. On Lueger and Vogelsang, see Anton Orel "Vogelsang und Lueger, ihre Bedeutung für die christliche Volksbewegung" in *Das Neue Reich* (1924).

201. Boyer, *Political Radicalism in Late Imperial Vienna*, 224.

202. Klopp, 346n.13.

203. According to Boyer, "the September meeting may have planted in Lueger's mind the idea of a 'Christian Social Party,' 'Christian' in its dual meaning of Jew hatred and quasi clericalism, 'Social' in its sense of reviving the Viennese Bürgertum" (*Political Radicalism in Late Imperial Vienna*, 225).

204. Spitzer describes Kielmansegg's significance: "[During his tenure as governor] he extensively co-determined the destiny of Vienna and Lower Austria. He was often in conflict with the rising mass movements, was considered a Liberal by many, a conservative by others. In any case, he was a sensible official who did not lack ideas of his own, courage, and social

engagement." Rudolf Spitzer, *Des Bürgermeisters Lueger Lumpen und Steuerträger* (Vienna, 1988), 35.

205. Kielmansegg, 409.

206. Whiteside, 146.

207. Ibid.

208. Boyer states that Lueger never forgave Cornelius Vetter for insulting Mandl — something difficult to prove — and that he "made sure that Vetter was denied a place on the antisemitic slate for the new metropolitan Council elections, destroying his career" (*Political Radicalism in Late Imperial Vienna*, 227, 228).

209. Kuppe, *Karl Lueger und seine Zeit*, 192.

210. Boyer has provided an incisive sketch of the *Volksblatt*'s publisher, Ernst Vergani, who got his political start as the mayor of Mühldorf in Lower Austria:

> He was elected to the Reichsrat and Landtag as a pan-German in 1886–87 and for a short time seemed to be the rising star in the Schönerian ranks, until his ego and venality got the best of him. A shrewd, autocratic, and cunning businessman, he ran his newspaper in the tradition of the Austrian Liberal press, accepting bribes, arranging special contracts, exploiting the city's vice structure, building expensive houses for himself [one of which he willed to the city during Lueger's mayoralty] and abusing mercilessly an army of underpaid and overworked editors and writers. . . . Vergani offered no one free publicity. Even groups with whom he was politically sympathetic . . . had to keep Vergani happy by means of gifts or subsidies. It was sometimes said in fin de siècle Vienna that the prestige of a journalist could be measured by the size of the bribe it required to control him. If this was the case, Vergani could certainly take pride in the price of his support. (*Political Radicalism in Late Imperial Vienna*, 225–26)

Chapter 3. The Master Politician: 1889–1897

1. Although there is no up-to-date and comprehensive source on Austrian Social Democratic party history, Ludwig Brügel, *Geschichte der österreichischen Sozialdemokratie,* 5 vols. (Vienna, 1922–1925), and Knapp are useful for the earlier period.

2. Knapp, 25.

3. See, for example, Geehr, *"I Decide Who Is a Jew!",* 87, 230, 231.

4. Lueger alludes to this in a letter to Vogelsang. See Geehr, *"I Decide Who Is a Jew!",* 234, 235. Quoting William Jenk's *Vienna and the Young Hitler* (New York, 1960), Whiteside has called attention to the *Volksblatt*'s "circulation of 50,000 — larger than any of the established 'great press' — " thus illustrating a kind of journalistic Gresham's Law that still seems to apply. Whiteside, 145.

5. The themes of these meetings are mentioned in Kuppe, *Karl Lueger und seine Zeit,* 201, 202.

6. Silberbauer, 116.

7. Gerhard Popp, *CV in Österreich 1864–1938* (Vienna, Cologne, and Graz, 1984), 153.

8. Friedrich Funder, *Aufbruch zur christlichen Sozialreform* (Vienna, Munich, 1953), 61.

9. Ibid.

10. Klopp, 346.

11. Boyer, *Political Radicalism in Late Imperial Vienna,* 228. One of Schönerer's henchmen, Karl Türk, had deprecated Austria's usefulness to Germany, should that country ever have needed Austria's help. Türk's remark, which raised "a storm of criticism," was made

in parliament a few weeks before Lueger's speech. Boyer explains that Lueger's remarks at a Catholic congress were useful in "undercut[ting] Liberal assertions about the undifferentiated, homogeneous nature of antisemitic radicalism."

12. "Abgeordneter Dr. Lueger," in *Das Vaterland* (April 30, 1889), 3. I have compared this paper's account with that of the *Volksblatt* and used the *Vaterland's*, because it is fuller and includes the significant audience response.

13. Ibid.

14. Silberbauer, 117, 118.

15. Klopp, 350.

16. Whiteside, 144–46.

17. Ibid., 147.

18. See, for example, "Zwei Reden gehalten in der Versammlung des Christlich-socialen Vereines" (Vienna, 1889), Österreichisches Institut für Zeitgeschichte Archiv.

19. Boyer, *Political Radicalism in Late Imperial Vienna*, 235. Seliger and Ucakar, quoting Funder, are in error in asserting "In July 1891 Lueger spoke for the first time of the 'Christian Social Movement' and the 'Christian Social Party.'" Seliger and Ucakar, II: 722.

20. *Protokolle*, 13384.

21. Dittes was a pioneer in the organization of teachers and a champion of teachers' rights. See Boyer, *Political Radicalism in Late Imperial Vienna*, 281–82, and the sources quoted therein.

22. Holleis, 9. A detailed treatment of the results is in Boyer, *Political Radicalism in Late Imperial Vienna*, 257, 258. Conflicting views of the election itself are provided by Lueger and the Liberal Guido Sommaruga. See *Landtag* (October 15, 1890), 13, 14.

23. On Uhl, see Felix Czeike, *Wien und seine Bürgermeister, Sieben Jahrhunderte Wiener Stadtgeschichte* (Vienna and Munich, 1974), 328ff.

24. Boyer has compared the radicalization of Viennese and Lower Austrian politics with equally radical Czech nationalist politics in Bohemia, indicating that Austrian aggressiveness was modeled on Czech behavior. His comparison recalls a statement of William Jenks, that "if Austria's fate lay in Radetzky's camp in the middle of the nineteenth century, its locus had moved to Bohemia's fields and mountains thirty years later." The interconnection of developments has become one of the hallmarks of political modernism. Boyer, *Political Radicalism in Late Imperial Vienna*, 256; Jenks, *Austria under the Iron Ring*, 239.

25. Kielmansegg, 383.

26. Ibid., 384.

27. Boyer, *Political Radicalism in Late Imperial Vienna*, 253.

28. Ibid., 252.

29. Whiteside, 144.

30. Kuppe, *Karl Lueger und seine Zeit*, 219.

31. Ibid., 226.

32. Boyer, *Political Radicalism in Late Imperial Vienna*, 273.

33. But Lueger thrived on the excitement and agitation preceding annual elections:

An honored colleague from the inner city has said that a certain excitement prevails from the new year onward, and that this excitement makes so-called objective deliberation impossible. It is true, gentlemen . . . that from new year's on, this certain excitement prevails — we call it election fever . . . but this excitement is very healthy (amusement) yes, very healthy, for it purifies the air of miasmas. (Renewed amusement.) It is as if one dug a drain in a swamp to allow stagnant water to drain and to purify itself. (*Landtag* [December 2, 1890], 607)

34. Ibid., 608.

35. Boyer, *Political Radicalism in Late Imperial Vienna*, 274. Boyer adds that "on an exact proportional basis [according to population], the suburbs should have received fifty-three seats rather than forty-five. Also, the Liberals gave the First and Second Districts an overproportional representation because of their reliability" (500n. 98). Boyer indicates that the "new cyclical system" and with it the elimination of the annual spring campaigns, which had afforded him the means to expose the Christian Socials, "decided [him] to take the language and behavior of the rally halls into the plenum of the Council and the Landtag." This tactic was nothing new as Felder would have attested. And soon the Socialists, similarly restricted, would behave the same way toward the Christian Socials in power.

36. Lueger had all but promised this disruption during a Landtag speech in December 1890: "You stipulate today the omnipotence of the future mayor of the city of Vienna. But this will not last too long. This omnipotence will be buffeted from all sides, and no matter how powerful one may be, he will not be able to withstand this continuous buffeting; even if he is made of iron, he will melt under these attacks, that, I guarantee all mayors." *Landtag* (December 5, 1890), 726.

37. Jenks, *Austria under the Iron Ring*, 235, 277.

38. See Kuppe, *Karl Lueger und seine Zeit*, 256–58.

39. Ibid., 258.

40. Ibid., 312.

41. Funder, *Vom Gestern ins Heute*, 51–55.

42. It was published between 1893 and 1938.

43. Funder, *Vom Gestern ins Heute*, 104.

44. Ibid.

45. Pulzer has called attention to the similarity between Bryan's oratory and his "fundamentalist rejection of modern knowledge" and that of some of the contemporary European anticapitalists. Pulzer, 47, 48.

46. Funder, *Vom Gestern ins Heute*, 104, 105. Publicists such as Funder liked to quote Lueger as having said "Praised be Jesus Christ!" See also Kuppe, *Karl Lueger und seine Zeit*, 317n. Lueger may have been less outspoken in using this greeting. See Geehr, *"I Decide Who Is a Jew!"*, 268–70.

47. Funder, *Vom Gestern ins Heute*, 105.

48. The Christian Social leaders were aware of this aspect of American populist politics and may well have patterned their appeals on the American model. See "Local-Nachrichten. Die Antisemiten gegen die Valuta-Regulirung," *Deutsche Zeitung* (May 20, 1892), 4, 5.

49. *Protokolle* (February 9, 1892), 5090–5138.

50. He refused the customary conciliatory handshake after the duel had been fought.

51. Geehr, *"I Decide Who Is a Jew!"*, 288, 289.

52. He refused challenges from Viktor Ritter von Ofenheim and Heinrich Friedjung.

53. Ernst Freiherr von Plener, a Liberal, has described in terms like Felder's the effects of Lueger's "brutal and spiteful" speeches in parliament. See Ernst Freiherr von Plener, *Erinnerungen von Ernst Freiherr von Plener*, 3 vols. (Stuttgart and Leipzig, 1911), II: 301, 302.

54. The economic situation is summarized in Boyer, *Political Radicalism in Late Imperial Vienna*, 300–304.

55. See Geehr, *"I Decide Who Is a Jew!"*, 277, 278. For the context of anti-Jewish animosity, which was well established before Lueger exploited and exacerbated it, see Pulzer, 128–37.

56. A list of Lueger memorabilia is in Hawlik, 172. See also Soukup, 293, 294. The largest public collection of Lueger memorabilia is housed in a depot of the Museum der Stadt

Wien. According to Dr. Heinz Schöny, a retired museum official, the Lueger legacy there is second only in size to that of Franz Grillparzer.

57. Kuppe, *Karl Lueger und seine Zeit*, 331.

58. Kielmansegg, 251, 252. It was suggested to Richter by higher officials that even if he were elected mayor, he could not count on the necessary imperial approval. Richter's wife had been so sure of her husband's success that she inspected the mayoral apartment in the town hall before Prix's widow had moved out. Unpublished memoirs of Heinrich Hierhammer, 2. The issue of confession was still alive in the 1986 Austrian presidential election. The statement of Socialist candidate Kurt Steyrer that he had left the Catholic Church cost him votes.

59. Boyer, *Political Radicalism in Late Imperial Vienna*, 349ff.

60. Ibid., 350, 351; on the Stadtrat, see Seliger and Ucakar, I: 417, 418; II: 969ff.

61. Lueger received sixty-five votes to Richter's one in the final balloting. Seventy-one ballots remained empty, prompting the Liberal *Fremden-Blatt* to comment that the "majority helped the anti-Semitic opposition to victory." "Die Vizebürgermeisterwahl," *Fremden-Blatt* (May 14, 1895), 3.

62. This is Boyer's contention, *Political Radicalism in Late Imperial Vienna*, 359.

63. *Amtsblatt* no. 32 (April 19, 1907), 901.

64. Boyer, *Political Radicalism in Late Imperial Vienna*, 361, 362. Boyer writes: "[Kielmansegg's] opposition to Lueger centered on the fundamental jurisdictional rivalry between city and state, which Lueger would only exacerbate by combining the offices of party leader and city executive of the *Residenzstadt*. The imperial bureaucracy had never had to face a bourgeois party which used its control of Vienna in national policy confrontations with the state."

65. *Niederösterreichisches Landesarchiv Präsidial Akt*, Zahl B2 ad 2653 (April 9, 1897).

66. Robert Weil (Homunkulus), *Rück näher, Bruder! Der Roman meines Lebens* (Vienna and Berlin, 1920), 46, 47.

67. Funder, *Vom Gestern ins Heute*, 144.

68. Ibid., 145.

69. Ibid., 147. The pope was said to have kept a picture of Lueger on his desk, much the same as did the contemporary Austrian conservative politician Erhard Busek. Silberbauer, 128.

70. Plener, II: 453.

71. Despatches from United States Ministers to Austria 1838–1906. T 157, roll 41, p. 283, no. 143. Bartlett Tripp to Hon. Edwin F. Uhl, acting secretary of state, Vienna, June 7, 1895.

72. Macartney, 661.

73. For the Lueger-Badeni struggle, see Boyer, *Political Radicalism in Late Imperial Vienna*, 373–82, and the sources quoted therein.

74. Ibid., 364, 365. According to Richard S. Levy, "dealing with bureaucrats in politics through decrees was already an established practice in Baden and Hesse which were also faced with the participation of teachers and low-level functionaries in the antisemitic party agitation there. It is a mark of how serious the situation was in Austria that such intervention did not work, while it did effectively seal off the civil service in the German states." Letter of September 22, 1987, to the author.

75. Kuppe, *Karl Lueger und seine Zeit*, 340.

76. "Die Bürgermeisterwahl," *Volksblatt* (October 29, 1895), 2.

77. Kuppe, *Karl Lueger und seine Zeit*, 344.

78. Boyer, *Political Radicalism in Late Imperial Vienna*, 361. In January 1933 some

thought governmental responsibility would either sober Hitler or reveal him as an incompetent rabble-rouser and thus discredit him. They should have known more Austrians.

79. Ibid., 374, 375. Many years later, the Liberal municipal councillor Dr. Alfred Mittler, who claimed to have been present at the negotiations over Lueger's confirmation, stated that Badeni's decision had been influenced by an unnamed Polish politician, "Badeni's right hand," who also had "other political blunders of Badeni on his conscience." *Amtsblatt*, no. 101 (December 17, 1909), 3061, 3062. With the formidable array of powers deployed against Lueger at the time, it seems unlikely that a gray eminence would have influenced Badeni's decision.

80. Liechtenstein referred to Lueger's confirmation as "a necessity of state." *Protokolle* (November 8, 1895), 21386.

81. Boyer, *Political Radicalism in Late Imperial Vienna*, 377.

82. Macartney, 660.

83. *Amtsblatt*, no. 32 (April 19, 1907), 901.

84. *Amtsblatt*, no. 92 (November 15, 1895), 1950.

85. Kuppe, *Karl Lueger und seine Zeit*, 350, 351.

86. Kielmansegg, 64.

87. Georg Nostitz-Rieneck, ed., *Briefe Kaiser Franz Josephs an Kaiserin Elisabeth 1859–1898*, 2 vols. (Vienna and Munich, 1966), II; letter of December 30, 1895, 111.

88. Tripp, dispatch of November 20, 1895. Tripp's remarks about the loyalty of the Viennese to the emperor may be exaggerated. A descendant of Vice-Mayor Heinrich Hierhammer informed me in February 1986 that Lueger was admired by some precisely because he did not accommodate the emperor as his predecessors had invariably done. Max Morold stated that when the emperor traveled from Schönbrunn to the Hofburg after the nonconfirmation, he was greeted with silence instead of being cheered on the Mariahilferstrasse, as had until now been the case. Millenkovich-Morold, 173.

89. My account of this development is based on Kielmansegg, 64, 65.

90. Ibid., 65.

91. Ibid., 268. Though the emperor had refused Lueger, the feeling in some areas was that Lueger had won in any case. Thus, when the Lueger March was played in St. Veit, one official remarked that in that area, they referred to the tune as "Badeni, get out!" Lueger was held by some to have been instrumental in Badeni's fall the following year. Millenkovich-Morold, 174, 196.

92. "Dr. Lueger über die Bürgermeisteraffaire," *Fremden-Blatt* (May 13, 1896), 7.

93. Knapp, 27.

94. Boyer writes: "On purely organizational terms the antisemites were no match for the disciplined, systematized cadre organization of the Socialists" (*Political Radicalism in Late Imperial Vienna*, 406).

95. Ibid., 382, 383.

96. Kuppe, *Karl Lueger und seine Zeit*, 356.

97. Ibid.

98. Schorske, 136.

99. Ibid.

100. Kuppe, *Karl Lueger und seine Zeit*, 358, 359.

101. Boyer, *Political Radicalism in Late Imperial Vienna*, 385.

102. *Fremden-Blatt* (May 13, 1896), 7.

103. "Vizebürgermeister Josef Strohbach†," *Deutsches Volksblatt* (May 11, 1905), 1, 2.

104. Boyer, *Political Radicalism in Late Imperial Vienna*, 385. "Once the municipal elite of the party began to be recruited from the ranks of the *Hausherren*, as occurred in

1895–96, the party finally arrived at a position where it was roughly comparable in its social constituency to the earlier Liberals. It had become, in other words, a Bürger party."

105. Ibid., 402.

106. Geehr, *"I Decide Who Is a Jew!"*, 316.

107. Hawlik quotes such authorities on Vienna's housing deficiencies during the Lueger era as Max Winter and Felix Czeike, and is obviously aware of the political connection between the landlords and Lueger, yet remains inconclusive about why Lueger did not attack the housing problem. He states that Lueger's other municipal building projects stretched the communal budget to the extreme, and that this is "the only possible explanation" for Lueger's inactivity. This argument seems naive at best. Hawlik, 211–13.

108. Boyer, *Political Radicalism in Late Imperial Vienna*, 400, 401. Viktor Adler touched on this during a Landtag speech in 1902 when he observed that Christian Social successes in Vienna had been facilitated by the incompetence of the Liberals and the need to accomplish many pressing tasks at the time Lueger's party came to power. *Landtag* (January 7, 1902), 109.

109. See Geehr, *"I Decide Who Is a Jew!"*, 9–12; on Chamberlain as mayor, see Michael Balfour, *Britain and Joseph Chamberlain* (Boston and Sydney, 1985), 77–108.

110. Seliger and Ucakar, II: 908, 909.

111. Seliger and Ucakar trace the issue of the communalization of gas to the 1860s. See Seliger and Ucakar, I: 614–17.

112. Seliger and Ucakar call attention to an apparent connection between municipalization and industrialization. Austria was the last of Europe's major nations to experience "municipal socialization," evidently because its political and economic systems had not achieved the necessary degrees of development and coordination. Seliger and Ucakar, II: 910.

113. Ibid., 891. Districts 12 to 21 had to wait for city gas until 1911.

114. Ibid.

115. Ibid., 816. Vienna's debts for various municipal projects of Lueger's increased to "from three to four times the amount of the annual municipal budget." The post-World War I currency devaluation freed Vienna of its domestic debts, but indebtedness to foreigners proved more difficult to eliminate. See Spitzer, 162, 163.

116. Seliger and Ucakar, II: 892.

117. Kuppe, *Karl Lueger und seine Zeit*, 363.

118. *Landtag* (January 14, 1896), 183.

119. "Lueger in Budweis," *Volksblatt für Stadt und Land* (October 3, 1896), 2.

120. Kuppe, *Karl Lueger und seine Zeit*, 367, 368.

121. According to Boyer: "Badeni . . . insisted that it would be better to wait until after the 1897 parliamentary elections in Mar. before allowing Lueger to take over. Lueger agreed, since this gave him more free time to devote to the 1897 electoral campaign" (*Political Radicalism in Late Imperial Vienna*, 524n.207).

122. Kuppe, *Karl Lueger und seine Zeit*, 370.

123. *NLPA*, Zahl B2 ad 2653 (April 9, 1897).

124. Ibid.

125. Ibid.

126. This speech was published in Vienna's leading papers. It also appears in Kuppe, *Karl Lueger und seine Zeit*, 377–83. Lueger's draft may be found in my *"I Decide Who Is a Jew!"*, 207–14. I have used Kuppe for this account.

127. Boyer, *Political Radicalism in Late Imperial Vienna*, 379.

128. Liberal opponents pointed out that Lueger was only continuing the project that they had initiated. But there was something to Lueger's response that only he could have purchased the necessary land for the reservoir, and at a relatively inexpensive price. Without

telling either the municipal council or the city council, Lueger had visited the Admont seminary and negotiated with the abbot. It was said by the monks that the abbot would not have dealt with anyone else but Lueger. Spitzer, 166.

129. See Geehr, *"I Decide Who Is a Jew!"*, 211, n. 10.

130. All Liberals had by this time resigned. "The new *Stadtrat* was designed to reflect the various constituencies and interests within the party (Catholics, Nationalists, teachers, property owners, artisans, etc.). Unlike the Liberals the Christian Socials selected their committee in proportion to the relative size of the three curias (two, First Curia, eight, Second Curia, fifteen, Third Curia). They also tried to provide each district with at least one representative on the body. In theory the party was committed to the abolition of the *Stadtrat*, but events soon showed the party elite the advantage of retaining it as an executive directorate of municipal policy" (Boyer, *Political Radicalism in Late Imperial Vienna*, 403-4).

131. Kuppe, *Karl Lueger und seine Zeit*, 383.

132. Ibid., 373, 374.

133. "Dr. Lueger should rule, and the Jews should croak." "Zur Beeidigung des Bürgermeisters," *Neue Freie Presse* (April 21, 1897), 7. A similar incident was recalled by N. H. Tur-Sinai, a distinguished scholar and former resident of Vienna:

> I can remember the "Lueger March," which used to be played in all the streets and courtyards of Vienna. I do not remember the official words, but the people would sing: "Lueger will live, and the Jews will croak." My late father, who was a brave, defiant man, obtained the consent of the majority of the tenants, and put up a plaque banning the playing of the "Lueger March" in the building we lived in. Nevertheless, a man with a barrel organ came along and played it, and when he refused to desist, despite several warnings, my father poured a bucket of cold water over him.
>
> "Cold Douche on Lueger March" was the headline over the *Arbeiterzeitung*'s report of the court proceedings that followed. My father was ten florins the poorer after them [sic] but he considered the money well spent. (N.H. Tur-Sinai, quoted in Josef Fraenkl, ed., *The Jews of Austria* [London, 1967], 316)

134. *Neue Freie Presse* (April 21, 1897).

Chapter 4. The Master Builder: 1897–1910

1. Referring to the Second Mountain Spring Water Reservoir, Kuppe goes a bit further than other biographers in remarking that one can only imagine how this resource spared Vienna many sicknesses and plagues during World War I, when troops and fugitives swelled the population. Kuppe, *Karl Lueger und seine Zeit*, 406.

2. See, for example, ibid., 384; and Skalnik, 114-30.

3. "Tagesneuigkeiten. Wien feiert Lueger," *Neues Wiener Journal* (September 20, 1926), 2.

4. The traditional position of Lueger as pioneer municipal politician is summed up by Ludwig Reichhold: "Lueger's true genius as a municipal politician was in opportunely recognizing the problems of a modern metropolis, and preparing for their solution, insofar as they had not already been solved by him: with him begins a new era of municipal politics that was mainly geared to satisfying the wants of a metropolitan population" (quoted in Hawlik, 125).

5. Karl Renner, *An der Wende zweier Zeiten. Lebenserinnerungen* (Vienna, 1946), 233.

6. *Landtag* (February 1, 1910), 1199.

7. The subtitle of Skalnik's biography.

8. Adam Müller-Guttenbrunn, bankrupt director of the Christian Social theater, indicated this when officials who were confiscating his property paused before an autographed portrait of Lueger. Müller-Guttenbrunn insisted that it, too, be forfeited. Adam Müller-Guttenbrunn, unpublished diary, Heft X (November 1903).

9. *Amtsblatt*, no. 39 (May 15, 1903), 855.

10. In 1896 Lueger argued in parliament that "It is in the interest of the empire that the poor be provided for, so that they would not endanger the rich. Therefore, if we provide for the poor, we do the rich a favor, and they need pay nothing" (quoted by Josef Scheicher, *Landtag* [October 13, 1909], 602).

11. Ibid. (January 11, 1892), 262. He said essentially the same thing in parliament later that year. See *Protokolle*, (May 11, 1892), 5839. It would be interesting to know if the Italian politician, Alcide De Gasperi, who "developed a great admiration for . . . Lueger" knew about his idol's opinions about Italian workers. See Elisa Carrillo, *Alcide De Gasperi: The Long Apprenticeship* (Notre Dame, 1965), 7.

12. *Landtag* (January 11, 1892), 262.

13. A Christian Social baker, Josef Bock, complained during a council session about the destructive effect of the cooperatives on individual private businesses. Lueger denied the authority of the municipal council in such matters, but said he would refer the pertinent interpellation to the appropriate official, though he was not hopeful that the situation could be remedied. *Amtsblatt*, no. 32 (April 21, 1903), 683. Socialists charged that "the Viennese building office, under orders from Lueger, . . . [refused] to grant a permit" for the creation of the Hammerbrotwerke, a bread factory belonging to the Social Democrats, within the city. Its location miles away increased the price of the bread because of added transportation costs. Charles A. Gulick, *Austria from Habsburg to Hitler*, 2 vols. (Berkeley and Los Angeles, 1948), I: 326.

14. *Amtsblatt*, no. 73 (September 12, 1905), 1837.

15. Wandruszka and Urbanitsch, eds., I: 378.

16. Seliger and Ucakar, I: 790, 792. For details about Viennese laborers' existences during the Lueger years, see Josef Ehmer, "Wiener Arbeitswelten um 1900," in Ehalt et al., eds., *Glücklich ist, wer vergisst . . . ? Das andere Wien um 1900* (Vienna, Cologne, and Graz, 1986), 195–213.

17. Seliger and Ucakar, I: 788, 792.

18. *Protokolle* (October 6, 1897), 378. On the successful completion of the gasworks, Karl Kraus commented that Lueger's triumphs had been made possible by the "ineptitude of his opponents," above all, "the papers of Vienna." See "Die Fackel," Anfang November 1899, no. 22, 20, 21; and "Die Fackel," Mitte Juni 1901, no. 80, 25, 26.

19. See Seliger and Ucakar, II: 896, 897.

20. Hawlik, 109.

21. Seliger and Ucakar, I: 618.

22. Ibid., II: 896.

23. Ibid., 894. The Socialists pointed to the inconsistency of investing in the "woods and meadows belt . . . dead capital," which devoured so much of the profit from the gas and electric works, when the municipality ran at a deficit. This particular criticism by Jakob Reumann is characteristic. See *Amtsblatt*, no. 86 (October 26, 1909), 2509–14.

24. Kuppe, *Karl Lueger und seine Zeit*, 395.

25. Seliger and Ucakar, II: 897. This episode, too, was not without anti-Semitic overtones. See *Amtsblatt*, no. 44 (June 2, 1903), 1021–30.

26. Kuppe, *Karl Lueger und seine Zeit*, 393 n.

27. Seliger and Ucakar, II: 899.

28. Maria Hornor Lansdale, *Vienna and the Viennese* (Philadelphia, 1902), 113, quoted in Jenks, *Vienna and the Young Hitler*, 57.

29. See Geehr, *"I Decide Who Is a Jew!"*, 189, 190.

30. Seliger and Ucakar, II: 903.

31. For Lueger's defense, see Geehr, *"I Decide Who Is a Jew!"*, 195–98. The life of a tram conductor's family during this era is described in Julius Deutsch, *Ein weiter Weg. Lebenserinnerungen* (Zürich, Leipzig, and Vienna, 1960), 13–32.

32. Seliger and Ucakar, II: 903.

33. On the spurious aspects of Christian Socialism as a labor movement, see Reinhold Knoll, *Zur Tradition der christlich-sozialen Partei* (Vienna, Cologne, and Graz, 1973), 184, 185. On Lueger and tramway personnel policies, see *Amtsblatt*, no. 48 (June 16, 1903), 1141–59.

34. Seliger and Ucakar, II: 904.

35. *Amtsblatt*, no. 102 (December 19, 1899), 2987.

36. Spitzer, 155.

37. Siemens's political orientation would be interesting to know.

38. For a catalog of Christian Social corruption, see Marie Götz, *Schmutzige Wäsche der Christlich Socialen. Eingesammelt von einer christlichen Waschfrau* (Vienna, n.d.).

39. Seliger and Ucakar, II: 905, 906.

40. Ibid., 906.

41. See, for example, *Amtsblatt*, no. 29 (April 9, 1907), 797, 799, 800; no. 98 (December 8, 1908), 2872.

42. Kuppe, *Karl Lueger und seine Zeit*, 395.

43. Seliger and Ucakar, II: 903; 1233n. 329.

44. *Amtsblatt*, no. 103 (December 24, 1907), 3168, 3169.

45. Seliger and Ucakar, II: 906; Kuppe, *Karl Lueger und seine Zeit*, 395.

46. Seliger and Ucakar, II: 906.

47. Ibid., 910.

48. See Geehr, *"I Decide Who Is a Jew!"*, 277, 278, 284–287.

49. *Amtsblatt*, no. 44 (May 29, 1903), 1027, quoted in Seliger and Ucakar, II: 910, 911.

50. Ibid., 796, 797 table 113; 816.

51. Ibid., 797 table 113.

52. The Liberal municipal councillor Oskar Hein may have voiced a secretly felt disappointment of Lueger in 1908 when he criticized the low yield of gas works revenues. During this session a critique and defense of Christian Social achievements in municipal socialization took place. The Liberals pointed out that Christian Social fiscal policies had burdened Vienna with record debts and were a continuation of the Manchester Liberalism that Lueger had earlier rejected, thus repeating a similar charge that had been made in parliament by the Socialist Anton Schrammel as early as 1897. *Amtsblatt*, no. 5 (January 17, 1908), 174–77; *Protokolle* (October 7, 1897), 422.

53. Seliger and Ucakar, II: 816.

54. Kuppe, *Karl Lueger und seine Zeit*, 403.

55. Kielmansegg, 383.

56. *Amtsblatt*, no. 26 (March 30, 1900), 657.

57. Ibid., 658.

58. "If we succeed [in building the reservoir]," he told an assembly of the Christian Social Workers' Association (Christlich-Sozialer Arbeiter Verein), "we will stand higher in this respect than imperial Rome itself." Leopold Kunschak, ed., *Reden gehalten in Wien am 19., 20. und 21. Juli 1899* (St. Pölten, 1899), 28.

59. Geehr, *"I Decide Who Is a Jew!"*, 194, 195.

60. Seliger and Ucakar, II: 872.

61. Ibid., 874.

62. Ibid.

63. See Chapter 3, n.115.

64. With apparent irony, Viktor Adler quoted "the two largest anti-Semitic papers in Vienna" during a provincial diet session to indicate the dissatisfaction within Lueger's own ranks over the increased size of the municipal labor force. In replying to Adler, Lueger stressed Christian Social achievements which benefited labor. *Landtag* (January 7, 1902), 109, 113–18. For additional criticism of Lueger's municipal projects, see *Protokolle* (March 12, 1902), 10213–24.

65. Beer prices were of long-standing interest to Lueger. See *Landtag* (December 14, 1891), 59ff.

66. See Kielmansegg on the political background, 370–73.

67. Here, as well as elsewhere, municipal employees were expected, at least passively, to support the Christian Socials. Lueger demanded that workers employed by the city give him their word that they were neither Social Democrats nor Pan-Germans, nor would they join these parties. *Amtsblatt*, no. 98 (December 8, 1908) 2871. When, shortly before the council session where Lueger spelled out his political requirements for municipal employees, Christian Social delegate Hermann Bielohlawek remarked in parliament that municipal workers voted "completely independently," someone interjected: "Even the caryatids [that decorate the parliament building] laugh when you say that!" (*Protokolle* [December 4, 1908], 7742).

68. In 1906 Lueger rationalized this by claiming that if the brewery had not existed, the brewers' guild would have raised the prices. Mack, 28–29.

69. The slaughterhouse was created to the accompaniment of anti-Semitic demagogy. Lueger told an electoral assembly in Margareten, Vienna's fifth district, that the entire cattle trade was in Jewish hands, and that a dealer, Saborsky, had boasted that no steer arrived at the central market without his approval. Lueger claimed that the municipal slaughterhouse would oppose "the terrorism of Jewish big capital." "Wählerversammlung in Margareten," *Reichspost* (January 25, 1905). In a letter to Lueger, Christian Social Magistrat director and future mayor, Richard Weiskirchner, attributed the unsatisfactory performance of the slaughterhouse to unfavorable purchases at the time of its inception. Weiskirchner to Lueger, IN 117.385 (July 18, 1905). Again, Lueger seems to have used Strohbach's skills as a businessman in the slaughterhouse venture. Strohbach warned Lueger about letting one Schnabel, who had come to grief in an earlier business venture, conceal himself behind a Christian and earn profits that should go to the municipality. Strohbach passed on to the mayor the advice of specialists who urged the building of a municipal margarine factory to process by-products, instead of allowing a middleman to skim the cream. Strohbach to Lueger, *IN* 31701 (June 22, 1904). According to Seliger and Ucakar, the municipal slaughterhouse was too little involved in the retailing, "so that there was no effective competition for the [retail] meat cutters. A positive influence on the trade and customs politics of the empire in the interest of the municipal population foundered on the internal political power relationships of the monarchy, which were also reflected in the dominant agrarian interests in the Christian Social party" (II: 881).

70. For a list of newly constructed and renovated schools of the Lueger era, see Soukup, 82–85.

71. *Landtag* (September 30, 1904), 65.

72. Kuppe, *Karl Lueger und seine Zeit*, 408.

73. In praise of Lueger's attitude toward education, Hawlik states:

However, as a high-ranking municipal politician, he recognized the meaning of a well-schooled, healthy youth, capable of meeting the challenges of the future. This unsentimental, yet far-sighted and responsible attitude allowed Vienna, under his leadership, to become one of the most modern school cities in the world. In school, adolescents should "not just be inculcated with knowledge, but also receive a religious, moral and fatherland-*völkisch* education." As sadder but wiser children of nationalistic consequences, we probably distance ourselves from the latter two points. Moreover, not all parents expect religious education for their children from the schools. (Hawlik, 133, 134)

74. One of Lueger's earliest biographers, Franz Stauracz, devotes nearly twice as much space to school curriculum as to the schools themselves. See Stauracz, *Dr. Karl Lueger,* 103–06, 188–93. See also Mack, 63–65.

75. Kuppe, *Karl Lueger und seine Zeit,* 427, 428.

76. Ibid., 409.

77. Seliger and Ucakar, II: 834.

78. Ibid., 869.

79. Ibid., 868, 869.

80. Ibid., 871.

81. *Amtsblatt,* no. 27 (April 1, 1904), 639.

82. Although a thoroughgoing study of Lueger's relationship to the workers is needed, useful insights and information about Socialist response to Lueger and Christian Socialism are in Robert S. Wistrich, *Socialism and the Jews: The Dilemmas of Assimilation in Germany and Austria-Hungary* (London and East Brunswick, N.J., 1982), 262–98. Wistrich's conclusion that "although some Jews suffered under Lueger's administration, they were probably discriminated against less than members of the two anti-clerical parties, the Pan-Germans and the Social Democrats" (297) is difficult to accept and harder still to prove.

83. Seliger and Ucakar, II: 824. Kuppe indicates an increase to 25,151 without indicating whether or nor he included teachers. Kuppe, *Karl Lueger und seine Zeit,* 397.

84. Ibid.

85. *Amtsblatt,* no. 5 (January 16, 1903), 69.

86. Spitzer, 173.

87. *Amtsblatt,* no. 79 (October 1, 1907), 2219.

88. For a summary of Kunschak's activities in the Christian Social party between 1891 and 1911, see Knoll, 203–10 and the sources quoted therein.

89. This is treated in more detail in Silberbauer, 121–44.

90. Shortly after the creation of the Christian Social party, Lueger declared himself an enemy of the higher clergy. Kuppe, *Karl Lueger und seine Zeit,* 239.

91. *Amtsblatt,* no. 73 (September 12, 1899), 2170.

92. Seliger and Ucakar, II: 858. During a municipal council session, Jakob Reumann complained about the clericalization of the nursing profession, that Catholic sisters in municipal nursing homes threatened to undermine the recovery of the patients because of their proselytizing zeal. *Amtsblatt,* no. 58 (July 19, 1904), 1466.

93. Silberbauer, 150.

94. Ibid., 152.

95. Kunschak, *Steinchen vom Wege,* 48.

96. On Kunschak and Vergani, see Anton Pelinka, *Stand oder Klasse? Die Christliche Arbeiterbewegung Österreichs 1933 bis 1938* (Vienna, Munich, and Zurich, 1972), 223.

97. Kunschak, *Steinchen vom Wege,* 48. He said he became "a prisoner of the magic that radiated from his being."

98. Ibid.

99. However, as late as 1892 at an assembly in which he shared the speaker's platform with the Socialist leader and later mayor, Jakob Reumann, Lueger acknowledged some common goals. He nonetheless rejected the implicitly Jewish influence over Social Democracy that made them bow before capital. Kralik, *Karl Lueger und der christliche Sozialismus*, 96.

100. Silberbauer, 145.

101. Silberbauer, 167.

102. Kunschak, *Steinchen vom Wege*, 51.

103. Ibid., 52.

104. Ibid., 53.

105. Schuhmeier's and Kunschak's debates became increasingly envenomed. Kunschak revealed bitterness that a brother who had lost his job was unable to find work for a year and a half because of a Social Democratic boycott. The feud ended in 1913 when Kunschak's brother shot and killed Schuhmeier.

106. *Amtsblatt*, no. 53 (July 4, 1905), 1425.

107. Ibid., no. 75 (September 17, 1907), 2093.

108. F. Bauer, "Leopold Kunschak als Politiker. Von seinen Anfängen bis zum Jahre 1934" (Ph.D. diss. University of Vienna, 1950), 38.

109. See, for example, *Amtsblatt*, no. 29 (April 9, 1907), 797, and *Protokolle* (July 12, 1907), 1227. During the latter session, Kunschak asserted that some government officials should be ashamed to be Austrians, because Prussia had appropriated 15 million marks to build worker housing in 1907.

110. Ibid., 1230.

111. Pelinka, 223.

112. Ibid., 222.

113. At the annual Ball of the City of Vienna in January 1907, Lueger evidently experienced a nervous attack that caused him to lose control of himself. Friends managed to lead him to a room adjoining the reception area. When Lueger's doctor appeared, the mayor cursed him and threw bottles and glasses at him. Lueger was then escorted with difficulty to his apartment. The report of this incident appeared in a Hungarian newspaper, which might give one pause as to whether or not to accept its validity. But shortly after this ball, Lueger was taken so seriously ill that it seemed for a time that he would die. He drafted his last will and testament. I accept the report of this incident as substantially valid. Lueger's attack may have been linked to his diabetes. Kuppe seems to have confused this incident with Lueger's last appearance at the Ball of the City of Vienna in January 1910. See Kuppe, *Karl Lueger und seine Zeit*, 520, 521. My account is based on "Lueger megörült. A trónörökös jelenlétében. Inzultálta az orvosát. Bécs város gyászban," *Szeged és Videke* (January 26, 1907), 3.

114. *Amtsblatt*, no. 37 (May 7, 1907), 1041. Lueger then stated that he could neither read nor write anymore.

115. As head of the party, Lueger prided himself on "looking around a little" from time to time to be sure that his supporters were still supporting him. A common tactic of his was to address a group that might not have shared in some of the benefits of others among their profession, but whom he deemed nonetheless important because of their potential influence on their peers. Such a group was that of the postilions, or post boys. On one occasion Lueger told the postilions that he thought they should have the same security for family and old age as a *Hofrat*, though they might not share the same measure of the *Hofrat*'s wealth. Though Lueger was vague about how security was to be achieved for the postilions, he reassured them that he was trying to better their lot. His speech boosted his listeners' morale. In such ways the mayor continued to inform his constituents of his con-

tinued interest in them and their problems. "Dr. Lueger bei den Postillonen," *Das Vaterland* (November 14, 1903), 4.

116. This is why "Rome allowed the subject peoples to exist," according to his notes. Karl Lueger, *Finanzwissenschaft, Dr. Stein, I. Heft,* Nachlass Karl Lueger, Städtische Sammlung Zahl 1257/12, Box I, Handschriftensammlung.

117. Macartney, 718.

118. "Die antisemitische Partei und die ungarische Frage," *Deutsches Volksblatt* (May 31, 1906), 4.

119. Lueger's account of his official visit is in *Amtsblatt,* no. 54 (July 6, 1906), 1361, 1362. As early as 1891 he referred to Rumania as "a natural ally of Austria," adding that adverse treatment of Rumanians in Hungarian territory had prevented closer friendship. Because of this unnatural state of affairs, Viennese industry had suffered. At the root of the problem was the Hungarian, and implicitly Jewish, grain dealer who, Lueger asserted, made "it impossible to conclude any favorable economic ties with this land." (*Protokolle* [June 24, 1891], 1138.)

120. "Le Docteur Lueger," *Revue Économique & Financière,* (June 8–21, 1906), 204.

121. Ibid., 205.

122. If agitation was Lueger's aim, he achieved the desired results. One of his followers cheered his visit to Rumania as a triumph over Hungary: "You achieved more for Austria than many foreign ministers. It is high time that we Austrians become active, for otherwise we will most certainly succumb to Hungary if it goes on like this. Dear mayor, use your time entirely for economic overtures to Rumania, for that will give us Austrians the greatest support." Rudolf Kasser to Lueger, *IN* 32855 (June 16, 1906).

123. Macartney, 598, 599.

124. "Der Kaiser und Herr Dr. Lueger," *Volkstribüne* (June 27, 1906), 2.

125. Friedrich Hertz, *Economic Problem of the Danubian States* (London, 1947), 51, quoted in Good, 123.

126. Spitzer, 18, 19.

127. *Amtsblatt,* no. 39 (May 16, 1902), 907.

128. Kielmansegg, 391. The Christian Social Landtag and parliamentary delegate Josef Scheicher blamed the Lueger cult on those close to him, adding that "great men do not need publicity." Josef Scheicher, *Erlebnisse und Erinnerungen,* 6 vols. (Vienna and Leipzig, 1912), IV: 418.

129. *Amtsblatt,* no. 27 (April 2, 1909), 886.

130. Ibid., no. 28 (April 7, 1903), 590.

131. Ibid., 591.

132. Millenkovich-Morold, 180. Morold's comment was in a letter to his parents, evidently written while Lueger was in office. Among the Nazi leaders, only Goebbels seems to have genuinely admired Lueger, enough, in fact, to have enthusiastically supported a major anti-Semitic film, *Wien 1910.*

133. In 1902, for example, a German Peoples' party representative, Wilhelm Voelkl, stated in parliament that he could not respect a man in Lueger's position who "scolds like any common, vulgar washerwoman. . . . He spoke of 'blockhead Germans'; he recently honored us in an assembly with expressions that I won't repeat before upright men; it was abuse of the most infamous kind. And this man deigns to say: Dr. Lueger never scolds. (Amusement.) Dr. Lueger is the most vulgar man who occupies a mayor's chair." *Protokolle* (October 17, 1902), 14689. Shortly thereafter, Lueger lent further support to Voelkl's remarks by chiding Franz Schuhmeier in parliament: "[F]rom all the treasures of German literature he knows only one sentence which 'Götz von Berlichingen' once said. (Boisterous peals of

laughter—Representative Schuhmeier: You have Goethe to blame for that!) That's right: if Goethe hadn't said it, Schuhmeier wouldn't have said it either—I believe that—because he isn't clever enough to have come up with something like that at all." (Lively amusement—Numerous interjections.) *Protokolle* (February 6, 1903), 17966. In reality, Lueger was probably fond of Schuhmeier, seeing in him, perhaps, the young oppositional agitator he himself had once been. See Wilhelm Ellenbogen, *Menschen und Prinzipien. Erinnerungen, Urteile und Reflexionen eines kritischen Sozialdemokraten* (Vienna, Cologne, and Graz, 1981), 66.

134. See, for example, *Amtsblatt*, no. 40 (May 19, 1905), 1035; *Landtag* (November 16, 1905), 318, 319.

135. Quoted in Richard Charmatz, "Dr. Karl Lueger," *Deutschland* (1905), 79.

136. Friedrich Funder, "Als er von uns ging," *Reichspost* (March 9, 1930), 4, 5.

137. "Bürgermeister Dr. Lueger über die Wahlen," *Reichspost* (May 17, 1907), 1.

138. *Protokolle* (October 2, 1905), 31779.

139. Ellenbogen, 66. Ellenbogen identifies the municipal councillor as "Blum." This appears to be an error, for there was no Social Democratic municipal councillor named Blum during Lueger's mayoralty.

140. For information on the fourth curia, see Seliger and Ucakar, II: 920. In 1900 nearly one-half of the male residents of Vienna more than twenty-four years old were excluded from voting in municipal council elections.

141. Spitzer, 54.

142. Ibid., 55.

143. Ibid. 57.

144. Macartney, 793n. 2. Lueger advocated empirewide suffrage in 1905, but as always, with a residency requirement to protect "the established population from the fluctuating one." *Protokolle* (October 2, 1905), 31783.

145. Seliger and Ucakar, II: 920. A fourth curia was added to the existing three in the rest of Lower Austria, as well as in Vienna. Until that time, women who were not residents of Vienna, Wiener Neustadt, or Waidhofen a.d. Ybbs, but who lived in other Lower Austrian communities, could give a man the power of attorney, and vote indirectly. The new electoral law deprived even the few formerly enfranchised female taxpayers of the vote, because the Christian Socials claimed that "the power of attorney had been abused." Spitzer, 60.

146. Seliger and Ucakar, II: 764.

147. Ibid., 766.

148. *Amtsblatt*, no. 100 (December 14, 1909), 2959.

149. Hitler was also impressed with Vienna's architectural splendor, but he saw the underside of the city as well: "the whole Ring Boulevard seemed to me like an enchantment out of *The Thousand-and-One-Nights*. . . . Outside the palaces on the Ring loitered thousands of unemployed, and beneath this *Via Triumphalis* of old Austria dwelt the homeless in the gloom and mud of the canals. . . . Dazzling riches and loathsome poverty alternated sharply." Adolf Hitler, *Mein Kampf* (Boston, 1943), 19, 23, 24.

150. Francis H. E. Palmer, *Austro-Hungarian Life in Town and Country* (New York and London, 1905), 190, 191. Poverty and its effects in fin de siècle Vienna are topics outside the scope of this study. There is a large literature on these topics. Recommended works include: Hans Maria Truxa, *Armenleben* (Vienna, 1905); Michael John, *Hausherrenmacht und Mieterelend. Wohnerfahrungen 1890–1923* (Vienna, 1982); Adelheid Popp, *Jugend einer Arbeiterin* (Vienna, 1977); Alfons Petzold, *Das Alfons Petzold Buch. Eine Auswahl des Dichters von Karl Ziak* (Vienna, n.d.); Ernst Kläger, *Durch die Quartiere des Elends und Verbrechens, Ein Wanderbuch aus dem Jenseits* (Vienna, 1908); Ferdinand Hanusch, *Die Namenlosen. Geschichten aus dem Leben der Arbeiter und Armen* (Vienna, 1910); Max Winter, *Das Schwarze*

Wienerherz. Sozialreportagen aus dem frühen 20. Jahrhundert (Vienna, 1982); and the appropriate parts of Ehalt, et. al.

Chapter 5. Running with the Hares, Hunting with the Hounds

1. See Skalnik, 80–82; Soukup, 132, 147.

2. P. G. J. Pulzer, "The Development of Political Antisemitism in Austria," in Fraenkel, ed., 429. This view is also suggested in Pulzer's earlier *The Rise of Political Anti-Semitism in Germany and Austria.* Schorske, 138, 139.

3. Hitler described "the great achievements of Lueger" to Joseph Goebbels; see Fred Taylor, ed. and trans., *The Goebbels Diaries 1939–1941* (New York, 1983), 23. See also Reinhold Hanisch, "I Was Hitler's Buddy," *The New Republic* (April 5, 1939), 241, 242.

4. "Ein antisemitisches Bubenstück," *Wiener Abendblatt* (August 14, 1897), 2, 3.

5. Pulzer, 189.

6. Boyer, "Karl Lueger and the Viennese Jews," 139. I have been unable to locate any passage in Hitler's writings or in his recorded comments where he referred to Lueger "as a dictatorial charismatic Führer-type."

7. Ibid., 126.

8. Ibid., 127.

9. Ibid., 129.

10. Ibid., 131.

11. Ibid., 132.

12. Ibid., 136.

13. Ibid., 126, 127.

14. Ibid., 138.

15. Robert S. Wistrich, "Karl Lueger and the Ambiguities of Viennese Antisemitism," *Jewish Social Studies,* vol. 45 (1984), nos. 3–4, 256.

16. Wistrich, *Socialism and the Jews,* 202.

17. Léon Poliakov, *The History of Anti-Semitism. Suicidal Europe: 1870–1933* (New York, 1985), 24; Steven Beller, "*Fin de Siècle* Vienna and the Jews: The Dialectics of Assimilation," *The Jewish Quarterly* 33 (1986), 32.

18. Skalnik, 82.

19. Hawlik, 199.

20. Josef Scheicher, *Aus dem Jahre 1920 – Ein Traum* (St. Pölten, 1900), 60. He wrote not only about the killing of "300 Jews and 20 Aryans in one day" in Vienna, by then the capital of the "*Ostmark,*" but also of the killing of thousands more in Poland and "Ruthenia." After having read some of Scheicher's virulently anti-Jewish speeches in the Landtag, it is hard to agree with Friedrich Heer that Scheicher, had he been living, would have been in the first transport to Dachau following the Anschluss in March 1938. Or perhaps if he had been in the transport, it would never have occurred to him that he had contributed importantly to paving the way for the National Socialist interlude in the first place by helping make anti-Semitism "politically acceptable." See Friedrich Heer, *Der Glaube des Adolf Hitler. Anatomie einer politischen Religiosität* (Munich and Esslingen, 1968), 113.

21. *Amtsblatt,* no. 100 (December 16, 1902), 2301. Bielohlawek's term "*Ausmerzung*" has other meanings besides "eradication." But during the same speech he categorically stated, "We want to destroy [*vernichten*] the Jews, we are not ashamed to say it" (2299). "Eradication" therefore endorses and amplifies his earlier remark.

22. *Landtag* (July 11, 1901), 356. Schneider was verbally reprimanded by the Landtag chairman for his remark; Lueger remained silent about Bielohlawek's.

23. Boyer, "Karl Lueger and the Viennese Jews," 130.

24. Ibid., 131. I am very much indebted to Marsha Rozenblit for this insight.

25. Marsha L. Rozenblit, *The Jews of Vienna 1867–1914: Assimilation and Identity* (Albany, N.Y., 1983), 196. A statement of the Israeli scholar Herbert Rosenkranz supports Rozenblit's assertion: "In 1931 . . . Walter Riehl, a national deputy and lawyer, demanded the legal emasculation of any Jew who had sexual relations with an 'Aryan' girl" (Fraenkel, 480).

26. Kielmansegg, 398.

27. Spitzer, 110. See, for example, the interpellation of Ernst Schneider, Richard Weis-kirchner, Albert Gessmann, Robert Pattai, and others protesting the attempts of Jews to de-fend themselves through the "Österreich-israelitische Union in Wien," in *Protokolle* (March 10, 1902), 10055–59. When one of Lueger's party members proposed changing the name of the "Judenplatz" in the first district to "Luegerplatz" as more befitting the dignity of the min-istry of the interior that was located there, Lueger said the idea should have occurred to him. *Amtsblatt*, no. 93 (November 21, 1899), 2693.

28. Kralik, *Karl Lueger und der christliche Sozialismus*, 149; Van Arkel, 31, 32. In a private letter in 1893, Lueger anticipated Schneider's proposed bounty "for the shooting of Jews" as an amendment to a law permitting "the killings of birds of prey." Robert A. Kann, *A Study in Austrian Intellectual History* (New York, 1960), 112n. For Lueger's letter see Geehr, "*I Decide Who Is a Jew!*", 255, 256. Father Deckert was haled into court for organizing a fraudulent lottery. A five-thousand-Gulden "villa," the grand prize in his scheme to raise funds for a new church, was exposed as a small collapsible and transportable house without any land to stand on. Bloch, 373, 374.

29. Boyer, "Karl Lueger and the Viennese Jews," 131, 132.

30. Wistrich, "Karl Lueger and the Ambiguities of Viennese Antisemitism," 260.

31. *Protokolle* (December 2, 1901), 7405, 7406.

32. Kielmansegg, 382. "'The main creator of Austrian Antisemitism was the Jewish-Liberal press, with its depravity and its terrorism,'" he was once said to have remarked. Fraenkel, 87. Lueger and other leading Christian Socials tried to bar a *Neue Freie Presse* re-porter from diet sessions. His right to attend was upheld by the presiding officer. *Landtag* (March 3, 1899), 230. For related attempts to silence apparently or implicitly Jewish opposi-tion, see *Landtag* (December 22, 1904), 40, and (October 24, 1905), 62.

33. *Protokolle* (May 26, 1894), 14623.

34. *Protokolle* (December 16, 1895), 22214; (November 16, 1899), 895. In the first instance, Lueger said the stone on which the boy Anderl von Rinn was martyred by the Jews was in a church not far from Innsbruck. (See illustration.) It was the interment of the remains of this martyr that aroused a national controversy in Austria in July 1985. In 1899, Lueger said he was "convinced" that Jewish sects practiced ritual murder.

35. Bloch, 367.

36. "Wählerverein des 5. Bezirkes," *Deutsches Volksblatt* (January 15, 1895), 4.

37. *Landtag* (May 12, 1899), 1079.

38. German Nationalists objected to the dissemination of this periodical in the public schools on the grounds that it violated imperial decrees and that it degraded the dignity of teachers. *Landtag* (January 7, 1902), 68. *Wiener Kinder* reflected official Christian Social val-ues. It was nationalistic, religious, sentimental, anti-Socialist, and glorified modern technology. The tone of its anti-Semitism anticipated that of *Der Giftpilz*, a "children's book" published by Julius Streicher, and introduced in evidence against him during the Nuremberg War Crimes trials.

39. The author Felix Braun recalled receiving a blow from an anti-Semitic youth that impaired his hearing for life. This incident occurred sometime after 1897, but during Lueger's

mayoralty. Braun adds that the agitation of the Christian Socials and of their press contributed to the growing anti-Semitism in rural areas, where the incident occurred. See Felix Braun, *Das Licht der Welt* (Vienna, 1962), 90. See also "Ein antisemitisches Bubenstück," which describes the August 1897 bombing of a Jewish shop in Vienna's second district, the Leopoldstadt, the site of the former Jewish ghetto. Boyer writes that "the charge that Jews were mistreated or attacked, especially around election time, deserves a most scrupulous examination, since politics in Vienna were not a game for the sensitive or the weak. An examination of Bloch's *Oesterreichische Wochenschrift* between 1892 and 1896, the high point of antisemitic agitation in the city, would show no more than a handful of suggestions that Jews had suffered physical abuse. Had such incidents occurred, Bloch would have reported them immediately with great fanfare. Verbal abuse of Jews, especially poorer Jews, was a common occurrence, however" ("Karl Lueger and the Viennese Jews," 131, n. 21). This seems gratuitous and glib. As a Galician Jew, Bloch knew very well what anti-Semitic violence was and it can just as well be argued that he would have been extremely cautious about reporting it, because the Jews of Vienna were a minority, and one that would have suffered had a wave of anti-Semitic violence broken out. Moreover, as a Galician, Bloch was an outsider to the Vienna Jewish community, whose own records must be examined before any conclusions can be reached about anti-Semitic violence in Vienna under Lueger. The issue of maltreatment of Jews during Lueger's mayoralty indeed "deserves a most scrupulous examination," but this issue lies outside the scope of this work. On the ritual murder trials, see Wandruszka and Urbanitsch, eds., 656 n. 49; on the 1898 Galician pogrom, see Siegfried Fleischer, "Enquete über die Lage der jüdischen Bevölkerung Galiziens," in Alfred Nossig, ed., *Jüdische Statistik* (Berlin, 1903), 209.

40. Kann, *A Study in Austrian Intellectual History*, 114. Kann also calls "attention . . . to the amazing similarity in style between Scheicher and Abraham" (112n.).

41. Ibid., 77, 78; on Abraham and the Jews, see 77–79. It was surely not merely by chance that Abraham's works were commissioned in a new edition by the city council in 1903. At that time, one of the most anti-Semitic of all Christian Social periodicals, the *Österreichische Frauen-Zeitung*, the official publication of Lueger's female supporters, declared that Abraham's works belonged "in every public and private library." "Theater, Kunst und Literatur" (September 13, 1903), 9, 10.

42. Letter of February 6, 1987, from Richard S. Levy to me.

43. Whiteside, 49.

44. At one point Lueger is alleged to have said to Ferdinand Kronawetter: "Well, we shall see which movement will become the stronger, the Democratic or the anti-Semitic. One will have to accommodate oneself accordingly" (quoted in Pulzer, 167).

45. Hans Tietze, *Die Juden Wiens. Geschichte, Wirtschaft, Kultur* (Leipzig and Vienna, 1933), 189. In 1902 Lueger was reminded of his words by the Liberal Oswald Hohensinner, who, during a municipal council session, introduced an interpellation trying to get a square or a street named after Fischhof. Lueger was evasive. He replied that such business belonged within the jurisdiction of the city council (whose proceedings were not reported), that Hohensinner had realized this, but had introduced the interpellation to get a public reading. This Lueger said he had done to show "how fair" he was. *Amtsblatt*, no. 37 (May 9, 1902), 850, 851.

46. Lueger's adviser was Ambros Opitz, an anti-Semitic publisher who became something of a court printer for the Christian Socials. Lueger provided Opitz with a manuscript about necessary legislative measures that would afford further protection to Austrian artisans. Northern Bohemia was a center of craft activity. Letter of Ambros Opitz to Karl Lueger (August 25, 1889), *IN* 41569. On Opitz, see Boyer, *Political Radicalism in Late Imperial Vienna*, 139.

47. *Protokolle* (February 13, 1890), 13384–93.

48. Ibid., 13393.

49. For information on Jewish occupational distributions that refutes anti-Semitic notions about Jewish concentrations, see Rozenblit, 47–70.

50. Rozenblit writes: "Professional occupations accounted for the same percentage (11%) of Jewish grooms in 1910 as they did in 1870. Many doctors or lawyers were Jewish, but Viennese Jews did not rush into careers in medicine or law in this period. Antisemitic discrimination against Jewish doctors may have contributed somewhat to this phenomenon. The public careers of some Jewish doctors were stymied by antisemites, and Jewish newspapers complained of an unofficial boycott of Jewish doctors" (52). Elsewhere she adds: "Jews formed a very substantial proportion of all medical and law *students* (italics mine) at the university. In the winter semester 1900, Jews comprised 22.8% of the law students, 39.6% of the medical students, and 18.2% of the philosophy students. . . . In 1890, Jews had formed 48.7% of the students in medicine" (221n. 10).

51. Pulzer, 163. For information on Rohling, and more particularly his favorite source of wisdom about the Talmud (Johannes Eisenmeuger, *Entdecktes Judentum* [1710]), see Jacob Katz, *From Prejudice to Destruction* (Cambridge, Mass., 1980).

52. *Protokolle* (October 20, 1891), 2529.

53. Ibid., 2538.

54. "Grosse Wählerversammlung in der Inneren Stadt," *Volksblatt* (April 4, 1905), 8.

55. *Protokolle* (December 7, 1892), 8300. Pulzer writes: "It is estimated that toward the end of the century some 5000 to 6000 [Jews in Galicia and Bukovina] died of starvation annually" (14).

56. *Landtag* (January 11, 1894), 116.

57. For public schools under the Liberals, see Seliger and Ucakar, I: 484ff.

58. Fraenkel, ed., xi, xii.

59. Schorske, 6.

60. Ronald W. Clark, *Freud, the Man and the Cause* (New York, 1980), 54.

61. *Landtag* (July 9, 1901), 296. During this same session, Lueger called syphilis "a kind of oriental disease," by which he implied a Jewish disease. His implication was immediately taken up by Schneider (297). Nothnagel was also blamed for the "Jewish dominance" at the University of Vienna Medical School. See *Protokolle* (October 27, 1898), 871–75. Nothnagel's support of the Dreyfusard Emile Zola triggered yet another attack on him by the *Reichspost*. See "Der Nothnagel ist da" (February 17, 1898), 5. In 1902 Lueger and other leading Christian Socials objected to the naming of Nothnagel to the Herrenhaus. See *Protokolle* (December 18, 1902), 17022, 17023.

62. Eduard Leisching, *Ein Leben für Kunst und Volksbildung. Erinnerungen* (Vienna, 1978), 66, 67.

63. *Amtsblatt*, no. 75 (September 19, 1905), 1908.

64. Letter of Josef Neumayer to Lueger (July 3, 1905), *IN* 31689. The *Reichspost* obituary began, "The well-known discoverer of the non-existence of Jewish ill breeding (*Unarten*), Herr Hofrat and University Professor Dr. Hermann Nothnagel, died last night of a heart attack." "Hofrat Nothnagel gestorben" (July 8, 1905), 3.

65. Mark Twain described Gregorig as "vast and conspicuous, and conceited and self-satisfied, and roosterish and inconsequential. . . . He looks very well indeed; really majestic, and aware of it. He crows out his little empty remark, now and then, and looks as pleased as if he had been delivered of the *Ausgleich*. Indeed, he does look notably fine. He wears almost the only dress vest on the floor; it exposes a continental spread of white shirt front; his hands are posed at ease in the lips of his trouser pockets; his head is tilted back com-

placently; he is attitudinizing; he is playing to the gallery." "Stirring Times in Austria," in *Literary Essays by Mark Twain* (New York and London, 1899), 231, 232.

66. At the time of Müllner's death in 1911, the *Neue Freie Presse* recalled his intervention on behalf of the equality of all citizens before the law in 1895. This prompted a spiteful article in the *Reichspost* in which Müllner's intervention was labeled a "polemic" that he might well long since have forgotten. See "Laurenz Müllner," *Neue Freie Presse* (November 29, 1911), 10; "Aus den Wiener Morgenblättern," *Reichspost* (November 29, 1911), 1.

67. *Landtag* (January 4, 1895), 66.

68. Ibid., 72, 73.

69. Ibid., 74.

70. Ibid., 75.

71. Bloch, 233.

72. For Bielohlawek's speech, see *Landtag* (October 15, 1903), 618–24.

73. According to Bielohlawek, "*Ich stehe heute noch auf dem Standpunkte Schönerers und sage: Die Religion des Juden ist mir einerlei, in der Rasse liegt die Schweinerei*" (ibid., 622).

74. Ibid. Bielohlawek's proposal anticipates the so-called Madagascar Plan of the Nazis, whereby, following the fall of France in 1940, Europe's remaining Jews were to be deported to Madagascar. This failed scheme was an important step in the chronology leading to the "Final Solution."

75. Ibid. (October 20, 1903), 669, 670. Steiner, who was recently called "one of the most gifted politicians of the Christian Social Party," rose from humble beginnings to become a delegate in the Landtag, municipal council, and parliament. Lueger entrusted him with the political organization of the suburbs, "and became one of his best friends." Steiner held several offices, including the chairmanship of the Christian Social party for Vienna and Lower Austria. He was instrumental in helping create Otto Wagner's Kirche am Steinhof. See Elisabeth Koller-Glück, *Otto Wagner's Kirche am Steinhof* (Vienna, 1985), 20, 21.

76. *Landtag*, (October 20, 1903), 671.

77. Ibid., 672, 673.

78. Ibid., 673.

79. Ibid. (October 27, 1903), 813. See "Ein Schreiben des Rektors der Wiener Universität," *Neue Freie Presse* (October 25, 1903), 7.

80. *Landtag*, (October 27, 1903), 820.

81. Ibid.

82. Ibid. (October 28, 1903), 864.

83. Ibid. (October 30, 1903), 913.

84. Ibid., 914.

85. Ibid., 921.

86. Ibid., 949–55. One who did not applaud Kielmansegg was Karl Kraus, who saw Kielmansegg's behavior during this incident as designed to strengthen the position from below that had long been shaky above. *Die Fackel* (November 11, 1903), 3.

87. *Landtag* (November 4, 1903), 1004–1007.

88. Ibid., 1004.

89. Ibid., 1005.

90. Ibid., 1005, 1006.

91. Ibid., 1010, 1011. An indication of the intensity of feeling surrounding this incident was a front-page article in the Christian Social *Deutsche Zeitung*. The thrust of "Four-footed anti-Semites" was that pets often perceived Jews before "Aryans" did. Josef Th., "Vierfüssige Antisemiten," *Deutsche Zeitung* (November 17, 1903), 1–4.

92. *Die Fackel* (November 11, 1903), 1–3, 7.

93. *Amtsblatt,* no. 94 (November 24, 1903), 2158.

94. Molisch, 165, 166.

95. "Ein Schreiben des Bürgermeisters Dr. Lueger an die Universitätsprofessoren," *Neue Freie Presse* (November 21, 1907), 2. Lueger's response to an earlier incident involving nationalistic student rowdyism is telling. When in May 1903 Christian Social municipal councillor Josef Wieninger complained about the rowdyism of "radical national students" on the Karlsplatz and Ringstrasse, Lueger blamed the university teachers and administrators for not maintaining the proper discipline over the Schönerians, Wolf supporters, and the few Jews who had also been present. *Amtsblatt,* no. 39 (May 15, 1903), 857, 858.

96. Letter of Ernst Count Sylva-Tarouca to Lueger (July 22, 1907), *IN* 40938.

97. This was a recurring theme in Lueger's speeches. See, for example, "Festversammlung des Salzburger Universitätsvereines," *Das Vaterland,* Beiblatt (November 20, 1905), 1. *Amtsblatt,* 100 (December 14, 1900), 2473–75. Lueger's views on education will be more fully treated in chapter seven.

98. "VI. allgemeiner österreichischer Katholikentag," *Volksblatt* (November 17, 1907), 10.

99. "Ein Schreiben Ernst Machs," *Neue Freie Presse* (November 26, 1907), 4.

100. For the Wahrmund affair, see Josef Wodka, *Kirche in Österreich: Wegweiser durch ihre Geschichte* (Vienna, 1959), 352; Johann Christoph Allmayer-Beck, *Ministerpräsident Baron Beck* (Vienna, 1956), 209–15; and Matthias Höttinger, "Der Fall Wahrmund," (Ph.D. diss., University of Vienna, 1949).

101. Allmayer-Beck, *Ministerpräsident Baron Beck,* 211.

102. William M. Johnston, *The Austrian Mind* (Berkeley, Los Angeles, and London, 1972), 60.

103. Macartney, 795n.3.

104. Franz Ferdinand is reported to have placed the "greatest trust in [the Christian Social] party," and saw in Lueger "his support." "The archduke spoke of you with veneration and <u>love</u> [underlined in original] . . . and sincerely hopes that you may be granted many years as our leader and that of all Christian Austria." Letter of Alfred Ebenhoch to Lueger (March 22, 1908), *IN* 40951.

105. Letters of Alfred Ebenhoch to Lueger (March 14 and 15, 1908), *IN* 40947 and 40952.

106. He was the author of *Der Dorflump von Dellach* and other "classics" of German literature.

107. Hans Arnold Schwer, *Die Wahrheit über die Morde in Polna* (Vienna, 1900). Schwer seems to fit the description of one of the "most ideologically hostile and combative actors in a political organization . . . [a] subleader . . . involved in the secondary policy levels of the party. . . . The second level political activists . . . especially journalists . . . [are] likely to be far more polarized than the population as a whole. Local and municipal sub-elites not only shape opinion by their frequent, intimate contact with the party's voters . . . but also exert the greatest pressure on that elite to maximize ideological distinctions, prevent compromise negotiations, and incite the voters to greater party loyalty" (Boyer, *Political Radicalism in Late Imperial Vienna,* 71).

108. "Ein Judentrick," *Badener und Mödlinger Bezirksnachrichten* (December 1, 1907), 1.

109. *Amtsblatt,* no. 95 (November 26, 1907), 2749, 2750.

110. *Landtag* (December 30, 1899), 41.

111. Boyer states that Lueger "made sure that the Jewish rabbis were given a prominent place in the new First Curia within the 1899–1900 franchise reforms in the city. One might argue that Lueger and Gessmann were forced to give the First Curia vote to the rabbis because

they had also included the Catholic pastors in that curia, but the important fact was that the issue was not a contentious one for the party" ("Karl Lueger and the Viennese Jews," 128, and n. 8). Nor could it have been a contentious issue, because of the imperial guarantees against discrimination because of religion and the sensitivity of Lueger to this issue. Not even Lueger would have dared such blatant discrimination, because of the possibility of imperial intervention. Lueger was also highly sensitive to suggestions that any of his party members might have violated such legal provisions. When it came to anti-Semitism, he was careful to distinguish between "religion" and "nation." See *Amtsblatt*, no. 84. (October 19, 1897), 2079, 2080. It would be interesting to know how many rabbis there were in the First Curia in 1899. Probably few.

112. Thus, his symbolical mingling with the Jews, as when Lueger attended a synagogue, was no more than symbolical: Lueger wore his badge of office during these visits. This emblem preserved his distinct and separate identity. Poliakov, 24.

113. During a municipal council session, Second Vice-Mayor Neumayer objected to the infestation of the judge's profession with Jews on the grounds that they completely lacked "the understanding, the feeling for moral-religious and national requirements and viewpoints of the Aryan nations." When this prompted protests from the Liberal minority, Lueger said one could hold any opinion about Jews whether the members of the minority liked it or not. When the objectors continued, Lueger expelled Liberal municipal councillors Lucian Brunner and Karl Wrabetz from that and the next three council meetings. *Amtsblatt*, no. 80 (October 5, 1897), 1973, 1974. In 1901 Lueger's name headed the list of those opposed to the appointment of a Jew as a lay judge on a parliamentary interpellation introduced by Magistrat director Richard Weiskirchner. *Protokolle* (March 14, 1901), 1356, 1357. On yet another occasion, a court decided against the expenditure of municipal funds to build churches, as Lueger had promised to do once he had become mayor. The court explained that this would violate the law, because churches served a particular religious community, rather than the entirety. Lueger criticized the judgment by arguing that if this were so, the municipal government could no longer support associations that practiced charity at Christmas. Nor could the city build public baths, "'for how many Jews go bathing?' (Amusement and applause.)" Spitzer, 189–191.

114. Nachlass Karl Lueger, St.[ädtische] S[amm]l[un]g. Z[ah]l. 1257/12, Karton II.

115. Boyer describes the "comic absurdity" arising out of "the confusion in 1908 when numerous Jewish merchants received large contracts from the city for materials needed for the Imperial Jubilee festival of that year. But, in general, an anti-Jewish contract policy was in force whenever conditions permitted, unless Jews made private 'deals' with individual members of the *Stadtrat*, which after 1907 was increasingly possible" ("Karl Lueger and the Viennese Jews," 129).

116. Nagl et al., IV: 1645, 1646. This is the present-day Volksoper.

117. Richard S. Geehr, *Adam Müller-Guttenbrunn and the Aryan Theater of Vienna, 1898–1903: The Approach of Cultural Fascism* (Göppingen, 1973), 48.

118. "Das Festbankett des Jubiläums-Stadttheaters," *Deutsches Volksblatt* (December 16, 1898), 8, 9.

119. Dr. Carl [sic] Lueger, *Reden gehalten in Wien am 20. Juli 1899* (St. Pölten, 1899), 28. Theodor Wähner, the publisher of the *Deutsche Zeitung*, which, Boyer states, "probably represented Lueger's thought in the period after 1897 more accurately than any other journalistic source," ("Karl Lueger and the Viennese Jews," 134) also praised the theater for providing the opportunity for German authors to have the word. Unlike "very many Viennese stages," the new theater was not "an eldorado for Jewry." *Amtsblatt*, no. 96 (December 1, 1899), 2821. Wähner pursued a German National course among the anti-Semites.

How much his paper actually "represented Lueger's thought in the period after 1897 more accurately than any other journalistic source" seems questionable. Wähner died in 1901. Lueger deemed the *Deutsche Zeitung* "worthless" by 1907. Its official function as "Christian Social organ" was taken over by the *Reichspost* in 1908. See Funder, *Vom Gestern ins Heute*, 322, 323.

120. Hawlik, 144.

121. See, for example, Geehr, *Adam Müller-Guttenbrunn and the Aryan Theater of Vienna*, 208.

122. In the latter version, the world-famous actor Werner Krauss played an especially virulent Shylock. According to the chief Nazi party organ, the *Völkischer Beobachter*:

> Words are inadequate to describe the linguistic and mimic variety of Werner Krauss's Shylock. . . . Every fiber of his body seems impregnated with Jewish blood; he mumbles, slavers, gurgles, grunts and squeaks with alarming authenticity, scurries back and forth like a rat, though he does so the hard way — knock-kneed; one literally smells his bad breath, feels the itching under his kaftan and — senses the nausea that overcomes him at the end of the court scene. Everything demonic is submerged in the impotent rage of the little ghetto usurer; in the wobbling of his body, in the frantic blinking of his eye lids and the arching of his arms, he becomes a caricature, especially together with the no less realistic Tubal of Ferdinand Maierhofer. An infernal puppet show. (Otto Horny, "Burgtheater. 'Der Kaufmann von Venedig' neu einstudiert," *Völkischer Beobachter*, May 17, 1943, 3)

The tone of this review was anticipated by that of the *Wiener Volksblatt* published by Hermann Bielohlawek. Anti-Semites were urged to hurry to the Aryan Theater production of the *Merchant*: "*Shylock personifies the entire Jewry of the world*; the only thing favorable about this Jewish beast in human form is that he did not cloak his ugliness" (Geehr, *Adam Müller-Guttenbrunn and the Aryan Theater of Vienna*, 153; emphasis in the original).

123. See Geehr, *Adam Müller-Guttenbrunn and the Aryan Theater of Vienna*, 151–52.

124. Ibid., 153, 154.

125. Ibid., 154, 155.

126. Ibid.

127. Ibid.

128. Ibid., 156.

129. Letter of Müller-Guttenbrunn to Ernst Vergani (March 31, 1899), *Nachlass Thim, Copirbuch*. On Jörg Lanz von Liebenfels, see Wilfried Daim, *Der Mann, der Hitler die Ideen gab* (Vienna, Cologne, and Graz, 1985); Bradley F. Smith, *Adolf Hitler: His Family, Childhood, and Youth* (Stanford, Ca., 1967), 124, 125, 147; Heer, 709–18. Though Hitler never admitted having read Lanz, Lanz claimed he was a model for Hitler. Daim, 12.

130. *Landtag* (October 23, 1903), 806. See also *Landtag* (April 20, 1903), 171, 172.

131. *Landtag* (October 23, 1903), 800, 806.

132. *Landtag* (June 11, 1907), 441, 442.

133. Geehr, *Adam Müller-Guttenbrunn and the Aryan Theater of Vienna*, 196.

134. The inspiration for the classical aspect of this caricature was doubtless Friedrich Schiller's poem "Pegasus im Joche."

135. John Polkinghorne, the vicar of Blean, states: "It is notoriously difficult to know how to assess speculative notions which subsequently prove to have more than a grain of truth in them but are insecurely anchored in contemporary knowledge. Are they deep intuitions or just lucky guesses?" ("The Facts of the Matter," *Times Literary Supplement*, September 13, 1985, 992). While any conclusions about the nature of Muller-Guttenbrunn's "speculative notions" must remain tenuous, the Aryan Theater project was an economic and artistic disaster. Nonetheless, some Christian Socials continued to oppose the "Jewish influence" in

the theater and opera world, and tried to block the subsequent construction of Jewish-managed playhouses. See *Amtsblatt*, no. 16 (February 22, 1907), 451 and no. 23 (March 19, 1907), 630. During World War I, Max von Millenkovich-Morold hoped to introduce a *numerus clausus* that would discourage the employment of Jewish actors and performance of "Jewish" plays. He contented himself, however, with discharging Jewish actors and assistants. Millenkovich-Morold, 277. Müller-Guttenbrunn's efforts, therefore, were not an isolated episode.

136. Quoted in Geehr, *Adam Müller-Guttenbrunn and the Aryan Theater of Vienna*, 381n. 24.

137. Austriacus, "Bürgermeister Dr. Karl Lueger," *Wiener Sonn- und Montags-Zeitung* (March 14, 1910), 1.

138. Considering newspaper reports of the turbulence in eastern Europe, Liechtenstein may have had apprehensions about the effects of the revolution on his own fortunes, when he wished that "the Lord grant the empire, fatherland and dynasty a happy disentanglement of the present crisis." Letter of Alois Liechtenstein to Karl Lueger (July 12, 1905), *IN* 31682.

139. On late czarist anti-Semitism, see Hans Rogger, *Jewish Policies and Right-Wing Politics in Imperial Russia* (Berkeley and Los Angeles, 1986). About two and a half million Jews fled Russia between 1881 and 1914, most because of the poverty they suffered.

140. *Amtsblatt*, no. 73 (September 12, 1905), 1836. Christian Social opposition to Jewish immigration was to continue. See *Protokolle* (March 27, 1906), 35688, 35689.

141. Schneider had proposed the abolishment of ritual slaughter, as well as the prohibition of the importation and sale of kosher meat, in the Landtag in 1898. His proposal was endorsed by Lueger and many other leading Christian Socials. *Landtag* (January 28, 1898), 302. Schneider's action both continued standard nineteenth-century practice and anticipated similar Nazi agitation in the Weimar Republic. Ritual slaughter was a major theme in the most virulent Nazi anti-Jewish film *Der ewige Jude*. See David Welch, *Propaganda and the German Cinema* (Oxford, 1983), 292ff. According to Richard S. Levy:

> This whole issue [of ritual slaughter] is a complex one. In Germany the Catholic Church and the Center Party defended kosher butchering as a matter of religious freedom. That Austrian Catholicism did not feel the need to do so reflects its dominant position in state and society. It never had to deal with a Kulturkampf or suffer minority persecution. I have read, in the German context, reasoned denunciations of kosher butchering on the basis of cruelty to animals (with no particular assault on Jews or Judaism). Animal lovers and antivivisectionists could be recruited to the antisemitic parties on the basis of this issue, however. Kosher slaughtering was in fact outlawed in the Kingdom of Saxony briefly during the 1890s. Kosher slaughtering and ritual murder charges were intimately connected in the minds of antisemites. Almost all the modern cases (Xanten, Konitz, etc.) have the victims found near Jewish butcher shops or have butchers as suspects. Kosher laws stood for all that was sinister and exclusivist in Jews, as far as suspicious gentiles were concerned. (Letter to author, September 22, 1987)

142. *Amtsblatt*, no. 52 (June 28, 1904), 1302, 1303; no. 80 (October 4, 1904), 1859.

143. See, for example, *Amtsblatt*, no. 36 (May 5, 1905), 865, 866, 885–910; *Protokolle* (May 11, 1905), 29361, 29362; *Landtag*, (November 9, 1904), 759–71.

144. *Amtsblatt*, no. 73 (September 12, 1905), 1826.

145. Ernst Waldinger has described the revulsion of youths, who greedily consumed everything readable, when confronted with the caricatures of *Kikeriki*, the predecessor of Julius Streicher's *Stürmer*. Fraenkel, 265, 266.

146. *Landtag* (November 3, 1905), 148. In the municipal council Lueger remarked that the demonstration of November 2 had again taught him, and "taught him very thoroughly, that certain elements were absolutely incorrigible." *Amtsblatt*, no. 89 (November 7, 1905), 2357.

147. The loyalty of the czarist troops prevailed and the throne was saved. See John Bushnell, *Mutiny Amid Repression: Russian Soldiers in the Revolution of 1905–1906* (Bloomington, Ind., 1985).

148. "Grosse Wählerversammlung," *Volksblatt* (December 6, 1905), 5.

149. Ibid., 6. On January 30, 1939, Hitler told the Reichstag that should the Jews unleash a new war they would perish.

150. *Amtsblatt*, no. 99 (December 12, 1905), 2609.

151. Ibid.

152. Ibid., 2610

153. Ibid. When the Liberal municipal councillor Oswald Hohensinner interjected that there were also Jews in the Christian Social party, Lueger commanded him to silence.

154. Ibid.

155. Ibid., 2611.

156. "Bürgermeister Dr. Karl Lueger," 1. Lueger's observation about Adler's racial origin recalled an earlier speech in which Lueger referred to the Social Democratic leader as his enemy. Were he not his enemy, Lueger's "old, Aryan blood" might move him to pity, "as was unfortunately frequently the case." But no, Adler should always show that he was Lueger's "most implacable enemy," so that Lueger should show no mercy "and fight as befits the leader of a great party." *Landtag* (July 12, 1901), 403.

157. Thus, his remarks in the municipal council were probably less an "open brag" about defending "the Jews on several occasions when his fellow party members planned antisemitic policies," as Boyer puts it, than a necessary attempt to de-emphasize his anti-Jewish demagogy, in general, and probably to calm some of the men of Jewish origin within the Christian Social party. Lueger showed he was disturbed during the municipal council meeting that some Jews had complained to the prime minister, Gautsch, "an old protégé of Francis Ferdinand's." Although the pretender to the throne was also an anti-Semite, Lueger would doubtless have wished to avoid risking the involvement of Gautsch in a cause célèbre, and thus antagonizing Franz Ferdinand, Lueger's own protector. Boyer, "Karl Lueger and the Viennese Jews," 128; Macartney, 793n. 1. I have compared the official *Amtsblatt* stenographic report of Lueger's remarks in the municipal council on December 7, 1905, with that of the *Reichspost* account cited by Boyer and used the *Amtsblatt* report because it is more complete. Responding to this incident, Karl Kraus remarked that "after the oratorical excesses of the mayor of a capital and residential city, an honorable anti-Semite must become a fanatical friend of the Jews" ("Antworten des Herausgebers," *Die Fackel*, no. 190 [December 11, 1905], 5).

At the time of the parliamentary elections of 1907, open "anti-Semitism was practically neglected in face of the Marxist menace." Lueger was then seriously ill and unable to campaign. For this campaign, the climax of the electoral reforms, see William Jenks, *The Austrian Electoral Reform of 1907* (New York, 1950), p. 184.

158. "Die Entrüsteten," *Reichspost* (December 12, 1905), 1, 2.

159. *Amtsblatt*, no. 100 (December 15, 1905), 2687–89.

160. Ibid., 2689. "Die Juden haben uns das Geld aus dem Sacke gestohlen!"

161. Ibid., 2695.

162. Publicly, at least, Lueger continued to identify the Jews with Social Democracy: "The Jews vote unanimously from the richest to the poorest for the Social Democrats. . . . I don't grudge the Social Democrats the Jews." *Amtsblatt*, no. 39 (May 15, 1906), 963. Opponents charged, however, that the Christian Socials prevented Jews from voting by withholding from them the necessary documents. Lueger promised to look into the matter. *Amtsblatt*, no. 57 (July 17, 1906), 1483.

In his attitude toward Jews, the emperor seems to have lived with cognitive dissonance.

It will be remembered that he wrote the empress that "the core (of anti-Semitism) is actually good, but the excesses are terrible." Yet, he told Prime Minister Taaffe at the beginning of the anti-Semitic movement that "every anti-Semitic movement must be nipped in the bud immediately (*muss sofort in ihrem Keime erstickt werden*). You will immediately have any anti-Semitic assembly dissolved. The Jews are brave and patriotic men and happily risk their life for emperor and fatherland." During World War I when Weiskirchner, Lueger's successor as mayor, proposed to transfer Jewish refugees who were streaming in from the eastern war zone to camps in Moravia, Franz Joseph replied: "If Vienna has no more room for refugees, I shall make Schönbrunn available for my Jewish subjects." See Nikolaus Vielmetti, ed., *Das Österreichische Judentum* (Vienna and Munich, 1974), 118; and Arthur J. May, *The Passing of the Habsburg Monarchy 1914–1918*, 2 vols. (Philadelphia, 1968), I: 311.

163. *Protokolle* (October 25, 1907), 2158.

164. See, for example, *Amtsblatt* no. 99, (December 9, 1904), 2403, 2404; no. 55 (July 10, 1906), 1415, 1416; and no. 29 (April 9, 1907), 826, 827. After this issue had once arisen, Lueger indicated that if the city council did not want to promote a Jewish official, there was nothing he could do about it. He had once interceded, "but one cannot expect that I . . . will always make a cabinet question out of this as it pertains to every Jew. That I won't do." *Amtsblatt*, no. 47 (June 11, 1901), 1099, 1100. Lueger's irritation over this subject was more transparent on yet another occasion when he dismissed allegations that an official had not been promoted because his wife was Jewish. "I would like to know, by the way, why [Oswald Hohensinner] is so much interested in Jews and Jewesses. That he . . . starts with such nonsense in the first meeting after the vacation is not good!" *Amtsblatt*, no. 75 (September 16, 1904), 1753.

165. "Karl Lueger and the Viennese Jews," 129n. 14. Boyer does admit, however, that "few Jews found avenues for advancement or promotion as easily available as under the preceding Liberal regime which itself had been extremely parsimonious in offering employment to Jews in municipal government" (128).

166. George Clare, *Last Waltz in Vienna: The Rise and Destruction of a Family* (New York, 1982) 22.

167. Ibid., 22, 24.

168. Ibid., 22, 23.

169. Rudolf Sieghart, *Die letzten Jahrzehnte einer Grossmacht* (Berlin, 1932), 312. As the director of the Austrian Länderbank, Lohnstein served as Lueger's financial adviser in municipal matters and as an intermediary in negotiations with foreign banks. In addition, he provided advice on the construction of a subway in Vienna, one of Lueger's unfulfilled projects. When in the spring of 1908 Lueger was recuperating from one of his increasingly frequent periods of illness, Lohnstein wrote him that he and his wife would like to visit the mayor for about a week. Though Karl Renner asserted in 1910 shortly before Lueger's death that Lohnstein had bid the Christian Socials farewell, evidently because of a sharply anti-Jewish polemic, *Kapitalismus, Bodenreform und christlicher Sozialismus* by Anton Orel, Lohnstein praised Lueger in his condolences to the surviving sisters as "always an exceedingly well-wishing friend and protector who, as long as I live, will be recalled with warm, thankful memories." Hildegard and Rosa Lueger also received condolences from Edouard Drumont, the anti-Semitic editor of *La Libre Parole* and leading anti-Dreyfusard, who called "the death of a great citizen like Lueger . . . a loss for the entire world." Letter of Ludwig August Lohnstein to Karl Lueger (March 24, 1908), *IN* 41544; *Landtag* (January 25, 1910), 1047; Nachlass Karl Lueger, St.[ädtische] S[amm]l[un]g. Z[ah]l 1257/12, Beileidsschreiben an Hildegard und Rosa Lueger, Karton II.

170. *Amtsblatt*, no. 75 (September 19, 1905), 1893, 1895.

171. Ibid., no. 51 (June 26, 1908), 1548. During the same session the Social Democrat

Jakob Reumann directed a sarcastic and castigating attack on Christian Social hypocrisy. Stating that the municipal council had before it "the edict of tolerance for Jewish capitalism," he charged that the Christian Social rapprochement demonstrated "the duplicity of their teachings. . . . I have . . . demonstrated how your anti-Semitism has gone bankrupt and said that this is a solemn moment for us. . . . God, what a wonderful success for you! How the whole financial world will rejoice that with this accord with the City of Vienna, the ice is broken" (ibid., 1543, 1544). Four years before the Liberal Ferdinand Klebinder had told Lueger: "If you fight big capitalistic Jews, that's a matter of taste; today you fight them, tomorrow you fraternize with them, and if you introduce a proposal on one hand to give only Christian children free theater tickets, you know very well that on the other, the theater is being built by a Jew" (*Amtsblatt*, no. 91 [November 11, 1904], 2153).

172. *Amtsblatt*, no. 100 (December 15, 1903), 2321; no. 102 (December 22, 1905), 2765; no. 29 (April 10, 1906), 714; no. 85 (October 23, 1906), 2205, 2206; no. 39 (May 15, 1908), 1206; no. 58 (July 20, 1909), 1802; no. 5 (January 18, 1910), 90.

173. "13. Bezirk," *Volksblatt* (October 19, 1909), 10.

174. "17. Bezirk, *Volksblatt* (October 19, 1909), 11.

175. *Landtag* (February 1, 1910), 1205.

176. Wistrich, "Karl Lueger and the Ambiguities of Viennese Antisemitism," 255.

177. Ibid., 254.

178. Bloch, *My Reminiscences*, 233.

179. Ibid., 7.

180. Redlich is quoted in Helmut Andics, *Luegerzeit* (Vienna and Munich, 1984), 347. Sigmund Mayer, *Ein jüdischer Kaufmann*, 298. Redlich and Zweig remain authorities in Austria for mitigating Lueger's anti-Semitism. They are cited by Norbert Leser, who denies that Lueger was a forerunner of Hitler. See A. Gaisbauer, "Lueger – eine Rehabilitierung?" *Österreich* (November 4, 1988), 4, 5, and the sources quoted therein.

181. On Hermann Levi, see Peter Gay, *Freud, Jews and Other Germans* (New York, 1978), 189–230.

182. *The Complete Diaries of Theodor Herzl*, 5 vols., trans. Harry Zohn, ed. Raphael Patai, (New York and London, 1960), I: 244.

183. Boyer, *Political Radicalism in Late Imperial Vienna*, 413.

184. Alexander Spitzmüller, " . . . *Und hat auch Ursach, es zu lieben*" (Vienna, Munich, Stuttgart, and Zurich, 1955), 74. Lueger's remark anticipates a similar statement on the same topic by Winston Churchill. In a Munich hotel in 1932 Churchill told Ernst Hanfstaengl, Hitler's foreign press chief, to tell his boss that "anti-Semitism may be a good starter, but it is a bad sticker" (Ernst Hanfstaengl, *Hitler: The Missing Years* (London, 1957), 185.

185. J. P. Stern, *Hitler*, 89.

186. Ibid. Viktor Adler touched on this once during a speech in the Landtag: "Almost everyone, . . . I know, speaks what he believes and holds to be true. You, *Herr Bürgermeister*, you believe what you say, and believe it only as long as you say it, and believe something else after you have spoken" (*Landtag* [July 11, 1901], 377).

187. *Amtsblatt*, no. 32 (April 20, 1894), 967; no. 2 (January 7, 1898), 82; no. 76 (September 21, 1909), 2199.

Chapter 6. The Lueger Gretl

1. Beskiba, 24, 25.

2. Boyer is contradictory here. On page 120 of his monograph on political radicalism

he states: "The history of the Christian Social women's movement properly belongs in the second volume of this study (which will deal with the period 1897–1920), since its major impact came after Lueger's political victories in 1895–96; but its origins lay in the formative years of the anti-semitic movement." On page 379 of the same work he states: "After 1896, when the government conceded the city to the Christian Socials the women returned to the political obscurity from whence they had come." Boyer, *Political Radicalism in Late Imperial Vienna.*

3. "Von der Weihnachts-Versammlung in der Volkshalle am 12. December 1899," ÖFZ (December 20, 1899), 1.

4. "Dr. Lueger and the Great Ladies of Vienna," *The World* (London), December 12, 1902), 1131.

5. Adagio, "Wochen-Bioskop, X, Dr. Lueger," *Wiener Sonn- und Montags-Zeitung,* (March 14, 1910), 3.

6. Alfred E. Frauenfeld, *Und trage keine Reu'* (Leoni am Starnberger See, 1978), 72. According to Frauenfeld, "the Viennese are eye people [*Augenmenschen*]."

7. Unpublished memoirs of Heinrich Hierhammer, 11.

8. "Nachtrag zum II. praktisch-socialen Curs," ÖFZ (July 29, 1899), 2. At the time the fourth curia was created and the few qualified women of Lower Austria were deprived of their franchise, Gessmann stated that it was logical that only a direct franchise should be exercised: "We Christian Socials are of the opinion that a distinction must be made in the political area between the two sexes." Quoted in Spitzer, 61.

9. For information on the early years of the league, see Antonie Schmolek, "Lueger und die christlichen Frauen," *Neuigkeits-Welt-Blatt* (September 19, 1926), 23.

10. Boyer, *Political Radicalism in Late Imperial Vienna,* 378, 379.

11. Spitzer, 119.

12. "Constituirende Versammlung des Vereines 'Christlicher Wiener Frauenbund,'" *Reichspost* (March 30, 1897), 3.

13. "Christlicher Wiener Frauen-Bund—Wiens christliche Frauen und Mädchen haben gesprochen!" ÖFZ (February 24, 1898), 2.

14. "Wochen-Rundschau," ÖFZ (July 22, 1906), 1. See also "Wochen-Rundschau," ÖFZ (July 29, 1906), 2.

15. "Grosse Bundes-Weihnachts-Versammlung," ÖFZ (December 8, 1901), 4. See also "Christlicher Frauenbund für Steiermark," ÖFZ (February 9, 1902), 6.

16. My inquiry about her birth and death dates to the Bundespolizeidirektion Wien was answered by a letter stating that Platter was born on March 7, 1874, in Stendal, Bohemia, and moved to Wels in Oberösterreich on November 3, 1933. This does not seem to have been the same person. Letter of Herr Emrich to me, August 21, 1970.

17. Beskiba, 31.

18. Kielmansegg, 387.

19. Another organ was the *Christliche Wiener Frauen Zeitung.* This was evidently the "hick paper" [*Winkelblättchen*] referred to by Beskiba (p. 31). The ÖFZ was of large format, initially at least. I have relied on the latter source, because it is more comprehensive in its reportage.

20. Klier was last referred to as the "founder of the league" by Platter in a letter of thanks on page one of the ÖFZ on October 28, 1906. In parliament Lueger claimed to have called the "women's movement in Vienna into being." *Protokolle* (October 6, 1897), 379.

21. Beskiba, 31.

22. "Erziehung," ÖFZ (December 3, 1905), 6; "Erziehung. Folgsamkeit ohne Widerspruch," ÖFZ (October 29, 1905), 6.

23. "Documente der Frauen," *ÖFZ* (March 23, 1899), 2. The *ÖFZ* called Mayreder and the other editors of the *Documente der Frauen* slanderers because they failed to be specific about the precise places in the *ÖFZ* where "the lowest instincts" and "the inexperience of women" were exploited.

24. F. K., "Vereins Rubrik. Von der Bundesreise nach dem Süden," *ÖFZ*, (July 6, 1902), 2-5.

25. Emma Kancler, "Die österreichische Frauenbewegung und ihre Presse (Von ihren Anfängen bis zum Ende des I. Weltkrieges)" (Ph.D. diss., University of Vienna, 1947), 114.

26. Ibid.

27. "Das Präsidium des Christlichen Wiener Frauen-Bundes," *ÖFZ* (June 3, 1900), 3.

28. Beskiba, 31, 32. In 1906 there were thirty-three *Ortsgruppen*. Kancler, 114.

29. "Ortsgruppe Meidling," *ÖFZ* (March 6, 1904), 7.

30. Beskiba, 32-34.

31. Marie Götz, *Die Frauen und der Antisemitismus* (Vienna, n.d.), 13. No translation can adequately capture the charm of the original in Viennese dialect: "Sie glaub'n gar net, wia so a Versammlung auf'n Geist und G'müth einwirkt. Da Lueger und da Fürscht, und dö andern Herr'n alle, dö san ja so unbändi b'lesen und b'lehrt. S' Herz wackelt ein' unbandi, wann ma all' das Wissenschäftliche hört, was da' g'redt wird." In a more serious vein, Götz asserted that the Christian Social leaders were trying to poison their children and families with anti-Semitism. "Hypocrisy, false respectability [*Biedermeierei*], hypocritical piety, celebrate veritable orgies, and the stupid women don't notice what a ludicrous role they play; they don't suspect that all the lovely words from the mouth of a Liechtenstein, from a Lueger, from a Scheicher, etc., are nothing more than a bold assault on common sense" (p. 11).

32. Beskiba, 32.

33. "Vereins-Rubrik Christlicher Wiener Frauen-Bund. Zur Bürgermeister-Beeidigung," *ÖFZ* (April 19, 1903), 5.

34. Ibid.

35. "Valerie Gréy gestorben," *Neue Freie Presse* (February 21, 1934), 3.

36. Lueger's mother functioned as an occasional administrative assistant. See the photostat of her letter to him in Soukup, 149.

37. Gréy seems to have been a reader of Honoré d'Urfé, the early-seventeenth-century novelist. A reference to Céladon, the ardent lover in d'Urfé's novel *Astrée*, appears both in Gréy's 1894 novel *Paula* and in one of Lueger's letters to Gréy. For information on d'Urfé, see Louise K. Horowitz, *Honoré d'Urfé* (Boston, 1984). Lueger and Gréy also shared an admiration for Schiller.

38. Nagl et al., III: 826.

39. Lueger belittled him in his letters. Gréy's first husband was a Kletzer.

40. "Viennese municipal records list Valerie Gréy's birth date as February 10, 1842, and February 10, 1845, and her name is given as Charlotte Valerie, born Loewe, and Valerie Charlotte Loewy. In the *Trauungsbuch des evangelischen Pfarramtes A. B., Jahr 1888, Reihezahl 136* (Vienna), her name appears as Caroline Valerie, born Loewy, and her birthplace and birth date as Pest, January 31, 1845. The last source would seem to be the more reliable, for the information was probably submitted by Gréy herself at the time of her second marriage." Geehr, *"I Decide Who Is a Jew!"*, 58n. 5.

41. Handwritten autobiographical sketch "Valerie Gréy," *IN* 45778.

42. Ibid.

43. Ibid.

44. A. Entsch, *Deutscher Bühnen-Almanach* (Berlin, 1881). January 1, 1881 (352), lists

the Gréy Theater at I. Canovagasse 5, the location of the Thalia Theater until 1879. Playbills in the Wiener Stadt Bibliothek collection (77065) include programs naming Gréy as the theater director.

45. Her students included Josef Kainz and Josefine Wessely. *Neue Freie Presse* (February 21, 1934), 3.

46. This was Robert Meixner, who was probably a relative of the comic actor Karl Meixner who taught elocution at Gréy's theater school.

47. Entsch, 353.

48. This letter is included in Geehr, *"I Decide Who Is a Jew!"*, 63, 64.

49. Ibid., 54.

50. Ibid., 65.

51. Ibid., 67.

52. Ibid., 70.

53. Ibid., 90.

54. Bloch, 227.

55. "Unbekannte Lueger-Briefe an eine Wiener Dame," *Neues Wiener Journal* (September 19, 1926), 5.

56. Geehr, *"I Decide Who Is a Jew!"*, 90.

57. Ibid., 81.

58. Ibid., 87.

59. Ibid., 88.

60. Boyer, *Political Radicalism in Late Imperial Vienna*, 226, 227.

61. A letter of Leopold Hollomay to Lueger (June 17, 1883), *IN* 40933, indicates that Mandl was interested in serving only himself and other Semites.

62. Geehr, *"I Decide Who Is a Jew!"*, 232.

63. Ibid., 91.

64. Stipek had succeeded Lueger as legal counsel to her theater in 1883. Entsch (1883), 371. Gréy's second husband proved professionally useful, for her bouts with the law continued. See "Ein angeklagter Advocat," *Illustrirtes Wiener Extrablatt* (October 6, 1899), 8.

65. Beskiba, 13.

66. Lueger's early biographer Mack relates the story of an attempt on Lueger's life on May 17, 1893, in which "two elegantly dressed men" offered Lueger a ride in a coach drawn by a horse that had eaten wine-soaked bread, and under whose tail had been tied a sponge soaked in styptic. Mack, 13, 14. Lueger described his own involvement in a brawl during a parliamentary session; see *Protokolle* (March 4, 1895), 17101, 17102.

67. Beskiba, 32.

68. Ibid., 6. Beskiba's impression recalls Lueger's words to Weiskirchner after the mayor's recovery from a serious illness: "If anywhere, the saying 'resting is rusting,' applies to the administration of a great city. It can't rest, the machine must go restlessly forward, even prematurely, even if one's strength is exhausted. It is not possible otherwise" (Mack, 45). Yet another municipal official commented on Lueger's relentless drive to achieve goals, "nothing was too far, nothing disturbed or impeded him." Millenkovich-Morold, 226, 227.

69. Beskiba, 18. Lueger's expensive preferences are passed over in silence by his earlier biographers, who were anxious to present him as a perfect man of the people, modest in his tastes and requirements.

70. Ibid., 67.

71. Ibid., 13.

72. Ibid., 19. Known to his closest friends as a "Viennese *Schnorrer*," nothing was more

certain to make Lueger melancholy than to lose at cards. Tarock was a favorite game of his. Soukup, 135.

73. Beskiba, 20.

74. Ibid., 11.

75. Ibid., 100.

76. Geehr, *"I Decide Who Is a Jew!"*, 93.

77. Ibid., 95.

78. Mack, 36, 37. Lueger's salary was 24,000 Gulden. He relinquished half of this.

79. Beskiba, 21. For details on Christian Social corruption, see Marie Götz, *Schmutzige Wäsche der christlich Socialen eingesammelt.*

80. Ibid.

81. Ibid., 56.

82. Ibid.

83. Ibid., 55. For Lueger's only known surviving poem, see Geehr, *"I Decide Who Is a Jew!"*, 47, 48.

84. Ibid., 82.

85. Ibid., 87.

86. Ibid., 106.

87. Kralik was a major irritant to the *ÖFZ*, which criticized his "malicious misuse of the freedom of expression." F. K., "Kaiserjubiläums-Stadttheater" *ÖFZ* (March 18, 1900), 3. On Kralik see Helmut Krenn, "Die 'Habakuk'-Reihe des Emil Kralik in der Arbeiterzeitung als Beitrag zur Wiener humoristisch satirischen Publizistik 1896–1906" (Ph.D. diss., University of Vienna, 1979).

88. Mels-Colloredo would make an interesting biographical subject. The only other aristocrat besides Liechtenstein to have vigorously agitated for the Christian Socials during the early period, he agitated among women's groups. As a priest, he seems to have been considered even more unattainable than Lueger to the Gretl, which together with his handsome appearance were the probable major ingredients of his success. He was a powerful speaker, according to all accounts, and his words had a deeper effect than the run-of-the-mill agitator, because of his noble and priestly status.

89. Habakuk, "Sezession," *Arbeiter Zeitung* (January 3, 1904), from "Konvolut von Zeitungsausschnitten über die christlich-soziale Partei, gesammelt von Marianne Beskiba," IN 83740.

90. See, for example, Carola W., "Die Geissel des 19. Jahrhunderts," *ÖFZ* (September 28, 1898), 2; F. K., "Der Mörder unserer Kaiserin vor seinen Richtern," *ÖFZ* (November 15, 1898), 1; F. K., "Wieder ein Fürstenmord!", *ÖFZ* (August 5, 1900), 1.

91. See, for example, S. Mühlhofer, "Erziehung," *ÖFZ* (May 7, 1898), 5. This author exhorted his readers to implant anti-Semitism in their children's hearts "at the tenderest age."

92. Letter of Franz Klier to Lina Morgenstern, quoted in *ÖFZ* (April 1, 1900), 8.

93. "Nachtrag zum II. praktisch-socialen Curs," *ÖFZ* (July 29, 1899), 2.

94. "Wochen-Rundschau," *ÖFZ* (January 25, 1903), 2.

95. "Aus der Frauenwelt. Die Negerinnen in Nordamerika," *ÖFZ* (July 17, 1904), 5.

96. Sharing this distinction with Lueger was Pope Leo XIII, who was quoted as follows: "The bad press has condemned Christian society; the good press must oppose the former and be disseminated with zeal, the lies refuted with great energy, and the truth defended." "Presse und Antisemitismus," *ÖFZ* (February 1, 1903), 3.

97. For Lueger's anti-Semitic remarks during the early years of the *Frauenbund*, see "Ortsgruppe Mödling," *ÖFZ* (December 12, 1899), 3; "Ortsgruppe Meidling," *ÖFZ* (March

25, 1900), 3. On the latter occasion, Lueger remarked that the women performed "the right duty" by supporting their husbands, just as the women "of the certain race" were "always destined to take over his business if her husband didn't pay." He regretted that Schneider was not present "in order graphically to portray the enemies of the Christian people."

98. "Presse und Antisemitismus," ÖFZ (February 1, 1903), 3. Lueger is responding to a statement of Friedrich III ("disgrace of the century") at his dedication of a synagogue in Berlin. Philo-Semitism from such a royal authority must have been upsetting to the Amazons. Friedrich's words were frequently featured in Verein zur Abwehr des Antisemitismus journals and pamphlets — a statement that had to be answered, clearly. For information on the Verein, see Richard S. Levy, The Downfall of the Antisemitic Political Parties in Imperial Germany (New Haven and London, 1975).

99. Hilsner served eighteen years of a life sentence before being pardoned in March 1918 by Emperor Karl. Hilsner was defended by Tomas Masaryk, the Czech Zola. On the Hilsner affair, see Johnston, 28.

100. "Grosse Frauenversammlung in Mödling," Reichspost (November 18, 1900), 4, 5.

101. "Vereins-Rubrik. Christlicher Wiener Frauen-Bund. Vom christlichsocialen Parteitag für Niederösterreich nördlich der Donau," ÖFZ (October 8, 1905), 3.

102. In a dramatized vignette, "which can very often be heard," a young Lueger Gretl explains to her initially skeptical mother why the Christian Social leader deserves the support of all "reasonable people":

Not only have the most profitable positions, the best real estate complexes, the best-known businesses been appropriated by Jewish speculative talent, but much worse [the Jew] has poisoned souls. Those who are nowadays still in the position to offer a girl employment in accordance with her rank . . . are mostly physically or morally old men. Jewish immorality has robbed them of the belief, inculcated since childhood, that marriage is a sacrament; rather, it is a business; what else could it be in this century of sad Jewish culture? If one is condemned to have to watch how the body and soul of a glorious old nation have been consumed by parasites, then every reasonable person must rejoice if a man makes his best effort to improve the material position of the disinherited, wishing to prepare for the union of the de-Christianized with God. And that's why I sing "Hoch Lueger!"

"Eine häusliche Scene, wie sie sehr häufig belauscht werden kann," ÖFZ (August 14, 1899), 3.

103. They were also urged to "Support the Christian Press!" An indication of the envy and backbiting among Christian Social journalists was afforded when Frauen-Zeitung readers were enjoined to agitate for Wähner's Deutsche Zeitung and Opitz's Reichspost, rather than for the Deutsches Volksblatt and Neuigkeits-Weltblatt, whose respective owners, Vergani and Kirsch, "had already become very well off." "Stützet die Christliche Presse," ÖFZ (March 18, 1900), 4.

104. "Wo kaufen die Christen?" ÖFZ (March 10, 1901), 2. More than two years later, the Frauen-Zeitung complained that the situation had worsened and that there was noticeable backsliding among the anti-Semites in other areas. "Wo bleibt der praktische Antisemitismus?" ÖFZ (December 6, 1903).

105. "Ortsgruppe Hernals," ÖFZ (December 12, 1899), 3.

106. "Ortsgruppe Mariahilf," ÖFZ (April 22, 1900), 2.

107. According to her, Schneider,

an enraged enemy of the Jews, championed and supported his principles with rare and . . . admirable consistency for decades. One can think as one chooses about the Jewish Question; recognition must be accorded to delegate Schneider for remaining true to his principles. During a time when the Christian Social movement still looked very "dubious," Schneider, with Gregorig and Schönerer, took the risk; he brought the idea of "anti-Semitism" into the Viennese sphere and made propaganda for the party that took the helm after a hard struggle. Many of the present "greats" attained their "party-political conviction" only after no more risk existed in assuming this stance and there was nothing to lose. But Schneider still speaks today as he did 30 years ago and this steadfastness of belief accrues to his honor. (Beskiba, 36)

108. "Ortsgruppe Hernals," *ÖFZ* (December 12, 1899), 3. On another occasion Schneider regaled Lueger Gretl with an account of his steamship passage to New York. On board were also seven hundred Russian Jewish emigrants on their way to swell the city's population, which "was already blessed with *700,000 Jews.*" [Emphasis in the original.] Schneider wondered that "the clever Americans [did] nothing against the Jewish emigration," though they excluded Chinese. "Ortsgruppe Rudolfsheim," *ÖFZ* (October 25, 1903), 4.

109. "Ortsgruppe St. Pölten," *ÖFZ* (March 13, 1904), 7.

110. "Ortsgruppe Hernals," *ÖFZ* (December 8, 1900), 3.

111. Elise von Reizenhofen, "Über Frauen-Emancipation," *ÖFZ* (December 2, 1900), 2. The members of the Ortsgruppe Wiener-Neustadt were informed that the type of private and public equality between the sexes advocated by the Social Democrats could never develop. Thanks to Christianity, women had been lifted out of their prehistoric slavery and now occupied an elevated position in society. The veneration of Mary symbolized this. "Ortsgruppe Wiener-Neustadt," *ÖFZ* (March 29, 1903), 8. In another article on women's franchise in Australia, the *ÖFZ* was of the opinion that female emancipation could only be spoken of in a qualified sense in that part of the world, for there and elsewhere, women of the Germanic and Anglo-Saxon races had never been oppressed. "Das Frauenstimmrecht in Australien," *ÖFZ* (August 30, 1903), 6. This and other articles made it clear that there could never be a thoroughgoing equality between the sexes, so far as the Christian Socials were concerned, because as one of them put it, that "contradicted . . . nature as well as Christianity." Professor Franz Spirago, "Eine vollkommene Gleichstellung der Frau mit dem Manne ist unzulässig, weil die Frau andere Anlagen besitzt als der Mann, und weil sie nur die Gehilfin des Mannes ist," *ÖFZ* (February 14, 1904), 8.

112. "Die christliche Weltanschauung," *ÖFZ* (March 31, 1901), 2.

113. Ibid.

114. "Die christliche Weltanschauung," *ÖFZ* (April 7, 1901), 4.

115. "Die christliche Weltanschauung," *ÖFZ* (April 28, 1901), 2.

116. "Der Frauenbund beim 'Kaufmann von Venedig,'" *ÖFZ* (November 26, 1899), 1. The *ÖFZ* reported the attendance of more than three hundred league members at a performance of *Der Rechtschaffene* on March 10, 1900. Loud applause greeted the play in many places, according to the front-page report:

> The "Christian Viennese Women's League" has achieved two things through this public demonstration: confirmed its agreement with the flagellation of the Semitic view of life, and then awakened anew among its members interest in the only Christian-German stage in Vienna. Proof of this sympathy for the Jubiläums-Theater and its efforts will certainly be richly and frequently demonstrated.

"Zum gemeinschaftlichen Besuch des Kaiserjubiläums—Stadttheaters vom 10. März," (March 18, 1900), 1. The *ÖFZ* was less happy with one of Müller-Guttenbrunn's later productions, Philipp Haas's *Andreas Gerhard*, which seemed to defend free love. Such practices were anathema to the *Frauenbund* and its journalistic organ, which occasionally functioned as a party censor, particularly in cultural matters. X., "Kaiserjubiläums-Stadttheater," *ÖFZ* (March 23, 1902), 5, 6.

117. F. K., "Unglaubliche Keckheit einer jüdischen Zeitung," *ÖFZ* (January 24, 1904), 2.

118. Eduard F. Sekler, *Josef Hoffmann: The Architectural Work* (Princeton, N.J., 1984), 29.

119. Lueger stated: "You know, Mariannscherl, I do like beautiful things, but the Secession, good grief! Some concept! You have to admit!" (Beskiba, 22). *"Weisst Mariannscherl, was schön is, g'fallt mir schon, aber die Sezession — u jegerl! — Das is do a a Verständnis, musst zugeben."*

120. *Protokolle* (March 20, 2901), 1520. The parliamentary inquiry in question asserted that Klimt's painting "would deeply injure the . . . public through crudity of conception and deficiency in aesthetics."

121. "Theater, Kunst und Literatur. Moderne Kunst?" *ÖFZ* (July 27, 1902), 3.

122. Puritanical and pietistic, the *ÖFZ* held up earlier times as golden ages. "Pursuit of pleasure is the sign, but also the great cancer of our time"; "Work, not pleasure, is the first duty in life"; "Back to the simplicity and the purity of morals of our fathers!" were characteristic, if unintentionally ironic, slogans. "'Lasset uns geniessen,'" *ÖFZ* (June 7, 1903), 2.

123. Martyrs were favorite subject material. The virtues of Elizabeth of France, sister of Louis XVI, guillotined in 1794, were commended to a women's auxiliary in Friedland, Bohemia. "Christlicher Frauenhilfsverein in Friedland (Böhmen)," *ÖFZ* (June 28, 1903), 5.

124. See, for example, Luise von Léon-Hunoltstein, "Über die Erziehung in höheren Ständen," *ÖFZ* (January 18, 1903), 2, 3. This contributor, who concentrated on the shortcomings of the upper classes, was refuted by another aristocrat who defended educators of the Herz-Jesu-Ordensfrauen. Proper religious education counted for more than the garden secular variety. See "Zur Abwehr," *ÖFZ* (March 1, 1903), 6; Luise Léon-Hunoltstein, "Einige Gedanken über das zwanzigste Jahrhundert" (September 14, 1902), 2, 3; (September 28, 1902), 1, 2; (October 12, 1902), 2; (November 23, 1902), 2.

125. "Etwas Heiteres," *ÖFZ* (October 4, 1903), 8.

126. "Wie es deutschen Mädchen in jüdischen Diensten geht,"*ÖFZ* (March 29, 1903), 3. This theme reappeared in *Der Stürmer.*

127. "Ortsgruppe Margareten," *ÖFZ* (March 27, 1904), 7.

128. "Ortsgruppe Brigittenau," *ÖFZ* (May 19, 1904), 5.

129. "Allerlei. Über Japan und seine Kultur," *ÖFZ* (June 19, 1904), 9, 10.

130. "Die Weihnachts-Festfeier des christlichen Wiener Frauen-Bundes in der Volkshalle," *ÖFZ* (December 27, 1903), 14.

131. Beskiba, 31.

132. "Vereins-Rubrik. Christlicher Wiener Frauen-Bund. Ausserordentliche Generalversammlung," *ÖFZ* (April 29, 1906), 4.

133. "Vereins-Rubrik. Christlicher Wiener Frauen-Bund, Zentrale des Christlichen Wiener Frauen-Bundes," *ÖFZ* (May 13, 1906), 4.

134. "Vereins-Rubrik. Christlicher Wiener Frauen-Bund. Ausserordentliche Generalversammlung," *ÖFZ* (April 29, 1906), 4.

135. "Oeffentliche Danksagung," *ÖFZ* (October 28, 1906), 1.

Chapter 7. Lueger and the "Gelatin Intelligentsia"

1. Geehr, *"I Decide Who Is a Jew!",* 36.

2. Ibid.

3. Ibid.

4. Ibid., 44.

5. Lueger and other leading Christian Socials sometimes chose to oppose Pan-Germans and Socialists on the grounds that they threatened Catholicism. See *Landtag* (December 22, 1904), 40.

6. Boyer, "Karl Lueger and the Viennese Jews," 133.

7. *Landtag* (December 9, 1890), 767.

8. *Amtsblatt*, 274.

9. In this, he probably reflected the influence of Richard von Kralik who for many years was an outspoken advocate of this project. As early as 1904, Lueger lent Kralik's undertaking at least tacit support. It was described to "all circles of Viennese society on May 2, 1904," in the Rathaus by the architects Karl Troll and Franz Biberhofer. The following month, Lueger read an invitation to the municipal council to visit an exhibit on the project in the Künstlerhaus on the Karlsplatz. In 1934 Lueger and Kralik's names were again linked to the Walhalla as part of a "heritage for the future." See *Amtsblatt*, no. 46 (June 7, 1904), 1116; Richard von Kralik, "Ein Traum vom künftigen Wiener Stadtbild," in *Schönere Zukunft*, no. 48 (August 26, 1934), 1265, 1266. Shortly before his death, Lueger evidently presided over a committee meeting that was to plan the details of the cornerstone laying for the Walhalla on August 18, 1910, Franz Joseph's eightieth birthday. Rudolf Kuppe, *Karl Lueger und seine Zeit*, 424. Neither I nor Vienna municipal archive officials could locate the official records of the meeting to which Kuppe refers. Kralik traced the origins of the Hall of Fame idea to a plan from 1883. Kralik believed the hall would complete "the building of our city." Richard Kralik and Hans Schlitter, *Wien. Geschichte der Kaiserstadt und ihrer Kultur* (Vienna, 1912), 744.

10. Although Kralik and Lueger's structure did not go beyond the planning stage, one of Kralik's disciples, Hans Eibl, designed a "Temple of Mankind," for which massive stained glass windows were actually created. See Richard S. Geehr, "Hans Eibl: A Religious Nature in a Psychopolitical Idiom," *Austrian History Year Book* (1981–82), 156–66.

11. Letter of Simon Aichner to Lueger (October 24, 1909), *IN* 40937.

12. *IN* 35104. This manuscript is incomplete and unpublished.

13. Bertha Zuckerkandl described Nigerl as "the reactionary, crabbed, spiteful, false-*gemütlich* underhanded Viennese." As a professional Viennese, Lueger rejected all aspersions on his native city and its inhabitants. When Rudolf Rigl, a journalist on the staff of the *Deutsche Zeitung*, complained about *Phäaken*, an iconoclastic novel castigating the venality of the Viennese, by Karl Conte Scapinelli, Lueger urged its boycott and referred to it with contempt. *Amtsblatt*, no. 83 (October 15, 1907), 2337, 2338. Bertha Zuckerkandl, *Österreich intim. Erinnerungen* (Vienna, Munich, 1981), 40. On at least one occasion he went further. "In 1906 Hermann Bahr's *Wien* was seized because Mayor Lueger found it unflattering." Johnston, 49, 50.

14. Bloch, 235.

15. Their property was in any case protected from such an eventuality by a building code that prohibited municipal housing on such lands. While Lueger's successors Neumayer and Weiskirchner began the construction of municipal housing on a larger scale than he had done, their efforts were dwarfed by the building projects of Karl Seitz during the 1920s and 1930s. Until the major revision of the building code in 1930, Seitz's projects were illegal, having been undertaken without proper authorization. His actions had been motivated by necessity and grew out of early post-World War I socioeconomic conditions. See Felix Czeike, *Wirtschafts- und Sozialpolitik der Gemeinde Wien 1919–1934*, 2 vols. (Vienna, 1958, 1959).

16. Kielmansegg, 365.

17. Ibid., 366. For Lueger's version of the Fogerty affair, see Geehr, "*I Decide Who Is a Jew!*", 174–84.

18. Ibid., 164; see also Lueger's motion during the meeting of the "Vereinigte Linke" (September 16, 1881), 164, 165. For the *Gürtelbahn* episode, see Brown, 263–65.

19. See, for example, Bloch, 235; Richard Charmatz, "Lueger, Karl," in Anton Bettelheim, ed., *Biographisches Jahrbuch und Deutscher Nekrolog* (Berlin, 1913), 123.

20. "Streiflichter. Schriftsteller Bartsch über Dr. Lueger," *Reichspost* (August 28, 1909), 2.

21. *Amtsblatt*, no. 100 (December 13, 1907), 2995.

22. Kielmansegg, 391.

23. *Amtsblatt*, no. 73 (September 12, 1899), 2157.

24. Ibid. Two years later in a municipal council session Josef Porzer, who was of Jewish descent, urged that a second steeple be added to St. Stephen's for "beautification." Bielohlawek then proposed that the Judengasse "a pesthole," be "regulated," but he doubted that this would happen, because "all of Israel would rise so that this worthy place, named *Judengasse*, would not be damaged." *Amtsblatt*, no. 7 (January 22, 1901), 145, 146. A court decision in 1899 had decreed that municipal funds were not to be spent "for projects which persons of all confessions could not enjoy or use." This meant that city moneys could not be spent on the maintenance of St. Stephen's or on churches "built where the old city-walls had once been." After an audience with Leo XIII, Lueger decided to oppose the court's verdict. He and his chief lieutenants stirred popular support through agitation. Though the decision of the court remained unchanged, "its subsequent review of individual appropriations was gratifyingly discreet" (Jenks, *Vienna and the Young Hitler*, 64). Referring to the outcome of the church maintenance issue, Friedrich Funder commented that no court decision is viable in the long run unless it has popular support. Lueger called the court decision an "assault on the autonomy of the imperial capital." Funder, *Vom Gestern ins Heute*, 236, 237.

25. See, for example, *Amtsblatt*, no. 8 (January 27, 1903), 131; no. 102 (December 20, 1904), 2504; no. 1 (January 1, 1909), 18. On the "German-Austrian Writers' Association," see Geehr, *Adam Müller-Guttenbrunn and the Aryan Theater of Vienna*, 70–72.

26. *Protokolle* (January 27, 1899), 2276. In addition, the Christian Socials criticized "the shamelessness of Jewry" for "usurping" the place of the implicitly Catholic Austrian intelligentsia in the learned professions. For a typical polemic, see "Die Wiedererlangung des aberkannten Doktorrates," *Reichspost* (July 8, 1904), 4, 5.

27. See *Landtag* (July 24, 1902), 646, 647; (September 22, 1903), 314, 315.

28. *Landtag* (October 7, 1904), 136, 137; (November 17, 1905), 353.

29. *Amtsblatt*, no. 35 (May 2, 1902), 800.

30. *Amtsblatt*, no. 91 (November 11, 1904), 2140–42.

31. Punning on the word *Pinkel*, meaning "dandy," and *pinkeln*, meaning "to piddle," Schuhmeier stated: "to say that the tickets should belong only to Christian children is more than absurd, because everyone knows that you want to exclude the little Jew-boy, the little dandy (loud peals of laughter) . . . but you can entertain old Jews at banquets" (ibid., 2141).

32. *Amtsblatt*, no. 101 (December 18, 1908), 3004.

33. *Amtsblatt*, no. 15 (February 20, 1906), 373; no. 46 (June 8, 1906), 1130; no. 75 (September 18, 1906), 1939.

34. Ibid.

35. *Amtsblatt*, no. 55 (July 9, 1901), 1329.

36. See Geehr, *Adam Müller-Guttenbrunn and the Aryan Theater of Vienna*, 113, 114; Adam Müller-Guttenbrunn, *Erinnerungen eines Theaterdirektors* (Leipzig, 1924), 100, 101.

37. "Theater, Kunst und Literatur. Die Verleihung des Bauernfeld-Preises an Artur Schnitzler," *Deutsches Volksblatt* (March 19, 1903), 9.

38. Ibid.

39. Hans Arnold Schwer's paper criticized Ibsen at the time of his death for not having bettered the world, for having "made it more discontented." Together "with Nietzsche and Tolstoy, he helped to revalue all standards. . . . His ideas spoiled many men, they appear to have left him undisturbed. He has nothing to say to us Christians; we quietly go the way Christ and the Church point." r., "Feuilleton. Henrik Ibsen," *Mödlinger Bezirksnachrichten* (June 24, 1906), 1, 2.

40. See Geehr, *Adam Müller-Guttenbrunn and the Aryan Theater of Vienna*, 167–70 and the sources quoted therein.

41. After his first parliamentary campaign in 1885, Lueger drafted a speech that contains some famous lines delivered by Ottokar von Horneck in Franz Grillparzer's play *König Ottokar's Glück und Ende*. Lueger wrote that the lines confirmed the description that Grillparzer sketched of his countrymen's character: "It is quite possible that there are people in Saxony and on the Rhine who read more; but, what is needed and pleases God, are a clear and forward look, an open and just mind. In this way the Austrian is anyone's equal; he thinks his thoughts and lets the others talk" (Geehr, *"I Decide Who Is a Jew!"*, 254).

42. Geehr, *Adam Müller-Guttenbrunn and the Aryan Theater of Vienna*, 149.

43. Ibid., 148. Robert Kann has called attention to the class conflicts between Emperor Frederick III, burgher patricians, and "primarily wealthy immigrant merchants," led by Konrad Vorlauf and Wolfgang Holzer, respectively. Both mayors were executed, and "in both cases Emperor Frederick III violated the rights of the burghers." Sigmund Mayer compared Holzer to Lueger, and also to John Wilkes, the late-eighteenth-century mayor of London. Kann, *A History of the Habsburg Empire 1526–1918*, 14; Sigmund Mayer, *Ein jüdischer Kaufmann*, 258.

44. Geehr, *Adam Müller-Guttenbrunn and the Aryan Theater of Vienna*, 148.

45. O. 1., "Stadttheater," *Arbeiter Zeitung* (October 4, 1899), 6.

46. O. 1., "Stadttheater," *Arbeiter Zeitung* (October 6, 1900).

47. The former tendency was represented by Richard von Kralik, the latter by Anton Baumann.

48. Geehr, *Adam Müller-Guttenbrunn and the Aryan Theater of Vienna*, 238, 239.

49. IN 75300. His addressee was Max von Millenkovich-Morold, who, as Burgtheater director during World War I, tried to introduce a *numerus clausus* in the hiring of Jewish actors.

50. r., "Feuilleton. Henrik Ibsen," *Mödlinger Bezirksnachrichten* (June 24, 1906), 1, 2.

51. Geehr, *Adam Müller-Guttenbrunn and the Aryan Theater of Vienna*, 400–409.

52. "Das Festbankett des Jubiläums-Stadttheaters," *Volksblatt* (December 16, 1898), 8, 9.

53. Lueger praised Johann Strauss as one whose name "will remain inseparable with the music life of our city." Letter of Lueger to Adele Strauss (June 3, 1899), IN 129126.

54. Letter of Hansi Niese to Lueger (June 30, 1904), IN 40917. Lueger indicated that she should be thanked for the letter but not be promised anything.

55. Letter of Peter Rosegger to Lueger (June 24, 1907), IN 31698. Lueger replied: "It is possible that I may go to the right, and you may go left, but at least we shall both arrive at the summit of the mountain together."

56. Letter of Peter Rosegger to Lueger (June 17, 1909), IN 40920.

57. *Amtsblatt*, no. 73 (September 11, 1906), 1881, 1882.

58. Kuppe, *Karl Lueger und seine Zeit*, 13.

59. The Männergesangsverein Archiv in Vienna possesses some forty congratulatory documents addressed to the *Verein* bearing Lueger's signature or a facsimile. For information on municipal subventions and religious music groups, see *Amtsblatt*, no. 79 (October 2, 1906), 2037–40; no. 77 (September 25, 1908), 2257–62. During the latter council session, anti-Semitism again became an issue.

60. Geehr, *"I Decide Who Is a Jew!"*, 315. The German anti-Semite Otto Böckel said much the same thing in his folksong collection. There is an element of antimodernity here — fear of loss, sense of declining values, distrust of the scientific. See Levy, *The Downfall of the Anti-Semitic Political Parties in Imperial Germany*, 43–47.

61. *Amtsblatt*, no. 4 (January 13, 1905), 96, 97.

62. Beskiba indicates that Lueger was blind in his left eye as early as 1906 (p. 42). Despite his impaired vision, Lueger evidently could read as late as the spring of 1908. Robert Ehrhart, *Im Dienste des alten Österreich* (Vienna, 1958), 153. Like so many other things about him, the "blindness" that made it "necessary" for interpellations, proposals, and the like to be read for him in council sessions, and papers read to him privately, may have been in part a pose.

63. Nearly forty years after Lueger's death, Rudolf Bibl, Lueger's one-time *Präsidialsekretär*, recalled an awkward incident when he had preceded the mayor into a carriage instead of following him. "So," said the mayor, "now you are the mayor and I am Dr. Bibl; Pumera is to blame for that." Lueger also insisted that his instructions to the coachman be conveyed through Pumera. Letter of Rudolf Bibl to Robert M. Prosl (June 12, 1949), *IN* 205.688. Anton Pumera was Lueger's servant bodyguard.

64. Geehr, *"I Decide Who Is a Jew!"*, 313.

65. "Eine antiungarische Demonstration Dr. Luegers bei der Haydn-Feier in Eisenstadt," *Neue Freie Presse* (May 28, 1909), 3.

66. The title of its front-page report, "The Iron Man in Eisenstadt" ("Der Eiserne Mann in Eisenstadt"), reflects the tenor of the article. *Reichspost* (May 28, 1909).

67. "Tagesneuigkeiten. Haydn, Lueger und ein paar Konflikte," *Arbeiter-Zeitung* (May 28, 1909), 4.

68. *Neue Freie Presse* (May 28, 1909), 3, 4.

69. *Amtsblatt*, no. 99 (December 10, 1907), 2921. Lueger may have been referring to a song "Nur in Wien" by Adolf Glinger, with couplets by Waldemar.

70. *Die Fackel* (Anfang October 1902), 26.

71. *Amtsblatt*, No. 6 (January 21, 1902), 136.

72. Beskiba, 22. Beskiba's understanding of painting may also be questionable if two of her indifferently modeled portraits of Lueger are an indication. See her 1895 portrait of Lueger in Geehr, *"I Decide Who Is a Jew!"* and that of Lueger as mayor in Soukup, *Lueger und sein Wien*.

73. *Amtsblatt*, no. 6 (January 21, 1902), 135. Lueger's quoted words were received with applause. Kornke's anti-Secessionistic polemic provides insights into the cultural ethos of some Christian Socials. See *ibid.*, 134–36. See also no. 97 (December 5, 1902), 2187–97; "Der Bau des städtischen Museums," *Neues Wiener Abendblatt* (November 28, 1902), 4; "Wiener Angelegenheiten," *Neues Wiener Tagblatt* (November 30, 1902), 4, 5.

74. Josef Engelhart, *Ein Wiener Maler erzählt. Mein Leben und meine Modelle* (Vienna, 1943), 207.

75. *Amtsblatt*, no. 3 (January 10, 1908), 82. On Lueger and Waldmüller, see Engelhart, 208–10.

76. *Landtag* (June 21, 1901), 31, 32. While the original proposal allowed for the purchase of Secessionist art works, selection was to be entrusted to a committee from the Christian Social controlled Landtag.

77. Almost no Jews "in the arts" were artists. Of the eleven percent of Viennese Jews "engaged in the professions" between 1870 and 1910, those engaged in the arts, actors, entertainers, etc., ranked last after doctors, lawyers, teachers, engineers, and journalists. Rozenblit, 49.

78. *Landtag* (November 14, 1905), 308, 309.

79. *Amtsblatt*, no. 97 (December 5, 1902), 2187-97; no. 99 (December 12, 1902), 2250-51. On Hoffmann, see Sekler. Valuable insights into the cultural political implications of the Secessionist movement are provided by Schorske, 208-78. Early in Lueger's mayoralty, Josef Bündsdorf, a municipal councillor and architect, tried to articulate a new theoretical basis for subsequent architectural development.

> Our artists are trained to compete, so that every single church will be awarded competitively. That is our duty, for we have very many artists who, by their work on many contemporary modern secular buildings, have consequently broken completely with the old. Renewed artistic impulses will be created in Vienna by new church construction which is based on old artistic traditions that must be strictly adhered to, even though these traditions are executed according to modern principles. Thereby we will have created a monument to ourselves. (*Amtsblatt*, no. 11 [February 7, 1899], 326)

Bündsdorf's ideas anticipate those of Hans Eibl.

80. *Amtsblatt*, no. 97 (December 5, 1902), 2196.

81. *Landtag* (January 7, 1902), 113.

82. Ibid.

83. *Amtsblatt*, no. 17 (February 27, 1900), Beilage, next to last unnumbered page.

84. *Amtsblatt*, no. 13 (February 13, 1903), 246. Lueger also was something of an auto enthusiast and was evidently fond of posing in cars. Karl Kraus once reported the mayor's words to "the participants of the automobile competition" as follows: "Princes, counts, barons, gentlemen with and without vons! You have . . . a powerful promoter in the governor of Lower Austria. As a count, his excellency is naturally an automobilist and he even drives to [the] court festivities [in] an *Automoperl*. The only one who is offended . . . is the prefect of police, my dear friend, whom you can see here, too. He is chased from one fright to another. For two days, he was afraid because of anarchists, and now he's afraid of automobilists." "Standesperson," *Die Fackel* (July 5, 1906), 24.

85. For Schneider's views on the superiority of Austrian mechanics, see *Landtag* (July 11, 1902), 383-85.

86. *Landtag* (October 1, 1909), 417; (October 19, 1909), 758. The Christian Social publication *Wiener Kinder* featured articles on technology and on great historical personalities, thus suggesting one of the ways in which the ruling party tried to impress its values on Vienna's youth.

87. Schorske, 269. Klimt would probably have agreed with Viktor Schklovsky, at least in principle, that "Art is always independent of life, its colors never reflect the flags that hang over the city."

88. Ibid., 304 n.

89. *Amtsblatt*, no. 99 (December 10, 1909), 2924.

90. Millenkovich-Morold, 227.

91. *Amtsblatt*, no. 58 (July 19, 1907), 1629.

92. *Protokolle* (May 6, 1898), 1177.

93. During the same session, Bielohlawek suggested that books proliferated because one Jew copied from another. Ibid.

94. To general amusement among the parliamentarians he once said that "some will perhaps smile now because I have a book in my hand," and proceeded to quote Goethe. *Protokolle* (July 11, 1907), 1139.

95. One Christian Social, Karl Fissthaler, referred to the *Postsparkasse* as "a nailed shoe sole." *Landtag* (January 14, 1908), 1188.

96. Ibid., 1189.

97. *Landtag* (November 12, 1903), 1254.

98. Wilfried Posch, "Der Streit um Alt und Neu: Adolf Loos," in Kristian Sotriffer, ed., *Das Grössere Österreich, Geistiges und Soziales Leben von 1880 bis zur Gegenwart* (Vienna, 1982), 183.

99. Ibid.

100. Quoted in Geehr, *"I Decide Who Is a Jew!",* 11. This was also said about Joseph Chamberlain. See John Vincent, review of *Joseph Chamberlain* by Enoch Powell, *Times Literary Supplement* (March 24, 1978), 343.

101. *Amtsblatt*, no. 51 (June 25, 1909), 1612. He was also proud of some architecturally unattractive structures, such as the Marienbrücke, for which he took credit. When Emperor William II once asked "how such an atrocity could [have been] constructed," Lueger is reported to have responded with "a very impolite answer." Robert A. Kann and Peter Leisching, eds., *Ein Leben für Kunst und Volksbildung. Eduard Leisching 1858–1938. Erinnerungen* (Vienna, 1978), 172.

102. *Amtsblatt*, no. 25 (March 27, 1906), 619.

103. "Wien im Blumenschmucke," *Reichspost* (April 8, 1909), 8.

104. Millenkovich-Morold, 227.

105. Bloch, 234. Bloch cited this anecdote not only as evidence of Lueger's vulgarity and banality, but also to indicate the occasionally elliptical quality of his anti-Semitism: "There are many Jews among the medical profession; the Jews are therefore hit *par ricochet*" (234, 235).

106. Millenkovich-Morold, 228. The allegedly extemporaneous character of all Lueger's speeches may have been exaggerated. See Funder, *Vom Gestern ins Heute*, 236.

107. *Amtsblatt*, no. 5 (January 18, 1910), 95.

108. See, for example, *Amtsblatt*, no. 6 (January 21, 1898), 254. Viktor Adler referred to the Christian Socials as the "Austrian Boxers." "Der Grazer Parteitag," *Die Fackel* (Anfang September 1900), 4.

109. Lueger expressed confidence that once in Vienna, Bohemians would "consider themselves Viennese and Germans after a short time, and their children no longer understand Bohemian; they speak Viennese, as we all do, and Viennese is a very good German language." *Landtag* (January 28, 1898), 317. In this way, Lueger revealed confidence in the Germanizing capabilities of Viennese cultural institutions, and in the assimilability of the Bohemians—particularly if they were Christian Social supporters.

110. The Liberal municipal councillor Alfred Mittler recalled that Lueger's first candidacy for parliament had been announced as "Karel Luegera" in Czech-speaking districts in 1885. *Amtsblatt*, no. 102 (December 22, 1908), 3061. A relatively early acknowledgment of Lueger's importance to the anti-Liberal Czech voting community of Vienna was provided in October 1889 when representatives of the Bohemian Electoral Committee asked Lueger to support two of their candidates to district committee elections in the ninth district. The Bohemians added that Lueger needed them as much as they needed him. They cited an article in *Das Vaterland*, which asserted that the United Christians and anti-Semites could never win in the second district unless they pursued a politics of reconciliation with the Czechs and Slavs, instead of emphasizing exclusive German nationalism. Letter of Bohemian Electoral Committee to Lueger (October 21, 1889), *IN* 41534.

111. Letter of Silesians and Moravians to Lueger (March 1908), *IN* 41550.

112. Ibid.

113. *Amtsblatt*, no. 80 (October 4, 1904), 1863, 1864.

114. *Protokolle* (February 21, 1901), 499.

115. *Landtag* (October 8, 1909), 490, 491.

116. *Amtsblatt,* no. 76 (September 21, 1909), 2198.

117. *Landtag* (June 25, 1901), 54.

118. *Amtsblatt,* no. 14 (February 16, 1909), 515, 516.

119. C. E. Williams, *The Broken Eagle* (London, 1974), 160.

120. *Protokolle* (October 24, 1899), 166.

121. See, for example, *Landtag* (February 13, 1896), 908, 909; *Protokolle* (October 2, 1905), 31777–84.

122. See, for example, *Bericht der (Gemeinderat) Sitzung vom 30/11 1875,* 1239. For details of development in Viennese public education, see Seliger and Ucakar, I: 484–89; II: 832–41.

123. Letter of Josef Dreisiebner to Lueger (May 14, 1885), *IN* 41560.

124. *Landtag* (February 12, 1897), 378.

125. Mayor Prix delivered a swan song of sorts for educational liberalism during his centennial commemoration of the death of Emperor Joseph II. See *Protokoll der öffentlichen Sitzung des Gemeinderathes der k.k. Reichshaupt- und Residenzstadt Wien, vom 20. Februar 1890,* 121, 122.

126. Seliger and Ucakar, I: 486. For further information on the school laws, see Gertrude Langer-Ostrawsky, "Wiener Schulwesen um 1900" and the sources quoted therein, in Ehalt et al., eds., 91–95.

127. This amendment was a continuing source of friction during Lueger's mayoralty. His opponents once pointed out in an interpellation that Vice-Mayor Josef Porzer, who was of Jewish descent, had proven his capability, and thus that of Jews "for all offices in an unambiguous way." Therefore, Lueger was requested to withdraw the advertisement for a head teacher's post which would have precluded a Jew from occupying it. The then Catholic majority of students was held to be an inadequate basis for excluding a Jew, for according to the law, the majority faith of the students for the past five years should be the determining factor. Lueger replied that he was not obliged to answer the interpellation, because "this whole thing has nothing at all to do with the Christian Social municipal council majority" and that he would not suspend the decision of the district school council to require a Catholic to occupy the post. *Amtsblatt,* no. 34 (April 27, 1906), 830, 381.

128. *Landtag* (October 22, 1903), 738.

129. Otto Glöckel, *Selbstbiographie* (Zurich, 1939), 47.

130. Kaspar Friedrich Schwarz, "Dr. Porzer und der Katholische Schulverein," *Reichspost* (May 29, 1914), 4. For information on the clerical effect on public school curriculum, see Oskar Achs, "Die Schulreform in der Ersten Republik (1918–1927)," in *Österreich in Geschichte und Literatur,* 13 Jg. (1969), Heft 5; A. Täubler, *Die Schule in Pfaffenklauen. Eine Kritik der niederösterr. Schulverderbungsgesetze mit Reden des Abg. Seitz* (Vienna, 1904); Karl Seitz, *Volksschule oder Pfaffenschule? Rede des Reichsraths-Abgeordneten Karl Seitz* (Vienna, 1902); and Seliger and Ucakar, II: 382 ff., and the sources quoted therein.

131. Karl Seitz, Aus den Erzählungen Seitz über seine Kindheit und Lebenserinnerungen, Nachlass Karl Seitz, Schachtel 77, Archiv der Stadt Wien.

132. Ibid., 5.

133. Quoted in Glöckel, 47.

134. *Landtag* (March 28, 1892), 596.

135. After more than a decade of Christian Social repression toward teachers belonging to other parties, Schuhmeier ironically recalled some of Lueger's earlier promises to uphold teacher freedom. See *Amtsblatt,* no. 102 (December 22, 1908), 3048.

136. See, for example, the speech of Julius Offner in *Landtag* (July 5, 1901), 228. Lue-

ger was sensitive about charges that Jews were being discriminated against in the teaching profession and responded sharply to the interpellation of one teacher, Oswald Hohensinner, that he should have raised this issue during a municipal council meeting. It is difficult to escape the impression that Lueger resented having such allegations being made part of the public record. *Amtsblatt*, no. 97 (December 2, 1904), 2299, 2300.

137. "Persönliche Erinnerungen an Dr. Lueger von Dr. Oskar Hein," *Neue Freie Presse* (September 19, 1926), 4. For information on temporary assistant teachers, see Boyer, *Political Radicalism in Late Imperial Vienna*, 120. Hitler himself is said to have used the Luegerian pronouncement when Joseph "Goebbels stood up at a large party in 1937 and announced that he and his wife could no longer remain on the premises because someone with 'non-Aryan' blood was present. It was [Leni] Riefenstahl who, he charged, was only three-fourths Aryan. . . . Hitler was so enamored of Riefenstahl that he gave her 'an official Aryan certificate' and decreed, 'It is I who will decide who is a Jew and who is not.'" Frank Deford, "The Ghost of Berlin," *Sports Illustrated* (August 4, 1986), 56.

138. *Amtsblatt*, no. 84 (October 18, 1901), 1963.

139. Seliger and Ucakar, II: 832; *Amtsblatt*, no. 17 (February 28, 1899), 509. When asked why teachers with 12, 13, 14, 15, even 16, 17, and 18 years of service were passed over for promotion, Lueger replied that "other, worthier people applied for the same position" (ibid.). He added: "The few infractions that have actually been presented here are really not worth talking about. I can only say that criticizing is easy, but work itself is hard!" (ibid., 510).

140. Ibid., 509.

141. *Landtag* (July 11, 1901), 364; (October 22, 1903), 739.

142. Here, Lueger may have been overstating Christian Social impartiality toward tradesmen. When Alois Liechtenstein was once asked why he wore such an ill-fitting coat, he replied that his tailor was a Christian Social and exerted considerable influence in his neighborhood. Kazimierez Chłedowski, *Pamiętniki*, 2 vols. (Wrocław, 1951), II: 169.

143. *Landtag* (January 20, 1898), 194. Gessmann, who had become convinced "that only the party that had the priests and teachers on its side could win political elections," systematically gathered information on the political views of politicians and teachers in the Lower Austrian communities. As the responsible official, Gessmann saw to it that only loyal Christian Social teachers were promoted. Spitzer, 188.

144. *Landtag*, 194.

145. Ibid., 185.

146. Ibid., 195.

147. Ibid., 196. Gessmann was referring to the Fickert case. See *Landtag* (June 5, 1899), 1528; *Amtsblatt*, no. 17 (February 28, 1899), 511. Auguste Fickert was a social reformer and founder, together with Rosa Mayreder and Marie Lang, of the periodical *Dokumente der Frauen*. She became a favorite target of Christian Social abuse. See Spitzer, 124–26.

148. Glöckel, 45.

149. *Amtsblatt*, no. 79 (October 2, 1900), 1811.

150. Ibid.

151. *Landtag* (July 11, 1901), 364. One of the suicides was the Social Democrat Karl Payerl. He despaired after seeing deserving colleagues passed over and Christian Socials with fewer years of service promoted instead. Spitzer, 186.

152. Rudolf Hawel, unpublished autobiography, *Aus meinem Leben, IN* 57983, 15; written reprimand to Rudolf Hawel from the Vienna District School Council (November 10, 1899), *IN* 56583.

153. Geehr, *Adam Müller-Guttenbrunn and the Aryan Theater of Vienna*, 198–202.

154. Hawel relates that the Liberal censor was persuaded to clear the play in its entirety only after papers reported that a scene that the censor had cut had actually taken place at a recent Christian Social meeting. Before these developments Heinrich Friedjung had commented favorably on the play's realism. Hawel, *Aus meinom Leben,* 17, 18.

155. C. S., "Theater, Kunst und Musik. 'Die Politiker,'" *Reichspost* (January 16, 1904), 12. For the "Lehrerstimme," see Glöckel, 42.

156. "Wien, 16. Januar.," *Neue Freie Presse* (January 17, 1904), 1.

157. O. 1., "Theater," *Arbeiter Zeitung* (January 15, 1904), 8.

158. Hawel also satirized the landlord class with the symbolical figure of Schmetterer, whose name means both "brayer" and "smasher." The stage description calls for a "portly, powerful man, large rings on his fingers, golden watch chain, pretentious appearance," thus recalling Karl Kraus's remark about Lueger's need for "fat sleek-headed men," like Josef Strohbach. Hawel, *Die Politiker* (Vienna and Leipzig, 1904), 14.

159. Fearing, perhaps, punitive action by the Christian Socials, one of Lueger's followers, a retired school official, protested his continuing loyalty to the mayor and party leader, apparently because of the oppositional school politics of his son. In the play, the Luegeresque character admonishes one of his supporters because of the rebellious behavior of his teacher son: "In politics no difference is made. He is the son — you are the father! You share a little guilt!" Art holds up the mirror to life. Letter of E. Filek von Wittinghausen to Lueger (July 15, 1905), *IN* 31674; Hawel, *Die Politiker,* 123.

160. Lueger himself was scrupulous about not favoring his own relatives or their friends with political appointments. He once failed to reply to a letter from a cousin requesting support for the appointment of a friend to a school directorship. Yet Liberals complained that nepotism was rampant among the Christian Socials, citing the promotion of Josef Gregorig's teacher son over more deserving colleagues, on one occasion. Letter of Jakob Luttenfeldner to Lueger (December 19, 1908), *IN* 40902; *Landtag* (February 27, 1899), 219.

161. Hawel, *Die Politker,* 29.

162. While the Christian Social politician Leopold Tomola asserted in 1902 during a municipal council session that the average number of students per teacher was forty-two, Schuhmeier interjected that there were 130 per teacher in some classes, presumably in workers' districts. *Amtsblatt,* no. 74 (September 16, 1902), 1694. Tomola performed the important function of appointing school directors.

163. *Amtsblatt,* no. 100 (December 14, 1900), 2475.

164. Ibid., 2474.

165. Mack, 66. According to Reinhold Hanisch, one of Hitler's closest associates during the Vienna years, young Adolf "talked a great deal about [the *Knabenhorte*] and about it being good for youth to be politically trained." Hanisch, 242. Bradley Smith has evaluated Hanisch's account and accepted it as substantially correct. See Smith, 164, 165. The inspiration for the militaristic *Knaben-* and *Mädchenhorte* may have been provided by the schools for officers' children that existed at least as early as the mid-eighteenth century. See Alfons Danzer, *Unter den Fahnen* (Vienna, 1889), 442ff.

166. Kriegsarchiv Präsidialakt 1913, no. 5624, k.k. Ministerium für Landesverteidigung.

167. Ibid.

168. Ibid.

169. *Amtsblatt,* no. 42 (May 25, 1909), 1285.

170. Ibid.

171. *Amtsblatt,* no. 36 (May 5, 1908), 1110.

172. As late as July 1901, Lueger mocked Viktor Adler for leading the true party of the plutocrats: "In the inner city on the occasion of the Reichsrat election for the fifth curia,

all Jews without exception, rich or poor, decided for the Social Democrats. . . . Naturally, the *Hofräte* and excellencies voted for the republican Ellenbogen. . . . Where are the plutocratic circles who go with us, my dear Dr. Adler?" In less than a year Lueger was to have his answer when Baron Albert Rothschild granted the municipality a right-of-way for the construction of the new reservoir pipe line. *Landtag* (July 12, 1901), 401.

173. Wandruszka and Urbanitsch, eds., IV: 49.

174. *Amtsblatt*, no. 78 (September 30, 1898), 2484.

175. "Gemeindezeitung — Zur Trennung der Schulkinder nach den Confessionen," *Reichspost* (October 5, 1898), 3.

176. Gessmann subsequently claimed that the Christian Socials wanted separate classes for pedagogic, rather than religious, reasons, because Jewish children could not write or perform manual labor on certain days. He added that the Christian Socials were not against the Jewish religion, but against the Jews who scorned Christianity and Catholicism. "Vollversammlung des Vereines 'Christliche Familie,'" *Deutsche Zeitung* (December 9, 1898), 2.

177. *Landtag* (October 14, 1904), 193.

178. Ibid., 204.

179. *Amtsblatt*, no. 13 (February 13, 1906), 313.

180. *Amtsblatt*, no. 99 (December 10, 1907), 2921, 2922. Lueger practiced delaying tactics on raising teachers' salaries. See *Amtsblatt*, no. 92 (November 16, 1909), 2690; no. 5 (January 18, 1910), 93, 94.

181. Franz Stauracz, *Darwinismus und Schule* (Vienna, 1897), 2.

> Words are thundering
> From lecterns everywhere:
> Mr. Darwin, there's no need to worry,
> We are staunchly fighting your battle!
> Even if many a professor is deserting you,
> We teachers remain steadfast.
> No matter whether your doctrine is in doubt,
> We won't abandon the monkey.
> Morning and evening our battle cry will be:
> Long live the ape theory!

This is parodistically based on "Die Wacht am Rhein."

182. Franz Stauracz, *Darwinistische "Haeckel"-eien — "Voraussetzungslose" Wissenschaft!* (Vienna, 1902), 79, 80.

183. "Franz Stauracz[†]," *Reichspost* (July 29, 1918), 5.

184. Franz Stauracz, *Dr. Luegers Leben und Wirken* (Klagenfurt, n.d.).

185. See, for example, Franz Stauracz, *Der Verein "Freie Schule," seine Protektoren und seine Ziele.* Separatabdruck aus dem "Korrespondenz-Blatt für den kathol. Klerus Österreichs," 1905.

186. Glaser, 303. See also Glöckel, 43, 44.

187. During a municipal council debate, a Liberal Marwalt, Ritter von Dorn, asserted that the "Freie Schule" did not aim to exclude religious education entirely, but to halt "coercive measures" to enforce religious training in Vienna's schools. *Amtsblatt*, no. 92 (November 16, 1906), 2433. For Seitz's criticism of abuses of religious teaching and educational theory, see *Landtag* (October 25, 1904), 317–30.

188. See, for example, *Landtag* (October 14, 1909), 631. On apprentice abuse by masters, see *Landtag* (January 26, 1910), 1103.

189. *Amtsblatt*, no. 73 (September 11, 1908), 2092, 2093; no. 16 (February 23, 1909), 588; no. 45 (June 4, 1909), 1376.

190. *Protokolle* (December 21, 1906), 41180.

191. *Amtsblatt*, no. 45 (June 4, 1909), 1376.

192. Jordan had been pilloried by Schwer's paper as a "Protestant and Jewish-Social-Democrat." Fr. Etn., "Die Christlich-Soziale Partei und das Schulwesen" (July 8, 1906), 3.

193. *Amtsblatt*, no. 101 (December 18, 1908), 2992.

194. Ibid., 2996.

Chapter 8. The Lueger Tradition

1. "Dr. Karl Luegers Tod," *Reichspost* (March 10, 1910), 2.

2. Anthony Burgess, "The War against Lucifer," *Times Literary Supplement* (November 9, 1984), 1273.

3. *Amtsblatt*, no. 24 (March 25, 1910), 636, 637.

4. Ibid., 646, 647.

5. One of the few papers that did not praise Lueger was the Pan-German *Tagblatt*, which hailed Lueger's death as the end of a "life's comedy." The *Tagblatt* also prophesied that Lueger's death would mark the beginning of the party's gradual disintegration. "Einer Lebenskomödie Ende," *Alldeutsches Tagblatt* (March 11, 1910), 1, 2. Karl Kraus observed that after Lueger had died, it was said that he had died ten times. Kraus perceived therein an undertone of political vindictiveness that remained unsatisfied "to the third and fourth exponent." Karl Kraus, "Glossen," *Die Fackel* (March 21, 1910), 53.

6. "Lueger," *Die Fackel* (March 21, 1910), 1.

7. Ibid.

8. Ibid., 2.

9. Ibid., 3.

10. Ibid.

11. Ibid., 4.

12. Ibid., 5.

13. Lueger's political testament made it clear that his successors should guard against specific interest groups from taking control of the party and that they should attend to the administration of the capital. "Der Wortlaut des politischen Testaments aus dem Jahre 1907," *Reichspost* (March 11, 1910), 2. Lueger's will also ordered his successors to adhere to his program on the Hungarian question. Josef Porzer, who was elected first vice-mayor after Lueger's death, was shouldered aside by Weiskirchner in 1912 after the resignation of Neumayer as mayor. According to the *Neue Freie Presse*, Porzer's half-Jewish ancestry made him an inappropriate choice as a Lueger successor. "Vizebürgermeister Dr. Josef Porzer," *Neue Freie Presse* (May 29, 1914), 10.

14. Kielmansegg, 365.

15. James Joll, "Backward Progress," *Times Literary Supplement* (July 5, 1985), 744.

16. "The mayor is better, and not even the hatred of the *Neue Freie Presse* is so implacable as to have granted death the prey of this particularly full life. In such moments political enmity is silent, and the independent and antiliberal press are united in endeavoring not to spare the public any details of the bladder flushing." "Am Krankenbett des Bürgermeisters," *Die Fackel* (February 22, 1907), 31.

17. *Protokolle* (February 5, 1906), 33749–53. On February 2, 1906, a panic occurred in an overcrowded church. One child was trampled to death and several others critically injured. Socialists, Liberals, and German Nationalists charged that the Magistrat had been negligent in enforcing safety regulations, because of the intimate friendship between ec-

clesiastical and municipal authorities. Schönerer's party recalled the Ringtheater fire of 1881 and the resulting political scandal, thereby suggesting that Lueger might share the fate of Newald. For details of this incident see "Massenunglück bei einer Kinderpredigt in der Altlerchenfelder Kirche. Panik durch falschen Feueralarm," *Neue Freie Presse* (February 3, 1906), 7–9; ibid., "Das Massenunglück in der Altlerchenfelder Kirche" (February 4, 1906), 10, 11.

18. Bloch, 236. Bloch added that this "was one thing that lifted him high above all his comrades."

19. Stefan Collini, "From Clerk into Guru," *Times Literary Supplement* (December 14, 1984), 1435.

20. *Landtag* (October 21, 1904), 253–86. So sure were the Christian Socials that the birthday celebration would take place that an elaborate *Fest-Programm* was printed. Unwilling to accept Kielmansegg's explanation that such celebrations were forbidden by law when parliament and the diet were in session, some Christian Socials blamed the prohibition on the machinations of the Jews and the Social Democrats. Schneider asserted that the former had employed "similar anti-government" tactics in France since 1789, and that these had invariably resulted in revolution and other acts of violence (264). However, Karl Seitz saw things differently, that the prohibition might be interpreted as a rebuff to Lueger's "boundless vanity": until now only Franz Joseph had been honored by a torchlight parade. Lueger craved a similar token of esteem (256). Seitz's remarks elicited a sharp response from Lueger, suggesting that Seitz had understood his motives only too well. Lueger was provided with demonstrations, but not the ones he had hoped for. Two days before his birthday, his attempts to dedicate a new fountain in the fifth district were drowned out by Socialist hecklers. The following day, thousands of Socialists participated in an anti-Lueger demonstration before the Rathaus.

21. Ibid., 285.

22. "Der 60. Geburtstag des Bürgermeisters," *Neue Freie Presse* (October 25, 1904), 9.

23. The symbolical sacrifice became a language of sacrifice during the Third Reich. J. P. Stern has suggested that the language of sacrifice "expresses . . . the death-wish at the heart of the will to power." J. P. Stern, 34. This was also implied by one of Lueger's contemporary biographers: "He made himself sick for his people and his Vienna, and being himself a martyr of suffering, he comforted the sick" (Mack, 43).

24. These views have been indicated by Robert Waissenberger. See his "Entre Rêve et Réalité," in Jean Clair, ed., *Vienne 1880–1938. L'Apocalypse Joyeuse* (Paris, 1986), 65.

25. Tomola, 5.

26. *Landtag* (October 21, 1904), 285. During this session Lueger indicated that he had "straightened out . . . certain parts of the population. . . . The teachers already know where truth and justice lie."

27. Tomola, 12.

28. Ibid. Referring to the same incident, Stauracz states that "the refusal of Prussia to participate in the discussions . . . filled all Austrians with displeasure." Stauracz, *Dr. Karl Lueger*, 12.

29. Tomola, 15.

30. Ibid., 37, 38.

31. Ibid., 34.

32. A passage suggests this, as well as the decline of Lueger's oratorical powers:

The opponents of the Christian Social party are conquered, but the citadels of their press have remained. In the long run, it won't work without an influential press. The leaders become older, the fire of their speeches is extinguished. The press remains a spiritual power, indispensable for every party. If we remain weaker in this point, if we allow the opponent to employ lies in larger measure than we use truth, then we gamble that the opponent will win the upper hand, perhaps at the decisive point, and break out of his old citadels in order to conquer his old positions again. (Stauracz, *Dr. Karl Lueger*, 167)

33. Funder, *Vom Gestern ins Heute*, 322, 323.

34. Stauracz, *Dr. Karl Lueger*, 180.

35. See, for example, ibid., 151–54.

36. Ibid., 185, 186. Stauracz himself should be numbered among the racists: "Baptism does not extinguish Jewish racial characteristics without further ado" (151).

37. Smith, 108ff.; Hitler, 55.

38. Stauracz, *Dr. Karl Lueger*, 192.

39. Ibid., 191.

40. Ibid., 136.

41. Ibid., 24. However, Stauracz does comment positively about Mandl's conversion to Christianity "under accompanying circumstances that remove all doubt about the purity of his motives" (157). Mandl died at about the same time Stauracz's biography was published.

42. Ibid., 139.

43. Ibid., 91–94. Though Stauracz praised the advantageous working conditions and pay of such categories as transportation workers and street cleaners, the quality of the labor performed, particularly by the street cleaners, left something to be desired, and the situation remained much as it had been when Lueger took office. Three years after his death, Mayor Weiskirchner complained that enough studies of inadequate municipal hygiene had been undertaken, and that it was time to take action, thereby repeating similar complaints of Lueger in 1897 and Neumayer in 1910. See Lueger's inaugural speech draft quoted in Geehr, *"I Decide Who Is a Jew!"*, 209. Seliger and Ucakar, II: 913.

44. Stauracz remarked that it was no wonder that Lueger was an exemplar for the youth and quoted the St. Gallen *Volksblatt* to prove his point:

And the thing that lends these qualities just the right brilliance is his irreproachable character, his impeccable private life. That is actually what makes the man, and encircles the brow of the ordinary citizen with a certain majesty. Stainless character and living, that is the highest fame of every man, the comfort during all temptations and persecutions, the noblest eulogy at the grave. (Stauracz, *Dr. Karl Lueger*, 120)

45. Mack's biography appeared in 1910, shortly after Lueger's death.

46. Mack, 25, 26.

47. Ibid., 78.

48. Ibid., 64.

49. Ibid.

50. Ibid., 80.

51. This had been anticipated by a *Reichspost* article from 1920, in which Kralik had praised Lueger as "one of the few thoroughly great statesmen of the nineteenth century." Like the classical statesmen of old, Lueger had based his political wisdom on religion. Kralik suggested that the recently ended war might have concluded differently, had Lueger with all his strength, and "with the whole magic of his personality," been at the right place in 1914. Kralik hinted at the desirable outcome in describing Lueger's "program":

It went far beyond the idea of "Great Austria" of the Rumanian Popovici, which the differing nationalities of Austria regarded as the bearer of a federation. Lueger wanted to carry the nation-connecting idea of Great Austria beyond the boundaries of the monarchy to the Aegean Sea. He thought of including the Balkan states with the Austrian lands as a league, a league of nations, like the "United States of South Eastern Europe." In any case, the idea was far more organic than the problematic League of Nations of Wilsonian origin seems to be today. But we will and must wait and see. In any case, the idea of Lueger should not be entirely forgotten.

Kralik added that Lueger had discussed this plan "in a few interesting interviews." Lueger may have entertained such ideas, but his public remarks suggest that he wished Austria to avoid entangling alliances, especially those that he could not control himself. How such a plan as Lueger's was to be achieved in the light of the rampant nationalism, particularly in the Balkans, Kralik does not indicate. Remarks such as his should therefore be treated with caution, or in this instance, perhaps read as a projection of his own wishes. Richard Kralik, "Dr. Karl Lueger," *Reichspost* (October 27, 1920), 1, 2.

52. Kralik, *Karl Lueger und der christliche Sozialismus*, 5.

53. The manuscript is in the Vienna Public Library, handwritten documents collection.

54. Kielmansegg's Lueger chapter in his *Kaiserhaus*, written early during World War I, strikes one as sardonic, the *Statthalter's* protestations of friendship toward Lueger "until his sad end" notwithstanding. Kielmansegg, 407. Another commentator writing at about the same time as Kielmansegg called Lueger "an ardent democrat," who "knew that democracy for the first time in Austrian history was on its trial." P. J. Connolly, S.J., "Karl Lueger: Mayor of Vienna," *Studies* (June 1915), 249, 226. See also P. J. Connolly, S.J., "Karl Lueger: His Rise to Power," *Studies* (September 1914), 280–91.

55. After having been spotted in a house of ill repute, clad only in a medal, Neumayer resigned, unceremoniously, the following day. The clergy was also disenchanted with Weiskirchner whose daughter was divorced. Only at his grave side was there a reconciliation of sorts.

56. See "Die Republik büsst ihre Würde ein," *Der Spiegel* (August 26, 1985), 108.

57. Some 80,000 participated in this ceremony, which included pageants, parades, speeches, and pass-by reviews. (See illustrations.) Lueger said it numbered among "the most noble and elevated" ceremonies that had ever taken place in Vienna, "perhaps, even in the world." *Amtsblatt*, no. 42 (May 26, 1908), 1309. Despite the ostensible purpose of the homage, Lueger managed to reap his share, perhaps the lion's share, of the adulation. At the unveiling ceremony eighteen years later, his popularity was uncontested. By then, the Lueger tradition was firmly established in the popular imagination. One hundred thousand participated in the festivities, which lasted some three hours. A giant parade included contingents from virtually every Christian Social association and organization, including a veteran's group of Lueger Gretl. Program of the *Dr. Karl Lueger—Denkmal-Enthüllungsfeier*, 1.

58. At an *enquete* in March 1986, "90 Years of Christian Social and Christian Democratic Communal Politics in Vienna," sponsored by the Karl von Vogelsang-Institut and Dr. Karl Lueger-Institut, Vogelsang was celebrated by University of Vienna Professor Reinhold Knoll, not only for providing the ideological foundation of Christian Social municipal politics in Vienna, but also for having been Lueger's teacher.

59. Seitz praised Lueger for having politically awakened the broad masses and for having democratized the municipal administration, for having municipalized the trams, electric and gas works, as well as the burial services, and thereby having removed important means of production from the hands of the capitalists. "Tagesneuigkeiten. Wien feiert Lueger. Enthüllung seines Denkmals.—100,000 Festgäste," Neues Wiener Journal" (September 20, 1926). Socialists such as Leopold Gratz and Norbert Leser continue to praise Lueger though, perhaps, with reservations. See Leopold Gratz, "Karl Lueger," in *Österreichische Porträts*, 2

vols. (Salzburg and Vienna, 1985), I: 379–97; Anneliese Rohrer, "Perspektive Minneapolis. Waldheim, Antisemitismus, und viele Vorurteile," *Die Presse* (June 2, 1986), 2.

60. Heer, 161.

61. See, for example, Richard Kralik, *Geschichte des Sozialismus der Neuesten Zeit* (Graz, 1925).

62. Kralik, *Karl Lueger und der christliche Sozialismus*, 8.

63. Ibid., 9.

64. Ibid., 23.

65. Felix Salten, *"Lueger,"* in *Geister der Zeit* (Berlin, Vienna, and Leipzig, 1924), 186.

66. Ibid.

67. Theodor Heinrich Mayer, *Die letzten Bürger* (Leipzig, 1927), 341.

68. This was L. Staackmann. Müller-Guttenbrunn's work is entitled *Der Roman meines Lebens.*

69. Hans Hauenstein, *Chronik des Wienerliedes* (Vienna, 1976), 255.

70. Kuppe was born in 1883 and died in 1950.

71. May, 516.

72. Schnee, *Bürgermeister Karl Lueger*, 20–34; Kuppe, *Karl Lueger und seine Zeit*, 205–16.

73. See Schnee, *Bürgermeister Karl Lueger*, 5, 14, 19, 52, 53. Interestingly enough, during the National Socialist period, some of Lorenz von Stein's ideas were held to have contributed to those of Julius Langbehn, an important mentor of the Nazi movement. See Fritz Werner, "Lorenz von Stein als Politiker," *Verwaltungsarchiv*, 47: 49–60. On Langbehn, see Fritz Stern, *The Politics of Cultural Despair* (Berkeley, Los Angeles, and London, 1961), 97–180.

74. Heinrich Schnee, *Karl Lueger. Leben und Wirken eines grossen Sozial- und Kommunalpolitikers* (Berlin, 1960).

75. Schnee states that Schönerer and Lueger had taught Hitler "the handiness of anti-Semitic electoral slogans." *Karl Lueger*, 53.

76. Schnee, *Bürgermeister Karl Lueger*, 5. A former *Gauleiter* of Vienna also took this tack. See A. Eduard Frauenfeld, *"Dr. Karl Lueger,"* *Zeitschrift für Politik* (Berlin, 1938), 28: 77–86.

77. Schnee, *Karl Lueger*, 19, 20.

78. Ibid., 110.

79. Ibid., 52, 53.

80. Ibid., 53.

81. Freiner, 524.

82. Richard S. Levy, *"Wien 1910*: A Comment," *Film and History* 15, no. 3 (September, 1985): 68.

83. Taylor, ed. and trans., 23. Immediately after he noted Hitler's admiration for Lueger in October 1939, Goebbels added: "I tell him about my preliminary work on the Jew-film, which interests him greatly."

84. In a conversation with the author, Erik Frey, who played the character Birkner in the film, indicated that the director, Karl Hartl, may have opposed the completion of this film.

85. Quoted in Richard Geehr, John Heineman, Gerald Herman, *"Wien 1910*: An Example of Nazi Anti-Semitism," *Film and History* 15, no. 3 (September, 1985): 53.

86. Another was Luis Trenker's *Der Rebell*, which depicted heroics of Andreas Hofer. See David Welch, *Propaganda and the German Cinema 1933–1945* (Oxford, 1983), 72.

87. Geehr, Heineman, Herman, 60.

88. Gerda Geehr and Richard S. Geehr, unpublished translation of *Wien 1910*.

89. *Wien 1910* was written by Gerhard Menzel and directed by E. W. Emo.

90. Geehr, Heineman, Herman, 56.

91. Erik Frey informed me he saw it in Vienna at that time.

92. When *Wien 1910* was first publicly screened in Vienna in the late 1970s, viewers were spattered with red paint by demonstrators, according to the manager of the Bellaria Kino, Ernst Birke.

93. Geehr, Heineman, Herman, 63.

94. Ibid. This point of view as it pertained to everyday problems in the old monarchy evidently left Third Reich Germans cold. Max Lippmann, "Wollt Ihr den totalen Film?" in Hans Peter Hofmann, ed., *Versunkene Welt* (Vienna, 1984), 203.

95. Welch, 324.

96. Soukup, 300.

97. Viennese seem to be sensitive to the accuracy of physical detail. Robert Prosl, the author of a 1949 Lueger play, *Der Pumera,* was advised by one who had spoken to Lueger on many occasions that he had been offended to hear the actor who portrayed the mayor utter the Prussianism "Raus!" instead of "Hinaus!" or "Naus!" or "Aussi!" The harsher form could only have been uttered by a *"Pifke"* [Prussian]. Letter of Franz Wimmer to Robert Prosl (June 8, 1949), *IN* 205.995.

98. Soukup, 132

99. Ibid., 147.

100. Skalnik, 167.

101. Ibid., 82.

102. Hawlik, 199.

103. Skalnik, 80.

104. See the exhibit catalog, *Dr. Karl Lueger. Dokumentation anlässlich der Lueger-Ausstellung Februar 1983* (Vienna, 1983).

105. Andics, *Luegerzeit.*

106. "Rathauskorrespondenz" (March 11, 1985), Blatt, 582.

107. Continuing controversy over Lueger was summarized by Kurt Stimmer, "Karl Lueger—umstritten wie kein andrer," *Wien Aktuell* (August, 1985), xxxviii–xl.

108. For Eckart, see Henry Grosshans, *Hitler and the Artists* (New York and London, 1983), 47–70.

109. Hawlik, 14.

110. Ibid., 15.

111. Ibid., 214.

112. John Bayley, "The Shadow of the Horseman," *Times Literary Supplement* (March 28, 1986), 339.

113. Spitzer, 9, 10.

Selected Bibliography

Archival Sources

Allegemeines Verwaltungsarchiv, Vienna, Eduard Pichl Nachlass.
Bibliothek der Katholisch—Theologischen Fakultät, University of Vienna, Karl von Vogelsang
    Nachlass.
Despatches from United States Ministers to Austria, 1838–1906.
Erzbischöfliches Diözesanarchiv, Vienna.
Felder, Cajetan. *"Infamien des Dr. Johann Nep. Prix, Meine Rechtfertigung Katzenpfoten."*
    Unpublished addendum.
Grundbuch, Wiener Invalidenhaus, Kriegsarchiv.
Handschriftensammlung der Wiener Stadtbibliothek.
Handschriftensammlung der österreichischen Nationalbibliothek.
Haus-, Hof-, und Staatsarchiv, Vienna, Friedrich Funder Nachlass.
Hierhammer, Heinrich. Unpublished Memoir.
Institut für Zeitgeschichte der Universität Wien.
Müller-Guttenbrunn, Adam. Unpublished Diaries.
Nachlass Albert Wiesinger, *Handschriftensammlung der Wiener Stadtbibliothek.*
Nachlass Karl Lueger, *Handschriftensammlung der Wiener Stadtbibliothek.*
Nachlass Karl Seitz, *Archiv der Stadt Wien.*
Nachlass Thim, *Forschungs- und Kulturstelle der Österreicher aus dem Donau-, Sudeten-*
    und Karpatenraum.
Niederösterreichisches Landesarchiv, Vienna, Präsidialakten, Statthalterei, 1880–1910.
"Opelt, Franz", Kriegsarchiv Präsidialakten.
Österreichische Gesellschaft für historische Quellenstudien.
Printed Document Collections of the Austrian National Parliament, Austrian National Library,
    Vienna Municipal Library.
Theatersammlung der österreichischen Nationalbibliothek.
Trauungsbuch des evangelischen Pfarramtes A. B. 1888.
Universitätsnationalien, Archive of the University of Vienna.

BIBLIOGRAPHY

Memoirs, Diaries, Reminiscences, Letters

Beskiba, Marianne. *Aus meinen Erinnerungen an Dr. Karl Lueger.* Vienna, 1911.

Bloch, Joseph Samuel. *My Reminiscences.* New York, 1973.

Braun, Felix. *Das Licht der Welt.* Vienna, 1962.

Chłedowski, Kazimierez. *Pamiętniki.* 2 vols. Wrocław, 1951.

Clare, George. *Last Waltz in Vienna: The Rise and Destruction of a Family 1842–1942.* New York, 1982.

Deutsch, Julius. *Ein weiter Weg. Lebenserinnerungen.* Zürich, Leipzig, and Vienna, 1960.

Eckstein, Friedrich. *"Alte unnennbare Tage!" Erinnerungen aus siebzig Lehr- und Wanderjahren.* Vienna, Leipzig, and Zürich, 1936.

Ehrhart, Robert. *Im Dienste des alten Österreich.* Vienna, 1958.

Engelhart, Josef. *Ein Wiener Maler erzählt. Mein Leben und meine Modelle.* Vienna, 1943.

Felder, Cajetan. *Erinnerungen eines Wiener Bürgermeisters.* Vienna, Hannover and Bern, 1964.

Frauenfeld, Alfred E. *Und trage keine Reu'.* Leoni am Starnberger See, 1978.

Funder, Friedrich. *Vom Gestern ins Heute.* Vienna and Munich, 1953.

Geehr, Richard S., ed. and trans. *"I Decide Who Is a Jew!" The Papers of Dr. Karl Lueger.* Washington, D.C., 1982.

Glöckel, Otto. *Selbstbiographie.* Zürich, 1939.

Grossmann, Stefan. *Ich war begeistert.* Berlin, 1930.

Hainisch, Michael. *75 Jahre aus bewegter Zeit. Lebenserinnerungen eines österreichischen Staatsmannes.* Ed. by Friedrich Weissensteiner. Vienna, 1978.

Hanfstaengl, Ernst. *Hitler: The Missing Years.* London, 1957.

Hanisch, Reinhold. *"I Was Hitler's Buddy." The New Republic.* April 5, 1939.

Hawel, Rudolf. Unpublished Autobiography: *Aus meinem Leben. Handschriftensammlung der Wiener Stadtbibliothek.*

Herzl, Theodor. *The Complete Diaries of Theodor Herzl.* Harry Zohn, trans., and Raphael Patai, ed. New York and London, 1960.

Hitler, Adolf. *Hitler's Secret Conversations.* New York, 1972.

Kann, Robert A., and Peter Leisching, eds. *Ein Leben für Kunst und Volksbildung — Eduard Leisching 1858–1938. Erinnerungen.* Vienna, 1978.

Kielmansegg, Erich Graf. *Kaiserhaus, Staatsmänner und Politiker.* Vienna and Munich, 1966.

Kubizek, August. *The Young Hitler I Knew.* Boston, 1955.

Kunschak, Leopold. *Steinchen vom Wege.* Vienna, n. d.

Mayer, Sigmund. *Ein jüdischer Kaufmann 1831 bis 1911. Lebenserinnerungen.* Leipzig, 1911.

Millenkovich-Morold, Max von. *Vom Abend zum Morgen. Aus dem alten Österreich ins neue Deutschland.* Leipzig, 1940.

Müller-Guttenbrunn, Adam. *Der Roman meines Lebens.* Leipzig, 1927.

———. *Erinnerungen eines Theaterdirektors.* Leipzig, 1924.

Nostitz-Rieneck, Georg, ed. *Briefe Kaiser Franz Josephs an Kaiserin Elisabeth 1859–1898.* 2 vols. Vienna and Munich, 1966.

Picker, Henry, ed. *Hitler's Tischgespräche im Hauptquartier.* Wiesbaden, 1983.

Plener, Ernst. *Erinnerungen von Ernst Freiherr von Plener.* 3 vols. Stuttgart and Leipzig, 1911.

Renner, Karl. *An der Wende zweier Zeiten. Lebenserinnerungen.* Vienna, 1946.

Schaeffle, Albert. *Aus meinem Leben.* 2 vols. Berlin, 1905.

Scheicher, Josef. *Erlebnisse und Erinnerungen.* 6 vols. Vienna and Leipzig, 1912.

Schnitzler, Arthur. *Jugend in Wien.* Vienna, 1968.

Schöffel, Joseph. *Erinnerungen aus meinem Leben.* Vienna, 1905.

Bibliography

Sieghart, Rudolf. *Die letzten Jahrzehnte einer Grossmacht.* Berlin, 1932.

Skedl, Arthur, ed. *Der politische Nachlass des Grafen Eduard Taaffe.* Vienna, 1922.

Somary, Felix. *Erinnerungen aus meinem Leben.* Zürich, 1959.

Spitzmüller, Alexander. *". . . Und hat auch Ursach, es zu lieben."* Vienna, Munich, Stuttgart, and Zürich, 1955.

Suess, Eduard. *Erinnerungen.* Leipzig, 1916.

Taylor, Fred, ed. and trans. *The Goebbels Diaries 1939–1941.* New York, 1983.

Weil, Robert (Homunkulus). *Rück näher, Bruder! Der Roman meines Lebens.* Vienna and Berlin, 1920.

Zuckerkandl, Bertha. *Österreich intim. Erinnerungen.* Vienna and Munich, 1981.

Additional Sources

Aba, B. *Moderne Grössen.* 2 vols. Vienna, 1883.

Adelmaier, Werner, "Ernst Vergani." Ph.D. diss. University of Vienna, 1969.

Allmayer-Beck, Johann Christoph. *Ministerpräsident Baron Beck, ein Staatsmann des alten Österreich.* Vienna, 1956.

———. *Vogelsang. Vom Feudalismus zur Volksbewegung.* Vienna, 1952.

Amtsblatt der K.K. Reichshaupt- und Residenzstadt Wien.

Andics, Hellmut. *Luegerzeit.* Vienna and Munich, 1984.

"Aus den Anfängen der Christlichsozialen Bewegung in Österreich. Nach der Korrespondenz des Grafen Anton Pergen," in Weinzierl, Erika, *Ecclesia Semper Reformanda. Beiträge zur österreichischen Kirchengeschichte im 19. und 20. Jahrhundert.* Vienna and Salzburg, 1985.

Balfour, Michael. *Britain and Joseph Chamberlain.* Boston and Sydney, 1985.

Barea, Ilsa. *Vienna: Legend and Reality.* London, 1966.

Bauer, F. "Leopold Kunschak als Politiker. Von seinen Anfängen bis zum Jahre 1934." Ph.D. diss. University of Vienna, 1950.

Beck, Elfriede. "Die Wienerin und ihre Zeit. Frauen- und Familienzeitschriften der 2. Hälfte des 19. Jahrhunderts als Zeitdokumente." Ph.D. diss. University of Vienna, 1964.

Beller, Steven. *"Fin de Siècle* Vienna and the Jews: The Dialectics of Assimilation." *The Jewish Quarterly* 33, 1986.

Benedikt, Heinrich, ed. *Geschichte der Republik Österreich.* Munich, 1954.

Berkley, George E. *Vienna and Its Jews.* Cambridge, Mass., Lanham, Md., 1988.

Berner, Peter, Emil Brix, and Wolfgang Mantl, eds. *Wien um 1900.* Munich, 1986.

Blasius, Dirk, and Pankoke Eckart. *Lorenz von Stein.* Darmstadt, 1979.

Botstein, Leon, and Linda Weintraub, eds. *Pre-Modern Art of Vienna, 1848–1898.* Detroit, Mich., 1987.

Boyer, John W. "Karl Lueger and the Viennese Jews." *The Leo Baeck Institute Year Book,* 26, 1981.

———. *Political Radicalism in Late Imperial Vienna: Origins of the Christian Social Movement 1848–1897.* Chicago and London, 1981.

Brown, Karin B. "Karl Lueger as Liberal: Democracy, Municipal Reform and the Struggle for Power in the Vienna City Council 1875–1882." Ph.D diss. City University of New York, 1982.

Brügel, Ludwig. *Geschichte der österreichischen Sozialdemokratie.* 5 vols. Vienna, 1922–1925.

Brunner, Heinrich. *Grundzüge der deutschen Rechtsgeschichte.* Leipzig, 1910.

BIBLIOGRAPHY

Bunzl, John, and Bernd Marin. *Antisemitismus in Österreich: Historische und Soziologische Studien.* Innsbruck, 1983.

Burger, Erwin. "Die Frage der Bestätigung der Wahl Dr. Karl Luegers zum Bürgermeister von Wien." Ph.D. diss. University of Vienna, 1952.

Bushnell, John. *Mutiny Amid Repression: Russian Soldiers in the Revolution of 1905–1906.* Bloomington, Ind., 1985.

Carsten, F. L. *Fascist Movements in Austria: From Schönerer to Hitler.* London and Beverly Hills, 1977.

Catalog. *Dr. Karl Lueger. Dokumentation anlässlich der Lueger-Ausstellung Februar 1983.* Vienna, 1983.

Charmatz, Richard. "Dr. Karl Lueger," *Deutschland.* 1905.

———. "*Lueger, Karl.*" In Anton Bettelheim, ed. *Biographisches Jahrbuch und Deutscher Nekrolog.* Berlin, 1913.

Clair, Jean, ed. *Vienne 1880–1938. L'Apocalypse Joyeuse.* Paris, 1986.

Clark, Ronald W. *Freud: The Man and the Cause.* New York, 1980.

Connolly, P. J., S.J. "Karl Lueger: His Rise to Power." *Studies.* September 1914.

———. "Karl Lueger: Mayor of Vienna." *Studies.* June 1915.

Czeike, Felix. *Liberale, Christlich Soziale und Sozialdemokratische Kommunalpolitik (1861–1934).* Vienna, 1962.

———. *Wien und seine Bürgermeister. Sieben Jahrhunderte Wiener Stadtgeschichte.* Vienna and Munich, 1974.

———. *Wirtschafts- und Sozialpolitik der Gemeinde Wien 1919–1934.* 2 vols. Vienna, 1958, 1959.

Czelechowski, Maria. "Hansi Niese." Ph.D. diss. University of Vienna, 1947.

Diamant, Alfred. *Austrian Catholics and the First Republic. Democracy, Capitalism, and the Social Order, 1918–1934.* Princeton, 1960.

Ebert, Kurt. *Die Anfänge der modernen Sozialpolitik in Österreich.* Vienna, 1975.

Eder, Karl. *Der Liberalismus in Altösterreich. Geisteshaltung, Politik und Kultur.* Vienna and Munich, 1955.

Ehalt, Hubert Ch., Gernot Heiss, and Hannes Stekl, eds. *Glücklich ist, wer vergisst . . .? Das andere Wien um 1900.* Vienna, Cologne, and Graz, 1986.

Ellenbogen, Wilhelm. *Menschen und Prinzipien. Erinnerungen, Urteile und Reflexionen eines kritischen Sozialdemokraten.* Vienna, Cologne, and Graz, 1981.

Engel-Janossi, Friedrich. "*Österreich und der Vatikan.* 2 vols. Graz, Vienna, and Cologne, 1958–60.

Entsch, A. *Deutscher Bühnen-Almanach.* Berlin, 1881.

Feldbauer, Peter. *Stadtwachstum und Wohnungsnot. Determinanten unzureichender Wohnungsversorgung in Wien, 1848 bis 1914.* Vienna, 1977.

Fraenkel, Josef, ed. *The Jews of Austria.* London, 1967.

Frank, Ferdinand. *Die österreichische Volksschule, 1848–1898.* Vienna, 1898.

Franz, Georg. *Liberalismus. Die deutschliberale Bewegung in der habsburgischen Monarchie.* Munich, 1955.

Frauenfeld, A. Eduard. "Dr. Karl Lueger." *Zeitschrift für Politik.* Vol. 28. Berlin, 1938.

Freiner, Johann. *Der Herrgott von Wien.* Dresden, 1940.

Friedländer, Otto. *Letzter Glanz der Märchenstadt. Das war Wien um 1900.* Vienna and Munich, 1976.

Frier, Bruce W. *The Rise of the Roman Jurists: Studies in Cicero's "pro Caecina."* Princeton, 1985.

Fuchs, Albert. *Geistige Strömungen in Österreich 1867–1918.* Vienna, 1949.

Funder, Friedrich. *Aufbruch zur christlichen Sozialreform.* Vienna, Munich, 1953.

Gärtner, Leopold. "Lueger und die Aussenpolitik der Österreich-ungarischen Monarchie." Ph.D. diss. University of Vienna, 1951.

Gay, Peter. *Freud, Jews, and Other Germans.* New York, 1978.

Geehr, Richard S. *Adam Müller-Guttenbrunn and the Aryan Theater of Vienna, 1898–1903: The Approach of Cultural Fascism.* Göppingen, 1973.

———. "Hans Eibl: A Religious Nature in a Psycho-Political Idiom." *Austrian History Yearbook*, 1981–82.

———, John Heineman, and Gerald Herman. "*Wien 1910*: An Example of Nazi Anti-Semitism." *Film and History.* Vol. 15, no. 3. September 1985.

Glaser, Ernst. *Im Umfeld des Austromarxismus. Ein Beitrag zur Geistesgeschichte des österreichischen Sozialismus.* Vienna, 1981.

Gold, Hugo. *Geschichte der Juden in Wien.* Tel Aviv, 1966.

Goldhammer, Leo. *Die Juden Wiens.* Vienna and Leipzig, 1927.

Good, David F. *The Economic Rise of the Habsburg Empire 1750–1914.* Berkeley, Los Angeles, and London, 1984.

Götz, Marie. *Die Frauen und der Antisemitismus.* Vienna, n. d.

———. *Schmutzige Wäsche der Christlich Socialen. Eingesammelt von einer Christlichen Waschfrau.* Vienna, n. d.

Grey-Stipek, Valerie. *Paula,* Leipzig, 1894.

Grimm, Gerhard, "Karl von Vogelsang-Publizist im Dienste christlicher Sozialreform." Ph.D. diss. University of Vienna, 1970.

Grover, Richard, and Felix Czeike. *Wien Lexikon.* Vienna and Munich, 1974.

Grosshans, Henry. *Hitler and the Artists.* New York and London, 1983.

Guglia, Eugen. *Das Theresianum in Wien. Vergangenheit und Gegenwart.* Vienna, 1912.

Gulick, Charles A. *Austria from Habsburg to Hitler.* 2 vols. Berkeley and Los Angeles, 1948.

Hahn, Manfred. *Bürgerlicher Optimismus im Niedergang.* Munich, 1969.

Hanson, Alice M. *Musical Life in Biedermeier Vienna.* London, 1985.

Hanusch, Ferdinand. *Die Namenlosen. Geschichten aus dem Leben der Arbeiter und Armen.* Vienna, 1910.

Harden, Maximilian. *Köpfe.* Berlin, 1911.

Harrer, Karl. "Dr. Richard Weiskirchner." Ph.D. diss. University of Vienna, 1950.

Hartmann, Gerhard, ed. *Der CV in Österreich. Seine Entstehung, seine Geschichte, seine Bedeutung.* Vienna, 1977.

Hauenstein, Hans. *Chronik des Wienerliedes.* Vienna, 1976.

Hausner, Eduard. "Die Tätigkeit des Wiener Gemeinderates in den Jahren 1884–1888." Ph.D. diss. University of Vienna, 1974.

Hawlik, Johannes. *Der Bürgerkaiser. Karl Lueger und seine Zeit.* Vienna and Munich, 1985.

Heer, Friedrich. *Der Glaube des Adolf Hitler. Anatomie einer politischen Religiosität.* Munich and Esslingen, 1968.

Heller, Erich. *The Disinherited Mind.* Cambridge, 1952.

Herden, Birgit. "Das Amt des Bürgermeisters der Stadt Wien in der liberalen Ära 1861–1895." Ph.D. diss. University of Vienna, 1967.

Hofmann, Hans Peter, ed. *Versunkene Welt.* Vienna, 1984.

Holleis, Eva., *Die Sozialpolitische Partei. Sozialliberale Bestrebungen in Wien um 1900.* Vienna, 1978.

Horowitz, Louise K. *Honoré d' Urfé.* Boston, 1984.

Höttinger, Matthias. "Der Fall Wahrmund." Ph.D. diss. University of Vienna, 1949.

Hron, Karl. *Wiens antisemitische Bewegung.* Vienna, 1890.

Huber, Augustin, K. *Ambros Opitz, 1846–1907. Ein Bahnbrecher der katholischen Bewegung Altösterreichs.* Königstein, 1961.

Iggers, Wilma Abeles. *Karl Kraus: A Viennese Critic of the Twentieth Century.* The Hague, 1967.

Janik, Allan, and Stephen Toulmin. *Wittgenstein's Vienna.* New York, 1973.

Jelavich, Barbara. *Modern Austria. Empire and Republic, 1815–1986.* Cambridge, London, New York, New Rochelle, Melbourne, Sydney, 1987.

Jenks, William A. *The Austrian Electoral Reform of 1907.* New York, 1950.

———. *Austria under the Iron Ring 1879–1893.* Charlottesville, Va., 1965.

———. *Vienna and the Young Hitler.* New York, 1960.

Jetzinger, Franz. *Hitlers Jugend. Phantasien, Lügen und die Wahrheit.* Vienna, 1956.

John, Michael. *Hausherrenmacht und Mieterelend. Wohnerfahrungen 1890–1923.* Vienna, 1982.

Johnston, William M. *The Austrian Mind.* Berkeley, Los Angeles, and London, 1972.

Jones, J. Sydney. *Hitler in Vienna 1907–1913: Clues to the Future.* New York, 1983.

Jung, Jochen. *Österreichische Porträts.* 2 vols. Salzburg and Vienna, 1985.

Kamp, M. E. *Die Theorie der Epochen der öffentlichen Wirtschaft bei Lorenz von Stein.* Bonn, 1950.

Kancler, Emma. "Die österreichische Frauenbewegung und ihre Presse (von ihren Anfängen bis zum Ende des I. Weltkrieges)." Ph.D. diss. University of Vienna, 1947.

Kann, Robert A. *A History of the Habsburg Empire 1526–1918.* Berkeley, Los Angeles, and London, 1974.

———. *A Study in Austrian Intellectual History.* New York, 1960.

Kant, Friedrich. "Der Niederösterreichische Landtag von 1902 bis 1908." Ph.D. diss. University of Vienna, 1949.

Kehle, Hertha. "Die Frauenzeitschrift: Ihre Anfänge und ihre Entwicklung in Österreich." Ph.D. diss. University of Vienna, 1951.

Kläger, Ernst. *Durch die Quartiere des Elends und Verbrechens. Ein Wanderbuch aus dem Jenseits.* Vienna, 1908.

Kleindel, Walter. *Österreich. Daten zur Geschichte und Kultur.* Vienna, 1978.

Klemperer, Klemens von. *Ignaz Seipel: Christian Statesman in a Time of Crisis.* Princeton, 1972.

Klopp, Wiard. *Leben und Wirken des Sozialpolitikers Karl Freiherrn von Vogelsang.* Vienna, 1930.

Knapp, Vincent J. *Austrian Social Democracy 1889–1914.* Washington, D.C., 1980.

Knapton, Ernest John. *France: An Interpretive History.* New York, 1971.

Knauer, Oswald. *Das österreichische Parlament von 1848–1966.* Vienna, 1969.

———. *Der Wiener Gemeinderat, 1861–1862.* Vienna, 1963.

Knoll, Reinhold. *Zur Tradition der christlichsozialen Partei.* Vienna, Cologne, and Graz, 1973.

Koller-Glück, Elisabeth. *Otto Wagners Kirche am Steinhof.* Vienna, 1985.

Kolmer, Gustav. *Parlament und Verfassung in Österreich.* 8 vols. Vienna and Leipzig, 1902–14.

Kosch, Wilhelm. *Deutsches Theater Lexikon.* Klagenfurt and Vienna, 1960.

Kossdorff, Karl-Heinz. "Die Wiener liberale Lokalpresse im 19. Jahrhundert (1850–1900)." Ph.D. diss. University of Vienna, 1969.

Kralik, Richard. "Die christlichsoziale Bewegung in Österreich," in *Österreichische Rundschau,* 1922, 15. and 16. Heft.

———. *Geschichte des Sozialismus der neuesten Zeit.* Graz, 1925.

———. *Karl Lueger Gedächtnisrede.* Vienna, 1926.

———. *Karl Lueger und der christliche Sozialismus.* Vol. I. Vienna, 1923.

———. and Hans Schlitter. *Wien. Geschichte der Kaiserstadt und ihrer Kultur.* Vienna, 1912.

Bibliography

Krenn, Helmut. "Die 'Habakuk'-Reihe des Emil Kralik in der Arbeiterzeitung als Beitrag zur Wiener humoristisch-satirischen Publizistik 1896–1906." Ph.D. diss. University of Vienna, 1979.

Kunschak, Leopold, ed. *Reden gehalten in Wien am 19., 20. und 21. Juli 1899.* St. Pölten, 1899.

Kunze, Margot. "Dr. Karl Lueger als Gemeinderat von 1875–1896." Ph.D. diss. University of Vienna, 1968.

Kuppe, Rudolf. *Festschrift zur [Dr. Karl Lueger] Denkmalenthüllung.* Vienna, 1926.

———. *Dr. Karl Lueger. Persönlichkeit und Wirken.* Vienna, 1947.

———. *Karl Lueger und seine Zeit.* Vienna, 1933.

Lahmer, Gundela. *Lorenz von Stein. Zur Konstitution des bürgerlichen Bildungswesens.* Frankfurt and New York, 1982.

Lehmanns Allgemeiner Wohnungs-Anzeiger. Vienna, 1888–1923.

Levy, Richard S. *The Downfall of the Anti-Semitic Political Parties in Imperial Germany.* New Haven and London, 1975.

———. "Wien 1910: A Comment." *Film and History.* Vol. 15, no. 3. September 1985.

Lewis, Gavin. *Kirche und Partei im politischen Katholizismus.* Vienna and Salzburg, 1977.

Lueger, Karl. *Sätze aus allen Zweigen der Rechts- und Staatswissenschaften, welche nach abgelegten vier strengen Prüfungen zur Erlangung der juridischen Doctorswürde an der k.k. Universität zu Wien, Karl Lueger, Advocaturs-Concipient in Wien, Freitag den 14. Januar 1870, um 12 Uhr Mittag, im k.k. Universitäts-Consistorialsaale öffentlich zu vertheidigen sich erbietet.* Vienna, 1870.

———. *Reden gehalten in Wien am 20. Juli 1899.* St. Pölten, 1899.

———. *Zwei Reden gehalten in der Versammlung des Christlich-socialen Vereines.* Vienna, 1889.

Macartney, C. A. *The Habsburg Empire, 1790–1918.* London, 1969.

Mack, Eugen. *Dr. Karl Lueger, der Bürgermeister von Wien.* Rottenburg a. Neckar, 1910.

May, Arthur J. *The Habsburg Monarchy 1867–1914.* New York, 1968.

Mayer, Arno J. *The Persistence of the Old Regime: Europe to the Great War.* New York, 1981.

Mayer, Sigmund. *Die Wiener Juden. Kommerz, Kultur, Politik 1700–1900.* Vienna and Berlin, 1917.

Mayer, Theodor Heinrich. *Die letzten Bürger.* Leipzig, 1927.

McCagg Jr., William O. *A History of Habsburg Jews 1670–1918.* Bloomington and Indianapolis, 1989.

McGrath, William J. *Dionysian Art and Populist Politics in Austria.* New Haven and London, 1974.

Mengelberg, Kaethe. *Lorenz von Stein: The History of the Social Movement in France, 1759–1850.* Totowa, N.J., 1964.

Metschl, Karl. *Wiener Lehrlings-Elend.* Vienna, 1907.

Miko, Norbert. "Die Vereinigung der christlichsozialen Reichspartei und des katholisch konservativen Zentrums im Jahre 1907." Ph.D. diss. University of Vienna, 1949.

Molisch, Paul. *Politische Geschichte der deutschen Hochschulen in Österreich von 1848 bis 1918.* Vienna and Leipzig, 1939.

Nagl, Johann Willibald, Jakob Zeidler, and Eduard Castle. *Deutsch-Österreichische Literaturgeschichte.* 4 vols. Vienna, 1930–37.

Nemetz, Melitta. "Bürgermeister und städtische Einrichtungen in der Zweiten Hälfte des 19. Jahrhunderts." Ph.D. diss. University of Vienna, 1943.

Neuwirth, Irene. "Dr. Cajetan Felder, Bürgermeister von Wien." Ph.D. diss. University of Vienna, 1942.

Ninkov, Benno. "Die politischen Anfänge Dr. Karl Luegers im Lichte der Wiener Presse." Ph.D. diss. University of Vienna, 1946.

Orel, Anton. "Vogelsang und Lueger, ihre Bedeutung für die christliche Volksbewegung." *Das Neue Reich.* 1924.

Oxaal, Ivar, and Walter R. Weitzmann. "The Jews of Pre-1914 Vienna. An Exploration of Basic Sociological Dimensions." *The Leo Baeck Institute Year Book* 30, 1985.

Oxaal, Ivar, Michael Pollak and Gerhard Botz, eds. *Jews, Antisemitism and Culture in Vienna.* London and New York, 1987.

Palmer, Francis, H. E. *Austro-Hungarian Life in Town and Country.* New York and London, 1905.

Patzer, Franz. "Der Wiener Gemeinderat von 1890–1952. Eine parteisoziologische Untersuchung." Unpublished monograph, Vienna, 1952.

Paupié, Kurt. *Handbuch der österreichischen Pressegeschichte.* 2 vols. Vienna and Stuttgart, 1960.

Pelinka, Anton. *Stand oder Klasse? Die christliche Arbeiterbewegung Österreichs 1933 bis 1938.* Vienna, Munich, and Zurich, 1972.

Petermann, Reinhard E. *Wien im Zeitalter Kaiser Franz Josephs I.* Vienna, 1913.

Petzold, Alfons. *Das Alfons Petzold Buch. Eine Auswahl des Dichters von Karl Ziak.* Vienna, n. d.

Pfarrhofer, Hedwig. *Friedrich Funder. Ein Mann zwischen Gestern und Morgen.* Graz, Vienna, and Cologne, 1978.

Pichl, Eduard. *Georg Ritter von Schönerer.* 5 vols. Berlin, 1938.

Poliakov, Léon. *The History of Anti-Semitism. Suicidal Europe: 1870–1933.* New York, 1985.

Pollak, Heinrich. *Dreissig Jahre aus dem Leben eines Journalisten. Erinnerungen und Aufzeichnungen.* 3 vols. Vienna, 1894–98.

Popp, Adelheid. *Jugend einer Arbeiterin.* Vienna, 1977.

Popp, Gerhard. *CV in Österreich 1864–1938. Organisation, Binnenstruktur und politische Funktion.* Vienna, Cologne, and Graz, 1984.

Pulzer, Peter G. J. *The Rise of Political Anti-Semitism in Germany and Austria.* New York, London, and Sydney, 1964.

Redlich, Josef. *Schicksalsjahre Österreichs, 1908–1919. Das politische Tagebuch Josef Redlichs.* Ed. Fritz Fellner, 2 vols. Graz and Cologne, 1953.

Reichhold, Ludwig. *Christentum - Gesellschaft - Sozialismus.* Vienna, 1969.

Riepl, Hermann Friedrich. "Die propagandistische Tätigkeit des Bauernorganisators Josef Steininger. Ein Beitrag zur Erforschung der bäuerlichen Standespresse Österreichs in der 2. Hälfte des 19. Jahrhunderts." Ph.D. diss. University of Vienna, 1962.

Ritter, Harry. "Austro-German Liberalism and the Modern Liberal Tradition." *German Studies Review.* Vol. 7. May 1984.

Rozenblit, Marsha L. *The Jews of Vienna 1867–1914: Assimilation and Identity.* Albany, N.Y., 1983.

Rutkowski, Ernst R. "Die revolutionäre Bewegung und die inneren Verhältnisse des Zarenreichs von 1877 bis 1884 im Urteil österreich-ungarischer Diplomaten." *Mitteilungen des österreichischen Staatsarchivs,* 9. 1955.

Salten, Felix. *Geister der Zeit. Erlebnisse.* Berlin, Vienna, and Leipzig, 1924.

Santifaller, Leo, et al. *Österreichisches Biographisches Lexikon 1815–1950.* Vienna, 1959–.

Scheicher, Josef. *Aus dem Jahre 1920 – Ein Traum.* St. Pölten, 1900.

———. *Arme Brüder.* Stuttgart, 1913.

Schick, Paul. *Karl Kraus in Selbstzeugnissen und Bilddokumenten.* Reinbek bei Hamburg, 1965.

Schmidt, Werner. "Lorenz von Stein. Ein Beitrag zur Biographie, zur Geschichte Schleswig-Holsteins und zur Geistesgeschichte des 19. Jahrhunderts." *Jahrbuch der Heimatgemeinschaft des Kreises Eckernförde e.V.,* 14, 1956.

Schmitz, Gertrud. "Die Entwicklungsgeschichte der christlichen Volksbewegung in Österreich." Ph.D. diss. University of Vienna, 1938.

Schnee, Heinrich. *Bürgermeister Karl Lueger. Leben und Wirken eines grossen Deutschen.* Paderborn, 1936.

―――. "Die politische Entwicklung des Wiener Bürgermeisters Dr. Karl Lueger." *Historisches Jahrbuch* 76, 1956.

―――. *Karl Lueger, Leben und Wirken eines grossen Sozial- und Kommunal-Politikers.* Berlin, 1960.

Schneider, Elfriede. "Karikatur und Satire als publizistische Kampfmittel. Ein Beitrag zur Wiener humoristisch-satirischen Presse des 19. Jahrhunderts 1849–1914." Ph.D. diss. University of Vienna, 1972.

Schnur, Roman, ed. *Staat und Gesellschaft. Studien über Lorenz von Stein.* Berlin, 1978.

Schorske, Carl E. *Fin-De-Siècle Vienna. Politics and Culture.* New York, 1980.

Schwer, Hans Arnold. *Die Wahrheit über die Morde in Polna.* Vienna, 1900.

Sekler, Eduard F. *Josef Hoffmann: The Architectural Work.* Princeton, 1984.

Seliger, Maren. "Liberale Fraktionen im Wiener Gemeinderat 1861 bis 1895." *Wien in der liberalen Ära. Forschungen und Beiträge zur Wiener Stadtgeschichte.* Vienna, 1978.

―――, and Karl Ucakar. *Wien. Politische Geschichte 1740–1934.* 2 vols. Vienna and Munich, 1985.

Silberbauer, Gerhard. *Österreichs Katholiken und die Arbeiterfrage.* Graz, 1966.

Skalnik, Kurt. *Dr. Karl Lueger. Der Mann zwischen den Zeiten.* Vienna and Munich, 1954.

Smith, Bradley F. *Adolf Hitler: His Family, Childhood, and Youth.* Stanford, California, 1967.

Sotriffer, Kristian, ed. *Das grössere Österreich. Geistiges und soziales Leben von 1880 bis zur Gegenwart.* Vienna, 1982.

Soukup, Richard. *Lueger und sein Wien.* Vienna, 1953.

Spitzer, Rudolf. *Des Bürgemeisters Lueger Lumpen und Steuerträger.* Vienna, 1988.

Stauracz, Franz. *Die Entwicklung der christlich-sozialen Partei und deren Hausfeinde.* Vienna, 1901.

―――. *Dr. Karl Lueger. Zehn Jahre Bürgermeister.* Vienna and Leipzig, 1907.

―――. *Dr. Luegers Leben und Wirken.* Klagenfurt, n. d.

Steiner, Herbert. *Die Arbeiterbewegung Österreichs 1867–1889.* Vienna, 1964.

Steiner, Kurt. *Politics in Austria.* Boston, 1972.

Stenographische Protokolle des niederösterreichischen Landtages.

Stenographische Protokolle über die Sitzungen des Hauses der Abgeordneten des österreichischen Reichsrats.

Stern, Fritz. *The Politics of Cultural Despair.* Berkeley, Los Angeles, and London, 1961.

Stern, J. P. *Hitler: The Führer and the People.* Glasgow, 1975.

Stöger, Gertrud. "Die politischen Anfänge Luegers. Ph.D. diss. University of Vienna, 1941.

Stöger, Walter. "Das Verhältnis der Konservativen zur christlichsozialen Partei." Ph.D. diss. University of Vienna, 1949.

Strasser, Anne Maria. "Publizistik und Agitation der österreichischen Frauenbewegung. Ein Beitrag zur Geschichte der Parteienpresse in der Zeit der österreich-ungarischen Monarchie." Ph.D. diss. University of Vienna, 1971.

Tapié, Victor. L. *The Rise and Fall of the Habsburg Monarchy.* New York, 1971.

Tietze, Hans. *Die Juden Wiens. Geschichte, Wirtschaft, Kultur.* Leipzig and Vienna, 1933.

Timms, Edward. *Karl Kraus: Apocalyptic Satirist — Culture and Catastrophe in Habsburg Vienna.* New Haven and London, 1986.

Tomola, Leopold. *Unser Bürgermeister Dr. Karl Lueger.* Vienna, 1904.

Truxa, Hans Maria. *Armenleben.* Vienna, 1905.

Twain, Mark [Samuel L. Clemens]. *Literary Essays by Mark Twain*. New York and London, 1899.

Uhl, Elisabeth. "Eduard Uhl. Bürgermeister der Stadt Wien, 1882–1889." Ph.D. diss. University of Vienna, 1950.

Vallentin, Hellwig. "Der Prozess Schönerer und seine Auswirkungen auf die parteipolitischen Verhältnisse in Österreich." *Österreich in Geschichte und Literatur*. 1972.

Van Arkel, Dirk. *Antisemitism in Austria*. Leiden, 1966.

Wagner-Rieger, Renate. *Die Wiener Ringstrasse. Bild einer Epoche*. 5 vols. Wiesbaden, 1975.

Wandruszka, Adam. *Geschichte einer Zeitung. Das Schicksal der "Presse" und der "Neuen Freien Presse" von 1848 bis zur 2. Republik*. Vienna, 1958.

————, and Peter Urbanitsch, eds. *Die Habsburgermonarchie 1848–1918*. Vienna, 1973–.

Weinzierl, Erika. "Antisemitismus in der österreichischen Literatur 1900–1938." *Mitteilungen des österreichischen Staatsarchivs* 20, 1967.

————, ed. "On the Pathogenesis of the Anti-Semitism of Sebastian Brunner 1814–1893," in *Ecclesia Semper Reformanda. Beiträge zur österreichischen Kirchengeschichte im 19. und 20. Jahrhundert*. Vienna and Salzburg, 1985.

Welch, David. *Propaganda and the German Cinema*. Oxford, 1983.

Werner, Fritz. "Lorenz von Stein als Politiker." *Verwaltungsarchiv*, 47.

Whiteside, Andrew G. *The Socialism of Fools*. Berkeley, 1975.

Wiktora, Oskar. "Die politische Haltung der *Neuen Freien Presse* in der liberalen Ära." Ph.D. diss. University of Vienna, 1948.

Williams, C. E. *The Broken Eagle*. London, 1974.

Winter, Max. *Das schwarze Wienerherz. Sozialreportagen aus dem frühen 20. Jahrhundert*. Vienna, 1982.

Wistrich, Robert S. "Karl Lueger and the Ambiguities of Viennese Antisemitism." *Jewish Social Studies*, 45.

————. *Socialism and the Jews: The Dilemmas of Assimilation in Germany and Austria-Hungary*. London and East Brunswick, N.J., 1982.

Wittmann, Maria Imma. "Die österreichische Frauenstimmrechtsbewegung im Spiegel der Frauenzeitungen. Mit einer einleitenden Darstellung der allgemeinen österreichischen Wahlbewegung von 1893–1906, im Spiegel der Presse." Ph.D. diss. University of Vienna, 1950.

Wodka, Josef. *Kirche in Österreich: Wegweiser durch ihre Geschichte*. Vienna, 1959.

Ziegenfuss, Werner. *Handbuch der Soziologie*. Stuttgart, 1956.

Zohn, Harry. *Karl Kraus*. New York, 1971.

Zöllner, Erich. *Geschichte Österreichs*. Munich 1984.

Index

Richard S. Geehr is Professor of History at Bentley College. He received his M.A. from Columbia University and his Ph.D. from the University of Massachusetts. He has also studied at the University of Vienna and has been awarded three Fulbright fellowships. Dr. Geehr's previous publications include *"I Decide Who Is a Jew!" The Papers of Dr. Karl Lueger* and *Adam Müller-Guttenbrunn and the Aryan Theater of Vienna: 1898–1903, The Approach of Cultural Fascism,* in addition to several journal articles on fin de siècle Vienna and early twentieth-century Austria.

The manuscript was edited for publication by Thomas Seller. The book was designed by Joanne Elkin Kinney. The typeface for the text is Palatino and the display is Muhle Condensed. The book is printed on 60–lb. Finch Opaque and is bound in Holliston Roxite B Grade Cloth.

Manufactured in the United States of America.

DEMCO